From a Whisper to a Movement

SUNY series, Studies in Human Rights

David L. Cingranelli and Alexandra S. Moore, editors

From a Whisper to a Movement

Investigating the Shared Rhetorical Spaces
of Whistleblowing and Social Protest

Edited by

JOSHUA GUITAR and ALAN CHU

SUNY
PRESS

Published by State University of New York Press, Albany

EU GPSR Authorised Representative:
Logos Europe, 9 rue Nicolas Poussin, 17000, La Rochelle, France
contact@logoseurope.eu

For information, contact State University of New York Press, Albany, NY
www.sunypress.edu

Library of Congress Cataloging-in-Publication Data

Names: Guitar, Joshua, 1986– editor | Chu, Alan, 1983– editor
Title: From a whisper to a movement : investigating the shared rhetorical spaces of whistleblowing and social protest / edited by Joshua Guitar and Alan Chu.
Description: Albany : State University of New York Press, [2025] | Series: SUNY series, studies in human rights | Includes bibliographical references and index.
Identifiers: LCCN 2024059968 | ISBN 9798855803280 (hardcover : alk. paper) | ISBN 9798855803297 (ebook) | ISBN 9798855803303 (pbk. : alk. paper)
Subjects: LCSH: Protest movements. | Whistle blowing. | Political participation. | Rhetoric. | Human rights.
Classification: LCC HM883 .F76 2025 | DDC 303.48/4—dc23/eng/20250518
LC record available at https://lccn.loc.gov/2024059968

*To all those who expose corruption and injustice
in the name of human rights.*

Contents

Acknowledgments

From Joshua: Above all else, thank you Natalie and Harper for your enduring support for all my work. Thank you, Natalie, for always listening to my long-winded explanations of my research projects, and thank you, Harper—in your two years of wisdom—for all your assistance with my writing. I just hope I found all the random keystrokes you have added to these documents along the way. As well, I offer a special thank-you to my professional network, especially those who have supported me through this project, namely Jack Sargent and all my Kean University colleagues, most notably those within the Communication, Media, and Journalism Department and the College of Liberal Arts. Finally, I am distinctly grateful for my students, especially the founding members of Anarchoic Chamber: Liliana Carredo and Kevin Stone. As I work to sharpen your skills, please know that you have helped sharpen mine and that you have positively shaped me in more ways than you know.

From Alan: To my mom, dad, and brother, who have led me to stories where a single person makes a terrifying decision but ends up changing the world. Thank you, Ken McAllister, for sharpening my vision and teaching me, however unconventionally, what it means to be a professional. And, as befitting her name, the queen's share of my gratitude always goes to Regina.

From Joshua and Alan: We both express our sincerest gratitude to the editorial team at State University of New York Press, especially Michael Rinella, whose guidance has been invaluable throughout. We are also grateful for the insight of our anonymous reviewers. Your feedback helped us substantially and our volume is markedly stronger because of your efforts. Most importantly, this project is only possible with the confidence, brilliance, and labor of the authors featured in this volume. We are immensely thankful for your contributions.

1

Racing to (Dis)Own Whistleblowers and Protests

Theorizing *Amongness* in the Shared Rhetorical Spaces of Democratic Agency

Joshua Guitar and Alan Chu

In contrast to other extensions of citizenship, whistleblowers and social protests typify democratic processes as they contest manifestations of authoritarianism, in turn creating sites of vibrant political discourse. This volume advances our understanding of the role of rhetoric within these spaces and its connections to the trajectory of democracy. As spaces that foster important meaning-making processes for democratic citizenship, the interrogation of the convergence of whistleblower and civic protest rhetoric is conditional to the progression of democratic ethics and human rights writ large. Indeed, "the public's tolerance for the persistent discord of a healthy democratic pluralism depends on discovering terms of convergence—minimal points of intersection with prevailing points of view—to legitimize the divergent stances of critics."[1] This collection of studies demonstrates the importance of the overlapping connections among singular instances of whistleblowing and collective protests as it pertains to urging democracy forward.

To lay the groundwork for this volume of rhetorical analyses, we highlight four important philosophical positions. First, we recognize that agency exists, and while we resist any designations regarding the extent to which this is so, we echo Shome in contending that "identities occur not just anywhere, but *somewhere*; social agency is derived not just anywhere but *somewhere*."[2] Second, we contend that individual agency can inform democratic social action, and vice versa. Third, while these actions can drive democracy and its discourses, not all of them do; sociopolitical implications matter. Fourth, these discursive processes of democracy are messy. This volume builds from the messiness.

In this chapter, we focus our attention on the divergent and often contentious descriptions of sociopolitical action. We claim that these discussions are far from trivial; they irradiate the state of democracy. Although we do not argue that the messier the discourse, the better it is for democracy, we recognize that dissensus and democracy are indivisible. Such discourses constitute requisite spaces to inform future action while consolidating, if not authoring, public perceptions of the events. Thus, we regard the subsequent, directional flow of public discourse as an indication of societal positionalities regarding the progression or regression of democracy.

As mass social protests often emerge from singular moments of discovery, the connected discourses expose unique spaces within the public forum rich with rhetorical significance. While not all whistleblowing utterances prompt public protests, and only some protests coalesce around specific disclosures of wrongdoing, recent history demonstrates that exposed abuses of power often spur collective action in the name of human rights. In this, we investigate the shared rhetorical spaces of singular agents and collective movements from the local to the global scale.

In approaching these studies, we advance beyond conventional definitions of whistleblowing while maintaining the core conditions that constitute the term. Similar to other published definitions on whistleblowing, which we discuss in greater detail later in this chapter, we recognize whistleblowers as vulnerable members of institutions who, motivated by democratic ethics, truthfully expose violations of human rights and abuses of power. However, while whistleblowing scholarship generally centers upon persons within more restricted organizational structures, like corporations or government agencies, we demonstrate how a variety of citizen-agent truth-tellers qualify as whistleblowers given their membership within a defined democratic body. Thus, the conception of whistleblowing for this volume urges a definitional amplification but also resists the contemporary usurpation of the term *whistleblowing* by partisan demagogues, like President Donald Trump's fabricated "Stop the Steal" campaign that paraded faux whistleblowers across the US after the 2020 election.

To accommodate our vision of whistleblowing, we argue in this volume that acts of whistleblowing can spark the formation of a public, thereby creating a scholarly exigency regarding conceptions of identity and constitutive rhetoric. Rhetoric has the power to alter "perceptions of events, people, and places and organiz[e] the scattered direct and indirect experiences of individual listeners into a broad and cohesive interpretation of reality."[3] "Because rhetoric functions to construct reality for listeners or readers and thereby influences their behavior,"[4] we position the singular contributions of whistleblowers and collective momentum of movements as two actions with outsized influences on the shaping of reality that have not been studied rigorously in convergence.

We begin with the contention that whistleblowing acts can occur from an assemblage of persons and places not typically associated with the term. Our critical scope affords us the ability to interrogate the rhetorical linkage among solitary whistleblowing acts and public protests. Accordingly, we conclude that individual and collective actions only deserve whistleblower or protest designations when they contest hierarchical power. This volume demonstrates how the political goal in advancing democratic rights galvanized by the singular whistleblower and the collective protest fosters symbolic expressions rich for academic inquiry.

An Effort to Define a Decennium of Wrongdoing

Although all historical eras contain their extraordinary events, those within the last decade have achieved unprecedented exposure with the advent of new media. In 2012, the death of Trayvon Martin sparked rejuvenated efforts for racial justice, coalescing into the Black Lives Matter social movement. As public attention has cycled past the killing of Martin by George Zimmerman, a civilian playacting as a police officer, Black Lives Matter has persisted, largely due to the exposure of the recurring tragedy of police killing unarmed Black citizens. Just as the world learned of Rodney King in the 1990s, in the 2010s we learned of Michael Brown, Alton Sterling, Philando Castile, Breonna Taylor, Sandra Bland,

and George Floyd, to name a few. With each disaster, another surge of public protests has demanded change.

Social tensions especially swelled during the presidency of Barack Obama, and the rhetoric of his successor, Donald Trump, exacerbated the growing unrest, which extended far beyond race relations. For instance, in a year that began with the 2017 Women's March as protesters worldwide demonstrated against Trump's presidency, predominantly due to his misogynistic rhetoric that led to fears of impending infringements upon women's rights, it concluded with an ongoing reckoning over the culture of sexual assault and workplace harassment that became popularized as the #MeToo movement.[5] The COVID-19 pandemic further divided an already hyperpartisan political context as far-right figures gathered to decry disease control measures like vaccination and lockdown policies.[6] In 2020, the extant polemics informed one of the most hotly contested presidential elections in US history, and as if the drama of the election was not enough, Trump, in defeat, launched his "Stop the Steal" campaign that attempted to overturn the results. This appeal culminated in one of the most frenzied events in US history as the US Capitol was violently overrun by a chaotic mass of Trump supporters.

Exhausting as it may be to relive and evaluate the rhetoric surrounding the events of the last decade, the critical interrogation of such discourses provides substantial epistemological value. While each of the aforementioned events can be analyzed on its own, this chapter approaches them in the aggregate. As each rhetorical act is intrinsically informed by its own idiosyncratic context, and in turn creates offshoots in unexpected directions, the variety of events makes it difficult to find commonalities. Nevertheless, this chapter helps uncover the connective tissue that binds disparate events, like Chelsea Manning's whistleblowing efforts and the January 6, 2021, violence at the US Capitol.

From Transgression to Democracy

Whereas rhetorical analyses largely unpack the nuances of singular texts or identify commonalities among a related set of artifacts, we are interested in the shared tension *among* the sites of contestation in this chapter and the ones to follow. Scholars have noted how these contentious discourses benefit democracy. Ivie, for instance, contends that "rowdy, rhetorical deliberations" are paramount "in a healthy pluralistic polity."[7] In this volume, we argue that evaluating these contentious discourses serves as a means to evaluate democracy. In other words, we contend that how a society constructs and navigates alike, and more often unconnected, actions of protest operates as a metric by which the presence of democracy, and ergo authoritarianism, can be measured.

To unpack the rhetorical implications of what we title the tension *in the among*, we channel a confluence of critical philosophies of democracy, most notably Derrida's différance[8] and "democracy to be,"[9] Rancière's rhetoric of the "in-between,"[10] and Mouffe's agonistic problematic.[11] Although the scholarly contributions of these theorists follow a similar trajectory, we do not intend to conflate their postulations, as each is complex in theory and application.[12] Instead, and appropriately for the sake of our analytical scope, we look to the shared tension *among* their contributions to democratic theory. Although other critical minds deserve attention, we deliberately aggregate Derrida, Rancière, and Mouffe given the similitude of their theories of, and the prominence of their work across, the critical study of democracy.

Such an approach serves two primary purposes. First, it provides entry to the advancement of democratic theory, which in turn, affords us the tools to better analyze democracy in practice. Although Derrida, Rancière, Mouffe, and others foster plurality through their theories, their contributions rely upon modernist presuppositions of binary relations. Moreover, as we will demonstrate in this chapter, contentious sociopolitical discourses often default to a fallacy of false dilemma. In theorizing the rhetoric *of the among*, we urge the discourses of democratic theory and democratic praxis away from dichotomized logics. Second, the practice of evaluating the meaning-making processes *in the among* of democratic theory exemplifies the epistemological scope that will be broadly applied to the discourses and spaces of the chapters to come. Although authors in this volume have chosen their own methods across the spectrum of rhetorical studies, they all intentionally contribute to the meaning-making processes at the intersection of whistleblowing and public protest.

The core of our argument builds from the important relationships that emerge *among* individual and collective attempts at actualizing democratic agency. At the individual level, few, if any, citizens typify democratic agency like whistleblowers. As members of defined bodies of people who truthfully expose the wrongdoing of those in power, whistleblowers contest authoritarianism through their existence alone.[13] Acting in the name of democratic rights, which are read here as human rights, our inclusive understanding of whistleblowers urges democratic progress through the attempted dismantling of hierarchical power. Protests operate similarly as they espouse collective civil liberties to expose and confront authoritarian power. Whistleblowers and protests, as exemplars of individual and collective democratic agency, spark democratic discourse and serve as rich artifacts for rhetorical inquiry.

From Différance, Agonism, and the In-Between to *In the Among*

Unquestionably, concurrently channeling Derrida, Rancière, and Mouffe could be read as lacking prudence. While their contributions maintain substantive theoretical overlap, they diverge in important, conflicting ways.[14] This suggests that navigating these variances would make for a rather convoluted methodological scope. However, when approached in the aggregate and with the understanding that the tension *among* the theories can reveal as much, if not more, as the theories themselves, such theoretical confluence can illuminate rhetorical processes that are otherwise underexplored. Admittedly, this approach and the corresponding analysis constitute most succinctly Derrida's deconstruction.[15] However, we instead synthesize the work of Derrida, Rancière, and Mouffe as it pertains to critical democratic theory and postulate the concept of *amongness* as that which can be constituted in the shared rhetorical tension *among* sites of political contestation and their respective discourses. Whereas each of these scholars of radical democracy theorizes the shared rhetorical spaces that manifest between sites and signs, we instead amalgamate the theories as a pathway for connecting the nonfamilial activities *among* sites and signs, most notably those that surround whistleblowing and protesting.

Derrida's concept of différance maintains that meaning is not found in the presence of things or the signs we use to identify them. Instead, we find meaning in the différance between reality and signs. Derrida contends that "the infinite différance is finite. It can therefore no longer be conceived within the opposition of finiteness and infinity, absence and presence, negation and affirmation."[16] Derrida's concept of différance prominently overlaps with Rancière's rhetoric of the "in-between,"[17] "which consists in occupying the space in-between, or the non-place between two positions."[18] As Bosteels states,

Similarly, with Dis-agreement, it is a question of being neither on the side of rational communicability nor on the side of absolute unrepresentability; neither in ready-to-wear sociologism nor in the hyperbole of the pure event. Now, in order for this third way to be tenable, even if the place of this third—as is that of the "third people" between the police and politics—is a non-place, it seems to me that the question of the historicity of thought imposes itself as a question that can no longer be postponed.[19]

Rancière describes political processes as the relationship *between* rational thought (logos) and our animalistic tendencies (alogia), or rather the tension between logic and its lack.[20] Rancière further remarks that politics produces and resides in a space fostering community and division.[21]

Similarly, Mouffe speaks of "shared symbolic space" where agonistic tensions within democracy occur.[22] As Mouffe states further, "Visualizing the dynamics of liberal-democratic politics as the space of a paradox whose effect is to impede both total closure and total dissemination, whose possibility is inscribed in the grammars of democracy and liberalism, opens many interesting possibilities."[23] In her work, Mouffe is keenly focused on the tense, spatial duality between democracy's core concepts of liberty and equality. Mouffe argues that whereas "the tension between equality and liberty cannot be reconciled,"[24] the processes "between the ethics of human rights and the political logic" require us to engage in decision-making processes.[25] These agonistic discourses occur within the spatial tension between liberty and equality. For Mouffe, this innate strain between democracy's core tenets produces a space of ongoing contestation where

power relations are always being put into question and no victory can be final. However, such an 'agonistic' democracy requires accepting that conflict and division are inherent to politics and that there is no place where reconciliation could be definitively achieved as the full actualization of the unity of 'the people.' To imagine that pluralist democracy could ever be perfectly instantiated is to transform it into a self-refuting ideal, since the condition of possibility of a pluralist democracy is at the same time the condition of impossibility of its perfect implementation.[26]

Thus, for Mouffe, democracy is not an achievable end per se, but rather, unavoidably exists within the agonistic discourse between liberty and equality, or rather, the rhetoric of "friendly enemies"—persons who share a common symbolic space but wish to organize that space in a different way,[27] a relationship Derrida refers to as "brother enemy."[28]

Derrida, Rancière, and Mouffe approach democracy through a recognition of its paradoxes, albeit with slightly different language. Mouffe advocates for an agonistic problematic, wherein democracy is not a destination but the contentious ongoing negotiation of equality and liberty. For Rancière, democracy is "based on nothing other than the absence of every title to govern."[29] Pertaining to classifying and defining, Rancière contends that democratic societies could manage their paradoxes by simply excluding "the democratic title because it is in contradiction with every title to govern."[30] Derrida speaks of a "democracy to come," paradoxically positioned and unmoored as "infinite heterogeneity"[31] that, as a concept, manifests unnaturally and can persist beyond borders, governments, and political orders.[32] In this, democracy is the formless space of the political.[33] For all three theorists, who indeed share a similar, if not familial, philosophical lineage, the concept of democracy exists paradoxically: Its greatest strengths are the tools of its own destruction; it strives for plurality but requires homogeneity; it persists, but only as painstaking process.

Despite their pluralistic determinations, all three rely, or are forced to rely, upon the language of modernism—structured to dissect and classify according to binary logic. Mouffe's agonistic problematic rectifies the tension between liberty and equality through a friend/enemy corrective. Rancière's work theorizes the political as "occupying the space in-between, or the non-place between two positions."[34] Derrida refers to democracy's paradoxes, like that of internal/external, as a perpetual "double-bind."[35] A reflexive analysis of Derrida, Rancière, and Mouffe indicates an urgency toward pluralism that is inadvertently framed as a dichotomous relationship. This chapter operates as a response to such frames while also channeling these theorists of radical democracy in situations of radical democratic action. As each subsequent chapter features authors utilizing different rhetorical methods to evaluate different case studies, the studies not only produce their own novel analyses, they inform a body of knowledge *among* the sites of whistleblowing and public protest. Thus, although each chapter can function as a standalone essay, when arranged together, the chapters advance knowledge *among* these cases to give us a broader sense of the state of contemporary democracy.

To be clear, we are not arguing for definitions and epistemologies based upon established theoretical positioning found in postmodern scholarship. Given our placement of whistleblowing as a form of agentive truth-telling, we recognize the paradoxicality of referencing the democratic philosophies of scholars like Derrida, Rancière, and Mouffe. After all, some deconstructionists and postmodernists argue that truth is contingent and agency is an illusion, which would mean that the activities of whistleblowing and protests could be perceived as infinitely relativistic and comprised of signs forever contested and uncertain. Such an arrangement is certainly not helpful to this volume. Instead, we broadly analyze the spaces *among* contested terms within discourses on democratic pragmatics. In other words, in this chapter, we engage, describe, and critique Derrida, Rancière, and Mouffe not to wholesale accept their logics of postmodernism or deconstruction, but to demonstrate that such logics counterintuitively operate according to false binaries while nevertheless offering us entry into spaces of radical democratic action. In this, we argue that democratic truths are not found between two thoughts, signs, or discourses, but *among* a multitude. As such, our analyses resist evaluating binary tensions and instead evaluate the meaning-making processes *among* rhetorical processes linking whistleblowing and social protest.

Whistleblowing: Definitions and Tensions

The divergent studies of whistleblowing and social protest are, in some sense, surprising given the panegyrics to democracy often ascribed to both activities. Both collective action and individual resistance share a rich and widely acknowledged lineage. Although recent scholarship identifies various whistleblowers early in US history,[36] the term *whistleblowing* became popular in news and legal discourse in the 1970s. Whistleblowing was first formally identified and protected in US law in 1978 with the Civil Service Reform Act (CSRA) and the Inspector General Act (IGA). The CSRA established that federal "employees should be protected against reprisal for the lawful disclosure of information which the employees reasonably believe" reveals "a violation of any law, rule, or regulation" or "mismanagement, a gross waste of funds, an abuse of authority, or a substantial and specific danger to public health or safety."[37]

Although the presence of laws helps concretize an important place for whistleblowers and protests in a democracy, more relevant to this volume is the contested public discourse over what can be considered an act of protest or whistleblowing. In this manner, federal statutes not only establish protection, they provide a legal definition that government officials use to delineate a civic act made in public interest from that which is not. However, public deliberations *among* these definitional ambiguities extend far beyond legalism and provide evidence for evaluating the state of democracy. In this chapter, we analyze the contested, multiperspectival discourses *among* the topics of whistleblowing and public protest to better illuminate the epistemological power of those tensions.

Given its centrality in major news events throughout the past few decades, scholars have increasingly labored to define and understand whistleblowing beyond US federal law. Generally, scholars have recognized whistleblowers as members of organizations who expose the wrongdoing of empowered people within those organizations.[38] Such actions disturb organizational hierarchies as whistleblowers speak truth about those in power.[39] Despite potential ulterior motives, whistleblowers intently "serve the public."[40] From a susceptible position, whistleblowers, as truth-tellers, augment democracy by fostering the "democratic principles of transparency, accountability, and participation."[41] Whistleblowers and their subsequent discourses foster democracy in invaluable ways, like exposing military brutality[42] and detangling the connections between governments and free press.[43] To expand the conceptions of whistleblowing to draw meaningful connections *among* whistleblowers and protests, we recognize whistleblowers as vulnerable members of institutions who, motivated by democratic ethics, truthfully expose violations of human rights and abuses of power. We consider this expansion to be invaluable as we draw connections *among* generally unconnected discourses.

For whistleblowers, the legal definition of whistleblowing carries immediate and obvious consequences. For instance, Chelsea Manning was denied whistleblower protections because she provided information about the wars in Iraq and Afghanistan to WikiLeaks, an outside agency. The US government also denied whistleblower status to Edward Snowden for taking his concerns public, although Snowden lacked legal protections as a subcontractor of the US government, since US law only protects federal employees and contractors.[44]

This ambiguity often directly leads to fueled contention over definitions. The Chelsea Manning discourse was saturated with such contestations: "To some, Manning is a heroic whistleblower; others, including the U.S. military, consider her a traitor."[45] Oftentimes, mediated discourses are responsible for the proliferation of various rhetorical binaries regarding whistleblowing. For example, a headline from a 2013 CNN article explored whether Manning was "an idealist who became disillusioned by what was being done in Iraq and elsewhere in the name of U.S. national interests" or a "a traitor who leaked classified material to WikiLeaks that [she] knew could assist terrorists."[46] These frames have been shown to influence public opinion.[47] Other reports position whistleblowers as different from truth-tellers but lack definitional clarity regarding the distinctions.[48]

In addition to media framing, US officials also influenced these dichotomous discourses. Although the public remained split on the whistleblowing status of both Manning and Snowden, Snowden gained more favor with the public, in part for relying upon reputable news agencies like the *Guardian* and the *Washington Post* to release the information, rather than WikiLeaks.[49] Agents and agencies within the US government labored to categorize Snowden as anything but a whistleblower. The US House Intelligence Committee opined that Snowden was a "disgruntled employee," not a whistleblower.[50] Members of US executive criminalized Snowden: "Edward Snowden is not a whistleblower. There actually is a specific process that is well-established and well-protected that allows whistleblowers to raise concerns that they have, particularly when it relates to confidential or classified information, to do so in a way that protects the national security secrets of the United States. That is not what Mr. Snowden did."[51] Obama also directly censured Snowden's potential as a whistleblower:

> I believe that those who have lawfully raised their voices on behalf of privacy and civil liberties are also patriots who love our country and want it to live up to our highest ideals. . . . If the concern was that somehow this was the only way to get this information out to the public, I signed an executive order well before Mr. Snowden leaked this information that provided whistleblower protection to the intelligence community—for the first time. So there were other avenues available for somebody whose conscience was stirred and thought that they needed to question government actions.[52]

Per US officials, patriots and whistleblowers act "lawfully" through "avenues available," or rather approved, by federal statutes. In essence, whistleblowing, and proxy designations like traitor, hero, and patriot, are defined by how the whistle is blown rather than by what is revealed.

As if the Manning and Snowden discourses were not confounding enough, the Trump presidency manufactured additional confusion regarding what is, and is not, whistleblowing. In one context, Trump adamantly denied the existence of the whistleblowers that sufficiently stirred Inspector General Michael Atkinson to investigate Trump's approach to international relations with Ukraine, which led to Trump's first impeachment. Whereas Manning and Snowden were denied whistleblower status for operating outside the law, Trump denied the existence of the whistleblowers because they were operating against him, despite following outlined legal protocols. In a November 4, 2019, tweet Trump quoted "there is no whistleblower."[53] Trump called the impeachment a "hoax" and argued, "What whistleblower? I don't think there is, I consider it to be a fake whistleblower because what he wrote didn't correspond to what I said in any way, shape, or form."[54]

Conversely, Trump's "Stop the Steal" team paraded a barrage of "whistleblowers" around the US after the 2020 election. Despite having a contentious relationship with whistleblowers over the years, Trump and many within the orbit of his administration sought and celebrated anyone willing to assume the title of whistleblower in their fight to overturn the election. In some cases, Trump-supporting "whistleblowers" from swing states like Georgia claimed they had evidence of corrupted Dominion voting machines.[55] These claims informed some rather bizarre media events, like self-proclaimed "whistleblower"[56] Melissa Carone's "testimony" before members of the Michigan House of Representatives.[57] Other "whistleblowers," like Richard Hopkins, were elevated by far-right organizations, like Project Veritas, with unsubstantiated claims of ballot tampering.[58] Not only did the "whistleblower" claims lack any verifiable evidence, the whistleblower designation was offered without any clarification. In short, whereas the Obama administration based their definitions of whistleblower upon method of reporting, Trump's categorizations revolved around political allyship.

Trump era discourse also contained a palpable strain among terms like *whistleblower* and *conspiracy theorist*. Discredited former researcher Judy Mikovits gained notoriety for her role in *Plandemic*, a highly debunked pseudo-documentary that propagated claims about the COVID-19 pandemic. Right-wing outlets celebrated Mikovits as a whistleblower[59] while reputable news organizations emphasized her as just another iteration of an extremist conspiracy theorist.[60] In other COVID-19-related cases, right-wing propagandists were regularly refuted for framing false claims as whistleblowing.[61] These "whistleblower or conspiracy theorist" contestations are not occurring in the dark shadows of the Internet; they persist in the mainstream. For instance, Fox News elevated Li-Meng Yan to whistleblower status for claiming that the scientific community is controlled by the Chinese Communist Party and conspired to engineer the COVID-19 virus.[62] Interviewed by Tucker Carlson on *Tucker Carlson Tonight* and amplified by Trump White House strategist Steve Bannon, Yan claimed to have evidence that the COVID-19 virus was manufactured by the Chinese government and intentionally released to the world.[63] Unsurprisingly, while Yan's claims lacked evidence, she was nonetheless positioned as a whistleblower by some, while other news agencies and health researchers raced to condemn Yan as a conspiracy theorist.[64] As it is, some conspiracies are true,[65] thus demonstrating the difficulty with using *conspiracy theorist* strictly in a pejorative sense.

In this way, not only do whistleblowers serve epistemic functions in their attempts to inform the public, but the strain *among* the discourses apprises the public on the state of their democracy. While knowledge receives less attention than liberty and equality in conversations about democracy, critical theorists like Freire[66] and hooks[67] look to center episteme within their work. The epistemic function of whistleblowing further augments the value of whistleblowers within democracy. As truth-telling, whistleblowing assists a public, especially in the navigation of mis/disinformation of our present media era. As well, while we can reasonably and justifiably assert that precarity will follow whistleblowers as long as authoritarian power exists—truth is their most valuable weapon. Truth and evidence *among* these discourses provide the public with a method to discern whistleblowing from pseudo-whistleblowing. Thus, while agents who advance mis/disinformation disturb epistemological processes, they also add tension *among* the discourses, which in turn affords citizens and scholars with a method for evaluating the state of democracy. In other words, we can assess the health of democracy by tracing whether the discursive currents *among* the political tensions favor truth and democratic processes, or fabrications and authoritarian power.

Although whistleblowing is a specific form of individual protest, we recognize the act as a part of the broader fabric of contesting hierarchical power relations. There are many documented ways in which whistleblower rhetoric adapts "a genre of rhetorical address to stabilize some communities while disrupting others."[68] In this, whistleblowers are like other protesters who "represent the global justice movement" as they "become evidence that the rhetorical substance of democracy (against corporate globalization) has sparked a passionate identification between protestors (or, more accurately, their subjectivities) and social subject."[69] Whistleblowers, as singular agents typifying democratic citizenship and democratic processes, inform collective action. Much like whistleblowers, collective actions entice definitional arguments. The subsequent discourses reveal the state of democracy.

Protest: Definitions and Tensions

Although the academic literature and popular discourse around the topics of whistleblowing and protests overlap peripherally through the concept of democratic agency, they are far more inextricable than generally assumed. Whereas whistleblowers represent individual agency, protests represent collective agency, or at least a collection of individual agents. Thus, despite the seemingly divergent discourses around the sites of contestation identified in this chapter, human agency weaves the fabric *among* both whistleblowing and protests.

Similar to whistleblowing, legal interpretations both validate protests as an activity and lead to definitional ambiguity. In the US, the First Amendment of the Constitution states that the people must be afforded the right to peaceably assemble. Although there have been many legal battles over the years regarding the application of the First Amendment, the US Supreme Court has largely upheld the right to peaceable assembly, like in the prominent cases of *De Jonge v. Oregon* (1937) and *Hague v. Committee for Industrial Organization* (1939). Despite these decisions in favor of free assembly, the terminological opacity within US law continues to create uncertainty. For instance, although the Anti-Riot Act of 1968—federal legislation that forbids interstate travel or the usage of interstate commerce to incite a riot—remains law, the Supreme Court decision in *Brandenburg v. Ohio* (1969) makes "proving a speaker's intent to incite violence" to be "difficult or impossible."[70] As such, defining the common elements that create or disqualify social protest is as vaporous as the activity of identifying a whistleblower.

Nevertheless, social political actions have long intrigued scholars interested in human communication and political processes, advancing terms to describe various actions like protests, social movements, demonstrations, marches, riots, counterpublics, uprisings, revolutions, among others. Although the plurality of social action terms affords descriptive nuance, our present social media ecosystem blurs the lines among these already overlapping topics. On the surface, the definitional opacity of these terms seems inconsequential, leading to generally assumed synonymity within public discourse. However, such social action designations inherently illuminate disparate power relations, which is particularly important in discourses surrounding democracy. Moreover, these power imbalances tend to fall along historic lines that demarcate the empowered from the oppressed. Thus, while the difference between a riot and a protest may seem inconsequential, these terminological variations matter greatly when media agents use terms like *riot*—which signifies a greater attention to violent chaos—to describe, for instance, Black sociopolitical actions. In other words, the rhetorical framing of these terms matters significantly as they function as coded language to devalue the sociopolitical actions of disempowered publics.

For all their difficulties, deliberative processes sustain democracy through a prerequisite process of interrogating power relations via social engagement. In this, "agency is communal, social, cooperative, and participatory and, simultaneously, constituted and constrained by the material and symbolic elements of context and culture."[71] Although individual and collective agency drive these processes, persistent authoritarian power relations inform the interactions. Yet, power is not simply the "ability to have power over another, or to overpower a situation"; it connects agency to the ability to influence a response that accounts for or avoids the "interconnections and interdependences of people, privilege, and social/political/economic opportunities."[72] Consequently, sociopolitical actions negotiate democracy in that democratic societies privilege "equality over supremacy" and channel discourses built upon "complementary differences," or "mutually beneficial interdependencies between parties with otherwise distinct and conflicted interests" to foster a "conjointly empowering web of differences."[73] Discursive spaces are formed and augmented by these sociopolitical actions, particularly as "protest movements have long relied upon the capacity of disobedient bodies to disrupt labor, traffic, commerce, and the flow of business as usual to instantiate new habits of congregating and behaving."[74] Given the multitude of ways individuals and collectives can disturb power relations, scholars have labored to define and describe key ways of advancing democratic labor.

One prominent site of scholarly deliberation pertains to sociopolitical action. Indeed, identification processes of individuals and collectives matter in the conceptualization of sociopolitical action. "Identification renders protest coherent . . . identification moves the individual to join a collective will. From this perspective, collective action not only forms as people conform to a positive principle, but may also form when people join against a common adversary."[75] Identification processes also matter in the description of sociopolitical investment. For instance, some scholars have differentiated between social movements and counterpublics, where social movement scholars tend to focus on rhetoric and materiality while scholars of counterpublics study dichotomous power relations and the discourses that surround them:

> "Social movement" often reflects the kinship between sociology and communication, while "counterpublic" tends to link our field to literary and political theory. Additionally, both terms have inspired robust theoretical debates. For instance, work classified (or classifiable) under the term "social movement" has assumed rhetoric as instrumental, constitutive, and more recently affective or immediate. "Counterpublic" work has problematized the material origins of discourse, where agent or agency is centered on subaltern identities, texts, or circulation.[76]

Warner contends that a counterpublic is uniquely aware of "its subordinate status" and publicly addresses indefinite strangers who "are presumed to not want to be mistaken for the kind of person who would participate" in the counterpublic's messaging.[77]

Academics also note that while much scholarship focuses on traditional forms of protests and marches, newer styles of sociopolitical action are growing, like radical cheerleading that "uses im/mediacy to disrupt the chains of identification that link protest, protestor, and cause"[78] as a "feminist performance and protest—a kind of intervention in political demonstration ('serious') and a subversion of cheerleading ('antifeminist')."[79] Regardless, these sociopolitical actions center "activists who were carried away by emotion, narrative, myth, spectacle, and above all, embodiment."[80]

More specifically, many scholars describe these sociopolitical actions according to their rhetorical backdrops and implications. Dimock, for example, distinguishes between dissent-style rhetoric and protest-style rhetoric, contending that dissent style attempts to achieve consensus through deliberation and civil discourse. Conversely, protest style rejects the decorum of civil discourse and emphatically blames the opposition for societal problems.[81] Ivie resists such strict demarcations, however, arguing that the rhetorical styles of dissent and protest should be viewed as "overlapping discourses" so as not to sacrifice any "critical edge" in the processes of advancing "democratic pluralism."[82] Ivie further states that "rather than thinking of dissent as a tool of consensus—an unlikely and even untoward prospect for diversity—or as a synonym for protest, rhetorical scholars should consider dissent's distinctive and essential contribution to democratic practice."[83] Other scholars identify different rhetorical styles, like Scott and Smith, who argue that social movements operationalize a rhetoric of confrontation.[84] Windt says that political protests can occur on a broad rhetorical spectrum, from traditional rhetorical means, like "speeches, essays, and peaceful demonstrations"[85] to the manipulation of "symbols by repudiating and profaning their traditional, conventional meanings, thus producing horror among people who had never examined their reasons for responding as they had toward these symbols."[86] The complexities of sociopolitical action in theory parallel the complexities of sociopolitical action in practice and public discourse.

We demonstrate the contentious, constitutive rhetoric among sociopolitical action through three prominent, contemporary public efforts: Black Lives Matter, #MeToo, and the January 6 events at the US Capitol. Our chapter lays the groundwork to further evidence the democratically essential, interconnected role of whistleblowers and protests in concert with the strains *among* the surrounding discourses, regardless of nation or geographical place. Principally, these discourses center upon how sociopolitical actions should be framed and defined.

Definitional tensions have manifested in Black Lives Matter events over the last decade. Some have opined that Black Lives Matter produced "rioting," instigated "looting," caused "arson," and engaged in "rage-fueled anarchy,"[87] while others ensured that Black Lives Matter was framed with a more objective tone, using terms like "protest," "demonstration," and "movement."[88] Some reports differentiated between "peaceful demonstrations" and "protests" that "erupted" across the US.[89] The "peaceful" qualifier made its way into the discourse quite regularly, when the definitional nuance among terms like *riots*, *protests*, and *demonstrations* was not enough. Some commented that the "demonstrations were largely peaceful during the day, but police and protesters clashed as night fell."[90] This designation appeared as an attempt to push back against right-wing framing of Black Lives Matter as "violent leftwing protesters and 'domestic terrorists'" by citing reports that showed that "93% of demonstrations have involved no serious harm to people or property."[91]

Protests that manifest to challenge other protests further complicate definitional contestations. News organizations took no pause in labeling the Charlottesville, Virginia, "Unite the Right" event as a protest that was met by pushback from counterprotesters.[92] Others described the Charlottesville "rally" as "white nationalist demonstrations that led to violence" which were met by "professed anti-fascist groups and individuals who staged counterprotests."[93] Although the Charlottesville events typify such complications, Black Lives Matter has regularly received backlash from "all lives matter" and "blue lives matter" counterprotests, where in at least one instance, a "counter protest reenacting George Floyd's death" featured a man kneeling on the neck of another man while yelling "if you don't comply, that's what happens" while others chanted "Black lives matter—to no one."[94] In these situations, some opinions fail to differentiate among the terms, describing all the collectives equally as "protest and counter-protest slogans such as Black Lives Matter, Blue Lives Matter and All Lives Matter."[95]

Much like Black Lives Matter, the #MeToo movement found salience through a grassroots online campaign and global in-person protests. Manifesting from a social media hashtag in 2017 when sexual assault allegations mounted against Hollywood mogul Harvey Weinstein, #MeToo rapidly became one of the most prominent social movements of the twenty-first century. In some ways, #MeToo has escaped some of the definitional argumentation that Black Lives Matter has endured. For instance, the public spent less time belaboring certain labels associated with #MeToo as news reports regularly described #MeToo activities as protests,[96] marches,[97] a movement,[98] a campaign,[99] and so on, without much pushback.

However, while the public generally avoided #MeToo descriptors like *riot*[100] and *anarchy*,[101] which were used regularly in Black Lives Matter discourse, patriarchal ideologues opposing #MeToo regularly referred to the movement as an angry mob. *New York Post* columnist Andrea Peyser described the "MeToo mob" as hell-bent on "ruining men with flimsy allegations,"[102] while her colleague made similar accusations, calling #MeToo a "career-destroying angry mob."[103] The "mob" designation was levied by celebrities, like Kanye West[104] and Terry Gilliam,[105] and by politicians like Trump[106] and US Senator Mitch McConnell.[107] Vocal opponents of #MeToo have also tended to associate the movement with "cancel culture" more broadly, advancing assumptions like "as seen with the #MeToo movement, the public has a low tolerance for people saying the wrong thing or taking a contrarian stance in regards to the ongoing cultural moment."[108]

Like all social movements, #MeToo withstood its share of juvenile ridicule within the name of the movement itself. Trump mocked #MeToo on countless occasions, making complaints like "there's an expression, but under the rules of MeToo I'm not allowed to use that expression anymore; in the old days, it was a little different."[109] #MeToo also experienced a litany of intentional misuse on social media, like when Kellyanne Conway, senior counselor to President Trump, congratulated Supreme Court Justice Brett Kavanaugh—a prime target of the #MeToo movement—on his confirmation to the US Supreme Court: "Millions of women are thrilled you are on the Court. #metoo."[110] Additionally, just like Black Lives Matter endured "All Lives Matter" and "Blue Lives Matter" responses, a #HimToo campaign swiftly gained popularity on social media, especially by Trump and his supporters as an attempt to devalue the unified voice of sexual assault survivors.[111] In the aggregate, far-right political agents contested the democratic rhetoric espoused by the recent human rights campaigns of Black Lives Matter and #MeToo. Unsurprisingly given the propensity for those in power to quell democratic uprisings, as right-wing political agents counterattacked the realities illuminated by these campaigns, Trump and his allies invoked reciprocal rhetoric in the "Stop the Steal" campaign that propagated a falsified reality surrounding the 2020 election.

After the events of January 6, commentators similarly quibbled about designations. Many media reports described the events with rhetorically heavy terms like "insurrection,"[112] "coup,"[113] "riot,"[114] and "siege."[115] Others countered such designations, arguing that insurrection was a legal term that should be saved for the judicial system.[116] Still others delineated between coups and self-coups.[117] Some national news agencies pondered these definitional questions[118] while others conveyed static definitions through differentiation.[119] Activities that reveal authoritarianism and the curtailment of civil liberties and political equality manifest in the discourses *among* whistleblowers, conspiracy theorists, protests, riots, and so forth. This rhetoric, which so closely connects to the project of democracy, is where our volume begins.

Whistleblowing and Protests
as Tensions Within the Same Sign

Critical theorists have long recognized that democracy is a paradoxical process of governance rather than an achievable end. As Mouffe contends, "To tackle the multiplicity of forms of subordination existing in social relations, about gender, race, environment and sexuality, a post-social democratic politics needs to be envisaged in terms of radical and plural democracy."[120] In this way, this volume is not an endeavor to locate or specify meaning, but rather as a rhetorical exploration to better understand the spaces *among* whistleblowing, protest, and democracy. This in turn helps us understand our individual and collective presence, and perhaps more importantly, how to articulate our right(s) to persist as citizens. While concepts like Derrida's différance examine the space *between* different signs and their material essences, we instead recognize the tensions *among* interconnected signs and discourses *among* the shared rhetorical spaces at and around sites of political contestation. Such an activity not only reveals the definitional disputes that mark the movements of democracy and authoritarianism within society; more importantly, it illustrates how we lack a language of democracy.

Yet, democracy exists, strives to exist, and is simultaneously threatened within *the among*. In one sense, discourses *among* contested terms afford us the capacity to engage in meaning-making processes. That is, we may never fully discern the particulars of protests, riots, and demonstrations, nor will we be able to prescribe a singular, static definition to each of these. However, without *the among*, democracy is but a fantasy. Thus, in another sense, while we desire a world without oppression, the messy responses ensure democratic discourse. So, while the riots, insurrections, and protests, and the whistleblowers, traitors, and conspiracy theorists stir public discord, they also foster clarity as we position terms and ideas *among* their counterparts.

In the end, our efforts in this chapter identify that the theories from Derrida, Rancière, Mouffe, and the like, exist in their own contradictory spaces, where they seek to interrogate modernist thinking while using modernist language. As Cixous[121] aptly posits, ideological power assumes hegemony largely because the only language we know is that which supports the ideologies of power. Instead, we should embrace the alterity of *the among* where meaning-making, despite enduring indefinitely, affords us episteme—which is as important as equality and liberty. So, just as Foust questions the binary logics/fallacies of critical democratic theorists,[122] we urge attention away from viewing sites as singular and toward the connective tissue that constitutes the space *among* them.

As such, we reframe and redirect the conversation to address some critical points. First, contemporary conversations, whether scholarly or popular, often do not observe the robust connections *among* topics like #MeToo, whistleblowing, Black Lives Matter, and cop watching.

Our recalculation of what it means to be a whistleblower bridges these important gaps so we can recognize how the conversations that follow these events influence each other and inform a democracy of becoming. Second, we urge theoretical conversations on democracy outward. Despite the profound contributions of democratic theorists like Rancière, Mouffe, and Derrida, they nevertheless default to binary speak. Democracy may well exist as a process of negotiating liberty and equality, but such a distinction restricts our attention from other formative conversations on topics of agency, citizenship, and collectivism. Third, we may never extinguish authoritarianism; however, we can identify and interrogate the sites of contestation where democracy, authoritarianism, and other external factors converge. For example, in that Black Lives Matter manifests from restrictions on democracy while the events of January 6, 2021, manifested from the restrictions on authoritarianism, the tensions among these two discourses afford us the capacity to recognize that the material damage of Black Lives Matter demonstrations, January 6 demonstrations, and institutional turnover function differently. As well, we can see how recording police, publicizing police brutality, exposing state records, and state-sponsored doxing operate uniquely. In other words, while January 6 events and some Black Lives Matter events both produced material damage, the implications are not the same. Similarly, a citizen pointing a camera at a cop is not the same as a cop pointing a camera at a citizen. The tensions *among* these events reveal the processes of power negotiation, and thus the processes of democracy. As such, democracy's progress can be evaluated *among* the entirety of these sites and their co-constituted tension.

Neither this chapter nor this volume pretends to theorize that which has already been theorized; however, we argue that this connective tissue in tension *among* these sites of contestation fundamentally link theory and praxis, philosophy and agency. To those wondering where democracy is and how it can be achieved, it is here, and not here, in the elastic fabrics *among*. In this volume, the authors are not necessarily indebted to logic specific to Derrida, Rancière, or Mouffe. However, they explore case studies that arise from *the among*—the shared rhetorical spaces at and around sites of political contestation as individuals and collectives experience the tensions of democracy. So, while we craft definitions of terms like *whistleblowers* and *protests*, our primary offerings are those that extend outward from *the among*, in all directions, to explore what we contend are the most robust discourses within democratic society—where individual and collective efforts that contest longitudinal power inform rhetorical implications worthy of being known, experienced, and actualized by a democratic populace.

So, we present chapters not in direct tension with one another, but as complementary to a shared discourse that reveals the state of democracy. The authors were charged only with approaching the intersection of whistleblowing and public protest from a rhetorical perspective. As such, we have intentionally included studies that span the entirety of the rhetorical spectrum, including classical, contemporary, and critical perspectives. Despite the variant epistemological approaches of the volume, we generally channel the studies as an academic call to action, akin to Cloud's charge: "Now and any time people rise to fight exploitation and oppression, let us be moved to greater critique and solidarity in the knowledge that we will make a difference."[123] Whereas citizens legitimize democracy through expressions of criticism and outrage,[124] we focus our attention on the human rights discourses *among* the whistleblowers, protesters, and members of the public forum to better understand the present state of democracy—lest "the champions of democracy and the knowledge it requires to thrive are lost."[125] As well, while McPhail was writing specifically about agents of whiteness, we contend that whistleblowers and protests demonstrate an invaluable "courage of conscience to acknowledge our complicity, embrace our implicature, and refuse to fall prey to the hopelessness engendered in the belief that [we] are essentially incapable of transformative change."[126] Thus, regardless of our positionalities, we can remain steadfast in the academic and social critique.[127]

Overall, our scholarly work here collectively values democracy in practice—where citizens not only protest authoritarianism but protest the authoritarian ideologies that impede democratic progress. In sum, these chapters urge us to think more deeply about the rhetorical spaces shared by whistleblowers, collective protests, power, and democratic rights like liberty, equality, and knowledge. In an ever-evolving state of becoming, democracy requires our constant attention. As we respond to this exigency, we hope these chapters augment ongoing scholarly conversations while motivating us to support and engage in democratic action, which cannot be "captured in the theory of politics of location."[128]

Notes

1. Robert Ivie, "Enabling Democratic Dissent," *Quarterly Journal of Speech* 101, no. 1 (2015): 53.

2. Raka Shome, "Space Matters: The Power and Practice of Space," *Communication Theory* 13, no. 1 (2003): 42.

3. Jose A. Guiterrez, John C. Hammerback, and Richard J. Jenson, *A War of Words: Chicano Protest in the 1960s and 1970s* (New York: Bloomsbury Academic, 1985), 6.

4. Guiterrez, Hammerback, and Jenson, *War of Words*, 6.

5. Joanna Walters, "Women's March on Washington Set to Be One of America's Biggest Protests," *Guardian* online, January 14, 2017, https://www.theguardian.com/us-news/2017/jan/14/womens-march-on-washington-protest-size-donald-trump.

6. Jason Wilson, "The Rightwing Groups Behind Wave of Protests Against COVID-19 Restrictions," *Guardian* online, April 17, 2020, https://www.theguardian.com/world/2020/apr/17/far-right-coronavirus-protests-restrictions.

7. Robert Ivie, "Rhetorical Deliberation and Democratic Politics in the Here and Now," *Rhetoric and Public Affairs* 5, no. 2 (2002): 281.

8. Jacques Derrida, *Speech and Phenomena: And Other Essays on Husserl's Theory of Signs*, trans. David B. Allison and Newton Garver (Evanston, IL: Northwestern University Press, 1973).

9. Jacques Derrida, *The Politics of Friendship*, trans. George Collins (New York: Verso, 2005).

10. Jacques Rancière, *Dis-agreement: Politics and Philosophy*, trans. Julie Rose (Minneapolis: Minnesota University Press, 1999).

11. Chantal Mouffe, *The Democratic Paradox* (New York: Verso, 2000).

12. See, for instance, Benjamin Arditi, *Politics on the Edges of Liberalism: Difference, Populism, Revolution, Agitation* (Edinburgh: Edinburgh University Press, 2007); Jane Mummery, *Radicalizing Democracy for the Twenty-First Century* (New York: Routledge, 2017); Ariana Reano, "Reconsidering the Paradox of Democracy," *Andamios* 5, no. 10 (2009): 309–333; Kathryn McNeilly, "After the Critique of Rights: For a Radical Democratic Theory and Practice of Human Rights," *Law and Critique* 27, no. 3 (2016): 269–288; Jen Hui Bon Hoa, "The Law or the Demos? Derrida and Rancière on the Paradox of Democracy," *Paragraph* 43, no. 2 (2020): 179–196; Helge Schwiertz, "Radical Democratic Theory and Migration: The Refugee Protest March as a Democratic Practice," *Philosophy and Social Criticism* 48, no. 2 (2022): 289–309.

13. Joshua Guitar, *Dissent, Discourse, and Democracy: Whistleblowers as Sites of Political Contestation* (Lanham, MD: Lexington Books, 2021), 174.

14. For a quality aggregate review of Derrida, Rancière, Mouffe, and other critical theorists of democracy, see, for instance, Mummery, *Radicalizing Democracy*.

15. Deconstruction endures throughout Derrida's work. For more substantive readings on the development of his theory, refer to the following works: Jacques Derrida, *Writing and Difference*, trans. Alan Bass (Chicago: University of Chicago Press, 1978); Jacques Derrida, *Of Grammatology*, trans. Gayatri Chakravorty Spivak (Baltimore, MD: Johns Hopkins University Press, 1997); Jacques Derrida, *Voice and Phenomenon*, trans. Leonard Lawlor (Evanston, IL: Northwestern University Press, 2011).

16. Derrida, *Speech and Phenomena*, 102.

17. Rancière, *Dis-agreement*.

18. Bruno Bosteels, "Rancière's Leftism, or, Politics and Its Discontents," in *Jacques Rancière: History, Politics, Aesthetics*, ed. Gabriel Rockhill and Philip Watts (Durham, NC: Duke University Press, 2009), 166.

19. Bosteels, "Rancière's Leftism," 174.

20. Rancière, *Dis-agreement*.

21. Rancière, *Dis-agreement*, 43.

22. Mouffe, *Democratic Paradox*.

23. Mouffe, *Democratic Paradox*, 10.

24. Mouffe, *Democratic Paradox*, 5.

25. Mouffe, *Democratic Paradox*, 140.

26. Mouffe, *Democratic Paradox*, 15–16.

27. Mouffe, *Democratic Paradox*, 13.

28. Derrida, *Politics of Friendship*, 159.

29. Jacques Rancière, *Hatred of Democracy*, trans. Steve Corcoran (New York: Verso, 2006), 41.

30. Rancière, *Hatred of Democracy*, 41.

31. Derrida, *Politics of Friendship*, 232.

32. Derrida, *Politics of Friendship*, 104.

33. Jacques Derrida, *Rogues: Two Essays on Reason*, trans. Pascale-Anne Brault and Michael Naas (Stanford, CA: Stanford University Press, 2005), 82.

34. Bosteels, "Rancière's Leftism," 166.

35. Derrida, *Rogues*, 35.

36. This idea was first conceptualized by Stephen M. Kohn in *The Whistleblower's Handbook: A Step-by-Step Guide to Doing What's Right and Protecting Yourself* (Guilford, CT: Lyons Press, 2011), but it is also analyzed in scholarly works like Allison Stanger, *Whistleblowers: Honesty in America from Washington to Trump* (New Haven, CT: Yale University Press, 2019), and Guitar, *Dissent, Discourse, and Democracy*.

37. Civil Service Reform Act, Pub. L. No. 95-454, 92 Stat. 1114.

38. Marcia P. Miceli and Janet P. Near, *Blowing the Whistle: The Organizational and Legal Implications for Companies and Employees* (Lanham, MD: Lexington Books, 1992), 15–17.

39. Stanger, *Whistleblowers*, 6.

40. Alan Chu, "In Tradition of Speaking Fearlessly: Locating a Rhetoric of Whistleblowing in the Parrhēsiastic Dialectic," *Advances in the History of Rhetoric* 19, no. 3 (2016): 248.

41. Hamilton Bean, *No More Secrets: Open Source Information and the Reshaping of U.S. Intelligence* (Westport, CT: Praeger, 2011), xiii.

42. Guitar, *Dissent, Discourse, and Democracy*, 118.

43. Alan Chu, "Whistleblower Epideictic and the Rejuvenation of the Fourth Estate," *Quarterly Journal of Speech* 109, no. 3 (2023): 212.

44. Guitar, *Dissent, Discourse, and Democracy*, 144.

45. Dave Davies, "Chelsea Manning Shared Secrets with WikiLeaks. Now She's Telling Her Own Story," NPR online, October 17, 2022, https://www.npr.org/2022/10/17/1129416671/chelsea-manning-wikileaks-memoir-readme.

46. Chelsea J. Carter, "Bradley Manning: Whistle-Blower or Traitor? He Awaits Judge's Verdict," CNN online, July 29, 2013, https://www.cnn.com/2013/07/28/us/bradley-manning-case/index.html.

47. Michael R. Touchton, Casey A. Klofstad, Jonathan P. West, and Joseph E. Uscinski, "Whistleblowing or Leaking? Public Opinion Toward Assange, Manning, and Snowden," *Research and Politics* 7 no. 1 (2020), https://doi.org/10.1177/2053168020904582.

48. Michael Ratner, "Edward Snowden Isn't the Only Truth Teller Who Deserves Clemency," *Guardian*, January 15, 2014, https://www.theguardian.com/commentisfree/2014/jan/15/edward-snowden-chelsea-manning-julian-assange-clemency.

49. Lauren Walker, "Glenn Greenwald: Why Americans Prefer Edward Snowden to Chelsea Manning," *Newsweek* online, July 20, 2015, https://www.newsweek.com/glenn-greenwald-why-americans-prefer-edward-snowden-chelsea-manning-355644.

50. Deb Riechmann, "Snowden Not a Whistleblower, Congressional Report Says," PBS, September 15, 2016, https://www.pbs.org/newshour/nation/snowden-whistleblower-congressional-report.

51. Nick Gass, "White House: Snowden 'Is Not a Whistleblower,' " *Politico* online, September 14, 2016, https://www.politico.com/story/2016/09/edward-snowden-not-whistleblower-earnest-228163.

52. Barack Obama, "Remarks by the President in a Press Conference," August 9, 2013, https://obamawhitehouse.archives.gov/the-press-office/2013/08/09/remarks-president-press-conference.

53. Donald Trump, Twitter post, November 4, 2019, 8:14 a.m., https://twitter.com/realdonaldtrump/status/1191342959695933441.

54. "Whistleblower Is a 'Fake': Trump," Reuters online, November 22, 2019, https://www.reuters.com/video/watch/idOVB6MJFTR.

55. Jacqueline Alemany, Emma Brown, Tom Hamburger, and Jon Swaine, "Ahead of Jan. 6, Willard Hotel in Downtown D.C. Was a Trump Team 'Command Center' for Effort to Deny Biden the Presidency," *Washington Post* online, October 23, 2021, https://www.washingtonpost.com/investigations/willard-trump-eastman-giuliani-bannon/2021/10/23/c45bd2d4-3281-11ec-9241-aad8e48f01ff_story.html.

56. Melissa Carone, Twitter profile, https://twitter.com/mellissa_carone, as of December 31, 2022.

57. "Uncut Explosive Testimony: Melissa Carone, Michigan House Oversight Committee," TFN Network online, December 4, 2020, https://www.youtube.com/watch?v=GEivbAXl1pg.

58. Jacob Shamsian, "Postal Service Finds 'No Evidence' of Project Veritas' Claim That Mail Workers Tampered with Ballots in the 2020 Election," *Business Insider* online, March 18, 2021, https://www.businessinsider.com/postal-service-finds-no-evidence-project-veritas-mail-ballot-claims-2021-3.

59. Jane Lytvynenko, "The 'Plandemic' Video Has Exploded Online—and It Is Filled with Falsehoods," *Buzzfeed News* online, May 7, 2020, https://www.buzzfeednews.com/article/janelytvynenko/coronavirus-plandemic-viral-harmful-fauci-mikovits.

60. Davey Alba, "Virus Conspiracists Elevate a New Champion," *New York Times* online, May 9, 2020, https://www.nytimes.com/2020/05/09/technology/plandemic-judy-mikovitz-coronavirus-disinformation.html.

61. Reuters Fact Check, "Fact Check—No Evidence over 48,000 People Died Within 14 Days of Receiving COVID-19 Vaccine," October 8, 2021, https://www.reuters.com/article/factcheck-vaccine-48000/fact-check-no-evidence-over-48000-people-died-within-14-days-of-receiving-covid-19-vaccine-idUSL1N2R41J6; Reuters Fact Check, "Fact Check—Report on 'CDC Whistleblower' Saying Vaccines 'Never Meant to Stop COVID' from Satirical Website," January 17, 2022, https://www.reuters.com/article/factcheck-cdc-satirearticle/fact-check-report-on-cdc-whistleblower-saying-vaccines-never-meant-to-stop-covid-from-satirical-website-idUSL1N2TX1GZ.

62. Bruce Y. Lee, " 'Whistleblower' Claiming China Created Covid-19 Coronavirus Has Ties to Steve Bannon," *Forbes* online, September 17, 2020, https://www.forbes.com/sites/brucelee/2020/09/17/whistleblower-claiming-china-created-covid-19-coronavirus-has-ties-to-steve-bannon/?sh=2c21445022d5.

63. Li-Meng Yan interviewed by Tucker Carlson in segment "Coronavirus Whistleblower Speaks Out About Possible COVID Origin on 'Tucker,' " Fox News online, September 15, 2020, https://www.youtube.com/watch?v=qFlqXPl_hZQ.

64. Jason Murdock, "Chinese Virologist Who Claimed COVID Was Made in Lab Says Her Mom Has Been Arrested in China," *Newsweek* online, October 7, 2020, https://www.newsweek.com/chinese-virologist-mon-arrested-china-covid-lab-conspiracy-theory-1536962; Craig Timberg, "Scientists Said Claims About China Creating the Coronavirus Were Misleading. They Went Viral Anyway," *Washington Post* online, February 12, 2021, https://www.washingtonpost.com/technology/2021/02/12/china-covid-misinformation-li-meng-yan/.

65. Edward Snowden, "Why Do Conspiracy Theories Flourish? Because the Truth Is Too Hard to Handle," *Guardian* online, July 1, 2021, https://www.theguardian.com/commentisfree/2021/jul/01/edward-snowdon-conspiracy-theories-belief-powerlessness.

66. Paolo Freire, *Pedagogy of the Oppressed* (New York: Bloomsbury, 2014).

67. bell hooks, *Teaching Community: A Pedagogy of Hope* (New York: Routledge, 2003).

68. Chu, "Whistleblower Epideictic," 226.

69. Christina R. Foust, *Transgression as a Mode of Resistance: Rethinking Social Movement in an Era of Corporate Globalization* (Lanham, MD: Lexington Books, 2010), 48.

70. Juliet Dee, "Charlottesville, January 6 and Incitement: Can Civil Conspiracy Laws Permit an End-Run Around *Brandenburg v. Ohio*?," *Communication Law Review* 22, no. 1 (2022): 2.

71. Karlyn Kohns Campbell, "Agency: Promiscuous and Protean," *Communication and Critical/Cultural Studies* 2, no. 1 (2005): 5.

72. Karma R. Chávez and Cindy L. Griffin, "Power, Feminisms, and Coalitional Agency: Inviting and Enacting Difficult Dialogues," *Women's Studies in Communication* 32, no. 1 (2009): 8.

73. Ivie, "Enabling Democratic Dissent," 55.

74. Dana L. Cloud, *Reality Bites: Rhetoric and the Circulation of Truth Claims in U.S. Political Culture* (Columbus: Ohio State University Press, 2018), 42.

75. Foust, *Transgression as a Mode of Resistance*, 46.

76. Christina R. Foust, Amy Pason, and Kate Z. Rogness, "Introduction: Rhetoric and the Study of Social Change," in *What Democracy Looks Like: The Rhetoric of Social Movements and Counterpublics*, ed. Christina R. Foust, Amy Pason, and Kate Z. Rogness (Tuscaloosa: University of Alabama Press), 1–2.

77. Michael Warner, "Publics and Counterpublics," *Public Culture* 14, no. 1 (2002): 86.

78. Foust, *Transgression as a Mode of Resistance*, 190.

79. Jeanne Vaccaro, "Give Me an F: Radical Cheerleading and Feminist Performance," *Women and Performance: A Journal of Feminist Theory* 14, no. 2 (2005): 43.

80. Cloud, *Reality Bites*, 168.

81. Aaron Dimock, "Styles of Rejection in Local Public Argument on Iraq," *Argumentation* 24, no. 4 (2010): 424.

82. Ivie, "Enabling Democratic Dissent," 53.

83. Ivie, "Enabling Democratic Dissent," 56.

84. Robert L. Scott and Donald K. Smith, "The Rhetoric of Confrontation," *Quarterly Journal of Speech* 55, no. 1 (1969): 1–8.

85. Theodore Otto Windt Jr., "The Diatribe: Last Resort for Protest," *Quarterly Journal of Speech* 58, no. 1 (1972): 10.

86. Windt, "Diatribe," 13.

87. James S. Robbins, "Rioting Is Beginning to Turn People Off to BLM and Protests While Biden Has No Solution," *USA Today* online, August 31, 2020, https://www.usatoday.com/story/opinion/2020/08/31/riots-violence-erupting-turning-many-away-blm-and-protests-column/5675343002/.

88. Larry Buchanan, Quoctrung Bui, and Jugal K. Patel, "Black Lives Matter May Be the Largest Movement in U.S. History," *New York Times* online, July 3, 2020, https://www.nytimes.com/interactive/2020/07/03/us/george-floyd-protests-crowd-size.html.

89. Ralph Ellis, Madison Park, and Jareen Imam, "Black Lives Matter Protesters Return to the Streets," CNN online, July 9, 2016, https://www.cnn.com/2016/07/09/us/black-lives-matter-protests/index.html.

90. Lynsey Jeffery, "Peaceful Anti-Police Brutality Protests Continue Across the Country," NPR online, June 6, 2020, https://www.npr.org/2020/06/06/871553038/largely-peaceful-anti-police-brutality-protests-continue-across-the-country.

91. Lois Beckett, "Nearly All Black Lives Matter Protests Are Peaceful Despite Trump Narrative, Report Finds," *Guardian*, September 5, 2020, https://www.theguardian.com/world/2020/sep/05/nearly-all-black-lives-matter-protests-are-peaceful-despite-trump-narrative-report-finds.

92. Meghan Keneally, "What to Know About the Violent Charlottesville Protests and Anniversary Rallies," ABC News online, August 8, 2018, https://abcnews.go.com/US/happen-charlottesville-protest-anniversary-weekend/story?id=57107500.

93. Farah Stockman, "Who Were the Counterprotesters in Charlottesville?," *New York Times* online, August 14, 2017, https://www.nytimes.com/2017/08/14/us/who-were-the-counterprotesters-in-charlottesville.html.

94. Carly Q. Romalino, "Counter Protest Reenacting George Floyd's Death in South Jersey Goes Viral," *USA Today* online, June 9, 2020, https://www.usatoday.com/story/news/local/south-jersey/2020/06/09/counter-protest-reenacts-george-floyds-death-during-south-jersey-rally/5326467002/.

95. Edward Helmore, "Largest US Police Union Asks Amazon to Pull 'Offensive' Black Lives Matter Shirt," *Guardian* online, December 23, 2016, https://www.theguardian.com/technology/2016/dec/23/amazon-black-lives-matter-police-union-t-shirt.

96. Rachel Abrams, "McDonald's Workers Across the U.S. Stage #MeToo Protests," *New York Times* online, September 18, 2018, https://www.nytimes.com/2018/09/18/business/mcdonalds-strike-metoo.html.

97. Megan Trimble, "Time's Person of the Year: #MeToo 'Silence Breakers,'" *US News and World Report* online, December 6, 2017, https://www.usnews.com/news/national-news/articles/2017-12-06/metoo-silence-breakers-named-time-magazines-person-of-the-year-2017.

98. Elizabeth Blair, "After One Year of Headlines, #MeToo Is Everywhere," NPR online, October 6, 2018. https://www.npr.org/2018/10/06/654993350/after-one-year-of-headlines-metoo-is-everywhere.

99. Nadia Khomami, "#MeToo: How a Hashtag Became a Rallying Cry Against Sexual Harassment," *Guardian* online, October 20, 2017, https://www.theguardian.com/world/2017/oct/20/women-worldwide-use-hashtag-metoo-against-sexual-harassment.

100. Darran Simon, "Trayvon Martin's Death Sparked a Movement That Lives on Five Years Later," CNN online, February 26, 2017, https://www.cnn.com/2017/02/26/us/trayvon-martin-death-anniversary/index.html.

101. Jaweed Kaleem, "Amid Milwaukee Unrest, a Conservative Black Sheriff Clashes with the City's Liberal White Police Chief," *Los Angeles Times* online, August 19, 2016, https://www.latimes.com/nation/la-na-milwaukee-sheriff-david-clarke-20160816-snap-story.html.

102. Andrea Peyser, "#MeToo Mob Comes for Bill Murray and Makes Mockery of the Movement," *New York Post* online, April 26, 2022, https://nypost.com/2022/04/26/metoo-mob-comes-for-bill-murray/.

103. Kyle Smith, "#MeToo Has Morphed into a Career-Destroying Angry Mob," *New York Post* online, September 22, 2018, https://nypost.com/2018/09/22/metoo-has-morphed-into-a-career-destroying-angry-mob/.

104. Ben Beaumont-Thomas, "Kanye West Condemns #MeToo Movement as 'Nineteen Eighty-Four Mind Control,'" *Guardian* online, November 5, 2021, https://www.theguardian.com/music/2021/nov/05/kanye-west-condemns-metoo-movement-as-nineteen-eighty-four-mind-control.

105. Anna Menta, "Terry Gilliam on Weinstein Accusers: 'A Night with Harvey—That's the Price You Pay,'" *Newsweek* online, March 16, 2018, https://www.newsweek.com/terry-gilliam-harvey-weinstein-me-too-849573.

106. Eugene Scott, "Trump Uses Kavanaugh to Embrace Another Culture War: The Backlash to #MeToo and Changing Gender Norms," *Washington Post* online, October 8, 2018, https://www.washingtonpost.com/politics/2018/10/08/trump-uses-kavanaugh-embrace-another-culture-war-backlash-metoo-changing-gender-norms/.

107. Emily Tillett, "McConnell: Senate Won't Be 'Intimidated' by 'Mob-Like Tactics' of Anti-Kavanaugh Protesters," CBS News online, October 7, 2018, https://www.cbsnews.com/news/mitch-mcconnell-face-the-nation-senate-wont-be-intimidated-by-mob-like-tactics-of-anti-kavanaugh-protesters/.

108. Tyler McCarthy, Celebrities Who Have Been 'Canceled' Over Scandals, Stances on Protests," Fox News online, June 11, 2020, https://www.foxnews.com/entertainment/celebrities-who-have-been-canceled-over-scandals-stances-on-protests.

109. Yohana Desta, "Trump Mocks #MeToo Movement Days After Decrying 'a Scary Time for Young Men,'" *Vanity Fair* online, October 11, 2018, https://www.vanityfair.com/hollywood/2018/10/donald-trump-mocking-me-too.

110. Lauren Tuck, "'That's Not How #MeToo Works Lady': Kellyanne Conway Slammed for Congratulatory Kavanaugh Tweet," *Yahoo! Life* online, October 7, 2018, https://www.yahoo.com/lifestyle/thats-not-metoo-works-lady-kelly anne-conway-slammed-kavanaugh-congratulations-tweet-125715321.html?guccounter=1.

111. Nanette Asimov, "#MeToo Movement Spurs #HimToo Backlash: 'People Don't Want to Believe,'" *San Francisco Chronicle* online, October 13, 2018, https://www.sfchronicle.com/nation/article/MeToo-movement-spurs-HimToo-backlash-People-13304270.php.

112. Kelly McLaughlin, "5 People Died in the Capitol Insurrection. Experts Say It Could Have Been So Much Worse," *Business Insider* online, January 23, 2021, https://www.businessinsider.com/capitol-insurrection-could-have-been-deadlier-experts-say-2021-1.

113. Fiona Hill, "Yes, It Was a Coup Attempt. Here's Why," *Politico* online, January 11, 2021, https://www.politico.com/news/magazine/2021/01/11/capitol-riot-self-coup-trump-fiona-hill-457549.

114. Rebecca Ballhaus, Joe Palazzolo, and Andrew Restuccia, "Trump and His Allies Set the Stage for Riot Well Before January 6," *Wall Street Journal* online, January 8, 2021, https://www.wsj.com/articles/trump-and-his-allies-set-the-stage-for-riot-well-before-january-6-11610156283.

115. Karoun Demirjian, Carol D. Leonnig, Paul Kane, and Aaron C. Davis, "Inside the Capitol Siege: How Barricaded Lawmakers and Aides Sounded Urgent Please for Help as Police Lost Control," *Washington Post*, January 10, 2021, https://www.washingtonpost.com/politics/inside-capitol-siege/2021/01/09/e3ad3274-5283-11eb-bda4-615aaefd0555_story.html.

116. Jeffrey Scott Shapiro, "Stop Calling Jan. 6 an 'Insurrection,' " *Wall Street Journal* online, January 5, 2022, https://www.wsj.com/articles/stop-calling-jan-6-an-insurrection-capitol-riot-civil-disorder-insurgency-protest-first-amendment-11641417543.

117. Arthur Goldsmith, "It Isn't Nitpicking—What Trump Attempted Was a Self-Coup, Not a Coup," *Boston Globe* online, January 10, 2022, https://www.boston-globe.com/2022/01/10/opinion/its-not-nitpicking-what-trump-attempted-was-self-coup-not-coup/.

118. David Bauder, "Riot? Insurrection? Words Matter in Describing Capitol Siege," AP News online, January 14, 2021, https://apnews.com/article/donald-trump-capitol-siege-riots-media-8000ce7db2b176c1be386d945be5fd6a.

119. Chandelis Duster and Dakin Andone, "Here's What 'Insurrection,' 'Coup' and 'Sedition' Mean," CNN online, January 13, 2022, https://www.cnn.com/2021/12/13/politics/insurrection-sedition-coup-january-6/index.html.

120. Mouffe, *Democratic Paradox*, 124.

121. Hélène Cixous, "The Laugh of the Medusa," trans. Keith Cohen and Paula Cohen, *Signs* 1, no. 4 (1976): 875–893.

122. Foust, *Transgression as a Mode of Resistance*, 45–49.

123. Cloud, *Reality Bites*, 168.

124. Karen Tracy, *Challenges of Ordinary Democracy: A Case Study in Deliberation and Dissent* (University Park: Pennsylvania State University Press, 2010).

125. Cloud, *Reality Bites*, 105.

126. Mark Lawrence McPhail, "Dessentializing Difference: Transformative Visions in Contemporary Black Thought," *Howard Journal of Communication* 13, no. 1 (2002): 93.

127. Karma R. Chávez, "Beyond Complicity: Coherence, Queer Theory, and the Rhetoric of the 'Gay Christian Movement,'" *Text and Performance Quarterly* 24, no. 3 (2004): 259.

128. Shome, "Space Matters," 43.

2

Wrangling the Ructions

Major Ian Fishback, Ph.D. and His Whistleblowing Campaign

REBEKAH L. FOX AND ANN E. BURNETTE

Bad things tend to happen to prophets.

—Helen Kennedy[1]

If one way to judge a democracy is to examine how its people treat whistleblowers, the twenty-first century has provided many chances for reflection on the health of democracies around the world. As Guitar argues, "The contextual dynamics of technological advancement in an era of increased state security concerns created an atmosphere ripe for a wave of whistleblowers."[2] An increased attention toward state security concerns often draws attention to the military's role in maintaining that security, and subsequent perceived tradeoffs between national security and individual liberties. The public discourse around these topics intensified as the images of prisoner abuse at Abu Ghraib prison emerged in the early stages of the Iraq War. The heavily publicized images, and powerful public backlash, prompted government officials to launch investigations. However, holding a few bad actors accountable at Abu Ghraib did not eliminate the use of questionable interrogation tactics in other military theaters, or restore the order necessary to sustain a healthy democracy.

In 2005, Major Ian Fishback, Ph.D. (1979–2021), who served two tours with the 82nd Airborne, and two tours with the 5th Special Forces Group in both Afghanistan and Iraq, blew the whistle on what he perceived to be violations of the *US Army Field Manual on Interrogation* while he was deployed to Afghanistan. As opposed to other whistleblowing cases, wherein the whistleblower's story is silenced or heavily marginalized as the event unfolds, we have both media coverage of Fishback and Fishback's original writings to allow a more complete examination of the whistleblowing process. However, Fishback's firsthand account is still primarily only available through media outlets. Thus, understanding the emancipatory potential of Fishback's whistleblowing accounts will still rely upon media discourse. Specifically, we seek to understand how the news media, whose overarching democratic goal in whistleblowing cases should be to inform the public, actually contribute to maintaining an antidemocratic status quo. In this chapter, we apply the abstraction model[3] to media coverage of Fishback to better understand how whistleblowers are conceptualized and, subsequently, how the American public is invited to engage the ideas brought forth by the whistleblower toward emancipatory ends.

Who Was Ian Fishback? The Making of a Warrior-Scholar

Ian Fishback was born in Detroit, Michigan, on January 19, 1979. He grew up in Newberry in Michigan's Upper Peninsula, where his parents, John and Sharon Fishback, were rural letter carriers. John Fishback had seen combat during his service in Vietnam. At Newberry High School, Fishback distinguished himself as a scholar and an athlete. He played on the football team and graduated with a 3.953 GPA in 1997. It was in high school, according to his father, that Fishback made the decision to seek a military career.[4] Fishback entered West Point and matriculated with a BS in Middle Eastern studies in 2001. During Fishback's service in the US Army, he completed four tours and was promoted to major before he left in 2014.

Fishback was not only a warrior but a scholar who simultaneously served in the Army while working on multiple academic degrees. He earned an MA in philosophy and political science at the University of Michigan in 2012 and taught at West Point from 2012 to 2015. He then enrolled in the University of Michigan to pursue a doctorate. In 2020, he was named a Fulbright Scholar to the Raoul Wallenberg Institute of

Human Rights and Humanitarian Law in Lund, Sweden. Fishback worked in Sweden from January to October 2021. For reasons that will become clearer throughout this chapter, he became "deeply disillusioned"[5] with the Army and the US and applied for citizenship in the European Union.[6] During this time, according to *The Washington Post*, Fishback "became overwhelmed by delusions that secret US government teams were tracking and planning to imprison or kill him."[7] He completed his doctoral dissertation, Method and the Morality of War,[8] and dedicated it to "the innocent victims of the Central Intelligence Agency." Once he returned to the US, "for several months he cycled through halfway houses and state-funded psychiatric facilities as his friends pushed to get him into a VA hospital."[9] Fishback died on November 19, 2021, in an adult foster care facility in Bangor, Michigan. He was forty-two years old.

What Do We Know and What Can We Learn from Fishback as a Whistleblower?

Fishback's experience as a "warrior-scholar" and whistleblower provides researchers with a well-documented look at how the whistleblowing process can influence an individual whistleblower, as well as the organizations and institutions to which they belong. There is a powerful curiosity around understanding who the person at the center of the controversy is and the circumstances they face. This curiosity has spurred scholars to explore the role of identity and tensions in identity[10] as well as motives of whistleblowers and the factors that affect their decisions.[11] Researchers have also examined the organizational dynamics of whistleblowing, including the measures that organizations might take in response,[12] the moral dimensions of whistleblowing,[13] the organizational hurdles associated with coming forward as a whistleblower,[14] the effect of leadership practices on whistleblowing,[15] and organizational retaliation against whistleblowers.[16] However, scholars have also broken through the "container" metaphor for organizations by examining whistleblowing in broader societal institutions. They have investigated implications for journalists,[17] the law,[18] and watchdog groups.[19]

Fishback's case also provides scholars who are interested in understanding the rhetoric of whistleblowing with a unique set of texts because he wrote extensively about his experience through a variety of outlets. Scholars interested in whistleblowers' descriptions of their own strategies[20]

could use Fishback's many public interviews, invited lectures, and pod-
casts to provide the foundation for a much-needed genre of whistleblowing rhetoric. Additionally, Fishback's dissertation provides yet another
primary text for the analysis of Fishback's reasoning behind his public
whistleblowing campaign. Still other scholars interested in exploring
the relationship between the rhetorical situation and the whistleblower's
motives, such as Chu, who concluded that both practitioners of parrhesia in ancient contexts and contemporary whistleblowers must exhibit a
rhetorical sensibility by taking into account factors such as their audience
and context,[21] would find plenty to analyze in Fishback's writings.

However, we are primarily interested in the powerful role the media
plays in shaping the public's understanding of whistleblowing. Almost
without exception, what the public comes to initially know about the
whistleblower is filtered through media coverage, which shapes public
knowledge through well-known media practices such as narrative framing.
Specifically, researchers have analyzed how media images of whistleblowers can compete with, cooperate with, or otherwise influence the ways
the state characterizes whistleblowers.[22] Other researchers have examined
the role of the media in casting the whistleblower as a hero[23] or the way
photographic images can further impact public debate.[24]

The issues highlighted by these studies have the potential to shed
light on the Fishback case. What is compelling about Fishback is the way
his disclosures about military practices influenced the public debate about
military torture, and the powerful role the media played in that process.
To further examine this dynamic, we turn to the abstruction model developed by Guitar.[25] Guitar used this model to explain how media depictions
of whistleblowers distract the public from the issues that whistleblowers
want to resolve. The abstruction model includes three components. The
first component is abstraction. The model contends that the media coverage of whistleblowers "abstract[s] situational truths through reduction,
distortion, and selective amplification processes."[26] Ructions constitute the
second component. Abstractions generate ructions or controversies that
invite debate about ancillary issues, thus diverting public discourse away
from the original complaint. Ultimately, these media depictions function
as the third component, obstruction. This discourse obstructs justice by
flooding the public with an oversaturation of elongated, inconsequential debates that "obstruct substantive public discourse on the concerns
raised by the political agents, in this case the whistleblowers."[27] In sum,

abstruction analysis examines the "aggregate reactions to individual agents who interrogate anti-democratic power" to "identify and explain the patterns of reactive, domineering appeals of agents and institutions of power when experiencing ideological vulnerability."[28]

Although generalized methods of ideological criticism provide a foundation that urges us to examine how rhetoric functions hegemonically, this specific method of criticism allows a rhetorical reading of the media coverage that enables us to interrogate the influence of these media narratives on the public tensions over the place of torture, especially as it applies to the project of maintaining democracies. The abstraction model allows us to see below the surface of the media narratives and evaluate how media function rhetorically to maintain the status quo.

Abstructing Warrior Fishback

In this section we examine Fishback's stated concerns as well as the media coverage[29] of his case through the lens of the abstraction model to understand how this coverage seemingly calls for the truthful exposition of "violations of human rights and abuses of power"[30] but actually works to maintain the status quo and statist power regarding the military's use of torture. Because Fishback had worked for seventeen months within the military chain of command to get clarification about legalities regarding torture, and because he had written extensively about his concerns, we are able to read Fishback's goals in his own terms throughout the whistleblowing process. This is unusual because the rhetoric of whistleblowers is not always clearly stated and recorded over such a long period of time. In fact, Guitar argues that "paramount to the abstraction process is the silencing of the whistleblower."[31] He illustrates this claim in several case studies. For example, he discusses how Chelsea Manning was imprisoned for nearly three years while awaiting a trail, during which time she was "forbidden by the State to speak publicly or with members of the press."[32] In the case of Edward Snowden, who was charged in 2013 with three felonies under the Espionage Act, Snowden was "denied clemency and the formal promise of a fair legal trial"[33] and still lives under asylum in Russia to avoid extradition to the US. By contrast, Fishback's case allows us to examine how resistance to the statist ideology is more subtly muted or contained through the abstraction process, instead of overt silencing.

FISHBACK STATES HIS CONCERNS

Although the following abstraction and ruction sections identify how the media covered Fishback, this section focuses on Fishback's writing to establish a sort of baseline in the discourse. While Fishback wrote about many topics related to torture, two overarching concerns emerged: (1) a lack of clear standards for interrogations that led to questionable moral decisions by individual soldiers, and by extension the American military, and (2) the denial of responsibility by high-ranking officials and the scapegoating of lower-ranking officials. First, Fishback was concerned about the lack of clear standards that were to be used during military interrogations. In the now famous 2005 letter to Arizona Senator John McCain (R), he argued that the abuses he witnessed in Iraq were committed because of a lack of clarification regarding what was allowed and what was prohibited. He wrote, "We did not set the conditions for our soldiers to succeed. We failed to set clear standards, communicate those standards and enforce those standards."[34] He further stated that the confusion around these standards led to "a wide range of abuses including death threats, beatings, broken bones, murder, exposure to elements, extreme forced physical exertion, hostage-taking, stripping, sleep deprivation and degrading treatment."[35]

In a podcast interview in 2017, Fishback argued that in the wake of 9/11, the US military began using interrogation tactics derived from the Survival, Evasion, Resistance, and Escape (SERE) training program. Fishback noted that those techniques were intended to be specific to the SERE program and not meant to be used as interrogation techniques.[36] Moreover, Fishback contended that these practices went against the Geneva Conventions.

Fishback and two other members of the 82nd Airborne said that members of their battalion had "abused prisoners by assaulting them, exposing them to extreme temperatures, stacking them in pyramids and depriving them of sleep to compel them to reveal intelligence—or, in some cases, simply to amuse the soldiers."[37] Fishback said that soldiers administered beatings "in part to let off steam and in part to soften up detainees for interrogation at the direction of intelligence officers who appeared to be from the CIA."[38] In addition to his concerns about the purpose and legality of abusive interrogation practices, Fishback worried US soldiers were not given clear directives about interrogation techniques yet were charged with violations. He explained, "It wasn't just a problem that we weren't following the Geneva Conventions; it was a problem that there was no clear standard to replace the Geneva Conventions."[39] In short, Fishback said soldiers were being "scapegoated" by higher-level officials.[40]

Fishback's allegations also "showed that abusive interrogation practices were not limited to relatively untrained reservists at Abu Ghraib, but extended to an elite Army unit serving on the front lines in Iraq."[41] Fishback voiced his concerns through the chain of command. However, Fishback said that his superiors ignored his allegations for seventeen months. According to Roth, the Army officers also refused to clarify the interrogation policy under President George W. Bush's administration.[42] Fishback and two other soldiers described the abuses they witnessed to Human Rights Watch, which released a thirty-page report.[43] The Army finally responded to Fishback by interrogating him, investigating his relationship with Human Rights Watch, and trying to persuade him to identify the other two soldiers who made allegations about abuse.[44]

Media coverage of US military personnel abusing and torturing prisoners at the Abu Ghraib prison turned a spotlight on the issues that Fishback was questioning. On November 1, 2003, the Associated Press released a story on abusive treatment of Abu Ghraib prisoners that resulted in prisoner deaths. In April 2004, the television show *60 Minutes II* broadcast a report on this abuse that included explicit photographs of US military personnel torturing prisoners. Journalist Seymour Hersh, who won the Pulitzer Prize for investigative journalism during the Vietnam conflict, published a 2004 story on the Abu Ghraib abuse in *The New Yorker* that included photos taken by US military prison guards. The American public would later learn from John Kiriakou, former CIA analyst and consultant for ABC News, that waterboarding was being used as an interrogation technique on al-Qaeda prisoners. Ultimately, eleven soldiers were convicted of crimes in military courts. The officer in command of Abu Ghraib, Brigadier General Janis Karpinski, was demoted to colonel, and Secretary of Defense Donald Rumsfeld twice offered to resign his position but President George W. Bush refused to accept his resignation.[45]

Reflecting on the hurdles associated with getting clarification, Fishback wrote, "My approach for clarification provides clear evidence that confusion over standards was a major contributor to the prisoner abuse. We owe our soldiers better than this. Give them a clear standard that is in accordance with the bedrock principles of our nation."[46] In what seems like an attempt to justify his request for clarification and to shine a light on those who would refuse that request, he wrote, "Since clear standards only limit interrogation techniques, it is reasonable for me to assume that supporters of this argument desire to use coercion to acquire information from detainees."[47] Fishback also wrote about his concerns that the state's use of torture eroded the moral standing of America on the international stage. He expressed concern about violating his sense of American values broadly when he wrote: "Some argue that since our actions are not as horrifying as Al Qaeda's we should not be concerned. When did Al Qaeda become any type of standard by which we measure the morality of the United States? We are America, and our actions should be held to a higher standard, the ideals expressed in documents such as the Declaration of Independence and the Constitution."[48] His concerns about morality also manifest on a more personal level. He wrote extensively about the need to prevent the moral injuries that could be sustained by the men and women inflicting this torture, and the military's responsibility to prevent those situations. He was troubled by the thought that he had let "his men commit a dishonorable act."[49]

Although Fishback wrote extensively about these concerns (and continued to interrogate pragmatic and philosophical issues related to torture in his PhD dissertation, subsequent interviews, and lectures), he seemed especially unsettled by what he perceived to be dishonesty and a denial of responsibility by high-ranking officials, as well as the scapegoating of lower-ranking service members. Fishback seemed particularly moved by Rumsfeld's claim that the military was actually obeying the rules of the Geneva Convention. He recalled, "I was immediately concerned that the Army was taking part in a lie to the Congress, which would have been a clear violation of the Constitution,"[50] and "bottom line: I am concerned that the Army is deliberately misleading the American people about detainee treatment within our custody."[51]

Recognizing that he was not the first person to push back against this dishonesty, denial of responsibility, and the price of blowing the whistle, Fishback asked, "How many other people have tried and been unable to bring things to light, given how hard it has been for me? . . . A lot of men I hold a great deal of respect for are going to hate me right now."[52] Some of these men were his immediate supervisors. His company commander asked Fishback to think about his career and "to remember the honor of the unit is at stake."[53] Later, Fishback revealed that the commander said he "would not stand up for me if I took my issues higher."[54]

While Fishback seemed particularly bothered by Rumsfeld's overt denial of wrongdoing, he was also concerned that if wrongdoing was discovered, the state would scapegoat lower-ranking service members. He drew a connection to the events surrounding the Abu Ghraib prison scandal as precedent. After the Abu Ghraib photos were leaked, officials began to frame the Abu Ghraib prisoner abuse scandal as an isolated situation, during which time low-ranking personnel (in the Guard or the reserves) were taking rogue actions, and that they had been discovered and punished. During Lynndie England's trial, prosecutors argued that England, alone, was responsible for abusing prisoners and that she "bore full responsibility for her own sick humor," finishing with the rhetorical question, "What soldier wouldn't know that's illegal?"[55]

When England's sentence was handed down in 2005, the Bush administration argued, "England is an example of how we hold people accountable."[56] However, these claims, along with Rumsfeld's insistence that torture was not occurring, caused Fishback to take a more public stand. He reasoned, "The way we have been treating detainees is immoral. . . . We had a serious command climate problem, across the board. One of the things that infuriates me is that the leaders are not accepting responsibility."[57] Fishback said the courts-martial for England and other low-ranking soldiers obscured the fact that unclear interrogation and treatment guidelines were accepted and promoted by the Army's chain of command.[58] He also raised the stakes by extending the blame from military officials to include the entire executive branch: "It's unjust to hold only lower-ranking soldiers accountable for something that is so clearly, at a minimum, an officer corps problem, and probably a combination with the executive branch of government."[59]

In 2005, Fishback sent signed letters detailing the abuse to top aides of McCain and Senator John Warner (R-VA). Warner was the chair of the Senate Armed Service Committee, and McCain was a member of the committee who had survived more than five years of torture during the Vietnam War. In one of his letters, Fishback argued, "Despite my efforts, I have been unable to get clear, consistent answers from my leadership about what constitutes lawful and humane treatment of detainees."[60] He maintained that this ambiguity contributed to the abuses he witnessed, which included murder, death threats, beatings, exposure to elements, and sleep deprivation.[61] Fishback concluded, "If we abandon our ideals in the face of adversity and aggression, then those ideals were never really in our possession. I would rather die fighting than give up even the smallest part of the idea that is 'America.' "[62]

Fishback's letter soon garnered significant attention. According to Fishback, his letter was leaked to other people on Capitol Hill. Fishback said he learned this when he was pulled from the Special Forces training and his team sergeant warned Fishback that he would not "make it through" the training.[63] Fishback speculated that his letter was leaked to the media the same day to "protect me in some way."[64] McCain also spoke of Fishback and his letter on the Senate floor. Fishback worked with McCain, and in October 2005, the Senate passed the Detainee Treatment Act of 2005 (DTA). The bill prohibited cruel, inhumane, and humiliating treatment of US-held detainees. Bush signed the bill on December 30, 2005. *Time* named Fishback one of the 2006 *Time* 100, and *Time* journalist Coleen Rowley wrote that Fishback "downplayed his heroism as nothing more than supporting clear standards in accordance with US values."[65]

Although Fishback stated his concerns clearly, he was not the only one influencing how the public perceived his actions. In the following section, we explore how media coverage of Fishback abstracts him as an individual and contributes to ructions in public discourse.

Abstractions and Ructions:
Distortions, Reductions, and Selective Amplifications

Abstracting Fishback

During the abstraction process, mediated discourses distort, reduce, or selectively amplify elements of the whistleblower's identity. In many cases, these distortions, reductions, and amplifications seem to invite the public to judge the personal credibility of the whistleblower (historically or at present) rather harshly. Often, during this phase, the audience absorbs a wealth of information about the whistleblower's personal life in what seems like a quest to explain the perceived resistant or disruptive behavior of the whistleblower. For example, the abstraction of Chelsea Manning painted her as being from a troubled home, mentally unstable, not physically built to be a soldier, "erratic and aimless," or in a state of "perpetual confusion."[66] As originally posited, abstraction generally focuses on disparaging details. However, abstraction can also occur through complimentary details to abstract the dissident, which in turn leads to debates about that detailed abstraction. In contrast to Manning and many others, a large portion of the abstraction of Fishback was focused on the rather positive aspects of his credibility as a citizen, soldier, and whistleblower. The bulk of the coverage contributes to a narrative of a small-town hero turned military hero turned whistleblowing hero.[67]

McCain directly voiced respect for Fishback's whistleblowing journey when he wrote, "I'm even more impressed by what a fine and honorable officer he is."[68] Letters to the editor included comments such as "it requires extraordinary courage to expose such vile practices. Our nation is blessed to have him among its defenders."[69] Or, in a *Time* article titled "Blowing the Whistle on Torture," Rowley wrote, "[Fishback] sends a shiver of respect down my spine."[70] One *New York Daily News* article titled "Capt. Tortured by Army Abuse of Prisoners" reads, "Army CAPT. Ian Fishback is smart, honest, and brave, with the face of a Boy Scout and spine of steel. . . . Fishback is everything the Army could want. But this perfect soldier is giving the Pentagon serious agita: He's accused Defense Secretary Donald Rumsfeld of lying to Congress about prisoner abuse."[71] Later, the same article pushed even harder to defend Fishback, by doubling down and directly calling out Fishback's fellow officers for their silence: "So, back to the honor code. If Fishback is lying, conjuring up the 17 months he spent investigating policy, Louisville Slugger leg-smashings, and soldiers 'blowing off steam' at PUC tents (Prisoners Under Control), as well as the subsequent warnings from superiors to shut up and mind his career, then where are all the West Pointers with enough integrity to blow the whistle on this whistleblower?"[72] Another letter to the editor expressed concern for Fishback's welfare, saying, "I hope Mr. McCain will help keep this young officer from becoming a victim of his idealism."[73] Even those who seemed cautious about Fishback's whistleblowing ascribed the highest motives to Fishback. While this type of coverage was primarily sympathetic to Fishback, it still functioned to focus attention on Fishback as a person, instead of Fishback's stated goals.

RUCTIONS AROUND FACTS, DEFINITIONS, VALUES, AND POLICIES

The ructions that emerged in response to Fishback's story addressed issues including the veracity of Fishback's report and the (im)morality of torture. We organize and consider them based on three standard types of claims offered in stasis theory. These claims are propositions of fact (what is or is not?), value (is it good or bad?), and policy (what should be done about it?), and serve as grounds for public debate.[74]

Propositions of fact

One category of ructions that came forward was the degree to which Fishback's allegations were accurate and thorough. Some media reports sought to establish the facts of the case. Reporters and commentators took up two issues of fact: (1) the exact nature of the events Fishback reported, and (2) who was to blame.

A *New York Times* article discussing Fishback's allegations tried to put those issues in context to illustrate the nature of abuse. The article noted that if one of the activities that Fishback alleged "took place in a bar, [it] might prompt witnesses to call the police."[75] In Afghanistan, however, "these soldiers were the police."[76] In a letter to the editor of *The Washington Post*, a sergeant in the Arkansas Army National Guard who had served in Iraq from April 2004 to March 2005 said that Fishback's "experience and observations are inconsistent with mine."[77] The writer added, "I do not challenge Capt. Fishback or his observations. But I saw US soldiers, both active-duty and National Guard, conduct themselves professionally on a daily basis."[78] An editorial in *The Chicago Tribune* reported that the "new report by Human Rights Watch, based on accounts from an Army captain and two sergeants allege that inhumane treatment was the norm."[79] The paper stated, however, that "these allegations have yet to be confirmed."[80]

The second question of fact that emerged in the ruction was who was responsible for the practices of abusive interrogations. One issue that received media attention was whether it was appropriate for US military personnel to guard prisoners who were being held as intelligence sources. A report in *The Los Angeles Times* discussed one of the sergeants who had come forward with Fishback. The article purported that the sergeant "had never been trained in handling prisoners"[81] and quoted the sergeant to say, "We never should have been allowed to guard people who tried to kill us."[82] News sources also reported that Fishback raised the questions of whether Army soldiers should have assisted with the detention of terrorist suspects and whether the blame for the abuse belonged higher up the chain of command."[83] Syndicated columnist Derrick Z. Jackson opined, "The 'confusion' started at the top, where then–White House counsel and now-US [Attorney General] Alberto Gonzales wrote the torture memo suggesting that the United States need not follow international prisoner-treatment laws."[84] Jackson also warned, "The more the White House stonewalls, the more explosive the truth will be."[85]

Fishback's concerns were amplified by media sources who repeated his claims. Richard Serrano, writing for *The Los Angeles Times*, argued, "In such a unit, evidence of a significant breakdown in discipline would call into question the Army's contention that previously disclosed abuses did not reflect systemic problems,"[86] and, "the review is the first major investigation by the military of widespread prisoner abuse outside the Abu Ghraib prison scandal, and the first time such a review has targeted soldiers in the regular Army rather than the National Guardsmen and reservists in the Abu Ghraib case."[87] Writing about abuses in Afghanistan specifically, Serrano noted that previous abuse cases involved relatively untrained National Guard and reservists, but "this is the first time that soldiers in the regular Army have been implicated in widespread abuse."[88] Again, media outlets recognized Fishback's concerns and amplified them by saying that "high-ranking officers have largely escaped accountability."[89] *Time* took a wider perspective when they examined allegations of abuse at Abu Ghraib through the time of Fishback's whistleblowing, concluding that there had been "400 allegations of detainee mistreatment since Abu Ghraib—and more than 230 of its personnel have been dealt with through courts-martial and nonjudicial punishments, but [the Army] has yet to find senior officers culpable."[90]

A specific subcategory emerged within the category of propositions of fact: specific questions of definitions. Media reports belabored two of these issues of definition: (1) whether the alleged activities should be considered torture, and (2) what legal codes applied to them.

Observers who parsed the definition of torture tested their understandings against sources that cited personal experience, common sense, and political leanings. *The New York Times* included the observation that Rumsfeld challenged a US Defense Department memo describing enhanced interrogation techniques. "I stand 8 to 10 hours a day," Rumsfeld wrote on the memo, "Why is standing limited to 4 hours?"[91] A letter to the editor of *The Washington Post* asked how it was "not common sense" that Fishback was describing behaviors that were "not lawful and humane."[92] The author added, "How could he or his troops be confused?"[93] *The Washington Post* editorial board recognized that the White House was complicating the definition of torture. They noted that "Mr. Bush has promised that all detainees will be treated humanely,"[94] but that the attorney general's office argued that humane treatment could not be expressed in a "succinct definition."[95] Furthermore, *The Washington Post* observed, Timothy Flanigan, a nominee for deputy attorney general, "could not even bring himself to declare particularly barbaric interrogation tactics either legal or morally off-limits."[96] According to *The Washington Post*, "anything short of outright torture" was protected and "nothing is absolutely forbidden."[97] The paper warned, "It is an odious thing that the top two law enforcement officers of the United States will both be people who resort to evasive legalisms in response to simple questions."[98]

Another ruction was the definitional debate over what interrogation techniques were legal. *The Washington Post* published the letter that Fishback had sent to McCain, which provided one standard of legality. Fishback asserted that "coercion" was "morally inconsistent with the Constitution."[99] *The Washington Post* also published deputy Flanigan's more complicated interpretation of legality: "Whether a particular interrogation technique is lawful depends on the facts and circumstances."[100]

Propositions of value

Ructions also clustered around a second stasis: propositions of value. In this case, media coverage grappled with the moral implications of torture. *The New York Times* described the abuse suffered by prisoners in Camp Mercury at the hands of the Army's 82nd Airborne division as "systematic."[101] The regularity of these practices was more ethically concerning than occasional violations of judgment. The paper also noted that personnel in this unit "routinely beat and abused prisoners in 2003 and 2004 to help gather intelligence on the insurgency and to amuse themselves."[102] The underlying purpose of these practices—to advance intelligence aims or to entertain personnel—also had moral implications. *The New York Daily News* also posed the question of whether torture performed for "fun" was more reprehensible.[103] This account also quoted one of the anonymous whistleblowers who said, "In a way it was sport."[104] *The New York Daily News* presented another moral consideration: that the harsh treatment caused moral as well as physical injury to the detainees. The same whistleblower observed that many of the detainees were ultimately released without having been linked to the insurgency and that "if he's a good guy, you know, now he's a bad guy because of the way we treated him."[105] Whereas questions of fact and policy around the topic of torture invite considerable dialogue, questions of value (is "it" good or bad) pose problems in the discourse because even if people who would agree that the (torturous) activities occurring are permissible or "good," they seldom refer to them as torture, thus the plethora of alternative phrasing—"enhanced interrogation," "abuse," and so forth.

Propositions of policy

Ructions also contended with the question of efficacy. In the stasis of policy, three issues arose: (1) whether torture works, (2) how the practice of torture affects those who conduct the torture, and (3) the whistleblowing process itself.

In an editorial, *USA Today* asked whether torture produces "useful information" and answered, "Abusing prisoners elicits intelligence of questionable worth."[106] The editorial recounted McCain's experience being tortured as a prisoner of war and concluded, "The tortured will say anything to stop the pain."[107]

A related question of efficacy is what effect prisoner abuse has on the people performing the abuse and the society they represent. At one level, the ruction concerns the situation of those who are the abusers. *The New York Times* reported on the "siege mentality" that resulted as "prison guards themselves are prisoners of the fear of attacks by insurgents, car bombers, and snipers."[108] The article even commented on the framing function of this ruction when it noted that "the 'torture question' puts prisoner abuse in a broader context of fear and rage, both in Washington and on the ground in Iraq."[109] A letter to the editor of *The Los Angeles Times* identified Fishback as one of the people who would be harmed by the abuse allegations and opined, "It is a sorry reflection on the state of our country that his personal adherence to honor, dignity, and justice will in all likelihood cost him his career dedicated to protecting America."[110]

Another dimension of this concern is whether US policies will continue to enjoy the support of US citizens in the aftermath of the torture allegations. According to *The Los Angeles Times*, McCain expressed concern about American support for the war in Iraq in the wake of the torture allegations and indicated that "continued allegations of abuse only turned more Americans against the war in Iraq."[111] McCain observed, "They're unhappy about a number of aspects of the war, and with some justification."[112] Other commentators speculated about the effect the torture allegations would have on the practical and moral role the US wants to play on the world stage. *USA Today* commented on the question of efficacy when it warned that abusing prisoners "unquestionably undercuts American values and produces international revulsion."[113] *The New York Daily News* expressed concern that the US would become a less respected world power by quoting McCain. "We've got to have it stopped," McCain said, "it is hurting America's image abroad."[114] *The New York Daily News* further quoted the senator saying, "We've got to make it clear to the world that America doesn't do it. It's not about prisoners. It's about us."[115]

In addition to the abstraction of Fishback as a whistleblower, media outlets invited the public to concentrate on certain aspects of the whistleblowing process itself, specifically the danger Fishback faced as a whistleblower, the military's process of investigation (both into the torture and into Fishback's whistleblowing), and criticism of whistleblowing in general. For example, a mother of Fishback's best friend who was an Episcopal minister, Cheri Ford, recalled, "I told him I was worried, and he said 'Nothing's going to happen to me. Think of how bad it would look.' When I said they could make the training really hard on him, he said 'well, that will make me a better soldier in the long run.' "[116] Although this account seems to be focusing on Fishback's resilience, it also captures a common concern about retaliation inherent in the whistleblowing process. One letter to the editor of *The Los Angeles Times* argued, "It is a sorry reflection on the state of our country that his personal adherence to honor, dignity, and justice will in all likelihood cost him his career dedicated to protecting America."[117]

Some sources, including *The Washington Post*[118] and *The New York Times*,[119] asked whether the military chain of command was also a factor. As opposed to answering questions about the appropriateness of torture, these authors seemed concerned about the appropriate pathway of speaking truth to power, and determining if Fishback and been prudent in his approach.

However, the media also included official statements from the administration about the whistleblowing process. *The Washington Post* included a statement from a Pentagon spokesperson, Lieutenant Colonel John Skinner, criticizing Fishback's relationship with Human Rights Watch (HRW), concluding, "Humane treatment has always been the standard no matter how much certain organizations want people to believe otherwise."[120] It would appear that the media were interested in foregrounding the internal and external personal struggles Fishback faced through the process, although those struggles were not specifically his original concerns.

DISCUSSION: OBSTRUCTING A CHANGE TO STATIST POWER

The abstractions of Fishback as a person, and the abstractions of the whistleblowing process, as well as the subsequent fact, value, and policy ructions in the public discourse, seem to invite important reflection on substantive issues. However, these abstractions and ructions subtly divert attention away from the original reason for the whistleblowing in the first place. When the press is busy discussing the appropriateness of Fishback's decision to blow the whistle and the subsequent path he took, such conversations branch around his original call to clarify standards about the military's use of torture. Because the topics are so closely related, and because they almost seem necessary for a comprehensive understanding of the process, the topic shifts are subtle and seem like logical extensions of original topics, yet remain functionally as distractions.

However, the discourse around Fishback as a whistleblower reveals at least two additional ways obstruction can occur. As such, we advance Guitar's theory of abstraction. Rather than functioning to distract attention away from originally stated goals, audiences can appear to stay on topic, but actually not be discussing the same phenomena through language inconsistencies related to conceptual slippage. Discourse may also seem to reflect that a topic has reached a decisive resolution when what has really occurred is a type of premature discursive closure. Additionally, rather than media coverage that is elongated over a span of time, the entire discourse around the whistleblower may go dormant, only to reemerge after some type of situational exigence, like the death of the whistleblower.

The conceptual slippage around the topic of torture may function to obfuscate any real changes in the actual treatment of detainees. In the surface-level discourse on the topic, we may perceive that we have a general understanding of what constitutes torture, but subtle slippage occurs when the public tries to grapple with the nuanced difference between "inhumane treatment," "degrading treatment," and "abuse." The opportunity for bypassing errors to occur in interpersonal conversations, all the way up to bypassing during policy creation and implementation, is ripe. Calls for clarification may seem to be answered, but the ambiguity in the language still exists and no actual clarification is provided.

In addition to distraction, Guitar suggests that obstruction occurs through elongation (public discourse is stretched over long spans of time).[121] In what seemed like a victory for Fishback and McCain, the DTA, as enacted, prohibits the inhumane treatment of prisoners by confining interrogation techniques to those within the *US Army Field Manual on Interrogation*. However, this "victory" may actually function to bring discourse to a premature close. In mid-December in 2005, before the DTA was passed, the Pentagon changed the manual to include a ten-page classified addendum. *The New York Times* reported, "In a high-level meeting at the Pentagon on Tuesday, some Army and other Pentagon officials raised concerns that Mr. McCain would be furious at what could appear to be a back-door effort to circumvent his intentions," with one official saying "this is a stick in McCain's eye. It goes right up to the edge. He's not going to be comfortable with this."[122] Ultimately, the DTA passed, but Bush issued a signing statement to accompany the act that effectively states that as president he has the right to waive the law's restrictions to protect national security. Marty Lederman, a Georgetown University law professor, interviewed in early 2006 by *The Boston Globe* said, "The whole point of the McCain Amendment was to close every loophole," but that "the president has re-opened the loophole by asserting the constitutional authority to act in violation of the statute where it would assist in the war on terrorism."[123] In some ways, the DTA may have inadvertently functioned as discursive closure around the topic of torture, giving officials and the American public the impression that it would actually prohibit torture across the board.

After the DTA vote, there was little media coverage about Fishback until his death in 2021. During the time between the DTA vote and Fishback's death, he opted to pursue questions around "just war" and the military's use of torture through a different path than the military or the media: academia. He changed his sphere of argument from the public forum to the academy, which allowed him to develop his position more fully through his dissertation and the Socratic style he often used on academic panels, but he effectively limited his reach due to the sequestered nature of academic writing in contrast to the "breaking news" cycle of the media.

In a slight departure from how Guitar discussed the elongation process contributing to obstruction,[124] the Fishback case reveals how the whistleblower's case may fall into dormancy, only to be revived in the whistleblower's death. Instead of an elongation of the process unfolding over a long period of time, media coverage may seem to "wrap up" on a topic through discursive closure, as discussed earlier, leading to a period of dormancy related to the topic. Any whistleblower's death, if publicized, can invite the public to revisit the original case. However, the circumstances around Fishback's death revived the original abstraction process and sparked an entirely new set of ructions around the topic of mental health care for military veterans.

One set of authors, writing in 2021, focused on Fishback's personal qualities, while reaffirming the tragedy within the tragic hero narrative. One author stated, "He had an enormous sense of purpose and rigidity, and rigidity doesn't make for resilience often . . . he died awaiting a bed at the [Veteran's Affairs]."[125] A writer quoted a friend of Fishback who said, "Ian's greatest quality is not his courage but his humanity."[126] That writer also quoted a friend who said of Fishback, "He was a moral absolutist."[127] One author elevated Fishback by calling him "one of the military's most prominent active-duty whistleblowers" who had "developed a reputation for uncompromising moral courage."[128] That author concluded by quoting a philosophy professor who befriended Fishback, who said of the former soldier, "He's a flawed, tragic hero."[129]

Another author seemed to raise the stakes in abstracting Fishback by positioning him as the single conscious objector among otherwise silent West Pointers, and implicating all Americans in a system that allowed Fishback to suffer and die. He wrote, "We should remember Ian Fishback as a hero twice over. He risked his life to fight America's wars, and risked his career to secure America's ideals. We have to do better for veterans like him, who give everything to protect our country and to make our country better."[130]

Moving from abstracting Fishback into subsequent ructions, many of the authors connected Fishback's whistleblowing on the irreparable harm that can be caused by witnessing or participating in torture and the circumstances of his death, positioning Fishback synecdochally around post-traumatic stress disorder and mental health treatment. One author wrote, "Just as he had revealed one injustice in his life, his death revealed another — the outrageous shortage of mental health treatment beds in America, including for veterans."[131] Another author opined, "Major Fishback said several years ago that his original testimony on abuses had been discredited by the Army, in part because doctors said he was suffering from post-traumatic stress disorder."[132] That author also quoted the Fishback family's public letter, which declared, "The system failed him utterly and tragically."[133] The title of one editorial summarized Fishback's symbolic role, "Army Whistle-Blower's Lonely Death Highlights Toll of Mental Illness."[134]

Fishback's whistleblowing case lay dormant in the media from 2005 until 2021 when it was revived as a result of his death. The media coverage cycled through the abstruction process once again. As seen earlier, this time, the abstruction process was distilled or condensed, and the authors wrote with a sort of clarity that comes from reporting on a factual historical event rather than debating a topic as it unfolds. In other words, these authors succinctly reminded readers about who Fishback was (a hero/warrior/whistleblower) in order to connect him to another ruction, a lack of adequate mental health care for veterans. There seems to be emancipatory potential in the discourse because the audience is invited to consider the longer narrative arc connecting the topic of torture and moral injury to the untimely death of a fallen warrior suffering from post-traumatic stress disorder, almost the same as the warning Fishback originally issued. However, related ructions centering on the toll the whistleblowing process may have taken on Fishback, and curiosities about the nature of his untimely death, rather than the military's use of torture, began to dominate the media coverage.

Conclusion

This analysis extends the abstruction model by identifying the rhetorical subtleties related to conceptual slippage and discursive closure, rather than complete distraction or overt silencing as ways that ructions occur. We also refine the model to include dormancy, rather than the more typical elongation of media coverage as a contributing factor to obstruction. This dormancy can be prompted by the death of the whistleblower, as in Fishback's case, or potentially, a new crisis, the emergence of new evidence in an unfolding case, and other reasons. The rhetoric of media coverage that marks the period of revival after dormancy seems to undergo a similar abstruction process, only more condensed and with a tone of completeness rather than unfolding debate. The revived discourse invites brief reflection over the past discourse, which provides an opportunity for the audience to connect the dots between disparate ructions, but this does not necessarily challenge statist power overall because new ructions take hold. Applying the abstruction model to the coverage of Ian Fishback provides a powerful case study of the functions of abstractions, ructions, and obstructions that typify media coverage of whistleblowers.

Fishback's case also reminds us that in the search for a healthy democracy whistleblowers play a significant role in giving voice to institutional practices that organizations would rather keep quiet. However, media coverage undercuts their efforts and diverts and truncates public discourse, rendering public response often more performative than substantive. Taking a critical perspective on media rhetoric that enables a false sense of emancipation offers validation to the work of the whistleblower and furthers the cause of democracy.

Notes

1. "Capt. Tortured by Army Abuse of Prisoners," *New York Daily News*, November 6, 2005.

2. Joshua Guitar, *Dissent, Discourse, and Democracy: Whistleblowers as Sites of Political Contestation* (Lanham, MD: Lexington Books, 2021), 113.

3. Guitar, *Dissent, Discourse, and Democracy*.

4. Sam Roberts, "Maj. Ian Fishback, Who Exposed Abuse of Detainees, Dies at 42," *New York Times*, November 23, 2021.

5. Greg Jaffe, "Ian Fishback, Army Officer and Whistleblower Against Detainee Abuse, Dies at 42," *Washington Post*, November 25, 2021.

6. Roberts, "Maj. Ian Fishback, Who Exposed."

7. Jaffe, "Ian Fishback, Army Officer."

8. Ian Fishback, "Method and Morality of War," PhD dissertation, University of Michigan, 2021.

9. Jaffe, "Ian Fishback, Army Officer."

10. Kate Kenny, *Whistleblowing: Toward a New Theory* (Cambridge: Harvard University Press, 2019); Daniel Ellsberg, "Secrecy and National Security Whistleblowing," *Social Research* 77, no. 3 (Fall 2010): 773–804; Dianne Gravley, Brian K. Richardson, and John M. Allison Jr., "Navigating the 'Abyss': A Narrative Analysis of Whistle-Blowing, Retaliation, and Identity Within Texas Public School Systems," *Management Communication Quarterly* 29, no. 2 (2015): 171–197; Kim R. Sawyer, Jackie Johnson, and Mark Holub, "The Necessary Illegitimacy of the Whistleblower," *Business and Professional Ethics Journal* 29, no. 1 (2010): 85–107.

11. Brian K. Richardson, " 'Death Threats Don't Just Affect You, They Affect Your Family': Investigating the Impact of Whistleblowing on Family Identity," *Management Communication Quarterly* 36, no. 1 (2022): 1–30; Logan L. Watts and M. Ronald Buckley, "A Dual-Processing Model of Moral Whistleblowing in Organizations," *Journal of Business Ethics* 146, no. 3 (December 2017): 669–683;

Brian K. Richardson, Zuoming Wang, and Camille A. Hall, "Blowing the Whistle Against Greek Hazing: The Theory of Reasoned Action as a Framework for Reporting Intentions," *Communication Studies* 63, no. 2 (April–June 2012): 172–193; George R. Mastroianni and George Reed, "Apples, Barrels, and Abu Ghraib," *Sociological Focus* 39, no. 4 (November 2006): 239–250; Michael Welch, *Scapegoats of September 11th: Hate Crimes and State Crimes in the War on Terror* (New Brunswick, NJ: Rutgers University Press, 2006).

12. A. J. Brown and Jane Olsen, "Whistleblower Mistreatment: Identifying the Risks," in *Whistleblowing in the Australian Public Sector: Enhancing the Theory and Practice of Internal Witness Management in Public Sector Organisations*, ed. A. J. Brown (Canberra: ANU Press, 2008), 137–161; Brian K. Richardson and Joseph McGlynn, "Rabid Fans, Death Threats, and Dysfunctional Stakeholders: The Influence of Organizational and Industry Contexts on Whistle-Blowing Cases," *Management Communication Quarterly* 25, no. 1 (2011): 121–150.

13. Lars Lindblom, "Dissolving the Moral Dilemma of Whistleblowing," *Journal of Business Ethics* 76, no. 4 (December 2007): 413–426.

14. Welch, *Scapegoats*; Welch, *Crimes of Power*; Kenneth Roth, "The Policies Behind Detainee Abuse," *Great Decisions* (2006): 55–66; Andrew J. Bacevich, "Requiem for the Bush Doctrine," *Current History* 104, no. 686 (December 2005): 411–413, 415–417.

15. Cheng Zeng, Stephanie Kelly, and Ryan Goke, "Exploring the Impacts of Leader Integrity and Ethics on Upward Dissent and Whistleblowing Intentions," *Communication Reports* 33, no. 2 (2020): 82–94.

16. Jessica R. Mesmer-Magnus and Chockalingam Viswesvaran, "Whistleblowing in Organizations: An Examination of Correlates of Whistleblowing Intentions, Actions, and Retaliation," *Journal of Business Ethics* 62, no. 3 (December 2005): 277–297.

17. Brent G. Johnson, Liz Bent, and Caroline Dade, "An Ethic of Advocacy: Metajournalistic Discourse on the Practice of Leaks and Whistleblowing from Valerie Plame to the Trump Administration," *Journal of Media Ethics* 35, no. 1 (2020): 2–16.

18. Junhong Zhu, "Is It Ethical to Be a 'Whistleblower' During Covid-19 Pandemic? Ethical Challenges Confronted by Health Care Workers in China," *Journal of Advanced Nursing* 76 (March 26, 2020): 1873–1875; Gil Shochat, "Legislation Aims to Increase Whistleblower Protections," *News Media and the Law* (Summer 2003): 8.

19. Jessie Bullock and Matthew Jenkins, "Best Practices in Civilian Oversight and Whistleblower Protection in the Armed Forces," *Transparency International* (2019), http://www.jstor.org/stable/resrep20476.

20. See Fred C. Alford, *Whistleblowers: Broken Lives and Organizational Power* (Ithaca, NY: Cornell University Press, 2001); Patrick D. Anderson, "On Moderate and Radical Government Whistleblowing: Edward Snowden and Julian

Assange as Theorists of Whistleblowing Ethics," *Journal of Media Ethics* 37, no. 1 (2022): 38–52.

21. Alan Chu, "In Tradition of Speaking Fearlessly: Locating a Rhetoric of Whistleblowing in the *Parrhēsiastic* Dialectic," *Advances in the History of Rhetoric* 19, no. 3 (2016): 231–250.

22. Lawrence T. Nichols, "'Whistleblower' or 'Renegade': Definitional Contests in an Official Inquiry," *Symbolic Interaction* 14, no. 4 (Winter 1991): 395–414; Zhenzhu Zhang and Steven J. Venette, "Rumormonger? Whistleblower? Martyr? How the US and Chinese Media Framed the Narrative of COVID-19 Doctor Li Wenliang," *Iowa Journal of Communication* 53, no. 2 (Fall 2021): 28–48; Guitar, *Dissent, Discourse, and Democracy.*

23. Lida Maxwell, "Celebrity Hero: Daniel Ellsberg and the Forging of Whistleblower Masculinity," in *Whistleblowing Nation: The History of National Security Disclosure and the Cult of State Secrecy*, ed. Kaeten Mistry and Hannah Gurman (New York: Columbia University Press, 2020), 96–123; Timothy Melley, "The Public Sphere Hero: Representations of Whistleblowing in US Culture," in *Whistleblowing Nation: The History of National Security Disclosure and the Cult of State Secrecy*, ed. Kaeten Mistry and Hannah Gurman (New York: Columbia University Press, 2020), 213–241.

24. Connal Parsley, "The Exceptional Image: Torture Photographs from Guantánamo Bay and Abu Ghraib as Foucault's Spectacle of Punishment," in *Law and the Visual: Representations, Technologies, Critique*, ed. Desmond Manderson (Toronto: University of Toronto Press, 2018), 229–247.

25. Guitar, *Dissent, Discourse, and Democracy.*

26. Guitar, *Dissent, Discourse, and Democracy*, 40.

27. Guitar, *Dissent, Discourse, and Democracy*, 40.

28. Joshua Guitar and Madeline Studebaker, "Abstracting AOC: Reifying the Reactionary Rhetoric of Patriarchal Ideology," *Communication and Democracy* 57, no 1 (2023): 27–51.

29. We analyzed the top ten newspapers in the United States (*Wall Street Journal, USA Today, New York Times, New York Daily News, Los Angeles Times, San Jose Mercury News, New York Post, Washington Post, Chicago Tribune*, and *Dallas Morning News*) for any instance of "Ian Fishback." The coverage clustered around two different time periods: when Fishback's letter to Senator McCain was leaked to the media in 2005, and when Fishback died in 2021. During the collection of these articles, we recognized that Fishback's case was being discussed in outlets that provided more space for discussion such as *Rolling Stone, Esquire*, and *The Nation*. As a result, we opted to include these articles since they, too, are considered mainstream.

30. Joshua Guitar and Alan Chu, "Racing to (Dis)Own Whistleblowers and Protests: Theorizing *Amongness* in the Shared Rhetorical Spaces of Democratic Agency," chapter 1 in the present volume, 2.

31. Guitar, *Dissent, Discourse, and Democracy*, 122.

32. Guitar, *Dissent, Discourse, and Democracy*, 122.

33. Guitar, *Dissent, Discourse, and Democracy*, 138.

34. Fishback in Eric Schmitt, "Officer Criticizes Detainee Abuse Inquiry," *New York Times*, September 28, 2005, A10.

35. Ian Fishback, Letter, *Washington Post*, September 28, 2005, A21.

36. Ian Fishback in Barry Lam, "Soldier Philosophers; Part One: Moral Exploitation," January 31, 2017, in *Hi-Phi Nation*, podcast, MP3 audio, 48:50.

37. Roberts, "Maj. Ian Fishback, Who Exposed."

38. Roth, "Policies Behind Detainee Abuse."

39. Fishback in Barry Lam, "Soldier Philosophers."

40. Fishback in Barry Lam, "Soldier Philosophers."

41. Roth, "Policies Behind Detainee Abuse."

42. Roth, "Policies Behind Detainee Abuse."

43. Josh White, "New Reports Surface About Detainee Abuse; Mistreatment Was Routine, Soldiers Say," *Washington Post*, September 24, 2005.

44. Roth, "Policies Behind Detainee Abuse," 62.

45. Donald Rumsfeld, interview by Larry King, *CNN Larry King Live*, CNN, May 25, 2006.

46. Fishback, Letter.

47. Fishback, Letter.

48. Fishback, Letter.

49. Fishback, Letter.

50. Fishback quoted in Richard A. Serrano, "More Iraqis Tortured, Officer Says: The 82nd Airborne Is Accused of Abuses in 2003 and Early 2004," *Los Angeles Times*, September 24, 2001, A1.

51. Fishback quoted in Serrano, "More Iraqis Tortured."

52. Fishback quoted in Moniz, "Captain Says Concerns About Prisoner Abuse Weren't Priority," *USA Today*, September 28, 2005.

53. Fishback quoted in Schmitt, "Officer Criticizes."

54. Fishback quoted in Serrano, "More Iraqis Tortured."

55. Derrick Z. Jackson, "The Buck Stops with Lynndie; But What About Those at the Top?," *Chicago Tribune*, October 3, 2005, 17.

56. Jackson, "Buck Stops with Lynndie."

57. Fishback, Letter.

58. Fishback, Letter.

59. Fishback quoted in Michael McAuliff, "Troop Abuse Allegations Rile McCain," *New York Daily News*, September 26, 2005.

60. Fishback, Letter.

61. Fishback, Letter.

62. Fishback, Letter.

63. Fishback in Barry Lam, "Soldier Philosophers."

64. Fishback in Barry Lam, "Soldier Philosophers."

65. Coleen Rowley, "Blowing the Whistle on Torture," *Time*, May 8, 2006, 112.

66. Guitar, *Dissent, Discourse, and Democracy*, 125, 126.

67. See, for example, John H. Richardson, "Acts of Conscience," *Esquire*, August 2006.

68. John McCain in Eric Schmitt, "Soldier Reports More Abuses to Senator," *New York Times*, October 5, 2005, A8.

69. William L. Hauser, Letter to the Editor, *New York Times*, October 11, 2005, 22.

70. Rowley, "Blowing the Whistle on Torture," 112.

71. Kennedy, "Capt. Tortured by Army Abuse of Prisoners."

72. Kennedy, "Capt. Tortured by Army Abuse of Prisoners."

73. Roland J. Scheck, Letter to the Editor, *Washington Post*, October 4, 2005, A22.

74. We do not plan to engage stasis theory (ancient or contemporary articulations) in this chapter. We are simply using the claim structure within stasis theory as an organizational framework.

75. Alessandra Stanley, "The Slow Rise of Abuse That Shocked the Nation," *New York Times*, October 18, 2005, E5.

76. Stanley, "Slow Rise."

77. Rowe P. Stayton, Letter to the Editor, *Washington Post*, October 4, 2005, A22.

78. Stayton, Letter to the Editor, A22.

79. "Beyond Abu Ghraib," *Chicago Tribune*, September 27, 2005, 18.

80. "Beyond Abu Ghraib."

81. Richard A. Serrano, "Officer's Road Led Him Outside Army," *Los Angeles Times*, September 25, 2005, A3.

82. Unnamed source quoted in Serrano, "Officer's Road."

83. Fishback quoted in McAuliff, "Troop Abuse Allegations," 19.

84. Jackson, "Buck Stops with Lynndie," 17.

85. Jackson, "Buck Stops with Lynndie," 17.

86. Serrano, "More Iraqis Tortured," A1.

87. Serrano, "More Iraqis Tortured," A1.

88. Serrano, "More Iraqis Tortured," A1.

89. "Beyond Abu Ghraib."

90. Adam Zagorin, "Another Abu Ghraib?," *Time*, October 3, 2005, 19.

91. Stanley, "Slow Rise."

92. Elizabeth Johns, Letter to the Editor, *Washington Post*, October 4, 2005, A22.

93. Johns, Letter to the Editor.

94. "Mr. Flanigan's Answers," *Washington Post*, September 28, 2005, A20.

95. "Mr. Flanigan's Answers."

96. "Mr. Flanigan's Answers."

97. "Mr. Flanigan's Answers."

98. "Mr. Flanigan's Answers."

99. Fishback, Letter.

100. Timothy E. Flanigan quoted in "Mr. Flanigan's Answers."

101. "Three in 82nd Airborne Say Beating Iraqi Prisoners Was Routine," *New York Times*, September 24, 2005.

102. "Three in 82nd Airborne."

103. Kennedy, "Capt. Tortured by Army Abuse of Prisoners."

104. Unnamed source quoted in Kennedy, "Capt. Tortured."

105. Unnamed source quoted in Kennedy, "Capt. Tortured."

106. "Clueless About Torture," *USA Today*, November 2, 2005, 12A.

107. "Clueless About Torture."

108. Stanley, "Slow Rise."

109. Stanley, "Slow Rise."

110. Katherine Moore, Letter to the Editor," *New York Times*, September 27, 2005, B12.

111. Richard Serrano, "New Iraq Abuse Allegations Get McCain Moving," *Los Angeles Times*, September 26, 2005, A17.

112. John McCain quoted in Serrano, "New Iraq Abuse Allegations."

113. "Clueless About Torture."

114. John McCain quoted in McAuliff, "Troop Abuse Allegations Rile McCain," 19.

115. McCain quoted in McAuliff, "Troop Abuse Allegations Rile McCain."

116. Cheri Ford quoted in Kennedy, "Capt. Tortured by Army Abuse of Prisoners."

117. Katharine Moore, Letter to the Editor, *Los Angeles Times*, September 27, 2005, B12.

118. White, "New Reports Surface."

119. "Three in 82nd Airborne."

120. John Skinner quoted in White, "New Reports Surface."

121. Guitar, *Dissent, Discourse, and Democracy*.

122. Eric Schmitt, "New Army Rules May Snarl Talks with McCain on Detainee Issue," *New York Times*, December 14, 2005.

123. Charlie Savage, "Bush Could Bypass New Torture Ban: Waiver Right Is Reserved," *Boston Globe*, January 4, 2006.

124. See Guitar, *Dissent, Discourse, and Democracy*.

125. Jennifer Steinhauer, "Vet Death Stresses Mental Illness Toll," *Chicago Tribune*, November 28, 2021, 5.

126. Christopher Nicholson quoted in Roberts, "Maj. Ian Fishback, Who Exposed."

127. Justin Ford quoted in Roberts, "Maj. Ian Fishback, Who Exposed."

128. Jaffe, "Ian Fishback, Army Officer."

129. Nancy Sherman quoted in Jaffe, "Ian Fishback, Army Officer."

130. Tom Malinowski, "Ian Fishback: A Whistleblower Who Reminded the US Military of Its Values," *Politico*, December 27, 2021.

131. Malinowski, "Ian Fishback: A Whistleblower."

132. Roberts, "Maj. Ian Fishback, Who Exposed."

133. Fishback family letter in Roberts, "Maj. Ian Fishback, Who Exposed."

134. Jennifer Steinhauer, "Army Whistle-Blower's Lonely Death Highlights Toll of Mental Illness," *New York Times*, November 24, 2001.

3

Shooting Bullets and Frames per Second

Recording the Police as Whistleblowing

David R. Dewberry

An alarming number of US citizens, many of whom are Black, are being killed by the police, and some of these incidents are recorded by citizens armed with cameras. This chapter argues that these citizens with cameras intentionally document and confront police misconduct, protest the perpetrators of that violence, and serve as a catalyst for protests and advocacy. In doing so, these citizens with cameras fulfill several democratic goals, even as they endure retaliation for their efforts. This characterization of citizens with cameras resonates with traditional ideas of whistleblowing, but it also problematizes those ideas in important ways.

To make this argument, this chapter is divided into six sections. The first two provide an overview of the theoretical perspective driving the chapter's analysis and an introduction to those who record the police. The subsequent three sections advance the chapter's argument. The section on the rhetorical nature of whistleblowing examines how recording the police reflects two rhetorical functions that constitute the sine qua non of whistleblowing: documenting and an individual moment of protest that sparks a collective protest. The section on flipping power relations discusses how those who record the police can equalize or invert power relationships between the state and citizens through the enactment of democratic ideals. The section on the consequences of recording police misconduct highlights the moral quandary that whistleblowers must confront. Do the citizens with cameras keep quiet and protect themselves or do they speak out for justice and face retaliation? These three sections suggest that pointing a camera at the police is a rhetorical practice that protests wrongdoing and exposes those transgressions to a larger audience, which results in the citizen with the camera becoming a key meaning-maker in contesting authoritarian police power through the actualization of democratic agency—namely, the freedom to record and protest police violence.

The chapter concludes by addressing how citizens with cameras challenge the conventional boundaries of what it means to be a whistleblower. Namely, whistleblowers need not necessarily be individuals within an institution; whistleblowers can operate within communities. Additionally, whistleblowers are typically seen as having privileged access to evidence of misconduct that is not publicly known. While police misconduct happens in public, this does not mean everyone witnesses it or knows about it. Citizens with cameras demonstrate they have unique access and opportunities through happenstance to document police misconduct in their communities. Finally, whistleblowers traditionally release evidence of misconduct to the press or some other entity. But the footage citizens with cameras record can bypass traditional media so that it is directly available for widespread distribution. These implications suggest that citizens with cameras typify the democratic agency that is ascribed to whistleblowers.

A Rhetorical Approach to Whistleblowing

This chapter examines the act of visually documenting law enforcement officials through a combination of classical and contemporary rhetorical theory. I rely on Quintilian to follow other scholars who have examined those who observe the police from a classical-inspired framework, namely through the lens of ancient myth/literature.[1] These scholars find similarities between spectators of police misconduct and the chorus in classical Greek tragedy.

The Greek chorus comparison to those who watch the police reflects Quintilian's heavy emphasis on morality and ethics when speaking out. The chorus has been described as the "moral barometer of the play . . . because chorus members constantly offered opinions on wickedness, punishment, and righteousness."[2] Those who record the police exhibit several key attributes of Quintilian's good person.[3] They have the integrity to recognize wrongdoing and desire justice, the sense of duty and responsibility to realize what must be done, and the courage and bravery to do what must be done: Document illegal or unethical acts, confront those who abuse their power, and stir others to action to combat abuses of power.

While Quintilian's focus is on oratory, contemporary rhetorical theory has expanded the scope of rhetoric to include the body. Scholars have examined how disempowered and disenfranchised groups have used their bodies rhetorically to confront injustice.[4] This is rhetoric through the frame of corporeality, or body-as-rhetoric. The body has physical and social meaning through its presence when directly witnessing and confronting police misconduct.[5] This is also true of the convergence of bodies with digital technology such as cameras.[6] In essence, the camera on the phone we carry can be seen as an extension of the body, and those who record the police exemplify body-and-technics-as-rhetoric.[7] Those who record the police with a camera allow for what Richardson calls a distant witness, "a person who views secondhand footage of a fatal police encounter and by doing so, may be moved to action."[8] This action is public protest: the confrontation of power through collective agency. As such, the secondhand footage is what Aguayo calls "documentary resistance" and serves as a "material force of social change."[9]

Taken together, this classical and contemporary rhetorical perspective guides us to an understanding of the relationships between democracy, whistleblowing, and rhetoric. Specifically, the classically inspired perspective provides a framework to understand how rhetoric and the democratic ideal of citizen oversight of state actors come together to form the foundation of whistleblowing regarding police misconduct against citizens in their communities. And the contemporary rhetorical perspective provides us a framework to understand how recording the police and sharing the documentation is not only a moment of verifying wrongdoing and call to attention, but also a moment of documentation that can be shared and used to spark larger protests. Understanding the individual and collective effort allows us to better understand the rhetorical linkages that unite whistleblowers and protests in the name of democratic rights.

Having explained the theoretical lens that informs this chapter's analysis, I now introduce and describe the people who record the police.

Citizens Recording the Police

There are many ways to categorize those who record law enforcement officials. For our purposes here, we can say there are two groups: those who actively seek and record the police and those who find themselves in situations that call for the police to be recorded. Cop watchers are a prime example of the first type of group who patrol the streets to police the police.

ORGANIZED COP WATCHERS

Cop watching (sometimes copwatching) is an organized form of activism and civic participation meant to bring accountability to the policing within the cop watchers' communities.[10] This accountability comes in documenting and raising awareness of the police's abuse and brutality against citizens. To accomplish this, cop watchers patrol the streets and neighborhoods in their community. During these patrols, they talk to their fellow citizens, observe the police's interactions with the public, and record those interactions.

Cop watching has roots in African American communities in and throughout Los Angeles during the late 1960s.[11] Groups such as the Black Panthers patrolled the streets on foot and in cars armed with notepads, cameras, and sometimes weapons. Decades later, in 1990, citizens in Berkeley, California, were concerned about how the police treated the homeless in their community. In response, they created a group called Copwatch.[12] The group focused on nonviolent observation of the police and not on direct intervention. These individual observations serve to not only document the police but also to advocate for the victims. The formal organizing of Berkeley's Copwatch influenced other communities to develop their own cop watching groups. Overall, the cop watch movement's goal is "to undermine the legitimacy of the police institution."[13] Cop watchers "believe making [the police institution's] essential violence visible will result in a withdrawal of legitimacy, and this alone will force change."[14]

SERENDIPITOUS RECORDERS

While cop watchers and others like them are proactive in documenting the police's interactions with the public, others document the police in a spontaneous, unorganized, and reactive manner. These are the people who are going about their lives and, through happenstance, come upon and record police misconduct. These videos frequently document the police's excessive use of force against members of marginalized communities. Such examples include George Holliday, who is responsible for "the most famous amateur video of all time—the police beating of Rodney King" in 1991.[15]

More recently, an "interminable stream of images of young, working-class, Black men being killed by the police have flooded commercial and social media."[16] The examples are numerous, and some key cases include Ramsey Orta, Feidin Santana, Abdullah Muflahi, Diamond Reynolds, Kevin Moore, and Darnella Frazier. Orta filmed Officer Daniel Pantaleo choking Eric Garner, who repeatedly pleaded "I can't breathe" until he died.[17] Santana was walking to work when he encountered Officer Michael Slager shooting and killing Walter Scott.[18] Muflahi was inside his convenience store as Officers Howie Lake II and Blane Salamoni pinned Alton Sterling to the ground and shot him, resulting in his death the next day.[19] Philando Castile was driving home with his girlfriend, Diamond Reynolds, and her child when the police pulled over Castile.[20] Reynolds live-streamed the stop that resulted in Officer Jeronimo Yanez shooting and killing Castile. Moore awoke in the morning when he heard a commotion outside.[21] He grabbed his phone and ran outside to record the police arresting Freddie Gray, who was screaming in agony as he was put into a transport van. Upon arriving at the station, Gray was taken to the hospital in a coma. Gray never regained consciousness and died a week later. Frazier was walking to the neighborhood grocery store when she came upon Officer Derek Chauvin kneeling on George Floyd's neck as he begged for water, air, and his mom. Frazier recorded for over ten minutes until Floyd's lifeless body was taken away.[22] While the examples are numerous, they all fundamentally exemplify a similar situation: Each of these incidents was brought to the nation's attention by a person—for lack of a better term, a serendipitous recorder—who came upon something wrong and documented it.[23] These serendipitous recorders—Orta, Santana, Muflahi, Reynolds, Moore, Frazier, and others—provide the examples that contextualize this chapter's argument.

From here on, I refer to those who follow and record police in an organized effort as cop watchers ("Cop Watchers" for organized groups and "cop watchers" for individuals in those groups). I use serendipitous recorders to describe those who happen upon police violence. And I use *citizen recorder* as an umbrella term for all who record law enforcement officials.

Whistleblowing as Documenting and Protesting

This book defines whistleblowers "as vulnerable members of institutions who, motivated by democratic ethics, truthfully expose violations of human rights and abuses of power."[24] To substantiate and legitimize the violations they observe, whistleblowers must have some form of documentation (e.g., copies, audio/visual recordings, etc.) of the unethical/illegal activities.

It is essential to recognize that in the moments when someone confronts wrongdoing and takes action to document it, that action is more than just evidence gathering. It is a moment when a person decides to oppose what is occurring. This is a moment of protest in the sense that there is a confrontation when the whistleblower vows in word or thought to act. As rhetorical action, whistleblowers then share the evidence with external audiences to expose violations of democratic governance. In turn, whistleblowing often fosters public outcry and demonstrations.

To Document

The recording of police serves several documentary functions. Recording is an effective way to document our world. It allows us to capture, preserve, and distribute experiences that would otherwise be fleeting. Recordings offer a permanent and stable form of documentation, which can address the constraints and liabilities of human memory, such as implicit biases, the trauma and intensity of the situation, and erosion of accuracy and detail over time.

Recordings can also serve an evidentiary purpose. In this sense, the camera is a witness. Through human action, the camera records what fills its lens with the evidence or proof of precisely what happened. Given the significant and severe consequences that might result in an encounter with the police, it seems especially prudent to record these interactions. While many police officers have body-worn and dash cameras, this is not to say that the citizen recording is redundant. Citizen recordings can be seen as complementary and adversarial.

Complementary

Citizen recording is complementary in several ways. Citizen recordings offer a more complete picture of events. The vision of police dash and body cameras is partial, and civilian recordings can fill the gaps. When the police do not have cameras, civilian recordings may be the only recorded evidence of what happened. Civilian recordings are also helpful as backups in cases where the officer's camera is damaged, inoperable (e.g., muted, accidentally deactivated, etc.), or intentionally or inadvertently not activated by the police.

Adversarial

While civilian recordings can offer multiple perspectives and a more complete record of what happened, the footage may also challenge the police's account. An officer may intentionally or unintentionally miss key details, misrepresent what happened or what was said during an encounter, or mischaracterize the individuals the police are interacting with. Civilian recordings also clarify the situations where an officer and the accused disagree over what happened and who said what. For example, Reynolds, who live-streamed the traffic stop that resulted in the police shooting and killing of her boyfriend, Castile, told herself as the situation unfolded, "Record this because if you don't, there's no telling where the story could end up, what they can make of this, what lies they can tell."[25]

Citizen recordings can also challenge the police's official report. Officer Slager stopped Scott for a routine traffic stop in 2015. Scott fled the scene on foot, and Slager chased him. Slager reported a struggle over his Taser, so he shot Scott five times in the back. The police report also indicated that officers performed CPR on Scott. A citizen video, shot by Santana, questions and contradicts that report. First, it is not entirely clear that there was a struggle over the Taser. The video simply shows the officer deploying his Taser and then throwing it to the ground as Scott runs away. Scott manages to get some distance away before the officer fires his weapon. At that point, the officer returned to the dropped Taser, picked it up, walked it back to Scott's body, and dropped it next to him.

Second, the video shows no evidence that CPR was performed. Slager was later sentenced to federal prison for his actions that day. This example demonstrates that civilian footage can show evidence of criminal activity by those authorized to enforce the law.

To Protest

Civilians recording the police also fulfill a second rhetorical function: protesting. Protesting is one way in which individuals and collectives advocate for social or political change that challenges the power dynamics of the status quo.[26] Due to their nature of expressing dissent or disapproval, protests are confrontational. To bring about change is to challenge the status quo, and to resist change is to confront what is being proposed. This confrontation brings attention, and that attention is how the message of the protest travels in and through public discourse.

Civilian recorder as protester and the moment of confrontation

To understand how holding a camera and pointing it at the police is a form of protest, we need to ask: Is pointing a camera at and recording someone considered speech? Scholars have noted that people can express ideas without verbal speech through sit-ins, holding signs, wearing armbands, and so forth.[27] This type of expression is commonly referred to as symbolic conduct, which is some action or activity that expresses an idea. The nature of such conduct is ambiguous. It is not always clear if some action is pure conduct (holding no symbolic meaning) or symbolic conduct.

To determine if the action is pure or symbolic conduct, we can consider whether that conduct is "sufficiently imbued with elements of communication."[28] For example, it seems reasonable that randomly throwing rocks at cars is not intended or would be primarily understood to overtly communicate any idea. On the other hand, wearing a black armband communicates the idea that the person is mourning another who has died. Police wear a black band around their badge when a fellow officer is killed, and during the US-Vietnam conflict, some saw the wearing of a black armband as a protest.[29] In these examples, the long tradition of wearing the band throughout history gives the conduct symbolic meaning, but so does the contemporary context in which the conduct takes place.

With regard to police misconduct, the context clarifies that holding a camera and pointing it at the police is sufficiently communicative. The context is determined by the wave of recorded police violence against African Americans, which we can trace back to the footage of LAPD officers beating Rodney King. A legal scholar who has written extensively on recording the police explains, "Because of the history of filming police officers in our country—both the history of patrols by African Americans during the civil rights movement and the recent history of anti-police brutality actions involving cameras—you cannot hold up a camera in front of a police officer without it being a political act or an act of dissent."[30]

Pointing a camera at police denotes "alarm or distrust of officers."[31] This is particularly true of serendipitous recorders, citizens who happen upon police in the streets. For example, Santana, who recorded Scott being shot and killed by police, heard screaming. Santana recalls, "I decided to pull my phone out and just record, to prevent some bad outcome. To intimidate the officer with my camera, I got closer; that way, he could be aware that someone was there."[32]

In Santana's situation and others like it, the people recording nonviolently confront police violence. This is similar to the concept of disciplined action, a form of nonviolent resistance that prioritizes discipline and action without resorting to violence despite the suffering in the situation. Here, disciplined action is "self-limitation and restraint," and action is some physical or corporeal presentation of oneself rather than complex verbal persuasion.[33] Reynolds remained remarkably calm as she sat in the car next to Castile as he died after being shot by the police. She did not scream or cry as she narrated to the camera what just happened in a concise, matter-of-fact style. All this while, Reynolds spoke respectfully to the officer who had just killed her boyfriend. Similarly, Frazier, who recorded Floyd's murder, recognized there was nothing she could do physically or otherwise to remove the police officer's knee from Floyd's neck. Still, she could record the incident as she and others around her watched in horror.

Civilian Recorder as Catalyst to Protest and Advocacy

The preceding section suggests that presenting one's body armed with a camera is a form of protest, but that protest is rooted in a specific time and location. However, what is recorded by that camera allows the moment to be saved and shared immediately or as it happens in real time when live streaming. The footage can provoke and foster collective protests. In the wake of the videos depicting the deaths of Garner, Scott, Sterling, Castile, Gray, and Floyd, there were massive and nationwide protests.[34] And in situations where the officers were criminally charged for their actions but acquitted, there were even more protests. Some were peaceful; others were not. In many situations, protests against police violence only begat more police violence.[35]

Cop watchers serve as a catalyst to help others document and protest police misconduct in their communities, and in this sense, Cop Watch groups engage in the "diffusion of protest."[36] These groups work to spread action repertoires—tactics and strategies to protest the abuse of power by law enforcement. As such, cop watchers not only protest by pointing the camera at the police, but they also advocate and educate others to do the same. After police shot and killed Michael Brown in Ferguson, Missouri, members from WeCopwatch traveled to the St. Louis suburb to help community members and protesters establish their group, the Canfield Watchmen.

Flipping the Power Relations

Some police find the presence of a camera as a threat, critique, or obstruction to their work.[37] Those who film cops find the perception that a camera is an impediment or dangerous absurd because police shoot bullets and cameras shoot frames per second. Presumably, police find cameras as threats because cameras document the reality of a community, which, consequently, can legitimize citizen concerns about wayward policing. As such, armed with cameras, members of communities plagued with police misconduct and brutality can confront the power relationship between state and citizen. In doing so, citizen recorders enact several democratic principles through documenting and protesting with a camera. These ideals address civilian oversight of the government and justice as a means of accountability, while allowing people to be informed and able to deliberate about their communities.[38]

OVERSIGHT

One way citizen recorders address the power differential is through what Blasi calls the checking value. Blasi argued that "free speech, a free press, and free assembly can serve in checking the abuse of power by public officials."[39] Through formal investigations, criminal charges, and even convictions, citizen recordings help hold police accountable. Frazier's recording of Floyd's last moments was a key piece of evidence against Chauvin, who was convicted. But just because there is footage of police misconduct does not mean it will secure indictments or convictions. Orta's video of New York Police Department Officer Daniel Pantaleo choking Garner to death was not enough to convince a grand jury to indict the officers involved. Holliday's footage of the LAPD beating King was a key piece of evidence in the trial of the officers, but the four officers were acquitted. Despite these outcomes, civilian footage serves as a means of oversight, sometimes leading to protest. The footage allowed an investigation into the officers' actions and a trial to debate the legality of their conduct.

JUSTICE

Recording the police also serves as a democratic value to promote justice. Civilian footage, as described earlier, provides evidence that can complement police or other recordings (e.g., security cameras, etc.). The idea here is that more evidence is better than less evidence. Although some might question the integrity or reliability of civilian footage, legal scholars hold that the existing rules of evidence will thwart the admission of questionable evidence in judicial matters, just as the rules apply to police body and dash cameras.[40] But civilian footage has the potential to have a more significant judicial impact than the police's footage in two ways.

First, civilian footage provides exculpatory evidence that benefits the accused. While the state must follow the Brady Rule, which requires prosecutors to disclose exculpatory evidence to the defense, the state is not necessarily obligated to maintain that evidence. The reasoning is that keeping such a massive amount of evidence "would be a tremendous burden on prosecutors and law enforcement agencies."[41] There is no such burden on civilian recordings, especially once the recordings are shared online. In addition, civilian footage may serve an exculpatory function when it provides evidence that substantiates the accused's version of events. Although the US judicial system is based on the premise that one is innocent until proven guilty, there is the belief that the police's narrative is favored. Frazier understood that her video could legitimize the bystander's account. Frazier explained she started recording Floyd's death by saying, "I opened my phone, and I started recording because I knew if I didn't, no one would believe me."[42]

Second, civilian footage may capture a crime that would otherwise go unreported or undocumented. For example, in 2012, Jennifer Gondola filmed police struggling to handcuff an uncooperative suspect in New Haven, Connecticut. The Black suspect was eventually detained after a white officer put his foot on the suspect's head and neck. An officer then approached Gondola and demanded she stop recording, but Gondola refused, saying it was her right to record the police. The officer replied that he had the right to review the tape, presumably because it had evidentiary value. Gondola quickly placed her phone in her bra, but to no avail. She was arrested, and a female officer retrieved the phone. The police department later suspended the officer for putting his foot on the suspect's head and neck, and the charges against Gondola were dropped.

NEWS AND DELIBERATION

There is one last democratic principle fulfilled by recording police, which arises from the intersection of news gathering and civic debate.[43] That is how civilian footage serves as a means to talk about whether the police's actions should be characterized as misconduct, if the actions were just, if the actions deserve praise or blame, or what should be done about the misconduct.

Civilian footage allows for more nuance in the public forum about the criminal justice system than what police reports and news media can provide, especially as it relates to social injustices pertaining to topics like race. Relying only on police reports for this conversation raises questions about credibility, as the example of Scott demonstrates. Further, police footage typically goes through a lengthy bureaucratic approval process, which requires time, while civilian footage can be distributed much quicker, or immediately when it is live-streamed. Relying on the news media also presents some concerns. Namely, traditional news footage of the police is filtered through the "political economic power of the mass media," which can frame and highlight particular perspectives over others, unlike the civilian recorder's "raw, unedited footage."[44] Moreover, it is impossible for traditional news crews to provide coverage of police misconduct in communities compared to the ubiquitous and omnipresent citizen with a camera.[45]

Consequences of Recording the Police

A vital part of any conceptualization of whistleblowing should include the treatment of the whistleblowers themselves. Some are praised for their heroic actions. For example, Edward Snowden has been praised for revealing the National Security Agency's mass surveillance program, which was later found to be illegal and most likely unconstitutional. Citizen recorders also experience such praise. Frazier was nominated for a Pulitzer Prize because her video was able "to reveal secrets that the corrupt seek to hide, to stand strong in a moment of personal peril, and to document a fleeting reality that is fraught with meaning."[46]

While some praise civilian recorders for their heroic actions, others often vilify the whistleblower, who have their personal and professional lives irreparably harmed. For his efforts, Snowden has been called a traitor, threatened with execution, and has been in exile in Russia for a decade. Likewise, for citizen recorders "who capture horrific acts of violence, returning to a normal life becomes impossible. They complain of harassment by police, threats against their life, and recurring trauma resulting from the death and brutality they have witnessed."[47]

A well-known Brooklyn cop watcher, Jose LaSalle is an example of how cop watchers have been harassed by the police. LaSalle was arrested by the NYPD as he documented and confronted officers stopping and frisking people. Once at the station for processing, officers celebrated his capture and taunted him with charges of committing a felony. Hours later, before seeing a judge, an officer removed LaSalle from his cell and told him he was free. LaSalle was later arrested again. The police explained he should not have been released without seeing a judge. LaSalle was then rereleased, again without seeing a judge. When he retrieved his possessions, LaSalle realized his phone had recorded the audio of the initial arrest, which revealed that officers conspired to charge him with a felony. With this, charges were dropped, and LaSalle received a generous settlement, validating his goal to hold officers accountable.

As serendipitous recorders, Santana and Muflahi echo the ethical dilemma all whistleblowers face: to reveal the misconduct and suffer the negative consequences or keep quiet and be left alone. After recording Scott being murdered, Santana ran. Like the situation with Gondola, Muflahi feared the police would take the footage and destroy it. Santana also feared for his life, so he initially kept quiet and gave a copy of the footage to his wife in case something happened to him. But when he heard the police department's official report contradicted what he had recorded, he revealed the truth. Santana said, "I had to forget about my personal dreams and stand up for justice. I understood that my only decision should be to give the video to Walter Scott's family so they can know the truth of what happened."[48]

Santana's decision resonates with the scholarship on whistleblowers' motivations for disclosing wrongdoing.[49] Scholars have found that people engage in whistleblowing for a number of reasons, which include preventing, stopping, or punishing wrongdoing.[50] More specifically, one scholar explains people decide to blow the whistle "to avenge slights and a sense that only they can stop the wrongdoing."[51] This is what we see with Santana's decision to release the recording. Santana recognized that he was the only one who could reveal the truth because he possessed the only evidence that demonstrably disproved the police's account.

The same applies to Muflahi. After recording officers shooting and killing Sterling outside his convenience store, Muflahi was placed into a patrol car for nearly six hours. Then, he was taken to the police station and locked in an interview room for two more hours before someone took his report and drove him back to his store. Muflahi recalled he was treated as if he had done something wrong during the entire process. Like Santana, Muflahi was initially afraid of speaking out but knew what must be done. He said, "I was scared to do anything with [the footage]. But my heart wouldn't let me just stay quiet and let it go. I had to let it out. People needed to see the video. His family needed to see the truth."[52] Both Santana and Muflahi were cautious and fearful of the personal consequences they might endure for releasing their documentation of wrongdoing. But each overcame their trepidation by calculating the benefit to the families and their communities over their own personal consequences. Santana and Muflahi recognized that the value of speaking out far outweighed any retribution they might face.

Implications for Understanding Whistleblowing

To this point, this chapter has introduced those who record the police and how they document, confront, and protest police misconduct. These citizens also spark public protests, fulfilling several democratic goals while enduring retaliation for their efforts. This portrayal resonates with traditional ideas of whistleblowing and also problematizes those depictions.

While there is no agreed-upon definition of whistleblowing, there is consensus that discussions should begin with Near and Miceli.[53] They define whistleblowing as "the disclosure by organization members (former or current) of illegal, immoral, or illegitimate practices under the control of their employers, to persons or organizations that may be able to effect action."[54] Those who record the police reflect this definition but problematize its organizational nature.

Near and Miceli conceptualize in detail the significant elements of the definition save one. Their discussion of the organization is vague and broad, starting with "any organization may be the target of a whistleblowing attempt: large or small, public or private, young or old."[55] There is not much guidance here, but the idea seems to be that whistleblowing needs some element that would allow an individual to report misconduct within an organization to an external audience, which could be another organization or just individuals that can implement change.[56] Consider the example of prominent whistleblower Daniel Ellsberg who worked on a Department of Defense report regarding the Vietnam War. Ellsberg worked in an organization, believed he found wrongdoing, and reported to external entities: Congress and the news media.

Indeed, the chapters of Cop Watchers across the country are organizations, but their focus is on the community. Serendipitous recorders are similarly described as being within a community rather than as part of a formal organization. Considering this, cop watchers better fit with this volume's definition of whistleblowers as members of a defined body—be it social, organizational, or otherwise—than conventional definitions such as those found in Miceli and Near. Additionally, cop watchers and citizens with cameras—whether they be cop watchers or serendipitous recorders—are there to alert those outside their communities of the reality of their worlds. Those outside the community can be people throughout the nation or state, and it could even be someone on the same block who has never seen the injustice that their neighbors have.

Most definitions of whistleblowing also highlight a recipient of the information, who can then enact change that serves to publicize the information to the public at large. As Ellsberg demonstrates, evidence of wrongdoing is submitted to the news or some agency that can exercise oversight (e.g., Congress, regulatory agencies, etc.), which then informs the public at large. There are examples of people recording the police who give their footage to external audiences such as the news and even the police themselves. Orta was offered $250 for his footage, but Orta did not want any money. He just wanted the footage on the news so people would know what happened. Holliday took his footage of King to the police, who were not interested, but Holliday found that the local news channel strongly desired the footage.

Yet, there are other examples of those who record the police that problematize this conceptualization of how misconduct is disclosed. These examples show how an individual confronts misconduct and then spreads that directly to the public. Reynolds and Frazier shared their footage of Castile and Floyd on Facebook, bypassing the traditional oversight entities. When citizen recorders blow the whistle, they are saying this is our experience, this is what is happening to our neighbors and in our communities.

In this sense, the neighborhoods and communities that cop watchers and serendipitous recorders patrol are the organization. The concept of organization is a key feature of whistleblowing definitions, and most of the scholarly discussions of whistleblowing are formal organizations (e.g., specific companies or government agencies).[57] But communities (e.g., a neighborhood) can also be described as organizations. "Community as organization" means people have a shared place and shared interests, and/ or a common identity.[58] Here, citizen recorders share the same geographic living space, an interest in revealing police misconduct (i.e., whistleblowing), and a common identity. This common identity arises from the activist movement they themselves constitute: to change the relationship between the police, who often live within and are tasked with patrolling the same communities, and members of their communities by documenting and protesting misconduct.

And, since a person pointing a camera can be seen as an instance of protest, the camera can facilitate change, which can be immediate. The mere presence of a citizen with a camera can cause an officer to stop or avoid engaging in misconduct due to the potential of publicity or accountability. In these situations, the possibility of whistleblowing may be enough to discourage wrongdoing, but the example of officers Pantaleo and Chauvin, unfortunately, suggest the opposite. Both were confronted with cameras (and others shouting) but continued until Garner and Floyd were dead. These examples demonstrate that the officers who engage in misconduct are the ones betraying the organization, which is the community and its members. Stanger describes whistleblowers' actions as betraying an organization to reveal the truth, but the discussion here suggests that the treachery to the organization is from wayward officers.[59] And whatever, if any, purpose these officers have in committing that betrayal is quite at odds with revealing the truth. Rather, it is the citizen-with-camera-as-whistleblower, who is defending their community and striving to protect and prevent harm to their neighbors, that is upholding the values of the organization and its members.

Others have defined whistleblowing based on unique or privileged access to evidence of wrongdoing. Jubb, for example, defines whistleblowing as being done "by a person who has or had privileged access to data or information of an organization."[60] Members of a financial organization may have access to bookkeeping records, or people working in national security may have access to classified information that reveals wrongdoing. This is a very material notion of privileged access. Access can mean more than authorized access. It can refer to the freedom, availability, or opportunity to access information that others do not have. Cop watchers sign up for patrols on a schedule to engage in their documentary and protest functions that others cannot fulfill due to other obligations such as work and family. Serendipitous recorders have unique access by nature of just being out and about. The lottery of happenstance can put a person with a camera at just the right time and place to observe and report the horrible things others may not have access or the ability to see themselves.

The scholarship on whistleblowing makes a clear distinction between source and journalist, but citizen recorders problematize this distinction. The typical relationship is one where the whistleblower is the source, and the journalist is the outlet or means for distributing that information to the public, although certainly, the whistleblower has alternatives to journalists (e.g., law firms, Government Accountability Project, etc.).[61] However, this distinction rests on a traditional understanding of journalism and news media. Contemporary perspectives recognize that citizen recorders fulfill a journalistic role in a new media paradigm.[62] As such, the citizen recorder becomes the source as well as the distributor of information by using social media. To rule out citizen recorders as whistleblowers because of traditional characterizations of who news reporters are is to miss the point of what citizen recorders do: publicize police wrongdoing within people's communities to facilitate accountability and achieve change.

In closing, it seems appropriate to ask whether this chapter's argument—that citizen recorders of police wrongdoing are whistleblowers—

stretch the traditional definition of whistleblowing too far. For those scholars who desire rigidity in defining whistleblowers, the answer is potentially, if not absolutely, yes.[63] It does seem prudent to ensure that the term *whistleblowing* maintains a proper meaning lest everyone has the potential to be a whistleblower, as the many false whistleblowing designations after the 2020 US presidential election have demonstrated. But, when it comes to race and policing, there is a lot of wrongdoing to expose. And this wrongdoing is severe but supported with actual evidence. Those who commit police violence should be accountable for their misdeeds because what they have done is often heinously wrong. But also, because the police are the ones supposed to be preventing and stopping wrongdoing, not committing it. And those who fall victim to police misconduct have and will undoubtedly continue to endure more of the same. Bystanders risk the same fate if they try to intervene in such situations. But, if the bystander is armed with a camera, there is hope for change. Through documentation, confrontation, and protest, cop watchers and serendipitous recorders critically empower a democratic populace regarding human and democratic rights. As such, classifying the rhetorical processes of citizen observers of the police as whistleblowing actions not only brings us new insights as we integrate important bodies of research that are too often separated, but we can also use this knowledge to interrogate the institutions of power that threaten human rights and democratic governance.

Notes

1. Hans Toch, *Copwatch: Spectators, Social Media, and Police Reform* (Washington, DC: American Psychological Association, 2012); Ben Brucato, "The New Transparency: Police Violence in the Context of Ubiquitous Surveillance," *Media and Communication* 3, 3 (2015): 39–55.

2. Toch, *Copwatch*, 4.

3. Marcus Fabius Quintilianus, *The Institutio Oratoria of Quintilian*, trans. H. E. Butler (Cambridge, MA: Harvard University Press, 1960), xii 1.16–1.35.

4. Karma R. Chávez, "The Body: An Abstract and Actual Rhetorical Concept," *Rhetoric Society Quarterly* 48, 3 (2018): 242–250; Raymie E. McKerrow, "Corporeality and Cultural Rhetoric: A Site for Rhetoric's Future," *Southern Communication Journal* 63, 4 (1998): 315–328.

5. Laura Verdi, "The Symbolic Body and the Rhetoric of Power," *Social Analysis* 54, 2 (2010): 99–115.

6. Catherine Gouge and John Jones, "Wearables, Wearing, and the Rhetorics That Attend to Them," *Rhetoric Society Quarterly* 46, 3 (2016): 199–206; James L.

Cherney, "Deaf Culture and the Cochlear Implant Debate: Cyborg Politics and the Identity of People with Disabilities," *Argumentation and Advocacy* 36, 1 (1999): 22–34.

7. Anthony M. Townsend, "Mobile Communications in the Twenty-First-Century City," in *Wireless World: Social and Interactional Aspects of the Mobile Age*, ed. Barry Brown, Nicola Green, and Richard Harper (London: Springer, 2012), 68–69.

8. Allissa V. Richardson, *Bearing Witness While Black: African Americans, Smartphones, and the New Protest #Journalism* (Oxford: Oxford University Press, 2020), 197.

9. Angela J. Aguayo, *Documentary Resistance* (Oxford: Oxford University Press, 2019), 4.

10. Toch, *Copwatch*.

11. Joshua Bloom and Waldo E. Martin Jr., *Black Against Empire: The History and Politics of the Black Panther Party* (Berkeley: University of California Press, 2013).

12. "Berkeley Copwatch Handbook," Berkeley Copwatch, 2021, accessed February 12, 2022, https://www.berkeleycopwatch.org/handbook.

13. Brucato, "New Transparency," 50.

14. Brucato, "New Transparency," 50.

15. Taylor Robertson, "Lights, Camera, Arrest: The Stage Is Set for a Federal Resolution of a Citizen's Right to Record the Police in Public," *Boston University Public Interest Law Journal* 23, 1 (2014): 120.

16. Christopher Robé, "El Grito de Sunset Park: Cop Watching, Community Organizing, and Video Activism," *Journal of Cinema and Media Studies* 59, 2 (Winter 2020): 62.

17. Brenna Ehlrich, "Ramsey Orta, Man Who Filmed Eric Garner's Arrest, Has Been Released from Prison," *Rolling Stone*, June 8, 2020, accessed February 12, 2022, https://www.rollingstone.com/culture/culture-news/ramsey-orta-eric-garner-prison-release-1011646/.

18. Caitlin Byrd, "The Quiet Struggle of Feidin Santana, the Man Who Filmed the Shooting of Walter Scott," *State*, May 13, 2021, accessed February 12, 2022, https://www.thestate.com/news/charleston/article251236739.html.

19. Joe Gyan Jr., "Store Owner's Detention After Alton Sterling Shooting Illegal and Inhumane, His Lawyers Tell Judge," *Advocate*, October 11, 2021, accessed February 12, 2022, https://www.theadvocate.com/baton_rouge/news/courts/article_555815d6-2a9e-11ec-bdb5-43e7df6cccbc.html.

20. Hettie Judah, "Diamond Reynolds: The Woman Who Streamed a Police Shooting Becomes a Renaissance Madonna," *Guardian*, June 26, 2017, accessed February 12, 2022, https://www.theguardian.com/artanddesign/2017/jun/26/luke-willis-thompson-philando-castile-autoportrait.

21. German Lopez, "Man Who Recorded Freddie Gray's Arrest: 'He Was Just Screaming—Screaming for Life,'" *Vox*, April 23, 2015, accessed February 12, 2022, https://www.vox.com/2015/4/23/8484185/freddie-gray-kevin-moore.

22. Joe Hernandez, "Read This Powerful Statement from Darnella Frazier, Who Filmed George Floyd's Murder," NPR, May 26, 2021, accessed February 12, 2022, https://www.npr.org/2021/05/26/1000475344/read-this-powerful-statement-from-darnella-frazier-who-filmed-george-floyds-murder.

23. Allissa V. Richardson, "Black Bodies at Risk: Exploring the Corporeal Iconography of the Anti-Police Brutality Movement," *Journalism* 23, 3 (2021): 599–613, 604.

24. Joshua Guitar and Alan Chu, "Racing to (Dis)Own Whistleblowers and Protests: Theorizing *Amongness* in the Shared Rhetorical Spaces of Democratic Agency," chapter 1 in the present volume, 2.

25. Camille Squires, "What Happened to the Witnesses," *New York Magazine: Intelligencer*, January 31, 2022, accessed February 12, 2022, https://nymag.com/intelligencer/2022/01/people-who-filmed-police-killings.html.

26. Mario Diani, "Protest, Political," in *The International Encyclopedia of Political Communication*, ed. Gianpietro Mazzoleni (New York: Wiley, 2015), 1272–1280; Luis Loya and Doug McLeod, "Social Protest," in *Oxford Bibliographies: Communication*, ed. Patricia Moy (Oxford: Oxford University Press, 2020).

27. Franklyn S. Haiman, *"Speech Acts" and the First Amendment* (Carbondale: Southern Illinois University Press, 1993).

28. *Spence v. Washington*, 418 US 405, 409 (1974).

29. *Tinker v. Des Moines Independent Community School District*, 393 US 503 (1969).

30. Jocelyn Simonson, "Filming the Police as an Act of Resistance," *University of St. Thomas Journal of Law and Public Policy* 10, no. 2 (2015): 86.

31. Mario Cerame, "The Right to Record Police in Connecticut," *Quinnipiac Law Review* 30, 417 (2012): 417.

32. Squires, "What Happened to the Witnesses."

33. Karuna Mantena, "Competing Theories of Nonviolent Politics" in *Protest and Dissent*, ed. Melissa Schwartzberg (New York: New York University Press, 2020), 95, 101.

34. Linda Poon and Marie Patino, "A Timeline of U.S. Police Protests," *Bloomberg*, June 9, 2020, accessed February 12, 2022, https://www.bloomberg.com/news/articles/2020-06-09/a-history-of-protests-against-police-brutality.

35. Adam Gabbatt, "Protests About Police Brutality Are Met with Wave of Police Brutality Across US," *Guardian*, June 6, 2020, accessed February 12, 2022, https://www.theguardian.com/us-news/2020/jun/06/police-violence-protests-us-george-floyd.

36. Sarah A. Soule, "Protest, Diffusion of," in *The Blackwell Encyclopedia of Sociology*, ed. George Ritzer (Oxford: Blackwell, 2007), 3685–3688.

37. Seth F. Kreimer, "Pervasive Image Capture and the First Amendment: Memory, Discourse, and the Right to Record," *University of Pennsylvania Law Review* 159, 335 (2011): 357.

38. Frederick Schauer, *Free Speech: A Philosophical Enquiry* (Cambridge: Cambridge University Press, 1982).

39. Vincent Blasi, "The Checking Value in First Amendment Theory," *American Bar Foundation Research Journal* 2, 3 (1977): 527.

40. Glenn Harlan Reynolds and John A. Steakley, "A Due Process Right to Record the Police," *Washington University Law Review* 89, 5 (2012): 1203–1210.

41. Reynolds and Steakley, "A Due Process Right to Record the Police," 1208.

42. Joanna Stern, "They Used Smartphone Cameras to Record Police Brutality—and Change History," *Wall Street Journal*, June 13, 2020, accessed February 12, 2022, https://www.wsj.com/articles/they-used-smartphone-cameras-to-record-police-brutalityand-change-history-11592020827?mod=djemptech_t.

43. Richardson, "Black Bodies."

44. Brucato, "New Transparency," 49; Bilge Yesil, *Recording and Reporting: Camera Phones, User-Generated Images and Surveillance* (Hershey, PA: IGI Global, 2011), 285.

45. *Glik v. Cunniffe*, 655 F.3d 78, 84, 1st Cir. 2011.

46. Roy Peter Clark, "Darnella Frazier, Who Filmed George Floyd's Murder by Police, Should Win a Pulitzer Prize," Nieman Lab, May 18, 2021, accessed February 12, 2022, https://www.niemanlab.org/2021/05/darnella-frazier-who-filmed-george-floyds-murder-by-police-should-win-a-pulitzer-prize/.

47. Oliver Laughland and Jon Swaine, " 'I Dream About It Every Night': What Happens to Americans Who Film Police Violence?," *Guardian*, August 17, 2015, accessed February 12, 2022, https://www.theguardian.com/us-news/2015/aug/15/filming-police-violence-walter-scott-michael-brown-shooting.

48. Squires, "What Happened to the Witnesses."

49. Marion Hersh, "Whistleblowers—Heroes or Traitors? Individual and Collective Responsibility for Ethical Behaviour," *Annual Reviews in Control* 26, 2 (2000): 243–262.

50. Philip H. Jos, Mark E. Tompkins, and Steven W. Hays, "In Praise of Difficult People: A Portrait of the Committed Whistleblower," *Public Administration Review* 49, 6 (1989): 552–561.

51. James Hollings, "Let the Story Go: The Role of Emotion in the Decision-Making Process of the Reluctant, Vulnerable Witness or Whistle-Blower," *Journal of Business Ethics* 114, 3 (2013): 502.

52. Squires, "What Happened to the Witnesses."

53. David Lewis, A. J. Brown, and Richard Moberly, "Whistleblowing, Its Importance and the State of the Research," in *International Handbook on Whistle-blowing Research*, ed. A. J. Brown, David Lewis, Richard E. Moberly, and Wim Vandekerckhove (Cheltenham, UK: Edward Elgar, 2014), 1–36.

54. Janet P. Near and Marcia P. Miceli, "Organizational Dissidence: The Case of Whistle-Blowing," *Journal of Business Ethics* 4, 1 (1985): 4.

55. Near and Miceli, "Organizational Dissidence," 4.

56. Granville King III, "The Implications of an Organization's Structure on Whistleblowing," *Journal of Business Ethics* 20, 4 (1999): 315–326; Ester Rocha and Brian H. Kleiner, "To Blow or Not to Blow the Whistle? That Is the Question," *Management Research* 28, 11/12 (2005): 80–87.

57. Ankit Kesharwani, "Whistleblowing: A Survey of Literature," *IUP Journal of Corporate Governance* 9, 4 (2010): 57–70.

58. Amanda Tattersall, *Power in Coalition: Strategies for Strong Unions and Social Change* (Ithaca, NY: Cornell University Press, 2013), 18.

59. Allison Stanger, *Whistleblowers: Honesty in America from Washington to Trump* (New Haven, CT: Yale University Press, 2019).

60. Peter B. Jubb, "Whistleblowing: A Restrictive Definition and Interpretation," *Journal of Business Ethics* 21, 1 (1999): 78.

61. Stephenson Waters, "The Ethical Algorithm: Journalist/Whistleblower: Relationships Explored Through the Lens of Social Exchange," *Journalism and Communication Monographs* 22, 3 (2020): 172–245.

62. Richardson, "Black Bodies at Risk."

63. Jubb, "Whistleblowing."

4

Shifting Power to Seek Change

Kategoria as a Form of Rhetorical Leadership

MARNIE LAWLER MCDONOUGH

Although organizations have long been plagued with scandal, the contemporary proliferation of media has fueled a societal fascination with stories of leadership transgressions. Facilitated by growing social platforms and forums to level allegations, public accusations of all kinds have increased. Society has witnessed "a series of corporate scandals that have betrayed consumer trust and destroyed shareholder value in many large enterprises,"[1] led in part by "successful people in power [who] sometimes behave badly."[2] Corporate malfeasance has become so pervasive that publications like *Fortune* and *Forbes* issue annual lists recounting top business scandals.[3] As the list of stakeholders, investors, board members, whistleblowers, victims, and survivors speaking out against organizational leaders grows, it is increasingly important to examine accusatory rhetoric that has been successful in effecting change.

Kategoria, a speech of accusation, is a classical rhetorical form that can be enacted to influence change and motivate action.[4] In this chapter, I argue that *kategoria* can be employed as a form of rhetorical leadership and utilized as a tool to disrupt value hierarchy to effect organizational change. The pervasiveness of public accusation indicates that a growing number of voices are seizing power and contributing to the conversation.

The increase in platforms and public support for allegations also creates forums for individuals who traditionally lack authority to speak. The #MeToo movement is responsible in part for revolutionizing the ways individuals publicly address wrongdoing by "creating the conditions that emboldened" people to come forward with a multitude of accusations.[5] These processes can institute "a domino effect," suggesting that when vulnerable members of a group begin to publicly accuse people in power, other group members "feel safe enough to come forward" with their own allegations.[6] The public speeches of accusation directed at organizational leaders have propelled various movements, driven by #MeToo, resulting in the assertion that "such callouts embrace the leveling effects of social media to empower marginalized voices."[7]

In this chapter, I examine an instance of leadership change at Michigan State University (MSU) that I contend was advanced by a group of women who spoke out together as a whistleblower collective (Sister Survivors). To begin, I discuss the implications of my examination that extend to both scholarship and society. Then, I elaborate on rhetorical leadership and how it can be used to encourage change. Finally, I establish the ways the Sister Survivors successfully employed *kategoria* to motivate change in an organization and how this study can inform future attempts at accusation.

Implications for Scholarship and Society

Revealing successful rhetorical strategies of *kategoria* has utility for rhetorical, leadership, and organizational culture scholars as well as crisis managers and other individuals seeking to effect change. Primarily, my study contributes to scholarship by situating *kategoria* as a form of rhetorical leadership. In rhetoric scholarship, *kategoria* has received little attention on its own and has been studied predominantly as the condition for better crafting *apologia*, or a speech of self-defense.[8] My examination positions *kategoria* as a tool for change and illustrates the potential utility of speeches of accusation that do not seek self-defense as the response. I demonstrate that vulnerable individuals who operate as whistleblowers can employ accusation to engage in rhetorical leadership that can motivate leadership change in organizations.

My investigation also enriches rhetorical and organizational communication scholarship by expanding understanding of speech forms that can be employed to enact change and who has access to accusation as a rhetorical form. In many cases, leadership is attributed predominantly to those with legitimate authority. I approach legitimate authority as the power held by an individual based on position or title and the given control over others as a result of their role.[9] An individual does not have to hold legitimate authority to enact leadership, particularly leadership through discourse, as evidenced by the #MeToo movement. Positioning speeches of accusation as a form of rhetorical leadership that is accessible by all individuals regardless of degree of power situates this study within an examination of whistleblowing as an impetus for social change. Exposing transgressions through rhetoric such as *kategoria* or whistleblowing (truthfully revealing wrongdoing from a vulnerable position within an organization)[10] is a means for serving justice as well as ensuring democratic rights for those without legitimate authority. At a time when enhanced understanding of speeches of accusation is critical for actualizing change at the leadership level, my study fuses theoretical and practical implications.

Rhetorical Leadership for Organizational Change

Given the proclivity for organizations to be resistant to change, it is important to examine who is capable of influencing change and how change has been successfully motivated in the past. The most effective organizations are those that evolve and adapt, guided by leaders who embrace change and are capable of navigating it.[11] Cultural change, while often necessary, is not an easy process for organizations. According to Heifetz and Linsky, adaptive change requires "individuals throughout the organization to alter their ways."[12] They posit that "to make real progress, sooner or later those who lead must ask themselves and the people in the organization to face a set of deeper issues—and to accept a solution that may require turning part or all of the organization upside down."[13] If organizational leaders are not willing to adapt in these situations, leadership changes may be demanded by other individuals within or outside of the organization.

Scholars contend that leadership is grounded in managing meaning and can be enacted through discourse.[14] In other words, individuals can assume a leadership role by deciphering complex situations and communicating meaning to others.[15] This perspective allows the possibility for individuals with varying degrees of power to employ rhetoric as a form of leadership. Husband's study on leader behavior explains the distinctions between power and influence as related to positions of leadership.[16] He maintains that power and influence are two different means to induce change, with power relating to a legitimate position of authority such as that of a leader in an organization. Influence, on the other hand, relates to goal identification and the ability to understand and respond to others' needs.[17] This critical distinction in leadership affords individuals without legitimate authority a ripe opportunity to act. Rhetorical leadership relies on "the ability to assess, shape, and meet unique symbolic demands" to motivate a specific purpose in situations that are often faced collectively.[18] Utilizing discourse to influence a collective goal is one tool for citizens, activists, survivors, and whistleblowers to seize power from vulnerable or disempowered positions. To understand how *kategoria* can be employed as a form of rhetorical leadership, scholars and society alike must develop a better understanding of the rhetoric that is capable of prompting organizational response in the form of concrete change.

Shaping meaning and engaging in rhetorical leadership is accessible to all individuals, regardless of legitimate authority, power, or position. Whistleblowers and accusers can seize power through discourse as a way to influence change. Gouran maintains that individuals "who have constructive motives and appreciate the common good" can—and possibly should—enact rhetorical leadership.[19] While the motives of whistleblowers can vary, some scholars maintain that exposing transgressions is a pure, altruistic act.[20] Certain factors influence the success of exercising leadership effectively, according to Gouran. One such factor germane to my study is the "recognition of power as distinct from leadership."[21] When individuals are able to recognize that power can be held in the absence of legitimate authority, they may be more likely to seize power and utilize rhetorical leadership as a means for achieving justice. Edward Snowden, one of the most significant whistleblowers in US political history, is a prime example of an individual seizing power to motivate change.[22] He is quoted as saying that he could not wait for someone else to act and that he made the choice to reveal information that he believed threatened democracy.[23] Morse posited that the current notion of leadership must expand beyond legitimate authority. She asserts that "there are skills, abilities, and circumstances that call on all to perform the leadership function."[24] This performance of leadership extends to those with less power than the organizations and leaders that they accuse. Understanding the ways accusation becomes a form of rhetorical leadership accessible to individuals with varying degrees of power can further embolden and prepare individuals to utilize *kategoria* to motivate change in organizations.

When employed as a form of rhetorical leadership, scholars have maintained that *kategoria* expands beyond the level of organization to disrupt systems of power. In his article advancing a theory of persuasion in social movements, Simons focused on "intentional symbolic acts" of individuals who wish to motivate change, claiming that leadership of social movements necessitates rhetorical requirements.[25] This understanding provides the foundation for our current conception of rhetorical leadership, particularly as it relates to employing speeches of accusation to shift power and motivate change. Individuals without legitimate authority can use discourse intentionally to assume a leadership role and motivate others. For the purpose of his study, Simons defined social movement as "an institutionalized collectivity that mobilizes for action to implement a program for the reconstitution of social norms or values."[26] This perspective explicates the influence that individuals can have by constructing a specific, rhetorical call for change that reorganizes systems designed to protect the powerful. Research conducted in the wake of #MeToo revealed that "women understand a little better their collective power, and they're using it" to influence and propel concrete change.[27] Zoller and Fairhurst contributed to this view of rhetorical leadership by moving beyond "the person in charge" model of leadership to being instead about "the way one or more actors engages the community and its mores in collective action," with the end of seeking justice for society, or in my specific case, an organization in peril.[28] In a similar way, the instance of *kategoria* selected for my study highlights a group of individuals with varying degrees of power joining together to form a whistleblowing collective. My examination elucidates the potential of accusatory speech as a rhetorical form to protect democratic rights of myriad stakeholders in an organization.

A Close Reading of *Kategoria*

For this study, I have selected a case in which accusers with less power than the accused have specified a desired organizational change and that change subsequently has been achieved by a relevant audience. As a genre of forensic rhetoric, accusation can function as whistleblowing, described by Near and Miceli as revealing transgressions of those in power to people capable of effecting action.[29] They contend, additionally, that once the whistle has been blown, the organization must respond.[30] By conducting a close reading of this text, a statement delivered by a group of individuals self-termed the Sister Survivors, I demonstrate how *kategoria* establishes guilt and, in its calculation, shifts value hierarchy to effect organizational change.

A contemporary view of *kategoria* is that accusation is "concerned with giving birth to an image."[31] This image is born because the accuser perceives "an exigence which (s)he would seek to modify through accusatory discourse."[32] When an individual without legitimate authority publicly asserts this image through *kategoria* with a defined, desired end, it is a form of protest—like whistleblowing—designed to shift power and enact change. Forensic rhetoric can enable the public to imagine possibilities for justice.[33] Harris and Werner "insist that forensic rhetoric is an important tool for social justice" and their extensive research concluded that such cases "have transformative potential."[34] The transformative potential of speeches of accusation is becoming increasingly established in society today, with a prime example being the #MeToo movement.

For my analysis, I focus on leadership change at MSU inspired by a whistleblower collective. As emphasized throughout this volume, "protests typify democratic processes as they contest manifestations of authoritarianism."[35] In the vein of #MeToo, individuals with a common goal came together at MSU to launch a movement. My artifact is a public grievance that sought forensic ends and in which concrete organizational action was the satisfactory response. Forensic oratory, as classified by Aristotle, is intended to provoke judgment concerning a past action as a means for justice.[36] This particular text exemplifies an instance of *kategoria* issued by voices that were amplified at a key time for potential impact in society.

Michigan State University

Historically, MSU has boasted a reputation for academic and athletic excellence, with the latter in part due to renowned physician and athletic trainer Larry Nassar. In 2016, after nearly twenty years of working for MSU in various roles, in addition to almost thirty years of affiliation with USA Gymnastics, allegations of sexual misconduct and abuse against Nassar became public.[37] By the end of 2018, almost two hundred survivors of abuse had come forward with claims against Nassar, many of which had been previously reported and overlooked.[38] These reports of sexual abuse and child molestation, described at the time as "medical research," date as far back as 1992, while Nassar was still a medical student at MSU.[39] In response to the legal accusations, Nassar pleaded guilty to multiple counts of criminal sexual misconduct during his tenure at MSU and was sentenced to 175 years in prison.[40] The university agreed to an unprecedented $500 million settlement to survivors for failure to protect them from Nassar.[41] However, survivors of Nassar's abuse demanded further accountability, especially given evidence that MSU leaders had ignored the survivors' claims and perpetuated a culture of abuse at the university.

The university experienced rapid turnover of leadership in the wake of the Nassar scandal. Lou Anna K. Simon, who served as president of MSU for thirteen years and allegedly ignored reports of abuse, resigned in January 2018 "amid growing calls for her to step down."[42] Following Simon's departure, John Engler was appointed interim president. A former Michigan governor and graduate of MSU, Engler was unanimously voted in by the board of trustees. In a statement at the time, Engler framed himself as a parent, asserting that he could understand the "frustration and anger" surrounding the Nassar scandal.[43] In his statement, he promised that he would care for the students of MSU as he would his own daughters.[44] As early as April 2018, allegations about Engler's wrongdoing—from coercion to lying—began to emerge.

Engler's tenure would not last long. According to *The Chronicle of Higher Education*, Engler's "selection was controversial from the start, and many saw him as a symbol of an intransigent culture that put political considerations ahead of morally sound decision making."[45] Engler's brief time as head of MSU has been described as "a year of tumult" during which he publicly made "eye-opening comments" including the suggestion "that some abuse victims enjoy 'the spotlight.' "[46] In addition, Engler was accused of "offering a cash payoff to a survivor" of Nassar's abuse as well as suggesting that another survivor was manipulating other women to speak out.[47] Nevertheless, Engler's institutional power made his position as interim president appear secure until the board was ready to appoint someone else to the role.

Survivors of Nassar's abuse, however, were appalled by Engler's appointment given his evident disregard for them and by the culture of abuse they claimed he continued to foster at the university. Many of these Sister Survivors wrote a public letter to the board of trustees demanding that Engler be immediately removed from his leadership position. Despite their lack of institutional power, many commentators credit the Sister Survivors' letter with Engler's removal from MSU leadership.[48] When the board of trustees pushed Engler out of his position in January 2019, one member remarked that the leader's "reign of terror was over."[49]

In what follows, I illustrate the ways the Sister Survivors' statement framed leadership as a decision as opposed to a circumstance to accentuate the need for change at MSU. Leadership enacted as a deliberate decision in an effort to influence change is the very nature of rhetorical leadership, which seizes power through discourse to manage meaning for a specific purpose. The Sister Survivors' accusation leveled at Engler, who by circumstance held legitimate authority given his role of university president, is an example of rhetorical leadership deployed by a group of individuals with unequal access to power. This act of rhetorical leadership established the Sister Survivors as a whistleblower collective who, from a vulnerable and disempowered position, utilized discourse as a tool to disrupt power and motivate change. By revealing leadership transgressions and amplifying the need to shift value hierarchy at MSU, the Sister Survivors engaged in not only social protest but also a deliberate form of rhetorical leadership.

The Sister Survivors' Statement

On June 19, 2018, over 120 abuse survivors issued a public statement calling for new leadership at MSU and demanding that the board fire Engler.[50] Considering that "Engler did not understand victims of abuse and has not fulfilled the promises he made when he took the job," a group of individuals attempted to enact change at MSU.[51] Condemning his leadership, the letter asserted that "MSU cannot move forward and become an institution of integrity and safety until John Engler is no longer President, and a new interim leader who will stand against an abusive culture is found."[52] The Sister Survivors called for this change in part to protect "those still silenced" and "those who are still at risk" and deserve justice.[53] The women's testimonies against Nassar are credited with securing his lengthy prison sentence, and their words continued to hold power as the scandal at MSU persisted.[54] On January 17, 2019, Engler "was asked to resign by a board that was prepared to fire him."[55] The Sister Survivors' letter calling for justice was the successful impetus for leadership change at MSU during Engler's interim presidency.

The Sister Survivors were bound by their conviction to serve justice and protect the democratic rights of others. However, not all of them attended MSU, which disqualifies them from the traditional definitions of whistleblowing. Yet, I posit that despite extending beyond the formal confines of a singular institution, this collective, as a group of individuals sharing related vulnerabilities, commands the attention of whistleblowing scholars, particularly because of their ability to actualize substantive change outside conventional boundaries of whistleblowing.

Accusation and Demands for Justice

By rhetorically constructing leadership as a decision rather than as a circumstance, it is possible to shape the necessity of organizational change and shift the power from those who hold legitimate authority to those seeking justice. A close reading of the Sister Survivors' statement through the lens of *kategoria* reveals that rhetorical strategies of establishing a dichotomy grounded in values, developing a specific image of leadership, and utilizing personal appeals can enable a power shift to exact change. These rhetorical tactics shift value hierarchy expectations to emphasize acceptable values germane to a specific instance. Shifting value hierarchy allows those with varying degrees of power to promote democratic action within organizations.

ESTABLISHMENT OF A CLEAR DICHOTOMY GROUNDED IN VALUES

Throughout the Sister Survivors' statement, clear rhetorical dichotomies emerge that construct leadership as a decision as opposed to a circumstance. These dichotomies present a choice to the audience. Emergent dichotomies constructed within the text include right or wrong and capability or incapability. The statement illustrates the critical distinction that leadership is a conscious decision and not simply a circumstance based on an empowered position.

In the text, right and wrong are delineated through direct statements of the ways that the Sister Survivors have adhered to the right side of justice. Historically, whistleblowers face significant risk to their personal and professional lives, as Snowden and Uber's Susan Fowler have chronicled.[56] The Sister Survivors acknowledged this outcome in their statement to speak out "at great personal cost because it was right."[57] This statement functions in several ways. First, it serves as a declaration of agency and active decision—"we *chose*" (emphasis mine) characterizes how the Sister Survivors utilize rhetorical leadership in the form of *kategoria* to seek justice.[58] The reminder that this decision comes "at great personal cost" underscores their lack of institutional power in this situation. As survivors of abuse and an abusive culture who have spoken out in the past, they likely have experienced the consequences of using their voices for justice against those in power. Finally, the statement directly contended that the Sister Survivors believe that issuing this accusation is the right thing to do for the future of the university and for justice—so much so that they are willing to consciously decide to put themselves at risk. What is right in this situation serves the greater good of the university moving forward, but it also must serve justice for the transgressions of the past. The only appropriate response to the *kategoria* is one that achieves justice by addressing both the past and the future.

Determining what is wrong establishes the guilt of the accused and accentuates organizational values. The Sister Survivors' letter detailed Engler's transgressions in each paragraph. They contended that Engler utilized "threats" and has "ridiculed, lied about, and shamelessly mocked" anyone who attempted to speak up about abuse or an abusive culture.[59] These descriptions encourage a value shift by positioning Engler's perceived values as misguided. The text maintained that Engler's mindset was "demeaning and derogatory" as well as "damaging," advancing the establishment of his guilt and exemplifying his firm standing on the side of wrong.[60] These quoted words do not describe someone who seeks justice for the abused. Prioritizing people can align the university on the side of justice, and the Sister Survivors established in their letter that Engler was not capable of doing that given his past actions.

Another dichotomy that emerges in this text is capability versus incapability. The language utilized within the Sister Survivors' statement distinguishes between the capability of the survivors of abuse to enact leadership and do what is right and Engler's incapability to lead and move the university toward justice. This dichotomy is emphasized through clear distinctions, including the use of the word "cannot" to describe Engler and his actions. For instance: "it is clear to us that he cannot" bring accountability, transparency, and change to MSU,[61] which are essential conditions of justice. The word "cannot" denotes an incapability as opposed to "will not," which indicates an active choice. Further evidence of this distinction is supported by the claims that the damage Engler has caused "cannot be repaired until he is gone" and "MSU cannot move forward" until Engler is removed from leadership.[62] The repetition of the word further underscores the Sister Survivors' active intention to encourage change. Additionally, the emphasis on Engler's "damaging mindset" illuminates his incapability to serve justice to survivors of abuse.[63] This dichotomy provides an opportunity for those enacting rhetorical leadership to demonstrate their capacity to respond to the inadequacies of those in power.

The Sister Survivors stress the dichotomy between capability and incapability by emphasizing their conscious choices. Throughout the text, the Sister Survivors utilized the phrase "we chose" multiple times, showcasing their agency.[64] Near the conclusion of the letter, the Sister Survivors contended that their determination for seeing justice achieved "will not cease" until MSU has a new leader.[65] The promise to persevere in their quest for justice until it is served emphasizes that they have the capability to continue to fight for themselves and other survivors of abuse. The first-person language that pervades the statement is marked predominantly by assertive verbs reflecting the decisions of the Sister Survivors: "we recognize," "we care," "we say 'no,'" and "we stand to protect."[66] These statements construct an image of the Sister Survivors as a group of individuals who have the capability to do what Engler has failed to do for MSU—create a safe environment where the culture of abuse is eradicated.

To further juxtapose their capability with Engler's incapacity, statements such as "we have made our motivations clear"[67] counterbalance Engler, highlighting the Sister Survivors' work to fix the culture of the university.[68] The following assertions about the past—"We stood against our abuser. We stood against an abusive culture."[69]—bolster the Sister Survivors' capacity to accomplish justice and change. The language not only illustrates the Sister Survivors' focus on the past to reinforce guilt, it showcases that they are looking to serve justice.

DEVELOPMENT OF A SPECIFIC IMAGE OF LEADERSHIP

The next rhetorical tactic uncovered in the Sister Survivors' letter is the development of a specific image of leadership that dissociates it as a circumstance of position from the decision to actively lead. The former is a noun—a position that is appointed or elected and holds legitimate power as a result of the title—while the latter is a verb—an active role chosen by an individual seeking an end. In this text, that dissociation is achieved through the rhetorical construction of an image of leadership that builds upon the dichotomies evident in the letter to accentuate Engler's guilt and the need for organizational change. Forensic rhetoric is marked by its concern with the past; in developing this image of leadership, the Sister Survivors are framing Engler's behavior as an unchangeable reality. This rhetorical device of dissociating leadership as a decision from leadership as a circumstance is another way the Sister Survivors shift power to achieve justice.

The Sister Survivors construct a specific image of leadership by describing what leadership is *not* by itemizing Engler's reported transgressions. This categorization solidifies his past behavior as antithetical to leadership and emphasizes his inability to change. These descriptions are marked by references to desirable values for a leader juxtaposed with Engler's lack of exhibiting and supporting those values. They posited that "President Engler has only reinforced the culture of abuse at MSU" by "creating an unsafe environment on campus."[70] The word "reinforced" in this instance suggests that he had the opportunity to encourage or enact change but instead his behavior fortified the very culture he was appointed to fix. The Sister Survivors underscore Engler's incapacity to lead, stating that title alone does not ensure ability:

> President Engler's abhorrent behavior—including gaveling down a survivor who only wanted him to listen and belligerently abrasive statements unmasking a survivor who only sought the comforts of confidentiality—has sent a chilling message across MSU's campus, causing damage that cannot be repaired until he is gone. . . . Our deepest concern is the impact his statements and behavior will have on survivors who are still living in silence, and in creating an unsafe environment on campus by communicating a demeaning and derogatory attitude towards survivors of abuse who still seek the confidence to speak up. This is not leadership.[71]

Generally, leadership is expected to be motivational, visionary, mentoring, and encouraging to steer a group toward a common goal.[72] The Sister Survivors implicitly constructed an image of good leadership through the contrast with Engler's ineffective leadership. The Sister Survivors' image illustrates that leadership is not necessarily a condition of circumstance but instead must be an active decision to adhere to what is required of a leader and what is just.

The Sister Survivors further developed this image of leadership by punctuating their statement with values that tie into the requirements of a leader and align with justice. Including value statements in a text can be persuasive as values offer the audience an opportunity to determine the values with which they align or wish to align. At the root of this *kategoria* is the end goal of justice, and this value is highlighted directly and indirectly throughout the text. After all, the other "sisters" who have not yet spoken up also "deserve justice" and need to feel safe "when they demand justice."[73] The value of justice lies in the fair, democratic treatment of individuals, and the Sister Survivors have constructed an image of Engler's leadership that is the antithesis of fairness, particularly toward the survivors of abuse. Justice is more than something to value, it is something that survivors "deserve." By rhetorically creating this image of leadership and Engler's incapacity to act as a leader, the Sister Survivors underscored the need for change.

PERSONAL APPEALS

Personal appeals directed to the six of eight MSU trustees who remained aligned with Engler—two had already publicly called for his removal[74]—were also included in the Sister Survivors' *kategoria*. As accusation requires an audience capable of taking action,[75] personal appeals directed to members of that audience encourage connection and comprehension of why the demanded change matters. These appeals create emotional association and relatability. This strategy helps shift value hierarchy to focus on what is most desirable given the current situation and ultimately motivates action to achieve change and justice.

Each appeal is constructed to address specific details that showcase the similarities between the board member and the Sister Survivors' case. The rhetorical appeal to personal issues works to shift alliances from Engler to the Sister Survivors. For instance, to the singular woman on the board aligned with Engler, the Sister Survivors maintained that "your choice as a woman to stand by in silence while hundreds of female sexual abuse victims are attacked and vilified is appalling."[76] The focus on biological sex—specifically using "woman" and "female" to enforce this shared experience—links this board member to the survivors. This statement is also unique in that it is one of only two times throughout the letter that the survivors referred to themselves as "victims," which changes the frame of the survivors' experience to elicit empathy.

The direct appeal to a board member who was a former National Football League player focused on his ability to "fight hard on the football field" despite his "unwillingness to fight over something that matters so much more: the safety of women and children."[77] Identifying his athleticism, which aligns with the Sister Survivors' experience as competitive gymnasts and public figures, highlights the value of perseverance. The text further developed the importance of this value by incorporating a metaphor grounded in their shared experiences as athletes. They pleaded: "You have six months left in your term. Please don't lose your willingness to fight hard for what is right at the end of the fourth quarter."[78] The time metaphor, through established sport cliches, symbolizes that it is not too late to align with the Sister Survivors.

Another example of a personal appeal grounded in connection was to the trustee undergoing serious health issues. The Sister Survivors acknowledged this and offered condolences but asserted to this trustee: "[You] must also recognize that you still have authority and a responsibility in this situation."[79] This statement addresses the legitimate power he held based on his position as a board member while also reminding him of his responsibility to the university and the survivors of abuse. By specifically stating "we know you are undergoing serious health issues," the values of personal well-being and safety come into focus and align this trustee to the Sister Survivors whose personal well-being and safety suffered.[80] This rhetorical connection demonstrates the Sister Survivors' ability to empathize with the trustee in the hopes that that sentiment will be returned. Focusing on specific details in each personal appeal forms human connections to highlight desirable values, shift power, and move toward needed change.

Another value that is pervasive throughout the personal appeals is that of family. Four of the six personal appeals mentioned children, for instance: "You are aligning yourself with misogyny, and against not only women, but even children," and "protecting John Engler over sexual assault survivors . . . and over the current students and children who attend and visit your campus—is horrifying."[81] There are several implications for the mention of children and the emphasis on the value of family. First, the notion of children recalls the need for leaders who value safety and protection. The idea of safety is highlighted by the comparison of protecting Engler—an adult male—over survivors, students, and children. The term "children" further enforces the value of family for the board members who are parents. The personal connection between survivors of abuse and board members' own children serves as additional motivation to protect others by enacting change. These rhetorical tactics indicate that even if trustees have shown inaction in the past, it is "never too late" to serve justice for the survivors of abuse.[82]

Conclusion

The Sister Survivors' letter provides a successful instance of *kategoria* and typifies the collective whistleblowing made famous by the #MeToo movement. In the letter, the Sister Survivors detail Engler's transgressions to establish his guilt and seek justice for survivors of abuse and MSU as a whole. Each of the rhetorical tactics uncovered in the text promote the superiority of certain values over others, affording the audience the choice to align with the more desirable values in this situation. The rhetorical tactics build upon each other, strengthening the persuasive power of each strategy. As a result, the board removed Engler from his position and the university promised changes to the board structure as well as the search process to name a future president.[83] The Sister Survivors successfully enacted rhetorical leadership to motivate the board of trustees and shift power from Engler, influence change, and accomplish justice.

The rhetoric that emerged from this instance of *kategoria* also serves as the basis for future speeches of accusation, especially as it is compounded and given magnitude through multiple voices. Value arguments, strategic framing of the past, construction of an image of leadership, and identifying with the appropriate audience are each fundamental to *kategoria* in the instance explored in my study. Introducing value hierarchy arguments into *kategoria* disrupts power systems by prioritizing which values are more desirable in the present to overcome the past. Successful speeches of accusation expose past behavior and frame it as an unchangeable reality. *Kategoria* identifies and enforces the most appropriate leadership characteristics juxtaposed with the leader's lack of those qualities. This juxtaposition builds on the strategic framing of the past by describing what leadership is *not* by itemizing a leader's transgressions, which solidifies an individual's actions as antithetical to leadership. These categorizations encompass the rhetorical strategies revealed in my analysis and can be employed in ways that relate to each instance of accusation, as evidenced in the Sister Survivors' text. Understanding these classifications is critical for future accusers seeking justice and organizational change.

This chapter shows that it is possible to redefine leadership and instill the notion that power by position or title alone does not necessarily make an individual a leader. The capability and power to lead and effect change is possible for individuals who do not hold legitimate authority via a title. This dissociation of leadership shifts power from those who hold legitimate authority to those who enact rhetorical leadership to motivate change and seek democracy within organizations. As leadership is grounded in the managing of meaning, individuals who are seeking change for the greater good of an organization can utilize discourse to influence that change. The recurrent strategies uncovered through my analysis can be reproduced and inform future attempts at accusation, particularly for individual whistleblowers—and whistleblower collectives—who wish to assume leadership through discourse.

Notes

1. Len Sherman, "Why Boards Must Step Up to Deter Corporate Scandal," *Forbes*, March 13, 2017, https://www.forbes.com/sites/lensherman/2017/03/13/why-boards-must-step-up-to-deter-corporate-scandals/#216d44471b79.

2. Rick Seltzer, "Of Moral Turpitude," *Inside Higher Ed*, July 31, 2017, https://www.insidehighered.com/news/2017/07/31/recent-scandals-show-leaders-failing-navigate-acceptable-behavior-standards-against.

3. See, for instance, Lucinda Shen, "The 10 Biggest Business Scandals of 2017," *Fortune*, December 31, 2017, https://fortune.com/2017/12/31/biggest-corporate-scandals-misconduct-2017-pr/; Lisette Voytko, "Here Are the Biggest Billionaire Scandals of 2020," *Forbes*, December 27, 2020, https://www.forbes.com/sites/lisettevoytko/2021/12/27/here-are-the-biggest-billionaire-scandals-of-2020/?sh=20940e947a19; "The Biggest Business Scandals of 2020," *Fortune*, December 27, 2020, https://fortune.com/2020/12/27/biggest-business-scandals-of-2020-nikola-wirecard-luckin-coffee-twitter-security-hack-tesla-spx-mcdonalds-ceo-ppp-fraud-wells-fargo-ebay-carlos-ghosn/.

4. See, for instance, Noreen Wales Kruse, "The Scope of Apologetic Discourse: Establishing Generic Parameters," *Southern Speech Communication Journal* 46 (Spring 1981): 278–291; Halford Ross Ryan, "*Kategoria* and *Apologia*: On Their Rhetorical Criticism as a Speech Set," *Quarterly Journal of Speech* 68 (1982): 254–261.

5. Jocelyn Noveck and Maryclaire Dale, "#MeToo, 4 Years In, 'I'd Like to Think Now, We Are Believed,'" *US News and World Report*, October 15, 2021, https://www.usnews.com/news/us/articles/2021-10-15/metoo-4-years-in-id-like-to-think-now-we-are-believed.

6. Anna North, "How Harvey Weinstein's First Accusers Paved the Way for More," *Vox*, October 12, 2017, https://www.vox.com/identities/2017/10/12/16459000/harvey-weinsteins-assault-accusers.

7. Spencer Kornhaber, "It's Not Callout Culture. It's Accountability," *Atlantic*, June 16, 2020, https://www.theatlantic.com/culture/archive/2020/06/callout-culture-black-lives-matter-adidas-bon-appetit-lea-michele/613054/.

8. Ryan, "*Kategoria* and *Apologia*."

9. See, for instance, G. Stoney Alder, "Managing Environmental Uncertainty with Legitimate Authority: A Comparative Analysis of the Mann Gulch and Storm King Mountain Fires," *Journal of Applied Communication Research* 25 (1997): 101; Vivian Giang, "7 Powers Leaders Can Use for Good or Evil," American Express, June 17, 2013, https://www.americanexpress.com/en-us/business/trends-and-insights/articles/7-powers-leaders-can-use-for-good-or-evil/; Michael Z. Hackman and Craig E. Johnson, *Leadership: A Communication Perspective*, 6th ed. (Long Grove, IL: Waveland Press, 2013), 141.

10. Joshua Guitar and Alan Chu, "Racing to (Dis)Own Whistleblowers and Protests: Theorizing *Amongness* in the Shared Rhetorical Spaces of Democratic Agency," chapter 1 in the present volume, 2.

11. See Hackman and Johnson, *Leadership*.

12. Ronald Heifetz and Marty Linsky, "A Survival Guide for Leaders," *Harvard Business Review*, June 2002, https://hbr.org/2002/06/a-survival-guide-for-leaders.

13. Heifetz and Linsky, "Survival Guide for Leaders."

14. See, for example, Gail T. Fairhurst and Robert A. Sarr, "Framing: Seizing Leadership Moments in Everyday Conversations," in *The Art of Framing: Managing the Language of Leadership* (San Francisco: Jossey-Bass, 1996), 1–22; Hackman and Johnson, *Leadership*.

15. Fairhurst and Sarr, "Framing," 2.

16. Robert L. Husband, "Toward a Grounded Typology of Organizational Leadership Behavior," *Quarterly Journal of Speech* 71 (1985): 103–118.

17. Husband, "Toward a Grounded Typology," 104.

18. Kathryn M. Olson, "The Practical Importance of Inherency Analysis for Public Advocates: Rhetorical Leadership in Framing a Supportive Social Climate for Education Reforms," *Journal of Applied Communication Research* 36, no. 2 (2008): 221.

19. Dennis S. Gouran, "Problematic Constraints on the Successful Exercise of Leadership, Their Negative Impact, Palliative Measures, and Argument as a More Effective Remedy," in *Recovering Argument*, ed. Randall A. Lake (New York: Routledge, 2018), 229.

20. Brian K. Richardson and Johny Garner, "Stakeholders' Attributions of Whistleblowers: The Effects of Complicity and Motives on Perceptions of Likeability, Credibility, and Legitimacy," *International Journal of Business Communication* 59, no. 3 (2022): 336.

21. Gouran, "Problematic Constraints on the Successful Exercise of Leadership," 229.

22. Glenn Greenwald, Ewen MacAskill, and Laura Poitras, "Edward Snowden: The Whistleblower Behind the NSA Surveillance Revelations," *Guardian*, June 11, 2013, https://www.theguardian.com/world/2013/jun/09/edward-snowden-nsa-whistleblower-surveillance.

23. Greenwald, MacAskill, and Poitras, "Edward Snowden."

24. Suzanne W. Morse, "Making Leadership Personal and Universal," *Innovative Higher Education* 17, no. 1 (Fall 1992): 72.

25. Herbert W. Simons, "Requirements, Problems, and Strategies: A Theory of Persuasion for Social Movements," *Quarterly Journal of Speech* 56, no. 1 (February 1970): 2–3.

26. Simons, "Requirements, Problems, and Strategies," 3.

27. Jeff Green, "#MeToo Has Implicated 414 High-Profile Executives and Employees in 18 Months," *Time*, June 25, 2018, https://time.com/5321130/414-executives-metoo/.

28. Heather M. Zoller and Gail T. Fairhurst, "Resistance Leadership: The Overlooked Potential in Critical Organization and Leadership Studies," *Human Relations* 60, no. 9 (September 2007): 1139.

29. Janet P. Near and Marcia P. Miceli, "Organizational Dissidence: The Case of Whistle-Blowing," *Journal of Business Ethics* 4, no. 1 (February 1985): 4.

30. Near and Miceli, "Organizational Dissidence," 4.

31. See Walter R. Fisher, "A Motive View of Communication," *Quarterly Journal of Speech* 56, no. 2 (1970): 132; Ryan, "*Kategoria* and *Apologia*," 255.

32. Ryan, "*Kategoria* and *Apologia*," 255.

33. See Leslie J. Harris and Jansen B. Werner, "Forensic Rhetoric and Racial Justice: Rhetorical Advocacy in the Reason Why the Colored American Is Not in the World's Columbian Exposition," *Communication Studies* 72, no. 4 (2021): 618–633.

34. Harris and Werner, "Forensic Rhetoric," 629, 621.

35. Guitar and Chu, "Racing to (Dis)Own Whistleblowers and Protests," 1.

36. *The Rhetorical Tradition: Readings from Classical Times to the Present*, ed. Patricia Bizzell and Bruce Herzberg (Boston: Bedford/St. Martin's, 2001), 30.

37. James Dator, "A Comprehensive Timeline of the Larry Nassar Case," *SB Nation*, July 31, 2019, https://www.sbnation.com/2018/1/19/16900674/larry-nassar-abuse-timeline-usa-gymnastics-michigan-state.

38. Dator, "Comprehensive Timeline."

39. Dator, "Comprehensive Timeline."

40. Dator, "Comprehensive Timeline."

41. Mitch Smith and Anemona Hartocollis, "Michigan State's $500 Million for Nassar Victims Dwarfs Other Settlements," *New York Times*, May 16, 2018, https://www.nytimes.com/2018/05/16/us/larry-nassar-michigan-state-settlement.html.

42. Dator, "Comprehensive Timeline."

43. Dator, "Comprehensive Timeline."

44. Dator, "Comprehensive Timeline."

45. Jack Stripling, "Michigan State U. Forces Out Engler Immediately," *Chronicle of Higher Education*, January 17, 2019, https://www.chronicle.com/article/Michigan-State-U-Forces-Out/245497?cid=cp179.

46. Rick Seltzer, "Words Matter at Michigan State," *Inside Higher Ed*, January 17, 2019, https://www.insidehighered.com/news/2019/01/17/michigan-state-board-moves-oust-interim-president-after-year-pressure-and-bad-press.

47. Lily Jackson, "John Engler Is Out at Michigan State. Here Are Three Moments That Got Him Booted," *Chronicle of Higher Education*, January 17, 2019, https://www.chronicle.com/article/John-Engler-Is-Out-at-Michigan/245500.

48. See, for instance, Alanna Vagianos, "Over 100 Larry Nassar Survivors Urge MSU to Fire Interim President John Engler," *Huffington Post*, June 19, 2018, https://www.huffpost.com/entry/larry-nassar-survivors-john-engler_n_5b291605e4b0f0b9e9a56efe; Tracy Connor, "MSU's John Engler Under Fire for Email that Insulted Nassar Victims," NBC News, June 20, 2018, https://www.nbcnews.com/news/us-news/msu-s-john-engler-under-fire-email-insulted-nassar-victims-n884866; Associated Press, "More than 120 Larry Nassar Victims Urge Michigan State Board to Fire Interim President John Engler," *Los Angeles Times*, June 19, 2018, https://www.latimes.com/nation/nationnow/la-na-michigan-state-engler-20180619-story.html.

49. Dan Murphy, "John Engler to Resign as MSU Interim President After Survivor 'Spotlight' Comments," ESPN, January 17, 2019, https://www.espn.com/college-sports/story/_/id/25779016/michigan-state-university-interim-president-john-engler-resign-comments.

50. Vagianos, "Survivors Urge MSU to Fire Interim President."

51. Murphy, "John Engler to Resign."

52. Vagianos, "Survivors Urge MSU to Fire Interim President."

53. Vagianos, "Survivors Urge MSU to Fire Interim President."

54. Amy Held, "More than 140 'Sister Survivors' of Larry Nassar Abuse Are Honored at ESPYs," NPR, July 19, 2018, https://www.npr.org/2018/07/19/630440282/more-than-140-sister-survivors-of-larry-nassar-abuse-are-honored-at-espys.

55. Seltzer, "Words Matter at Michigan State."

56. See, Greenwald, MacAskill, and Poitras, "Edward Snowden"; Elizabeth Lopatto, "To Expose Sexism at Uber, Susan Fowler Blew Up Her Life," *The Verge*, February 19, 2020, https://www.theverge.com/2020/2/19/21142081/susan-fowler-uber-whistleblower-interview-silicon-valley-discrimination-harassment.

57. Vagianos, "Survivors Urge MSU to Fire Interim President."

58. Vagianos, "Survivors Urge MSU to Fire Interim President."

59. Vagianos, "Survivors Urge MSU to Fire Interim President."

60. Vagianos, "Survivors Urge MSU to Fire Interim President."

61. Vagianos, "Survivors Urge MSU to Fire Interim President."

62. Vagianos, "Survivors Urge MSU to Fire Interim President."

63. Vagianos, "Survivors Urge MSU to Fire Interim President."

64. Vagianos, "Survivors Urge MSU to Fire Interim President."

65. Vagianos, "Survivors Urge MSU to Fire Interim President."

66. Vagianos, "Survivors Urge MSU to Fire Interim President."

67. Vagianos, "Survivors Urge MSU to Fire Interim President."

68. See, for example, Connor, "MSU's John Engler"; Associated Press, "More than 120."

69. Vagianos, "Survivors Urge MSU to Fire Interim President."

70. Vagianos, "Survivors Urge MSU to Fire Interim President."

71. Vagianos, "Survivors Urge MSU to Fire Interim President."

72. See, for example, Hackman and Johnson, *Leadership*.

73. Vagianos, "Survivors Urge MSU to Fire Interim President."

74. See, for example, Connor, "MSU's John Engler."

75. See Ryan, "*Kategoria* and *Apologia*."

76. Vagianos, "Survivors Urge MSU to Fire Interim President."

77. Vagianos, "Survivors Urge MSU to Fire Interim President."

78. Vagianos, "Survivors Urge MSU to Fire Interim President."

79. Vagianos, "Survivors Urge MSU to Fire Interim President."

80. Vagianos, "Survivors Urge MSU to Fire Interim President."

81. Vagianos, "Survivors Urge MSU to Fire Interim President."

82. Vagianos, "Survivors Urge MSU to Fire Interim President."

83. Seltzer, "Words Matter at Michigan State."

5

Whistleblower Rhetoric

Mistreatment of Migrant Children in US Detention Facilities

SVILEN TRIFONOV

In 2021, thousands of families with children fled from terror and poverty in Central America and headed toward the United States. Rather than an isolated incident, this has become a pattern repeating every few years during the past two decades. This time, however, due to the Title 42 rule implemented by the administration of President Donald Trump, migrants and asylum seekers were prevented from crossing the US border due to COVID-19 concerns. Soon after taking office, President Joseph Biden's administration created a temporary exception from expulsion of unaccompanied migrant minors without fully revoking Title 42. The result of this exception was the entry of more than one hundred thousand unaccompanied minors seeking asylum who were then promptly detained for processing in federal facilities as well as privately contracted makeshift camps in proximity to the US-Mexico border.

These recurring events inform a rhetoric of an "immigration crisis," now a common topos in US politics. For instance, an investigation by the Applied Research Center in 2011 revealed that President Barack Obama's administration had separated migrant children from their families, leading to more than five thousand children living in a foster care system that prevented them from being reunited with their families who had either been deported or detained, awaiting to appear before an immigration judge.[1] More recently, in 2018, the US public was appalled by the "children in cages" incident during Trump's presidency, which was an egregious violation of human rights as migrant children were treated inhumanely, contradicting core US values and narratives of "a nation of immigrants," and eluding even basic human decency.[2] Since 2017, "one of every three people held in a Border Patrol facility was a minor."[3] Making matters worse, during Trump's presidency, "the United States sent at least 21,300 asylum-seeking children together with their families to dangerous Mexican border cities under Remain in Mexico."[4]

The problems with migrant children detention and denial of due process did not end after Trump was out of office. Indeed, three separate whistleblower reports documenting mistreatment of migrant minors were submitted to Congress right after Biden had committed to reverse Title 42 and "the last four years of cruelty by his predecessor."[5] According to Ari Sawyer, "with efforts to account for and process those children and their families on indefinite hold, the Biden administration has left vulnerable asylum seekers stranded."[6] It appears that regardless of which president is in office, the US government has consistently treated migrant children like criminals and denied them of their basic human rights.

This chapter focuses on this rather inhumane aspect of US immigration policy and its enforcement through an examination of the whistleblowers who speak up against the violence perpetrated on migrant children. Following the 2018 public outcry at the released images of children held in cages by the Trump administration, and the more recent whistleblower reports of similar (if not worse) treatment of migrant children, public sentiment shows increased concern over the way migrants are treated at the border. A 2021 NPR poll found that "two-thirds of respondents are concerned about ensuring proper care for unaccompanied migrant children detained at the border."[7] The poll found similarly that a majority of Americans support the proposal to create a pathway to citizenship for children who were brought into the country by their parents without documentation. But the poll also found that broader proposals for pathways to citizenship for all undocumented immigrants did not enjoy the same support, indicating the familiar trope that the path should only be for "deserving" migrants.

As a result, a perplexing but all-too-familiar paradox of US immigration discourse emerged. The whistleblower reports documenting neglect and mistreatment of migrant children in custody, reckless failures to follow safety protocols, and egregious processing errors resulting in losing children triggered an emotional response from the US public, urging renewed calls and proposals for reform of immigration policy and practices that would address the unacceptable, if not horrifying, situation of detained migrant children. At the same time, these calls also prompted a political blame game that divided the US public into those who blamed Trump for his "zero tolerance" policy, specifically the Remain in Mexico and Title 42 programs, and those who blamed Biden for failing to address the detained children crisis.

How are we to make sense of the rhetorical implications of these whistleblower reports? On the one hand, we can applaud them for raising public awareness and increasing support for releasing migrant children from detention and opposing family separation.[8] But on the other hand, we cannot ignore their relative inability to promote actual changes in border and immigration enforcement practices. This chapter seeks to address this perplexing dichotomy by contextualizing these whistleblower reports within the history of US immigration policy and enforcement practices, as well as assessing how they function rhetorically within this larger discursive network of US immigration rhetoric that has been characterized and driven by alienizing logics and the politics of biopower. The whistleblower reports and subsequent reactions illustrate the US public's struggle to both empathize and express outrage against the mistreatment of children, and at the same time justify said mistreatment as the correct and rational response to the perceived need to secure the US-Mexico border and to enforce US immigration law. As a result, the whistleblower reports are important rhetorical and cultural artifacts that invite the public to assuage its moral outrage and rehearse common tropes about America's founding myth of "a nation of immigrants."

Approaching them as rhetorical artifacts, I argue that these whistleblower reports function in two important ways. First, they appeal to the US government and its system of checks and balances. Even though the problems are internal, it is up to the government to resolve them. But, since the system itself does not recognize the value of migrant life, instead treating it as a policy issue or as a problem to be managed, the best such an appeal could hope for is moderate improvement of facility conditions. At its core, the basic premise that the system is designed to control and detain migrants who enter unlawfully prevents it from recognizing important nuances and concerns arising from the fact that the migrants in question are children. As long as Biden, or any other president, seeks to uphold the system and enforce immigration law (as is their job), such issues are bound to recur. The whistleblower reports thus become part of the historic record—positively seen as an enactment of a citizen's duties in a democratic system, but also accomplishing little in challenging the alienizing logics of the bureaucratic order of US immigration policy and enforcement. They become evidence of Michel Foucault's argument that parrhesia depends on the existence of a democratic constitution, just as democracy requires the existence of truthful speech, thus creating a vicious and self-serving circle.[9]

This leads to the second rhetorical function of the whistleblower reports—appealing to the demos, or the public. The whistleblowers, acting on their duty as ethical citizens, seek to persuade the US public to see the value of migrant life by documenting and revealing atrocities observed at the detention facilities. But in doing so, their appeals run into the double bind of US immigration discourse of the past several decades in which (im)migrants are both celebrated for their hard work but also chastised for their illegal entry; their presence is validated by the mythic narrative of a "nation of immigrants" but also negated by the mythic narrative of a "nation of laws." The irreconcilable character of this double bind has been repeatedly reified by presidents, with Obama famously and repeatedly stating, "We are a nation of laws, but we are also a nation of immigrants,"[10] and recently with Biden's proclamation that "we will always be a nation of borders."[11] These evocatively sounding double binds do not, or have not, allowed US immigration discourse to move in a progressive direction. I argue that, despite their best intentions and moral foundations, these whistleblower reports fail to influence immigration discourse or policy because they do not address or resolve the aforementioned double binds. Even as they bring attention to unethical and problematic practices, the whistleblower reports remain grounded in the logics of the nation-state that require the audience to see citizen-alien distinctions and that legitimate bordering practices. What's more, I argue that these whistleblower reports invite an absolution cycle[12]—one that paradoxically urges the public to feel guilt and responsibility about migrant children and thus rehearse core American values, but that also rationalizes their detention as necessary to uphold the nation's immigration policies.

To analyze these whistleblower reports, I engage in rhetorical criticism by incorporating the practice of close textual reading of the whistleblower reports through a critical perspective to illustrate their analytic, interpretive, and evaluative potential.[13] My critical perspective and criteria for evaluation follow Michael McGee and Raymie McKerrow's fragmentation thesis,[14] allowing me to approach the reports of whistleblowers as textual fragments produced in the context of and reflective of broader sociopolitical discourses about citizenship and immigration in the US. The rhetorical implications of such fragments are not always immediately manifest or achieved independently; instead, they function together as fragments in a broader discursive and political landscape about borders, immigration, and belonging.

Notably, this reconceptualization of rhetorical texts as fragments operating in broad contexts does not invalidate or preclude close reading as an integral step of the analytical process. Rather, it allows the critic to offer a richer understanding of how texts operate within a political culture. In doing so, critical rhetoric is not a strictly defined method; it is an orientation toward the demystification of power within discursive and political regimes[15]—one that is particularly apt, given that one goal of this volume is to challenge the conventional boundaries of what it means to be a whistleblower.[16] As an orientation, it requires us to examine the relationship between rhetorical texts, ideology, and power.[17] Regarding this chapter, the dominant discursive framework of borders and immigration enforcement represents both the context in which the whistleblower reports operate and simultaneously functions as the object of their parrhesiastic speech. In the context of the volume, the analysis reveals limitations, boundaries, and paradoxes inherent to the parrhesiastic speech of government whistleblowers united in democratic agency but constrained by the biopowers of the state.

Before I present my analysis, I offer brief discussions of the scholarship on whistleblowing and on US immigration discourse. Whistleblowing is a particularly interesting form of rhetoric because, as this essay demonstrates, its existence is both entirely dependent on democratic principles, while also upholding those very same democratic principles. This double bind of whistleblower rhetoric, in the context of US immigration discourse, sheds light on the political stalemate of the past two decades because it helps explain the paradox of a nation that largely favors immigration reform but at the same time seeks to reify and protect its traditional borders—both physically and rhetorically.

Whistleblowing, Parrhesia, and Democracy

Sometimes positively seen as "truth-speaking" and other times pejoratively perceived as "leaking," whistleblowing has numerous and contested definitions, both in scholarship and in public discourse. For the purposes of this essay, I echo Joshua Guitar's definition of whistleblowers as "individuals who publicly reveal unlawful or unethical behaviors of the state, regardless of means,"[18] and recognize whistleblowers, as defined in this volume, as members of a defined body who truthfully expose wrongdoing from a position of vulnerability.[19] Guitar's definition aligns with previous definitions from scholars who have similarly focused on the disclosure of illegal or unjust practices of individuals, organizations, or the state.[20]

Whistleblowers are individuals who make the decision to speak up against what they perceive to be unjust or unlawful, even as the state (or organization) is purportedly the arbitrator of justice and law. As such, they engage in a process of personal deliberation as they weigh the risks of retaliation with their sense of responsibility to speak out in the name of human rights. In the US, the federal government, as well as some private organizations, provide protections for whistleblowers.[21] However, in reality, whistleblowers have often faced public repercussions such as being labeled leakers, traitors, or cowards, as well as experiencing other forms of informal and extralegal repercussions, with the most notable examples including Edward Snowden and Chelsea Manning, who received severe public backlash over their disclosures.

Rooted in the Greek term *parrhesia*, meaning to speak candidly, whistleblowing is an exercise in free speech against the power structures of the state. Guitar explains that "tenuously positioned, whistleblowers assume significant risks as they exact fearless speech while simultaneously acknowledging severe power disparity."[22] Michel Foucault's work on parrhesia is central to understanding the connections between the term's origins in Hellenistic Greece and the modern-day democratic context of nation-states and systems of power.[23] Modern examples of whistleblowing can be seen as an exercise of democratic citizenship, as the ethical responsibility of citizens to speak out against injustices inflicted upon others, even at the risk of retaliation.[24]

This essay focuses on instances of government employees and human rights advocates blowing the whistle on inhumane treatment of migrants held in detention centers near the US-Mexico border. The analysis demonstrates the meaning-making relationships that emerge among individual attempts to contest state power and to actualize democratic agency in the name of human rights. The fact that the voices of whistleblowers have been filtered through the reports written by an organization like the Government Accountability Project does not strip them of their parrhesiastic character because, as Pramod Nayar explains in his study of WikiLeaks, truth-telling against systems of power and the nation-state cannot and should not be personalized or individualized.[25] Even as they may differ from the Hellenistic parrhesiastes, modern-day whistleblowers speak in the same tradition of what Foucault describes as not a tolerant democracy where everyone is allowed to speak, but instead a risky and provocative practice that has transformative potential in challenging the powers of the state.[26] Especially in the context of immigration, where the state has ultimate, and often unchecked, power over the treatment of moving bodies, whistleblowing offers a potential avenue to hold the state accountable and, perhaps, to even disrupt the governing regime of migrant bodies.

Rhetoric of US Immigration in Context

Wielded as both a god and devil term,[27] *immigration* has been a historically politicized term that prompts the US public to debate the merits and dangers of allowing foreigners to enter a country that was originally built by immigrants.[28] The terrorist attacks of 9/11 brought new concerns about foreigners and immigration, renewing discussion about border security and ultimately ushering in an era of renewed anxiety about the impact of immigration on the US economy, demographics, and national identity. Specifically, renewed fears of the so-called "illegal aliens"[29] defined media and political discourses about immigration in the new century.[30] These fears were grounded in a perception that the United States had lost control of its borders and that foreigners were altering the character of the nation.

The early twenty-first century also set the stage for the US government to heighten immigration policy enforcement through a combination of the highly militarized US-Mexico border apparatus, a vast and rapidly expanding network of detention facilities, and the deportation raids of the Immigration and Customs Enforcement (ICE) agency in the interior.

The three-pronged approach aimed to reduce the number of foreigners seeking unauthorized entry into the US and to remove foreigners already living in the country without authorization.[31] Accordingly, the media landscape reflected and amplified discourses about immigration, borders, and threats to the US nation's security and identity, especially in recent years with major news outlets obsessing over "caravans" of migrants from Central and South America.[32] Discourses about "illegal aliens" captured the nation's attention and eventually enabled Trump to build a successful presidential campaign based on fears of immigrants and porous borders. Collectively, these developments illustrate long-standing anxieties about the need to police and protect the normative borders of US citizenship and identity (racial, cultural, economic, and gendered), particularly against immigrants from Mexico and Central America.[33]

From a disciplinary perspective, immigration and rhetoric scholars have paid significant attention to the topics of borders and citizenship as they relate to questions of race and the US national identity's presumed normative whiteness.[34] In various ways, rhetoric scholars of US immigration and citizenship speak to Kent Ono and John Sloop's argument that borders, both material and figural, can draw people in or outside of citizenship based on their race, culture, gender, sexuality, and/or language.[35] Official policies and dominant discursive frames that target Latino/a/x immigrants as always/already "illegal" produce the conditions of exclusion, upholding the borders of US citizenship in racialized ways that protect regimes of normative whiteness.

Scholars of immigration have also discussed in detail the mechanisms of border enforcement that gradually extended the state's sovereign power to control its borders into the disciplinary power to surveil, control, and exclude certain immigrant bodies as "illegal." This extension of state power ultimately defines the biopolitics of immigration. Using Judith Butler's discussion of "life management" processes and the "grievability" of bodies, Joanna Zylinska defines the biopolitics of immigration as a dominant regime in which power determines "which bodies come to matter and why,"[36] establishing the exclusion of bodies that do not belong in order to define and protect the constitution of the polis, or the state. What Nicholas De Genova describes as "the border spectacle" at the US-Mexico border, becomes a stage on which "numerous singular lives are being barred from the life of the legitimate community, in which standards of recognition allow one access to the category of 'the human.'"[37]

Indeed, the history of US immigration policy and border enforcement reveals the state's position that *the object* of immigration politics is migrant life. Simply put, the US nation-state implements immigration policy and enforces its borders as a way to regulate migrant life in relation to the nation. Foucault distinguishes this power from disciplinary state powers that "rule a multiplicity of men to the extent that their multiplicity can and must be dissolved into individual bodies that can be kept under surveillance, trained, used, and, if need be, punished.[38] Instead, biopower takes disciplinary power a step further by establishing control over people not as bodies, but as species. In this case, the "species" is the Latino/a/x foreigner, discursively reimagined as the "illegal alien" or the "migrant asylum seeker" who is manifest in both individual bodies but also as a general population of people who threaten the US nation. For Foucault, "biopolitics deals with the population, with the population as political problem, as a problem that is at once scientific and political, as a biological problem and as power's problem."[39] Over time, US immigration rhetorics helped establish an image of Latino/a/x immigrant bodies as always-already outside the nation, making them a population to be controlled and excluded. Xenophobically seen as a foreign population separated by a border fence, their lives are unintelligible in the context of the US nation—not as human bodies, but as a statistic and a population to be managed, controlled, and detained. Thus, the biopolitics of immigration help explain the seeming contradiction in the fact that migrant asylum seekers have not technically broken the nation's immigration laws and policies and yet are treated as detainees in prisonlike camps and facilities. Within the context of US immigration history, contemporary political discourses about migration, and the intersection of sovereign power and biopower, the foreign Latino/a/x body is treated as a threat first and human second.

Blowing the Whistle on Immigrant Detention Facilities

The problem of inhumane treatment of migrants detained in federal facilities is not new. In 1993, the US Supreme Court heard the case *Reno v. Flores*, later revisiting it and codifying it as the 1997 Flores Settlement Agreement, which established standards for the detention of immigrant children, including standards for the facilities in which they were housed, the duration of their detention, and the conditions of their release. Since 1997, government watch groups and human rights organizations repeatedly brought attention to the former Immigration and Naturalization Services (INS) and now Customs and Border Protections (CBP) agencies for routinely violating the standards set by the Flores Settlement Agreement.[40]

The early 2010s saw a vast increase in the number of asylum seekers escaping violence from Central American countries.[41] This increase was also highly publicized (and politicized) as the US media reported on the "caravans" of migrants and asylum seekers that reached the US border in 2014, 2017, 2019, and again in 2021–2022.[42] Since 2014, the number of unaccompanied children migrants apprehended at the US-Mexico border has fluctuated, reaching a high of more than 76,000 in 2019, declining to just over 30,000 in 2020 due to the COVID-19 pandemic, and spiking to a new all-time high of more than 112,000 in 2021.[43] The Obama, Trump, and Biden presidential administrations worked to contain the influx of migrants, issuing similar calls for people to not approach the US border and threatening that they would be turned away or arrested.[44] Yet, as migrants continued to arrive at the US-Mexico border, international law required the U.S. grant them entry as asylum seekers. Overwhelmed by the number of migrant children, the three most recent presidential administrations opened temporary shelters and influx facilities to house the thousands of children waiting to be processed.

Perhaps the most consistent element between the three administrations has been the repeated violations of the Flores Settlement Agreement and the continued mistreatment of migrants in detention. In 2018, a Human Rights Watch report outlined the barbaric and inhumane conditions of detention facilities in Arizona and Texas, bringing attention to the practice of housing migrants in frigid holding cells, dubbed "freezers."[45] In 2019, legal teams investigated the conditions and treatment of migrant children in a holding facility near El Paso, Texas, finding that the facilities failed to provide adequate care, food, water, and sanitation for hundreds of children and teens, most of whom were forced to take care of each other.[46] The teams also uncovered that, despite US law prohibiting holding of children in Border Patrol custody for more than seventy-two hours, many migrant children were held for weeks, and some for months. Even those who were eventually released from custody were transferred to different facilities under the jurisdiction of the Department of Health and Human Services (HHS) where there are no limits on how long migrant youth may be housed. In an example from 2015, two teenage migrants spent almost a full year at HHS facilities despite their father awaiting their release in the US.[47]

In 2021, the largest temporary facility established by the Office of Refugee Resettlement (ORR), the Fort Bliss Emergency Intake Site, drew public attention when several federal workers detailed to the facility filed a whistleblower complaint to Congress alleging that "the employees of the private contractor running the facility had no child welfare experience, no Spanish language skills, and no relevant prior training."[48] The findings were presented and corroborated in three separate but related whistleblower reports from the Fort Bliss facility. All three reports were published publicly and sent to Congress by the Government Accountability Project, a nonpartisan, public interest group with over fifty years of experience as "the nation's leading whistleblower protection and advocacy organization."[49] As such, the organization serves as a conduit for the parrhesiastic speech of government detailees who witnessed violations of migrant detention policies and practices at the Fort Bliss facility.

The three complementary reports occurred within nine months. The first whistleblower report was based on the disclosures of Laurie Elkin and Justin Mulaire and was sent to Congress on July 7, 2021. The second report focused on the testimony of Arthur Pearlstein and Lauren Reinhold and was sent to Congress on July 28, 2021. Most recently, on April 5, 2022, a third whistleblower report based on the testimony of Kaitlin Hess was sent to Congress making similar allegations and documenting egregious errors resulting in losing children, failure to follow safety protocols, and general neglect for the children in custody.

These recent whistleblower cases, which I deem as rhetorical artifacts or fragments, are the objects of my examination. I approach rhetorical criticism with a specific orientation toward critical rhetoric to help explain the artifacts' role, influence, and place in broader US discourses about migration, border enforcement, and relationships of power. Situating the texts within the context of US immigration rhetoric allows me to illustrate the ways in which alienizing logics, the biopolitics of migrant life, along with the competing tropes of "a nation of immigrants" and "a nation of laws," achieve the dual functions of inviting public outrage and criticizing immigration enforcement policies and practices, while at the same time reaffirming and validating the logics of bordering and enforcement.

Hostility, Indifference, and Resistance Toward Migrant Children

The focus in all three whistleblower reports is on testimony of observed misconduct and malfeasance by federal contractors and employees at the

Fort Bliss migrant detention site. Specifically, the report disclosing the testimony of the whistleblowers Elkin and Mulaire organized their observations around three themes: hostility, indifference, and resistance. The themes are supported with numerous examples of the two whistleblowers observing practices that illustrate systemic problems in the detention and treatment of migrant minors by the US government and their contractors. These range from "losing" children in the system, prolonged detention of children, inability (and unwillingness) to provide mental and physical care for detained children, and gross health and safety violations in the detention facility at Fort Bliss. All of these violate the rules and principles established by the 1997 Flores settlement, but as I documented earlier, violation of such rules has been a pattern for the past several decades.

As examples of hostility, they mentioned that federal contractors "blasted music" and blared bullhorns at the children early in the mornings to wake them.[50] Additional examples outlined contractors questioning children's need for medical care and outright refusal to assist children in dire medical situations. The other whistleblower, Hess, reported federal contractors at the Fort Bliss facility "regularly threatening children with deportation."[51]

The hostility was also complemented by the sheer indifference of federal contractors who "seemed to view their job more as crowd control than youth care."[52] Furthermore, employees refused to interact with children, ignoring their pleas for help, and even questioning whether they really needed medical attention, despite being specifically told that migrant children had experienced numerous traumas during their "long and dangerous journey from their homes in Central America . . . ranging from being victims of sexual assault or other crimes to witnessing others die along the journey."[53] Coupled with the fact that the children "were separated from their parents and family, their community and culture," the whistleblowers' report testifies to the patterns of hostility and indifference shown by federal detailees and privately contracted workers who were "wholly unsuitable" for providing care for children in distress.[54]

The theme of indifference is further supported by the whistleblowers' testimony of observing case management failures that resulted in children being "lost in the system," not seen by case managers for extended periods, and sometimes erroneously transferred between facilities. The detention facilities, described as "tents," were dirty and had a foul odor, "dust and sand were everywhere," "clean bedding and clothes were not regularly provided," and children had to "plead for clean underwear."[55]

When Pearlstein suggested that detailees use federal business credit cards to purchase underwear and other supplies for the kids, a senior federal manager rejected his suggestion, saying, "I don't have time for this shit."[56] Hess similarly reported that children were "held for weeks without basic needs such as clean underwear or bedding and without case management meetings to facilitate their release from HHS custody," and they noted the atrocious conditions of "an unsafe environment for children including harmful noise levels, 24 hour lighting in sleeping areas, and sleeping arrangements that impeded supervision."[57] The indifference of the staff, Elkin and Mulaire argued, was best demonstrated by their lack of qualifications as the company that provided the staff specialized in "fire, water, mold and other specialty cleanup and restoration services," all under the motto "As if it never happened."[58] The whistleblowers Pearlstein and Reinhold detailed the mismanagement and waste of private contractors from three companies, none of which had experience with child care.

Finally, the theme of resistance is supported by examples of contracted staff resisting efforts by the whistleblowers to assist children in need or to report the observed issues. Often advised to report issues to a "suggestions box" and sometimes encountering refusals by staff to address clear policy violations, Elkin and Mulaire contacted Congress to air their concerns. That was met with resistance as federal detailees were instructed not to report issues or provide "feedback" during the first ten days on the job, a de facto "gag order," which is illegal under the provisions of the Whistleblower Protection Act of 1989 and the Whistleblower Protection Enhancement Act of 2012.[59] Hess further reported that the detention facility was plagued by "a culture of secrecy lacking any method to address numerous concerns in which bullying, rioting, and sexual harassment of children were unaddressed."[60] In the whistleblower report focusing on the testimony of Pearlstein and Reinhold, they recalled that when detailees attempted to report incidents of sexual harassment, such as when "construction workers lewdly and loudly gawked at girls as they walked outside," tent management resisted taking the complaints.[61]

Combined, the hostility, indifference, and resistance of federal contractors toward detained migrant children was compounded by the physical environment of vast, overcrowded, noisy, and filthy tents. All the whistleblowers explain in their own words how this environment violated basic expectations of human rights, but it is best explained by Hess, who noted: "This feels like a prison. . . . This is not a place for children. This is not a place for adults. It was way worse than I could have imagined."[62]

In his report, Pearlstein recalls that when interviewing children regarding their prolonged stay in the detention facility, children "told him they felt like they were in prison and often begged 'please get me out of here, I don't know if can take it anymore.' "[63] The reports explain that the whistleblowers felt compelled to speak out after witnessing "the despair of children who felt (often accurately) that they were being ignored or forgotten," but were met with "non-responsiveness at best and unlawful deterrence at worst."[64]

The overall situation depicted by the three themes compels the audience to feel outraged at the mistreatment of children in federal facilities. The themes also function rhetorically as evidence for the argument presented to Congress. In each of the whistleblower reports, the authors from the Government Accountability Project "request" and "urge" Congress to investigate promptly[65] or ask to "continue to investigate"[66] the situation. Despite using the testimony from whistleblowers to document "violations of law, rule and policy, gross mismanagement, gross waste of resources, abuses of authority and specific dangers to public health and safety,"[67] the authors never directly urge Congress to act and address the core problem—the detention of migrant children. Crucially, the authors of one of the reports conclude that "whatever one might think about immigration policy, the reality is that these children are here now . . . ,"[68] suggesting that their mistreatment is wholly separate from the broader issue of immigration policy.

Effectively, this demonstrates a key problem in these whistleblower reports in their unwillingness and/or inability to challenge the norm that migrant children *must* be processed and detained in the first place. Each of the three reports urges Congress to investigate detention practices and conditions but falls short of asking Congress to end the practice altogether. As such, these whistleblower reports function as rhetorical fragments embedded and dependent on a preexisting system driven by bureaucratic logics of enforcement and control. Within this system, the foreign body—even a child's—must be controlled and processed. Despite appeals to human rights, the authors speak from a discursive paradigm that makes it impossible to separate the human condition and the status as a foreigner. Thus, the reports do not challenge the logics of detention and systems of power that make it possible for migrant children to be held in government facilities and treated as subhuman; instead, they work within those systems to plead for the improved treatment of detained migrant children. Within this frame, the hostility, indifference, and resistance of government employees and private contractors is scrutinized only because of its egregious nature and cruelty. But the detained migrant child remains constructed as an Other—one that deserves better treatment, but one that nonetheless needs to be detained. As such, these whistleblower reports illustrate a boundary that remains—between citizen and foreigner, as the whistleblower exercises the citizenship duty to speak out against observed injustices and inhumane practices, but never goes the extra step of questioning or erasing the borders between citizen and alien.

We thus return to the question posed earlier in this chapter—How are we to make sense of the rhetorical influence of these whistleblower reports? Indeed, we can celebrate and applaud the decision of federal detailees to speak out and testify about the observed injustices and inhumane treatment of migrant children in detention facilities. These whistleblowers speak for those who are not allowed to speak, whose voices are ignored, and whose place is not perceived as legitimate in US public discourse. They speak out from a sense of duty, as concerned democratic citizens and as concerned human beings, having witnessed the inhumane and unsafe treatment of migrant children, as well as the mismanagement and waste by private contractors with no child care experience. In the process of disclosure, they speak parrhesiastically based on their own observations and experiences. Filtered through the medium of an official report created by the Government Accountability Project, their parrhesiastic speech is channeled to address both Congress and the US public, urging them to investigate the situation and to show decency toward the hundreds of detained children in federal facilities.

Yet, as textual fragments, they also appear within a discursive landscape dominated by concerns about immigration, border security, and the logics of alienization.[69] As products of that discursive landscape, which explains their reluctance and even failure to seek change, even as they urge the public to feel sympathy toward migrant children and as they ask Congress to investigate and to resolve issues in the treatment of migrant children, the reports and the parrhesiastic speech of federal detailees never advocate for reforms to immigration policy that would disallow the detention of migrant children altogether.

Despite these shortcomings, the whistleblower reports did indeed prompt the government to act. Despite the lack of specific details, the Biden administration and the agencies responsible (ORR and HHS) committed to implementing changes in detention practices, as well as to reducing the maximum time migrant children are held in detention in accordance with the 1997 Flores settlement. When asked about the whistleblower accounts, an HHS spokesperson said: "The care and well-being of children in our custody continues to be a top priority for HHS. We act quickly to address any concerns and have proactively closed sites that didn't meet our standards."[70] With regard to the broader public, news reports and coverage of the whistleblower disclosures were widespread and received moderate public attention.[71] But ultimately, they failed to reach the gravity and urgency of the previous disclosures of "children in cages" that sparked nationwide protests and marches in 2018.[72]

Does that mean these recent incidents at Fort Bliss were less atrocious? Or that the whistleblower disclosures failed at raising the attention of the public and Congress? I argue that the relative lack of public and government response results from the broader tendency to rationalize, and even normalize, the mistreatment of detained migrants as isolated incidents at best, and as an expectation of policing the US-Mexico border at worst. When placed within the discursive landscape of US immigration rhetoric, and within their historical context, these recent whistleblower reports lose the rhetorical appeal characteristic of other whistleblower reports. They appeal to a public that is, in some ways, desensitized to the abuse of migrant children in detention, due to repeated reports of similar incidents and the competing coverage of threat from "migrant caravans." Nevertheless, the whistleblower reports of atrocities inflicted by the state on migrant children are important rhetorical artifacts and enactments of citizenship, speaking truth to power, and holding the state accountable.

Conclusion

Immigrant rights advocates gained significant visibility over the past two decades.[73] Their rhetoric has been effective as well, as a majority of the US public now agrees that undocumented immigrants who cross the border "illegally" while fleeing violence in their own countries should be offered a path to citizenship.[74] At the same time, however, competing rhetorical forces have raised fears about illegal immigration and the erosion of the rule of law, ushering in regulations and restrictions that have greatly increased US border surveillance and enforcement. The detention of migrant children falls into a gray area between these two competing rhetorical forces, as the public repeatedly wrestles to sympathize and rationalize their treatment at detention facilities. Unfortunately, the whistleblower reports fall into that same gray area, rendering them ineffectual against the alienizing logics of US immigration discourse.

The parrhesiastic speech of federal detailees examined in this chapter offers important lessons about whistleblowing practices in the context of US immigration politics and rhetoric. As Foucault explained, parrhesiastic speech can only occur within a discursive landscape that champions democratic principles.[75] The positive, albeit limited, influence of these whistleblower reports owes its success to legal and discursive systems that allow and invite speech that challenges power structures and systems. At the same time, Foucault also cautioned that democracy itself requires, and depends on, the existence of truthful speech.[76] As such, the whistleblower reports are elevated as examples of good citizenship and as evidence that, despite the problematic practices outlined by them, the US system and its power structures can be, to some degree, accountable to its citizens. The effect of this rather complex iteration of the genesis paradox is seen in the lack of actual policy change as migrant children continue to be detained, as incidents of their mistreatment in detention facilities become recurring episodes that reignite national outrage caused by the lack of political interest to reform immigration.

Perhaps the most frustrating element, or slippage point, is the fact that the detained migrant children do not even fall under the pejorative label of "illegal aliens." The children did not cross the US-Mexico border illegally. They appeared at the border with the intent to seek asylum and protection from the violence in their home countries. Despite international laws guaranteeing asylum and refugee protections, the recent incidents demonstrate that the treatment of migrant children seeking asylum violates these protections. Furthermore, they demonstrate the way in which the nation-state, as well as the US public largely, see these children as de facto illegal immigrants—guilty before committing any crime. Their (mis)treatment by private contractors at the Fort Bliss Emergency Intake Site illustrates that they are not seen as children, or even as human beings, but rather as a "crowd" to be controlled, a problem to be resolved, and a statistic that needs to be bureaucratically treated. The US biopolitics of migrant life render detained children meaningless and expendable. In this context, the whistleblower reports, despite their limitations, nonetheless seek to humanize migrant children. The parrhesiastic speech of federal detailees, appalled at what they saw, urges the US government to investigate and address problems with migrant detention practices, and to treat detained migrant children in a more humane and respectful manner.

In the end, even as it poses challenges and questions about US values (life, children, nation of immigrants) and democratic values in general, migrant detention is allowed to continue regardless of which president is in office because at its core, the US system treats migrants as alien outsiders first and people second. Whistleblower reports about the mistreatment of migrant children invite US media and the public to rehearse aspirational, if not always realized, US values, allowing them to feel guilt and voice their outrage, but they ultimately offer absolution[77] by rationalizing detention practices as necessary in the name of upholding the nation's immigration policies and law.

Notes

1. Julio Ricardo Varela, "Abuse of Migrant Children Didn't Start with Trump. It Didn't End with Him, Either," MSNBC, April 10, 2022, https://www.msnbc.com/opinion/msnbc-opinion/mistreatment-migrant-children-u-s-border-spans-administrations-n1294203.

2. Clara Long, "Written Testimony: 'Kids in Cages: Inhumane Treatment at the Border,'" Human Rights Watch, July 11, 2019, https://www.hrw.org/news/2019/07/11/written-testimony-kids-cages-inhumane-treatment-border.

3. Anna Flagg and Julia Preston, " 'No Place for a Child': 1 in 3 Migrants Held in Border Patrol Facilities Is a Minor," Politico, June 16, 2022, https://www.politico.com/news/magazine/2022/06/16/border-patrol-migrant-children-detention-00039291.

4. Human Rights Watch, "US: Border Program's Huge Toll on Children," Human Rights Watch, February 4, 2022, https://www.hrw.org/news/2022/02/04/us-border-programs-huge-toll-children.

5. Hayes Brown, "Biden's Immigration Promises Are Running Up Against Reality," MSNBC, February 24, 2021, https://www.msnbc.com/opinion/biden-s-immigration-promises-are-running-against-reality-n1258692.

6. Human Rights Watch, "US."

7. Joel Rose, "Despite Concerns About Border, Poll Finds Support for More Pathways to Citizenship," NPR, May, 20, 2021, https://www.npr.org/2021/05/20/998248764/despite-concerns-about-border-poll-finds-support-for-more-pathways-to-citizenship.

8. Sophia Jordán Wallace and Chris Zepeda-Millán, "Americans Support Releasing Migrant Children from Detention and Oppose Family Separation, New Data Shows," Washington Post, March 12, 2021, https://www.washingtonpost.com/politics/2021/03/12/americans-support-releasing-migrant-children-detention-oppose-family-separation-new-data-shows/.

9. Michel Foucault, *The Government of Self and Others: Lectures at the Collège de France, 1982–1983* (Houndmills: Palgrave Macmillan, 2010), 155; Michel Foucault, *The Courage of Truth: The Government of Self and Others II: Lectures at the Collège de France, 1983–1984* (Houndmills: Palgrave Macmillan, 2011), 60–61.

10. Barack Obama, "Remarks by the President in Address to the Nation on Immigration," White House, 2014, https://obamawhitehouse.archives.gov/the-press-office/2014/11/20/remarks-President-address-nation-immigration; Josue David Cisneros, "A Nation of Immigrants and a Nation of Laws: Race, Multiculturalism, and Neoliberal Exception in Barack Obama's Immigration Discourse," *Communication, Culture and Critique* 8, no. 3 (2015): 356–375.

11. Joseph Biden, "FACT SHEET: The Biden Administration Blueprint for a Fair, Orderly and Humane Immigration System," White House, 2021, https://www.whitehouse.gov/briefing-room/statements-releases/2021/07/27/fact-sheet-the-biden-administration-blueprint-for-a-fair-orderly-and-humane-immigration-system/.

12. Kenneth Burke, *Permanence and Change*, 2nd ed. (Los Altos, CA: Hermes, 1954), 234.

13. Michael Leff, "Interpretation and the Art of the Rhetorical Critic," *Western Journal of Speech Communication* 44, no. 4 (1980): 337–349.

14. Michael McGee, "Text, Context, and the Fragmentation of Contemporary Culture," *Western Journal of Speech Communication* 54, no. 3 (1990): 279; James Jasinski, *Sourcebook on Rhetoric: Key Concepts in Contemporary Rhetorical Studies* (Thousand Oaks, CA: Sage, 2001), 119.

15. Raymie McKerrow, "Critical Rhetoric: Theory and Praxis," *Communication Monographs* 56, no. 2 (1989): 91–111.

16. Joshua Guitar and Alan Chu, "Racing to (Dis)Own Whistleblowers and Protests: Theorizing *Amongness* in the Shared Rhetorical Spaces of Democratic Agency," chapter 1 in the present volume, 2.

17. For a discussion on the connection between rhetoric and ideology, see Maurice Charland, "Constitutive Rhetoric: The Case of the *Peuple Québécois*," *Quarterly Journal of Speech* 73, no. 2 (1987): 133–150. http://doi.org/10.1080/00335638709383799; Maurice Charland, "Rehabilitating Rhetoric: Confronting Blindspots in Discourse and Social Theory," in *Contemporary Rhetorical Theory: A Reader*, ed. John Lucaites, Celeste Condit, and Sally Caudill (New York: Guilford Press, 1990), 464–473; Michael McGee, "Social Movement: Phenomenon or Meaning?," *Central States Speech Journal* 31, no. 4 (1980): 233–244; McKerrow, Critical Rhetoric.

18. Joshua Guitar, "<Snowden> Is (Not) a Whistleblower: Ideographs, Whistleblower Protections, and Restrictions of <Free> Speech," *First Amendment Studies* 54, no. 1 (2020): 3.

19. Guitar and Chu, "Racing to (Dis)Own Whistleblowers and Protests," 2.

20. Marcia Miceli and Janet Near, *Blowing the Whistle: The Organizational and Legal Implications for Companies and Employees* (Lanham, MD: Lexington Books, 1992); Fred C. Alford, *Whistleblowers: Broken Lives and Organizational Power* (Ithaca, NY: Cornell University Press, 2001); Myron Peretz Glazer and Penina Migdal Glazer, *The Whistleblowers: Exposing Corruption in Government and Industry* (New York: Basic Books, 1989); Roberta Ann Johnson, *Whistle-Blowing: When It Works and Why* (Boulder, CO: Lynne Rienner, 2003); Alan Chu, "In Tradition of Speaking Fearlessly: Locating a Rhetoric of Whistleblowing in the Parrhēsiastic Dialectic," *Advances in the History of Rhetoric* 19, no. 3 (2016): 231–250.

21. Whistleblower Protection Enhancement Act, 5 U.S.C. § 2302(b)(13).

22. Guitar, "<Snowden> Is (Not) a Whistleblower," 4.

23. Foucault, *Government of Self and Others*, 155; Foucault, *Courage of Truth*, 60–61.

24. Alan Milchman and Alan Rosenberg, "Michel Foucault: Crises and Problemizations," *Review of Politics* 67, no. 2 (2005): 335–351; Theresa Sauter and Gavin Kendall, "Parrhesia and Democracy: Truthtelling, WikiLeaks and the Arab Spring," *Social Alternatives* 30, no. 3 (2011): 10–14.

25. Pramod Nayar, "WikiLeaks, the New Information Cultures and Digital Parrhesia," *Economic and Political Weekly* 45, no. 52 (2010): 27–30.

26. Foucault, *Government of Self and Others*, 36–37.

27. On god and devil terms, see Richard Weaver, *The Ethics of Rhetoric* (Chicago: Henry Regnery, 1953).

28. D. Robert DeChaine, "Afterword: Tracking the 'Shifting Borders' of Identity and Otherness; Productive Complications and Ethico-Political Commitments," in *The Rhetorics of US Immigration: Identity, Community, Otherness*, ed. E. Johanna Hartelius (University Park: Pennsylvania State University Press, 2015), 280.

29. Lisa A. Flores, "Constructing Rhetorical Borders: Peons, Illegal Aliens, and Competing Narratives of Immigration," *Critical Studies in Media Communication* 20, no. 4 (2003): 376.

30. Aviva Chomsky, *Undocumented: How Immigration Became Illegal* (Boston, MA: Beacon Press, 2014); Nicholas De Genova, "The Legal Production of Mexican/Migrant 'Illegality,'" *Latino Studies* 2, no. 2 (2004): 178. See also Leo Chavez, *Shadowed Lives: Undocumented Immigrants in American Society* (Fort Worth, TX: Harcourt, Brace, and Jovanovich, 1992).

31. Ruth Ellen Wasem, "Brief History of Comprehensive Immigration Reform Efforts in the 109th and 110th Congresses to Inform Policy Decision in the 113th Congress," Congressional Research Service, 2014; ACLU, "Arizona's SB 1070," https://www.aclu.org/feature/arizonas-sb-1070; Valeria Fernández, "Arizona's 'Concentration Camp': Why Was Tent City Kept Open for 24 Years?," *Guardian*, 2017, https://www.theguardian.com/cities/2017/aug/21/arizona-phoenix-concentration-camp-tent-city-jail-joe-arpaio-immigration.

32. David Cisneros, "Looking 'Illegal': Affect, Rhetoric, and Performativity in Arizona's Senate Bill 1070," in *Border Rhetorics: Citizenship and Identity on the US-Mexico Frontier*, ed. D. Robert DeChaine (Tuscaloosa: University of Alabama Press, 2012), 133–150. For examples of media coverage on "the caravans" of migrants, see Patrick Oppmann and Natalie Gallón, "A Look Inside the Journey of Central American Migrants Bound for the US," CNN, November 26, 2018, https://www.cnn.com/2018/11/26/americas/migrant-caravan-profiles; Jake Lahut, "Fox News Is Bringing Back Its Caravan Coverage Playbook from the 2018 Midterms, but the Circumstances Have Changed," *Business Insider*, June 7, 2022, https://www.businessinsider.com/fox-news-caravan-coverage-2018-compared-to-now-immigration-asylum-2022-6; Nicole Darrah, "Trump on Migrant Caravan: 'Onslaught of Illegal Aliens' Represents 'Disgrace' to the Dems," Fox News, October 21, 2018, https://www.foxnews.com/politics/trump-on-migrant-caravan-onslaught-of-illegal-aliens-represents-disgrace-to-the-dems; Jose Torres and Lizbeth Diaz, "Migrant Caravan in Mexico Heads for U.S. Border as Americas Summit Starts," Reuters, June 6, 2022, https://www.reuters.com/world/us/migrant-caravan-mexico-heads-us-border-americas-summit-starts-2022-06-06/.

33. Josue David Cisneros, *The Border Crossed Us: Rhetorics of Borders, Citizenship, and Latina/o Identity* (Tuscaloosa, AL: University of Alabama Press, 2014).

34. Cisneros, "Looking 'Illegal' "; D. Robert DeChaine, "Bordering the Civic Imaginary: Alienization, Fence Logic, and the Minuteman Civil Defense Corps," *Quarterly Journal of Speech* 95, no. 1 (2009): 43–65; Flores, "Constructing Rhetorical Borders"; Kent Ono and John Sloop, *Shifting Borders: Rhetoric, Immigration and Proposition 187* (Philadelphia: Temple University Press, 2002).

35. Ono and Sloop, *Shifting Borders*.

36. Joanna Zylinska, "The Universal Acts: Judith Butler and the Biopolitics of Immigration," *Cultural Studies* 18, no. 4 (2004), 526; Judith Butler, *Bodies That Matter* (New York: Routledge, 1993), xii.

37. Zylinska, "Universal Acts," 526; Nicholas De Genova, "Spectacles of Migrant 'Illegality': The Scene of Exclusion, the Obscene of Inclusion," *Ethnic and Racial Studies* 36 (2013): 1180–1198; Kent Ono, "Borders That Travel: Matters of the Figural Border," in *Border Rhetorics: Citizenship and Identity on the US-Mexico Frontier*, ed. D. Robert DeChaine (Tuscaloosa: University of Alabama Press, 2012), 22; Jennifer Potter, "Brown-Skinned Outlaws: An Ideographic Analysis of 'Illegal(s),' " *Communication, Culture and Critique* 7, no. 2 (2014): 228–245.

38. Michel Foucault, *Society Must Be Defended: Lectures at the Collège de France* (New York: Picador, 2003), 242.

39. Foucault, *Society Must Be Defended*, 245.

40. Rebeca López, "Codifying the Flores Settlement Agreement: Seeking to Protect Immigrant Children in U.S. Custody," *Marquette Law Review* 95 (2012): 1635; Wendy Young and Megan McKenna, "The Measure of a Society: The

Treatment of Unaccompanied Refugee and Immigrant Children in the United States," *Harvard Law Review* 45 (2010): 247.

41. Emily Kassie, "Detained: How the US Built the World's Largest Immigrant Detention System," *Guardian*, September 24, 2019, https://www.theguardian.com/us-news/2019/sep/24/detained-us-largest-immigrant-detention-trump.

42. Oppmann and Gallón, "Look Inside"; Lahut, "Fox News Is Bringing Back"; Torres and Diaz, "Migrant Caravan in Mexico."

43. Congressional Research Service, "Unaccompanied Alien Children: An Overview," Congressional Research Service, 2021.

44. Devin Dwyer, "Obama Warns Central Americans: 'Do Not Send Your Children to the Borders,'" ABC News, June 26, 2014, https://abcnews.go.com/Politics/obama-warns-central-americans-send-children-borders/story?id=24320063; Katie Rogers and Sheryl Gay Stolberg, "Trump Calls for Depriving Immigrants Who Illegally Cross Border of Due Process Rights," *New York Times*, June 24, 2018, https://www.nytimes.com/2018/06/24/us/politics/trump-immigration-judges-due-process.html; "Kamala Harris Tells Guatemala Migrants: 'Do Not Come to US,'" BBC, June 7, 2021, https://www.bbc.com/news/world-us-canada-5738 7350.

45. Human Rights Watch, "In the Freezer: Abusive Conditions for Women and Children in US Immigration Holding Cells," Human Rights Watch, 2018, https://www.hrw.org/report/2018/02/28/freezer/abusive-conditions-women-and-children-us-immigration-holding-cells.

46. Cedar Attanasio, Garance Burke, and Martha Mendoza, "Attorneys: Texas Border Facility Is Neglecting Migrant Kids," AP News, June 21, 2019, https://apnews.com/article/texas-immigration-us-news-ap-top-news-border-patrols-46da2 dbe04f54adbb875cfbc06bbc615.

47. Adrienne Gaffney, "What It's Like to Be a Teen Living in an Immigration Detention Center," *Teen Vogue*, 2017, https://www.teenvogue.com/story/teens-living-in-immigration-detention-center.

48. Congressional Research Service, "Unaccompanied Alien Children," 32–33; Priscilla Alvarez, "Government Watchdog Launches Review into Troubled Fort Bliss Facility for Migrant Children," CNN, 2021, https://www.cnn.com/2021/08/02/politics/fort-bliss-migrants-ig/.

49. Government Accountability Project, Mission Statement, https://whistle blower.org/our-story-2/.

50. David Seide and Dana Gold, "Protected Whistleblower Disclosures of Gross Mismanagement by the Department of Health and Human Services at Fort Bliss, Texas Causing Specific Dangers to Public Health and Safety," Government Accountability Project, July 7, 2021, 8.

51. David Seide, Dana Gold, and Andrea Meza, "Ongoing Whistleblower Concerns About Unaccompanied Immigrant Children at Emergency Intake Sites," Government Accountability Project, April 5, 2022, 2.

52. Seide and Gold, "Protected Whistleblower Disclosures," 9.

53. Seide and Gold, "Protected Whistleblower Disclosures," 7.

54. Seide and Gold, "Protected Whistleblower Disclosures," 7–9.

55. Seide and Gold, "Protected Whistleblower Disclosures," 8–10.

56. David Seide, "Second Protected Whistleblower Disclosures of Gross Mismanagement by the Department of Health and Human Services at Fort Bliss, Texas Causing Specific Dangers to Public Health and Safety," Government Accountability Project, July 28, 2021, 5.

57. Seide, Gold, and Meza, "Ongoing Whistleblower Concerns," 2.

58. Seide and Gold, "Protected Whistleblower Disclosures," 9.

59. United States Code, Title 5, Section 1201; United States Code, Title 5, Section 2302(b)(13).

60. Seide, Gold, and Meza, "Ongoing Whistleblower Concerns," 2.

61. Seide, "Second Protected Whistleblower," 5.

62. Keegan Hamilton, "Migrant Children Face Danger, Trauma, and Separation at 'Hellhole' Border Tent Camp," *Vice News*, 2022, https://www.vice.com/en/article/bvnkvm/whistleblower-kaitlin-hess-migrant-kids.

63. Seide, "Second Protected Whistleblower," 8.

64. Seide and Gold, "Protected Whistleblower Disclosures," 13.

65. Seide and Gold, "Protected Whistleblower Disclosures," 13.

66. Seide, "Second Protected Whistleblower," 10.

67. Seide, "Second Protected Whistleblower," 10.

68. Seide and Gold, "Protected Whistleblower Disclosures," 13.

69. Mae Ngai, *Impossible Subjects: Illegal Aliens and the Making of Modern America* (Princeton, NJ: Princeton University Press, 2004); D. Robert DeChaine, *Border Rhetorics: Citizenship and Identity on the US-Mexico Frontier* (Tuscaloosa: University of Alabama Press, 2012).

70. Rene Kladzyk, "A Tale of Two Cities: Comparing the Fort Bliss Sites for Afghans and Migrant Children," El Paso Matters, 2021, https://elpasomatters.org/2021/09/16/a-tale-of-two-tent-cities-comparing-the-fort-bliss-sites-for-afghans-and-migrant-children/.

71. Camilo Montoya-Galvez, "Migrant Children in U.S. Tent Camp Faced Depression and Filthy Conditions, Whistleblowers Say," CBS News, July 28, 2021, https://www.cbsnews.com/news/immigration-fort-bliss-migrant-children-whistleblower-complaint; Elizabeth Trovall, "Whistleblower Complaint Outlines Mismanagement, Abuse at Texas Shelters for Migrant Kids," *Houston Chronicle*, September 9, 2021, https://www.houstonchronicle.com/news/houston-texas/immigration/article/Whistleblower-outlines-mismanagement-and-abuse-at-16444752.php; Julia Ainsley, "Whistleblowers Allege Poor Care for Migrant Kids by Contractor Specializing in Disaster Cleanup," NBC News, July 7, 2021, https://www.nbcnews.com/politics/immigration/whistleblowers-allege-poor-care-migrant-kids-contractor-specializing-disaster-cleanup-n1273124.

72. Ellen Knickmeyer, " 'No More Children in Cages': Thousands March Against Family Separations in 700 Protests Across U.S.," *National Post*, June 30,

2018, https://nationalpost.com/news/protests-planned-nationwide-over-trump-immigration-policy.

73. Megan E. Morrissey, "A DREAM Disrupted: Undocumented Migrant Youth Disidentifications with U.S. Citizenship," *Journal of International and Intercultural Communication* 6, no. 2 (2013): 145–162; Svilen Trifonov, "DREAMer Narratives: Redefining Immigration, Redefining Belonging," in *Migration, Identity, and Belonging: Defining Borders and Boundaries of the Homeland*, ed. Kumarini Silva and Margaret Franz (New York: Routledge, 2020); Tania A. Unzueta Carrasco and Hinda Seif, "Disrupting the Dream: Undocumented Youth Reframe Citizenship and Deportability Through Anti-Deportation Activism," *Latino Studies* 12, no. 2 (2014): 279–299.

74. Rose, "Despite Concerns About Border."

75. Foucault, *Government of Self and Others*, 155; Foucault, *Courage of Truth*, 60–61.

76. Foucault, *Government of Self and Others*, 155; Foucault, *Courage of Truth*, 60–61.

77. Burke, *Permanence and Change*, 234.

6

"This Is an Information War"

Mediated and Rhetorical Contestations over the War in Northern Ethiopia

AZEB NISHAN MADEBO

Between November 2020 and November 2022, the Ethiopian government and the Tigray People's Liberation Front (TPLF)—Ethiopia's previous ruling regime hailing from the northernmost regional state of Tigray—warred over administrative boundaries and political power. During this time, Western news media, governments, and international organizations condemned the Ethiopian and Eritrean governments for their handling of the conflict. In addition to the war's humanitarian toll in the regional states of Tigray, Amhara, and Afar, the Ethiopian government was criticized for deploying hate speech and disinformation to gain public support against the TPLF and its armed allies. However, many Ethiopians and Eritreans observing the conflict grew to believe that similar rhetorical and war tactics used by opposition groups (the TPLF and its ethnonational allies) received less critical attention from Western media, government, and nongovernment organizations. Convinced that the West's response to the conflict was aiding the TPLF, Ethiopians and Eritreans perceived it as an "information war," and tactically employed social media and protest to make collective claims, influence international narratives on the war, push for policies, and determine the war's outcome.

This chapter analyzes the rhetorical and political context that gave rise to #NoMore—a 2021 online campaign created by Ethiopian and Eritrean organizers Simon Tesfamariam, Neyibu Asfaw, and Hermela Aregawi. The #NoMore campaign mobilized a broad set of protest participants by presenting coherent rhetorical messages and targets that appealed to a wide array of Ethiopian, Eritrean, and allied observers of the conflict. #NoMore organizers and participants sought to challenge Western intervention and narratives regarding Africa, particularly the war in northern Ethiopia, by organizing online campaigns and street protests against the TPLF and what many Ethiopians and Eritreans saw as biased Western news media. Central to #NoMore's public appeal was Hermela Aregawi, an Ethiopian American, ethnic Tigrayan journalist and former #TigrayGenocide activist. Leaving her job at CBS Los Angeles (CBSLA) and severing ties with the #TigrayGenocide campaign, Aregawi played the role of whistleblower, or "truth-teller," by publicly questioning the #TigrayGenocide campaign and Western media coverage of the conflict. Her actions united Ethiopian and Eritrean observers who were frustrated by #TigrayGenocide protesters' framing of the conflict as well as Western intervention and media.

Employing critical rhetorical methods in situ, I discuss and analyze how Ethiopian and Eritrean activists mobilized, circulated, and contested narratives about the war in order to influence international public opinion about the conflict. Using what Middleton and colleagues describe as "participatory critical rhetoric,"[1] I use in situ observations (or "rhetorical fieldwork") to analyze the mediated discourses, advocacy practices, and the affective and political motives of those who created and participated in #NoMore. Endres and colleagues define *in situ rhetoric* as "naturally occurring rhetoric that is accessed, documented, and interpreted as it occurs in the moment of rhetorical invention."[2] Thus, rhetorical fieldwork entails collecting data on the experiences of rhetorical phenomena as they unfold.[3] Throughout this chapter, I analyze data collected through participant observation, in situ dialogue, and the observations I made of digitally mediated discourses and news media coverage of the conflict.

Following my fieldwork in Ethiopia (November 2019–May 2020), I spent time between June 2019 and January 2022 conducting rhetorical fieldwork of different Ethiopian social media campaigns, digitally mediated conversations, and protest events. My observations of over 850

Ethiopia-related accounts on Twitter, Instagram, Clubhouse, and Telegram involved daily scrolling, reading, listening, viewing, and tracking of rhetorical themes and debates. At times, I actively participated by attending Zoom meetings, asking questions during Clubhouse discussions, and directly communicating with content creators on platforms like Instagram. In addition to online participant observations, I attended street protests in Los Angeles for the #TigrayGenocide (June 2019) and the #NoMore campaigns (January 2022). The observations I made by immersing myself in the digitally mediated discourses and street protests added a layer of embodied and emplaced knowledge of the protests' rhetorical and affective dimensions. I successively spent one month in Ethiopia during what was coincidently the "Great Ethiopian Homecoming" campaign.[4] Rooted in #NoMore's galvanization of protesters, the Great Ethiopian Homecoming campaign asked diaspora Ethiopians to return and invest in Ethiopia as a defiant act against Western news media and governments like the US, which issued sanctions and advised foreign nationals to leave Ethiopia as the TPLF advanced toward Addis Ababa.

Ethiopia's Contemporary Political Conjuncture

Between 2014 and 2018, Ethiopians at home and across the diaspora mobilized against the Ethiopian government and its ruling party—the Ethiopian People's Revolutionary Democratic Front (EPRDF). Though the EPRDF came into power in 1991 as a multiethnic coalition, it was formed and controlled by the TPLF—a party with Marxist-Leninist and secessionist roots. Forged during Ethiopia's 1960s student movements, the TPLF had the stated aim of liberating the Tigray region from Ethiopia. However, after ousting the then-ruling military regime and coming into power in 1991 as the dominant wing of the EPRDF coalition, the TPLF led the reconstitution of Ethiopia into an ethnic federation and granted ethnic groups (described in the Ethiopian constitution as distinct "nations, nationalities, and peoples") with the constitutional right to self-determination and secession.

After nearly three decades of authoritarian rule, overwhelming demands for change by antigovernment protesters forced the TPLF-led EPRDF to implement a series of reforms. Protesters denounced the TPLF-EPRDF for stoking ethnic division and maintaining undemocratic control over Ethiopia's economic resources and political power. While the constitution and ethnic-federal arrangement devolved authority to Ethiopia's ethnoregional states and ethnic groups, the TPLF-EPRDF ruled using a highly centralized and repressive approach that prioritized economic growth over democracy and human rights.

In general, antigovernment protesters represented two ideological perspectives: (1) supporters of ethnic nationalism and federalism frustrated by the TPLF's authoritarian rule for undermining ethnic groups' constitutional rights to self-determination and political representation, and (2) supporters of Ethiopian nationalism who feared that ethnic federalism undermined the Ethiopian state, its national cohesion, and civic participation. Antigovernment protesters who supported ethnonationalism and ethnic federalism protested the TPLF's authoritarian rule mainly because the party's centralized and repressive rule deviated from Ethiopia's decentralized and ethno-federal arrangement. The TPLF, representing an ethnic population that is about 6 percent of Ethiopia, controlled the EPRDF coalition and Ethiopian state, despite people with ethnic Oromo and Amhara background comprising over 60 percent of the Ethiopian population. On the other hand, antigovernment protesters who disagreed with ethnic federalism and the TPLF's control protested the TPLF-EPRDF's authoritarian rule because the reconstitution of Ethiopia into an ethno-federal state in the early 1990s was done through undemocratic means that legitimated ethnic discrimination and undermined Ethiopia's national integrity. While antigovernment protesters differed in their support of ethnic federalism and Ethiopian nationhood, many resented TPLF's undemocratic rule and repressive strategies.

2018–2020 Reforms and Political Conflict

In response to the 2014–2018 protests, Abiy Ahmed was seated as the new chairman of the EPRDF and made premier of Ethiopia through internal party and government negotiations. Ahmed, coming from the ethnic Oromo wing of the EPRDF coalition, presented himself as a champion of Ethiopian national unity, democratization, economic liberalization, and national reconciliation—positions that garnered him overwhelming support from Ethiopians who were otherwise divided by national politics or suspicious of his past with the EPRDF and the Oromo People's Democratic Organization (OPDO). Soon after coming into power, Ahmed initiated a wave of reforms that garnered local and international support.[5] His government promptly ended Ethiopia's state of emergency, created greater gender and ethnic parity within the government, and freed thousands of protesters and journalists jailed during TPLF-EPRDF rule. In a surprising and controversial move, outlawed and exiled political leaders, armed groups, and media were invited to return to Ethiopia and granted amnesty if they agreed to participate peacefully in Ethiopia's reforms. Economically, Ahmed's government assured greater liberalization and a move away from the highly centralized developmental state model established during TPLF-controlled EPRDF rule. While the TPLF-EPRDF's centralized development model had materialized in double-digit GDP growth for over a decade, the promise of privatization assuaged the demands of protesters and investors for greater liberalization.

In addition to these changes, Ahmed's government quickly brought an official end to Ethiopia's decades-long border conflict with Eritrea. The 1998–2000 border war was followed by eighteen years of hostility and impasse until Ahmed's government accepted the Algiers "comprehensive peace agreement" of 2000. By relinquishing the disputed borderlands awarded to Eritrea, the agreement promised a cessation of hostilities and an increase in economic and political cooperation between Eritrea and Ethiopia.[6] However, while Ahmed was awarded the 2019 Nobel Peace Prize for ending hostilities with Eritrea, the details of the agreement were not revealed to the public and involved a process that further sidelined and aggrieved the TPLF. The omission of Tigray's regional leaders presented a problem because the contested territories, situated between Eritrea and Tigray, were administered and claimed by Tigray. A history of political grievances, conflict, and competition among the leaders of Eritrea, Ethiopia, and the state of Tigray thwarted the possibility of any collective agreement coming to fruition.

By the end of 2019, the EPRDF and its allying parties dissolved and formed a countrywide party called the Prosperity Party (PP). Forced out of its leading position within the EPRDF and sidelined in the reform process, the TPLF left the coalition and retreated to the regional state of Tigray, where it still had widespread support and control. Unlike the EPRDF—which was composed of four unequal, distinct, and largely ethnic-based parties that claimed to represent the national interests of their ethnic and regional constituents—the PP took shape as a single, countrywide or "pan-Ethiopian," party that claimed to represent the interests of all Ethiopians. However, the TPLF contested the merger, declaring it "illegal" and "unconstitutional." For the TPLF, the formation of the PP was an attempt by Ahmed to consolidate his power and undermine Ethiopia's ethno-federal arrangement. Ahmed's rhetoric of Ethiopian national unity and the formation of the PP were recast by the TPLF and other proponents of ethnic federalism and self-determination as harbingers of future political reforms aimed at undermining ethnic groups' nationalist claims to territorial and administrative rights.[7]

Ahmed's single-handed and swift implementation of political change, along with his failure to negotiate with the TPLF and other opposition groups, drew criticism from skeptical Ethiopians and worsened tensions between ethnonational groups like the TPLF and the central government.[8] Furthermore, Ahmed's rhetoric of unity and the return of political opposition groups failed to result in the "national dialogue," reconciliation, and peace process Ethiopians hoped to see. Despite Ahmed's hopeful rhetoric, Ethiopia saw a rise in politically motivated assassinations and ethnic massacres between 2018 and 2022. The government's inaction toward armed groups targeting ethnic and religious minorities in regions like Oromia heightened perceptions of ethnic discrimination, ethnonational sentiments, and skepticism toward the PP.

Citing COVID-19, the Ethiopian government "indefinitely" postponed federal and regional elections in 2020. However, the TPLF—declaring the postponement an attempt by Ahmed and the Ethiopian government to rule beyond their constitutionally allotted term—defied the government by forming an election commission and carrying out regional elections in September 2020. The TPLF won over 98 percent of the votes and all the 152 available seats in the regional council, while the remaining 38 seats were distributed among the four opposition parties that took part in the election.[9] The TPLF proclaimed that its election process was democratic and constitutional, and the Ethiopian government was illegitimate. Warning that any interference by the federal government in Tigray's elections would warrant war, the TPLF maintained that the region would protect its constitutional rights to self-determination. In response to the TPLF's defiance, the Ethiopian government retaliated with sanctions and refused to recognize the election in Tigray. Conflict over administrative power, the use of inflammatory rhetoric, growing ethnic division augmented by widespread violence against civilians, and a lack of governmental checks and balances[10] eventually led to a war in which the Ethiopian government, Eritrea, and the regional states of Amhara and Afar fought against the TPLF.

During the night of November 3, 2020, the conflict and hostile rhetoric between the Ethiopian government and the TPLF escalated into a war. The TPLF completed what it described as a "preemptive strike" on the Ethiopian National Defense Force's (ENDF) military base located in the Tigray regional state.[11] According to reports, ENDF soldiers allied with the TPLF killed other ENDF soldiers, stole armaments, and attacked Eritrea and the regional state of Amhara.[12] The Ethiopian government, allied regional forces, and Eritrea—which were reportedly preparing for armed conflict—responded the next day with a military intervention.[13] Though the federal government proclaimed a bloodless and swift "law enforcement operation" to restore authority,[14] it declared a six-month state of emergency[15] in Tigray. Using the declaration, it cut telecommunication services, imposed a curfew, and restricted access to Tigray.[16] The military intervention resulted in human rights violations against ethnic Tigrayan civilians and fighters[17] while the involvement of Eritrean forces further complicated the conflict—even though Ethiopian government officials denied Eritrea's involvement until the end of March 2021.[18]

Genocide versus Terrorism:
Wartime Rhetoric and the Struggle for Narrative Control

Concerned with the war's humanitarian toll and political outcome, as well as the veracity and circulation of competing information coming from Ethiopia and the Tigray regional state, diaspora Ethiopians mobilized to influence narratives about the war and its outcome. Between November 2020 and January 2021, two competing rhetorical frames emerged to explain the war as either a genocidal campaign against ethnic Tigrayans or as a necessary military intervention prompted by and against a terrorist organization (the TPLF). Most Ethiopians I spoke to during this phase of the conflict explained the war as senseless, divisive, and politically motivated while arguing that the Ethiopian government had no option but to go to war against Tigray's rebellious political leadership. On the other hand, the ethnic Tigrayans I spoke to perceived the war as a matter of survival for their nation, using human rights language like "genocide," "crimes against humanity," and "extermination" to describe the actions of the Ethiopian government and its allied forces. Divided along these lines, protesters tactically used digital media and street protests to influence international narratives and policies aimed at the war.

Soon after the start of the war, Tigrayan protesters organized to demand UN[19] and Western government intervention in the conflict.[20] Tigrayan campaign organizations like Omna Tigray[21] and Stand With Tigray[22] emerged across social media. Protesters used the hashtags #TigrayGenocide, #StopWarOnTigray, #IStandWithTigray, and #ReconnectTigary to amplify international awareness, fundraise, boycott Ethiopian businesses,[23] and compel policymakers to help ethnic Tigrayans by implementing a no-fly zone, a humanitarian corridor, and sanctions against Ethiopia and Eritrea. Much of the initial advocacy focused on bringing attention to the gender-based violence, mass displacement, and starvation risk faced by Tigrayans caught in war.

In addition to demanding humanitarian intervention, Tigrayan protesters (sometimes identifying themselves as Digital Woyane and the Tigray Diaspora Force)[24] portrayed anti-TPLF activists, Prosperity Party supporters, and proponents of Ethiopian nationalism as existential threats to Tigray and Tigrayans. For example, Omna Tigray often featured images and stories of Tigrayan war victims while framing the conflict as a matter of survival necessitating a nationalist response from Tigrayans.[25] At times, Tigrayan activists collaborated with Oromo nationalists who supported the Oromo Liberation Army (OLA)—an armed, ethnonational, and secessionist group allied with the TPLF during the war. Activists and TPLF politicians[26] framed Ethiopian and Eritrean forces as genocidal by circulating images and accounts of extrajudicial executions, arrests, rape, and starvation.[27] They positioned the Ethiopian state and ethnic groups like the Amhara—generally supporters of Ethiopian statehood and nationhood—as ideological, political, and historical enemies of Tigrayan self-determination and nationalism.

In other words, the war was framed by #TigrayGenocide supporters as being *against* a group of people persecuted for their ethnic identity and beliefs. This frame obscured the political and ideological differences that existed among the different groups who fought the TPLF and the grievances many Ethiopians held against TPLF's repressive rule. While campaigns like #TigrayGenocide urged humanitarian assistance to affected Tigrayans, they often omitted, denied, or justified human rights violations perpetrated by the TPLF and its allies. The rhetorical leveling of Ethiopians and Eritreans as genocide apologists,[28] a singular focus on ethnic Tigrayan victims of the war, the push for international intervention and economic sanctions, and the lack of accountability placed on the TPLF limited the possibility of cross-ethnic dialogue and mobilization on behalf of affected civilians.

Though the TPLF framed its military campaign as a preemptive act of self-defense against genocidal forces, the Ethiopian government, its military allies, and anti-TPLF activists countered by characterizing the TPLF's actions as terrorism. They asserted that the TPLF started the war to undermine the current government and undemocratically regain a dominant economic and political position in Ethiopia.[29] The Ethiopian government tied the TPLF and OLA to a series of ethnic massacres and political assassinations and maintained that the ousted party was trying to destabilize the new government's authority and reforms by sowing ethnic division. On May 6, 2021, the Ethiopian government designated the TPLF and OLA as terrorist organizations—indicating its unwillingness to negotiate with both organizations.

As the stakes for framing the war intensified, Western news media played an important role in shaping international perceptions of the conflict and the kinds of interventions sought by activists and policymakers. The Ethiopian communities I observed speculated that international journalists and analysts were advancing a pro-TPLF political agenda by adopting activists' framing of the conflict as a war against ethnic Tigrayans (rather than the TPLF) and providing fewer and less critical coverage of the violence perpetrated by TPLF-allied fighters. For instance, many Ethiopians expressed frustration with CNN because its reports pushed for economic sanctions, like ending Ethiopia's African Growth and Opportunity Act program eligibility. In some instances, CNN's journalists appeared to take a partisan stance by pushing to designate the war as a genocide.[30] Many observers believed that news media framing of the war—and the implicit attachment of moral binaries to ethnic groups during an ethnicized conflict—established grounds for Western institutions and politicians to intervene and give directives. Therefore, many Ethiopians and Eritreans feared that Western media and pressure would force the Ethiopian government to negotiate with the TPLF and concede to its demands.

While the ensuing sanctions and attempts to frame the war as a genocide failed to compel the Ethiopian government to negotiate with the TPLF, it compounded the adverse economic effects experienced by Ethiopians who were already affected by COVID-19 and high inflation rates (20.4 percent in 2020; 26.8 percent in 2021).[31] Rather than catalyzing humanitarian support for those severely affected in northern Ethiopia, skewed framing of the conflict and claims of genocide entrenched and exacerbated Ethiopians' ethnopolitical divisions, one-sided responses to the humanitarian crisis, and mistrust of Western institutions and news media.

In response to these grievances and political stakes, several anti-TPLF, pro-Ethiopia, pro-Eritrea, and progovernment groups formed online to amplify, challenge, and influence media reports and international responses toward the conflict. Ethiopians and Eritreans who regarded the conflict as an information war against the TPLF disagreed with the genocide frame and the interventions solicited using claims of genocide. Using social media to organize campaigns like "One Ethiopia" and "Unity for Ethiopia," they employed hashtags like #UnityforEthiopia, #EthiopiaPrevails, #EritreaPrevails, #OneEthiopia, and #TPLFisaTerrorist to influence the wartime narrative and proclaim the sovereignty of Ethiopia and Eritrea, and the right of Africans to defend themselves against terrorism.[32] In addition to fact-checking and refuting news media and journalists, social media users targeted what they saw as the propagation of mis/disinformation by activists, analysts, lobbyists, politicians, and human rights organizations.

At this time, fact-checking, whistleblowers, whistleblowing events, and other forms of information disclosure became catalysts for mobilizing protesters, corroborating information, and challenging narratives. For instance, former Facebook employee Frances Haugen disclosed that Facebook knowingly allowed ethnic conflict to be inflamed in Ethiopia.[33] Hermela Aregawi, a news reporter and insider to the #TirgayGenocide campaign, publicly spoke out against the campaign and its political commitments. Internal communication between United Nations officials and audio of UN-Ethiopia employees asserting that the UN was engaged in partisan politics within Ethiopia were leaked.[34] These events raised questions about the role of media and international organizations in the conflict and were seen by Ethiopian and Eritrean observers as instances of whistleblowing and truth-telling.[35] Recognizing the conflict as an informational and psychological war, the Ethiopian government and social media users mobilized to create Twitter accounts like @ETFactCheck, @FdreService, @Qnie_Addis dedicated to fighting the "information war" against the TPLF and fact-checking news media, activists, and organizations like the UN, Amnesty International, and Human Rights Watch (HRW). Although the activists represented a spectrum of ethnic identities and political leanings, those I observed expressed the need to unite, preserve Ethiopia, and prevent the TPLF from undemocratically regaining power.

However, anti-TPLF protesters and proponents of Ethiopian nationalism did not always have a cohesive agenda to galvanize a unified and mass protest, though they mostly agreed that the TPLF and its political agenda harmed Ethiopia and the Horn of Africa more broadly. The anti-TPLF campaigns I observed during the first year used an array of hashtags like #RisingEthiopia, #UnityforEthiopia, #OneEthiopia, #EthiopiaPrevails, and #TPLFisaTerrorist but struggled to lay a common ground for mass mobilization. Organizing meetings and conversations over applications like WhatsApp, Telegram, Zoom, Clubhouse, and Twitter Spaces, participants often debated and tried to address the issue of creating a movement that could unite people under the common goal of challenging Western and TPLF narratives about the conflict and preserving the Ethiopian state. However, organizational hurdles and the culpability of the Ethiopian and Eritrean governments complicated these goals. The Ethiopian government's role in stoking ethnic conflict and Abiy Ahmed's dismissive response to the humanitarian crises divided anti-TPLF activists among those supportive and those critical of the PP and Ahmed's leadership. While participants who used these hashtags differed in their opinions and support of PP, they were often rhetorically constructed by international analysts and #TigrayGenocide activists as progovernment and prowar counterprotesters.

The #NoMore Movement and the Politics of Refusal

One year after the start of the war, protesters organized to showcase their support for Ethiopia and Eritrea as well as denounce the TPLF, Western intervention, and news media coverage of the conflict using #NoMore. Much of the activism that emerged before November 2021 amplified issues that affected particular ethnoregional groups (#AmharaGenocide, #OromoProtests, and #TigrayGenocide) or involved anti-TPLF and pro-Ethiopia campaigns like #UnityforEthiopia.[36] By contrast, #NoMore emerged a year into the war as "a month-long campaign to bring awareness to and end the war on Ethiopia,"[37] and eventually mobilized protesters across North America, parts of Europe, and Africa. Offering Ethiopians and Eritreans a broadly conceived and coalition-based campaign, #NoMore aimed to resist "mainstream media's propagation of disinformation and division" and combat international, namely US-led, intervention efforts, institutions, and policymakers' roles in the conflict:

> The mainstream media framed this regime-change war as an ethnic "genocide" with arguably one of the most intense disinformation campaigns ever witnessed. While the war raged on, the US and its allies proceeded to instigate coups, threaten invasions and pass sanctions against multiple other African countries (Eritrea, Somalia, Mali, Guinea, Burkina Faso, etc.), making it clear that Ethiopia was fighting a broader Pan-African war in defense of African sovereignty. . . Fed up with the mainstream media's propagation of disinformation and division in support of US aggression and exploitation, a number of African organizers, mainly emanating from the Horn of Africa, began to coalesce on social media and communicate on messaging apps about a campaign of resistance.[38]

Unlike previous campaigns against the TPLF, I argue there were three reasons #NoMore mobilized and unified Ethiopians and Eritreans. First, the circumstances in the war were changing in favor of the TPLF. The TPLF and Tigray Defense Force (TDF) fighters, after regaining control of the Tigray region in June 2021, began a southward offensive toward the regional states of Amhara and Afar, and the capital city of Addis Ababa.[39] Though #TigrayGenocide activists framed the offensive as a peaceful and necessary military maneuver to end the genocidal war and siege on Tigray, the TPLF and its allied fighters used violent means to seize towns in the regional states of Amhara and Afar. They often committed human rights violations akin to those that took place in Tigray during the first phase of the conflict.[40] The support given to the TPLF and its allied fighters by Tigrayan activists led to outcries from other Ethiopians about #TigrayGenocide activists' stated humanitarian principles and ambitions.[41]

By November 2021, representatives of the TPLF, OLA, and other ethnonational and secessionist groups publicly met in Washington, DC, to declare their political and military alliance.[42] The allied opposition groups claimed to represent the ethnonational interests of nine different ethnic groups in Ethiopia and vowed to "form a transitional government" by "bring[ing] down Prime Minister Abiy Ahmed by force or negotiation."[43] Though some dismissed the alliance as a publicity stunt, the rebels' military advances toward Addis Ababa alarmed observers. The Ethiopian government responded to TPLF's military gains by implementing a state of emergency in Addis Ababa, arresting ethnic Tigrayan residents and supporters of TPLF, and mobilizing Addis Ababans to protect the capital.[44] This turn of events between June 2021 and December 2021 heightened nationalist sentiments among Ethiopians as well as Amhara Ethiopians who sought to defend the Amhara region from the TPLF and its allied fighters.

Second, there was growing discontent with Western media and institutions among Ethiopians and Eritreans. The targets of their frustration were news organizations like CNN, the Associated Press, Reuters, and the BBC, which anti-TPLF protesters sometimes labeled as "fake news." Those frustrated expressed that instead of duly scrutinizing the engagements of all parties to the conflict, Western media reports dramatized the conflict and treated non-Tigrayan victims of the war with indifference. For instance, many complained that media like CNN downplayed or omitted important context about events leading up to the war, devoted less coverage to the toll of the TPLF's expansion of the conflict, and provided whitewashed and exaggerated accounts of the insurgents' advances to Addis Ababa. Furthermore, CNN reporter Nima Elbagir's designation of the war as an ethnic genocide against Tigrayans aggrieved those who saw the TPLF as the primary instigator of the conflict. In addition, protesters on Twitter and Facebook lamented that these platforms failed to prevent the spread of disinformation from pro-TPLF accounts while selectively deactivating and repressing the engagements of anti-TPLF activists online. Rather than providing fair, accurate, context-driven, peace-and-solution-oriented reporting, many believed that Western media fueled ethnic and political cleavages within Ethiopia and the Ethiopian diaspora by taking sides in the conflict.

In addition to Ethiopians and Eritreans' loss of confidence in Western media, the public statements by the UN, United States Agency for International Development (USAID), World Health Organization, World Peace Foundation (WPF), Amnesty International, HRW, and Crisis Group corroded trust in the West. For example, the statements of public figures like Samantha Power (USAID), Laetitia Bader (HRW), Alex de Waal (WPF), and Martin Plaut upset those who felt that Western actors either misunderstood the conflict or knowingly used simplistic frames and patronizing rhetoric to address Africans and the conflict. Additionally, leaked information on Twitter and YouTube led some Ethiopians to conclude that organizations like the UN and the UN's World Food Programme (WFP) were engaged in interventions that aided the TPLF's war efforts. For instance, leaked audio recordings and an email exchange showed UN employees' biases, as well as evidence that food aid, trucks, and fuel from the WFP—meant to feed and distribute aid to civilians in Tigray—were being used by the TPLF to feed and transport fighters. With growing mistrust of Western institutions, many believed that the West conspired with the TPLF despite Ethiopians' desires for change.

As a result, #NoMore—a campaign used by Eritreans and Ethiopians to collectively rally against mis/disinformation, Western intervention, and the TPLF—emerged online. Aregawi and the #NoMore movement embodied many protest participants' grievances against Western media, institutions, the TPLF, and Ethiopia's ethnic politics. Founded by organizers with Ethiopian and Eritrean heritage—Aregawi (Tigrayan-Ethiopian), Tesfamariam (Eritrean), and Asfaw (Ethiopian)—the #NoMore movement differed in leadership and scope from previous pro-Ethiopia and anti-TPLF campaigns, even though many of its participants used #NoMore in conjunction with other hashtag campaigns like #EthiopiaPrevails, #UnityforEthiopia, and #TPLFisaTerrorist. #NoMore's mission and the organizers' diverse backgrounds appealed to a broader coalition of protesters than similar anti-TPLF campaigns. Differing from #TigrayGenocide, #OromoProtests, and #AmharaGenocide, which advocated on behalf of specific ethnic groups and against the actions and interests of actors inside Ethiopia, #NoMore was able to appeal to participants across ethnic, national, and state boundaries.

Users engaged in the #NoMore campaign could use the hashtag and phrase to denounce the TPLF by saying, for example, not only "#NoMore TPLF" but also "#NoMore: Western intervention, disinformation, CNN, fake news, colonization, and war." In other words, the campaign enabled participants to rhetorically challenge an array of institutions and actors they saw as culpable for the war. For instance, denouncing the unsolicited influence of external actors believed to aid the TPLF, participants of a November 2021 #NoMore campaign I observed in Los Angeles asked the West to leave Ethiopia alone by demanding: "African solutions for African problems," "Hands off Ethiopia and Eritrea," "#NoMore sanctions on Ethiopia and Eritrea," "#NoMore taxpayers money spent to destabilize sovereign countries [sic]" and demanded that African institutions like the African Union mediate the conflict.

However, #NoMore's focus on external targets led to criticism and internal tensions. First, the movement was often criticized for not holding the Ethiopian and Eritrean governments accountable for their role in the conflict. #NoMore activists, by focusing their protest on external actors and the TPLF, often avoided holding the Ethiopian and Eritrean governments accountable for their use of violence, disinformation, and repression. At times, the campaign's rhetoric of pan-Ethiopian and Pan-African unity was used to repress activists who sought to simultaneously hold Western institutions, the TPLF, and the Ethiopian and Eritrean governments accountable for the humanitarian crises in Ethiopia. For example, some #AmharaGenocide activists who took part in #NoMore felt marginalized for refusing to set aside their grievances against the Ethiopian government and the OLA. Tensions with #AmharaGenocide activists highlighted #NoMore's avoidance of contentious issues, which complicated the campaign's priorities and ability to maintain a unified front against external intervention. Still, #NoMore galvanized popular protest among Ethiopians and Eritreans because of its broad reach and Aregawi's whistleblowing.[45]

Whistleblowing

As Guitar and Chu argue,[46] whistleblowers, vulnerable and guided by democratic ethics, reveal abuses of power and human rights violations. A diaspora Ethiopian and ethnic Tigrayan based in Los Angeles, Aregawi worked as a journalist and news anchor for CBSLA. During the initial phases of the war, she advocated as part of the broader #TigrayGenocide campaign. Using her news anchor background, she appeared on Instagram Live and Clubhouse discussions hosted in collaboration with accounts like @omnatigray, @tigraytimes, and @makeinjeranotwar.[47] However, she eventually left CBSLA and shifted her support from #TigrayGenocide to anti-TPLF, Pan-African, and pan-Ethiopian campaigns by the end of 2021. In a series of tweets and media appearances that predated and corresponded with the official launch of #NoMore, Aregawi explained that her journalistic integrity, discontent with pro-TPLF and diaspora-led activism, and what she witnessed as misinformative and unethical media coverage of the conflict changed her perspective on the war and compelled her to speak out.

In one of her first public critiques of the TPLF, she used Twitter to question why mainstream media had not investigated TPLF's diversion and use of WFP trucks and aid meant for Tigrayan civilians.[48] Responding to an October 22, 2021, @nytimesworld tweet that stated, "For months, U.N. officials have complained about Ethiopian obstacles to truck convoys of aid for victims facing famine in the Tigray conflict. On Friday, a U.N. humanitarian air flight to Tigray also was thwarted," Aregawi tweeted @nytimesworld: "CORRECTION: For [months], Ethiopian govt was allowing hundreds of aid trucks to get into Tigray & turns out rogue UN [officials] gave the trucks & other [equipment] to rebel groups who then killed thousands. This [downward pointing arrow emoji pointing to @nytimesworld tweet] is NOT journalism. It's fueling war in a foreign country. Another @declanwalsh [trash bin emoji]."[49] By directing criticism toward Western journalists and news media like New York Times World on her social media accounts, Aregawi became one of the few Tigrayans to validate the views and grievances of anti-TPLF activists who were dismissed using the genocide frame. Her social media engagements, criticism of the TPLF, and #TigrayGenocide were perceived as whistleblowing events by Ethiopians and Eritreans who felt that they were in a war against misinformation but faced the risk of being labeled genocide supporters if they posed the same critical questions or openly spoke out against the TPLF.

In addition to using Twitter, Aregawi appeared on independent media programs like BreakThrough News (BTN) and African Diaspora News Channel. She also created her own YouTube channel, HermelaTV,[50] and news blog, Mela Media,[51] to critically recount her shifting perspectives on the conflict and the #TigrayGenocide campaign.[52] For example, during a November 2021 interview with the African Diaspora News Channel,[53] Aregawi positioned herself as a truth-teller and explained why she was compelled to speak out against #TigrayGenocide and misinformation on news media. She argued that the misinformation stemmed from the "digital war" fought and "orchestrated" by pro-TPLF activists. According to Aregawi, while the "physical war" was "fought by TPLF in Ethiopia," "digital warriors" in the diaspora started the digital war to "feed" TPLF's narrative to the media.[54] Positioning herself as a concerned journalist and ethnic Tigrayan, she explained:

> Because I am ethnic Tigrayan myself . . . I was working with the #TigrayGenocide activists . . . I never fully bought into

the hashtag, I just thought it was a humanitarian cause so I worked with them. I saw how orchestrated they are. This apparatus is there to weave a certain story, a story of this minority political group [TPLF]. That is what we're up against. I've been a journalist for ten years, much of it in what you might call corporate media. The reason I have taken some time from that is because *I am so disgusted by how the lie has become the truth!*[55]

Despite her initial belief that #TigrayGenocide's advocacy was humanitarian, she recounts realizing that the campaign advanced covert political and ideological goals. Moreover, she argues that pro-TPLF activists' engagements were part of the very apparatus that worked to reinforce and make the TPLF's "lie" into a "truth." In many of her early media appearances, Aregawi argued that TPLF leaders not only started the war, but that they evaded responsibly and attained support from Tigrayans and international audiences by rhetorically "flipping" the story and framing the war as genocide:

When the Ethiopian government reacted [to TPLF's attack], the TPLF said this is a genocide. . . . They said this is about the ethnic Tigrayans that live in that region. This is a genocide. . . . That is just absolutely not true. . . . [The TPLF rebels] aren't just some underdogs that are trying to get their way with the current government. They've been in power for a long time. . . . They are just trying to force their way back into power. . . . A majority of a hundred million people do not want them to come back [into power]. They do not even represent the ethnic Tigrayan people. . . . So, the only people the TPLF are interested in fighting for is their own political power.[56]

As her views and questions became increasingly critical of the TPLF, #TigrayGenocide participants sidelined and attempted to repress her speech but designated her a supporter of the "genocidal" war—even petitioning on Change.org to have her fired from CBSLA:

Anytime someone says something that doesn't support their argument they go after them. They started a petition to get me fired from my job because they called me "pro-Tigray genocide."

Somehow, I am pro my own ethnicity being genocided because I spoke up and asked some questions about "why are we fighting the war at this point? In June the Ethiopian government declared a humanitarian ceasefire. Why did we not declare a ceasefire? Why did the TPLF not declare a ceasefire? Why did they continue to arm militias and push them into neighboring regions of Amhara and Afar where thousands of people died? All I did was ask a few questions and it sparked this petition to get me fired. It sparked all this harassment. So, it tells you how powerful they are.[57]

By labeling her a *génocidaire*, Aregawi argued that #TigrayGenocide deployed genocide as a frame to disempower her and repress any criticism of the TPLF. Her ethnicity, background in journalism, and effort to hold the TPLF accountable compromised the campaign's goal to designate the war a genocide as a means for diverting negative attention away from the TPLF and its allied fighters and compelling international intervention in Ethiopia. For the Ethiopians who saw the TPLF as the primary instigator of the conflict, the favorable news coverage received by the TPLF risked restoring the TPLF's position of power in the Horn of Africa. Aregawi explains, "But there is a hundred million plus people in the Horn, including Eritreans, including Somalis who have lived through the terror of TPLF that are fighting against this narrative which is why we started the hashtag #NoMore. Because we got fed up! For how long are the killers gonna be the victims and the victims gonna be the killers?"[58] Although pro-TPLF interests actively discouraged her from whistleblowing, she stood out as an ally and movement leader to anti-TPLF activists who had their concerns dismissed by mainstream media. Aware of this, Aregawi described how she was uniquely positioned to speak out against the TPLF and its efforts to propagandize news media like CNN and *The New York Times*. In this context, independent media became vital to Aregawi and #NoMore activists who sought to correct biased reports and keep "corporate" media in check:

If we don't have independent media to be able to write the story, because the very places that we used to look up to like the CNNs and *NY Times* are simply spitting out propaganda, then somebody has to fill that space. And I felt the responsibility not just as a journalist but a journalist of ethnic Tigrayan descent because I felt like my voice would actually potentially make a difference. Because when an Ethiopian of another ethnicity says what I am saying, they say "you're pro Tigray genocide." So, I felt convicted because there just wasn't enough of the truth in that space and I think slowly but surely, we are starting to correct the narrative.[59]

Throughout these media engagements, Aregawi drew attention to the political underpinnings of #TigrayGenocide and reinforced anti-TPLF activists' claims that the TPLF is a corrupt party that does not represent the interests of all ethnic Tigrayans. Reflecting during an interview with BTN, Aregawi explained that during her participation with #TigrayGenocide, she noticed misconduct in fundraising and the suppression of critical questions regarding the campaign's humanitarian scope.[60] Though she initially believed activists were engaged in humanitarian efforts, she eventually realized that some of the campaigns and its associated organizations were mobilizing and fundraising to fund the TPLF's war efforts. Aregawi also described that pro-TPLF campaigns ethnicized and politicized the humanitarian crisis in Tigray by refusing support from other Ethiopians who were prefigured at the onset of the conflict as inherently antagonistic toward Tigrayan nationalist interests.[61]

Aregawi used her ethnic identity, journalism background, and experiences advocating for #TigrayGenocide to bring a new dimension to the activism efforts of anti-TPLF protesters. Through her outspoken social media posts and appearances, Aregawi reinforced anti-TPLF activists' claims that (1) the TPLF started the war, (2) #TigrayGenocide activists did not represent the interests of all ethnic Tigrayans, and (3) the TPLF was using Tigrayan lives and the rhetoric of genocide to advance its political interests. Though some anti-TPLF activists remained skeptical of Aregawi or saw her media engagements as a diversion, Aregawi blew the whistle on #TigrayGenocide and mainstream news media by using alternative media like YouTube and Twitter.

Aregawi, Tesfamariam, Asfaw, and the #NoMore Movement's rhetoric captured many of the issues that aggrieved Eritrean and Ethiopian observers: the United States' sanctions and policies on Africa, Western intervention by intergovernmental organizations like the UN, biased media coverage, and the TPLF and its ethnonational allies' undemocratic claims to power. #NoMore offered protesters a platform to collectively voice their frustrations on behalf of their respective homelands, the Horn of Africa region, and the Third World more broadly. While some protesters were suspicious of Aregawi's changing views, she became one of the few diaspora Ethiopians with an ethnic Tigrayan background to publicly speak out against the TPLF. #NoMore vindicated the national sentiments, future desires, and grievances of those who had been labeled "genocide enablers" for their stance against the TPLF and suspicion of #TigrayGenocide. Because of this, #NoMore and Aregawi were able to corroborate and rally Ethiopians and Eritreans who had been echoing the same sentiment espoused by the #NoMore Movement but were largely ignored or dismissed as supporters of a genocidal war.

Conclusion

Social media protests like #NoMore, whistleblowers, fact-checkers, analysts, and even conspiracy theorists derived their significance during the war because they challenged the skewed information being presented by "reputable" Western media and human rights organizations who were at the forefront of shaping international discourse and responses to the conflict. However, by dramatizing human suffering and oversimplifying complex socioeconomic dilemmas, reporters ultimately stoked division instead of critical dialogue and conflict resolution. While Ethiopians and Eritreans have important problems to resolve, Western media and institutions reduced genuine questions and grievances about governance, land distribution, economic precarity, ethnic identity, and the future of the Ethiopian state to essentializing and simplistic frames of violence and inhumanity. As this chapter demonstrates, Western regimes of power and knowledge disseminating and operating on oversimplified wartime narratives and human rights discourse impede rather than promote peaceful resolution to conflicts. Disempowered subjects use whistleblowing and protest to tell their stories and determine their political futures when established institutions and safeguards for intervention fail them.

Notes

1. Michael Middleton, Aaron Hess, Danielle Endres, and Samantha Senda-Cook, *Participatory Critical Rhetoric: Theoretical and Methodological Foundations for Studying Rhetoric In Situ* (Lanham, MD: Lexington Books, 2015).

2. Danielle Endres, Aaron Hess, Samantha Senda-Cook, and Michael K. Middleton, "In Situ Rhetoric: Intersections Between Qualitative Inquiry, Fieldwork, and Rhetoric," *Cultural Studies? Critical Methodologies* 16, no. 6 (2016): 511–524.

3. Endres et al., "In Situ Rhetoric."

4. Dereje Desta, "Some in Diaspora Respond to Call for Ethiopian Homecoming," Voice of America, January 1, 2022, https://www.voanews.com/a/some-in-diaspora-respond-to-call-for-ethiopian-homecoming/6375906.html.

5. Paul Schemm, "Ethiopia Says It Is Ready to Implement Eritrea Peace Deal and Privatize Parts of the Economy," *Washington Post*, June 5, 2018, https://www.washingtonpost.com/world/africa/ethiopia-says-its-ready-to-implement-eritrea-peace-deal-and-privatize-parts-of-the-economy/2018/06/05/f5813936-68e4-11e8-9e38-24e693b38637_story.html.

6. Government of Eritrea, "Peace Agreement Between Eritrea and Ethiopia: Ministry of Foreign Affairs—Eritrea," ReliefWeb, OCHA, December 16, 2000, https://reliefweb.int/report/eritrea/peace-agreement-between-eritrea-and-ethiopia-ministry-foreign-affairs; United Nations, "Agreement Between the Government of the State of Eritrea and the Government of the Federal Democratic Republic of Ethiopia," General Assembly Security Council, December 13, 2000.

7. The description of Ethiopian nationalism and de-ethnicization efforts as "homogenizing" and "unitary" state formation projects by proponents of ethnic federalism are contested by Ethiopian nationalists because cultural and linguistic diversity can be preserved without the use of a federal and political arrangement that employs single-category ethnic identification and territorialization.

8. This failure is also attributed to the TPLF, which refused to participate in the central government with a diminished status and played an antagonistic role against the PP.

9. Medihane Ekubamichael, "TPLF Wins Regional Election by Landslide," Addis Standard, September 11, 2020, https://addisstandard.com/news-tplf-wins-regional-election-by-landslide/.

10. This limits the capacity of Ethiopia's courts to independently determine constitutional issues.

11. Cameron Peters, "Ethiopia Says It's Captured the Capital of Its Rebellious Tigray Region," *Vox*, November 28, 2020, https://www.vox.com/2020/11/28/21724049/ethiopia-captured-tigray-capital-mekele-tplf.

12. Teodrose Fikremariam, "TPLF Admits Sparking Tigray Conflict in Ethiopia," *TesfaNews*, November 14, 2020, https://tesfanews.net/tplf-spokesman-admits-sparking-tigray-conflict-ethiopia/; Giulia Paravicini and Dawit Endeshaw, "Ethiopia Sends Army into Tigray Region, Heavy Fighting Reported," Reuters, November 4, 2020, https://www.reuters.com/article/us-ethiopia-conflict/ethiopia-sends-army-into-tigray-region-heavy-fighting-reported-idUSKBN27K0ZS?il=0.

13. Though November marks the official start of the war, the TPLF, Ethiopia, and Eritrea are believed to have begun preparing for armed conflict before November 2020.

14. Jason Burke, "Fighting Reported in Ethiopia After PM Responds to 'Attack' by Regional Ruling Party," *Guardian*, November 4, 2020, https://www.theguardian.com/world/2020/nov/04/ethiopia-on-brink-as-pm-orders-military-response-to-attack.

15. Federal Democratic Republic of Ethiopia, Office of the Prime Minister, "Federal Council of Ministers Declares State of Emergency in Tigray Region," Embassy of Ethiopia, November 4, 2020, https://ethiopianembassy.org/federal-council-of-ministers-declares-state-of-emergency-in-tigray-region-november-4-2020/.

16. UN OCHA, "Ethiopia: Tigray Region Humanitarian Update—Situation Report No. 1," ReliefWeb, UN Office for the Coordination of Humanitarian Affairs, November 7, 2020, https://reliefweb.int/report/ethiopia/ethiopia-tigray-region-humanitarian-update-situation-report-no-1-7-november-2020.

17. The fighters are often collectively called the Tigray Defense Force (TDF) by allies, Tigrayans, and the TPLF.

18. James Jeffrey, "Abiy Ahmed Finally Came Clean About Eritrean Troops. What Next?," Al Jazeera, April 2, 2021, https://www.aljazeera.com/news/2021/4/2/abiy-ahmed-finally-came-clean-about-eritrean-troops-what-next.

19. Omna Tigray (@omnatigray), "UNSC Act Now on Tigray Campaign . . . ," Instagram, January 19, 2021, https://www.instagram.com/p/CKP64HZHjPT/.

20. Omna Tigray (@omnatigray), "Our Demands for the Biden-Harris Administration . . . ," Instagram, January 15, 2021, https://www.instagram.com/p/CKFzDQcn0mc/.

21. Omna Tigray (@omnatigray), "Who Are Tigrayans and Where Is Tigray? An Introduction to the History, Region, and the Tigrayan People . . . ," Instagram, April 1, 2021, https://www.instagram.com/p/CNIUqj3n5xd/.

22. Stand With Tigray, "About Us," accessed August 11, 2022, https://www.standwithtigray.com/.

23. Omna Tigray (@omnatigray), "#BOYCOTTETHIOPIANROSES CHOSE LOVE, NOT WAR . . . ," Instagram, February 13, 2021, https://www.instagram.com/p/CLQKXbvHSZl/.

24. "Digital Woyane" (or "Digital Warriors") refers to a 1940s rebellion that took place in Tigray against Emperor Haile Selassie's rule. "Tigray Diaspora Force" and "Tigray Digital Force" are wordplays on Tigray Defense Force (TDF), the TPLF-allied rebel fighters.

25. Omna Tigray (@omnatigray), "#The Tale of Two Ideologies: Federalism and Unitarism in Ethiopia Explained," Instagram, January 31, 2021, https://www.instagram.com/p/CKul9TbHdVO/.

26. Tghat, "Debretsion's Statement (Translation)," February 15, 2021, https://www.tghat.com/2021/02/15/debretsions-statement-translation/.

27. Though activists attached ethnic identities onto victims and accounts of violence throughout the war, the accounts and identities were not always verifiable or accurate.

28. Betty, "Pure Betrayal—Addis Ababians Supporting the Genocidal War on Tigray," Omna Tigray, May 2021, https://omnatigray.org/pure-betrayal-addis-ababians-supporting-the-genocidal-war-on-tigray/.

29. The question of who started the war is highly contested between the two sides of the conflict. #TigrayGenocide and TPLF supporters argue the Ethiopian government started the war and TPLF was forced to defend Tigray and its constitutional rights. Proponents of the Ethiopian government argue the war was started by the TPLF to destabilize Ethiopia and regain power.

30. Nima Elbagir, Gianluca Mezzofiore, Katie Polglase, and Barbara Arvanitidis, "Ethiopia Used Its Flagship Commercial Airline to Transport Weapons During War in Tigray," CNN, October 8, 2021, https://www.cnn.com/2021/10/06/africa/ethiopian-airlines-investigation-tigray-war-intl-cmd/index.html; Nima Elbagir and Arnaud Siad, "Ethiopia to Lose Access to Lucrative US Trade Program Following CNN Investigation," CNN, December 24, 2021, https://www.cnn.com/2021/12/24/africa/ethiopia-us-trade-agoa-intl/index.html. A November 2021 webinar, hosted by CNN's Elbagir and Yale MacMillan's Genocide Studies Program, was criticized by many Ethiopian and Eritrean observers for framing the conflict as a genocide. Elbagir's reporting and participation in the webinar was critiqued by anti-TPLF activists because the kinds of violent events she framed as genocidal in the context of Tigray were also taking place in other parts of Ethiopia at the hands of TPLF-allied forces. In addition, anti-TPLF observers believed that the genocidal frame was deployed from the onset of the war by TPLF and pro-TPLF actors to justify interventions that benefited the TPLF. See the discussion at https://youtu.be/sToOht20S1M and the postwebinar statement by Yale here: https://macmillan.yale.edu/news/responding-crisis-northern-ethiopia.

31. "Inflation, Consumer Prices (Annual %)—Ethiopia," World Bank, accessed October 28, 2022, https://data.worldbank.org/indicator/FP.CPI.TOTL.ZG?locations=ET.

32. Claire Wilmot, Ellen Tveteraas, and Alexi Drew, "Dueling Information Campaigns: The War over the Narrative in Tigray," *Media Manipulation Casebook*, September 14, 2021, https://mediamanipulation.org/case-studies/dueling-information-campaigns-war-over-narrative-tigray.

33. Allison Simon, Samuel Gebré, and Claire Wilmot, "Leaked Documents Reveal How Facebook Failed to Contain Hate Speech in Ethiopia," *Continent*, November 13, 2021; Kenya Insights, "How Facebook Is Fanning the Flames in Ethiopia," November 13, 2021, https://kenyainsights.com/how-facebook-is-fanning-the-flames-in-ethiopia/; Eliza Mackintosh, "Facebook Knew It Was Being Used to Incite Violence in Ethiopia. It Did Little to Stop the Spread, Documents Show,"

CNN, October 25, 2021, https://www.cnn.com/2021/10/25/business/ethiopia-violence-facebook-papers-cmd-intl/index.html.

34. Maggie Fick, "U.N. Officials Recalled from Ethiopia over Audio Recordings," Reuters, Thomson Reuters, October 13, 2021, https://www.reuters.com/world/africa/un-official-recalled-ethiopia-over-audio-recordings-letter-2021-10-12/.

35. Robbie Gramer and Colum Lynch, "U.N. Officials Downplayed Sexual Violence in Ethiopia in Leaked Call," *Foreign Policy*, August 27, 2021, https://foreignpolicy.com/2021/08/27/united-nations-officials-downplayed-sexual-violence-ethiopia/; Birhanu Abera, "Western Media Fueling Information War in Ethiopia," Walta Media, November 6, 2021, https://waltainfo.com/western-media-fueling-information-war-in-ethiopia/.

36. "Lets Stand Together for Our Common Cause: Unity for Ethiopia," Unity for Ethiopia, accessed August 28, 2022, https://www.unityforethiopia.net/.

37. #Nomore, "About #Nomore," #NoMore—Global Movement of Solidarity for the Horn of Africa, accessed October 28, 2022, https://www.nomore.global/about/.

38. #Nomore, "About #Nomore."

39. "Addis Ababa Asks Residents to Prepare to Defend Ethiopian Capital," Al Jazeera, November 2, 2021, https://www.aljazeera.com/news/2021/11/2/ethiopian-government-tells-residents-to-prepare-to-defend-capital.

40. Zecharias Zelalem, " 'They Are Out for Revenge': Evidence of War Crimes as Rebels Roar Out of Ethiopia's Tigray Region," *Telegraph*, August 17, 2021, https://www.telegraph.co.uk/world-news/2021/08/17/revenge-evidence-war-crimes-rebels-roar-ethiopias-tigray-region/.

41. #TigrayGenocide participants' support of the offensive and denial of the TDF's violence in parts of Amhara and Afar regions resulted in some Ethiopians and Eritreans criticizing #TigrayGenocide for having double standards when it came to its stated human rights agenda. Similar criticism was made toward anti-TPLF campaigns that supported the offensive against the TPLF despite the violence perpetrated against Tigrayans.

42. Humeyra Pamuk and Maggie Fick, "New Alliance Wants to Oust Ethiopia's PM by Talks or Force," Reuters, November 5, 2021, https://www.reuters.com/world/africa/nine-ethiopian-groups-form-anti-government-alliance-2021-11-05/.

43. Pamuk and Fick, "New Alliance."

44. Under the state of emergency, the Ethiopian government implemented mass arrests using processes that violated civilians' rights. A majority of those targeted for questioning and arrest (for allegedly aiding the TPLF's war efforts) were of ethnic Tigrayan background.

45. Omna Tigray (@omnatigray), "#The Tale of Two Ideologies: Federalism and Unitarism in Ethiopia Explained," Instagram, January 31, 2021, https://www.instagram.com/p/CKul9TbHdVO/.

46. Joshua Guitar and Alan Chu, "Racing to (Dis)Own Whistleblowers and Protests: Theorizing *Amongness* in the Shared Rhetorical Spaces of Democratic Agency," chapter 1 in the present volume, 2.

47. Omna Tigray (@omnatigray), "Hermela Aregawi—Live Interview Host," Instagram, February 7, 2021, https://www.instagram.com/p/CK__J5dHVNu/; Tigray Times (@tigraytimes), "Los Angeles Nationwide Protest," Instagram Live post, March 10, 2021, https://www.instagram.com/p/CMQ0OWEnDye/; Tigray Times (@tigraytimes), "LATEST NEWS #WARONTIGRAY, NEXT PROTEST & SURPRISE GUESTS," Instagram, March 9, 2021, https://www.instagram.com/p/CMNFw5wH1zt/?utm_source=ig_web_copy_link.

48. Awasa Guardian, "Tigrayan Reporter: TPLF Blocked Aid to Not 'Make Abiy Look Good,'" *Awasa Guardian*, September 23, 2021, https://awasaguardian.com/index.php/2021/09/23/tigrayan-reporter-tplf-blocked-aid-to-not-make-abiy-look-good/.

49. Hermela Aregawi (@HermelaTV), "Correction: For mnths, Ethiopian govt was allowing hundreds of aid trucks to get into Tigray & turns out rogue UN ofcls gave the trucks & other equip to rebel groups who then killed thousands . . . ," Twitter post, October 22, 2021, https://twitter.com/hermelatv/status/1451778220307615749?lang=en.

50. Soon after leaving CBSLA, she started as an independent journalist with the help of anti-TPLF activists who donated over 80,000 USD to her GoFundMe campaign.

51. Hermela Aregawi, "Are Missing Aid Trucks Being Used for War in Tigray?," Mela Media, November 17, 2021, https://www.melamedia.org/post/this-is-the-story-of-the-day.

52. "Hermela Aregawi: Why 'I Had a Responsibility to Speak Out' on Ethiopia," BreakThrough News, January 5, 2022, https://www.youtube.com/watch?v=LXQa_xo26eQ; Hermela Aregawi, "Tigray War: Is the Ethiopian Govt Really Targeting Civilians?," HermelaTV, October 22, 2021, https://www.youtube.com/watch?v=j2jGSD0zxcM.

53. "Exposing the Plot Against Ethiopia by the Western World, Discussion with Hermela Aregawi," African Diaspora News Channel, November 13, 2021, https://www.youtube.com/watch?v=Q8htd9mWv98.

54. African Diaspora News Channel, 6:14–6:28.

55. African Diaspora News Channel, 6:28–8:00, emphasis added.

56. African Diaspora News Channel, 2:00–4:36.

57. African Diaspora News Channel, 7:59–8:46.

58. African Diaspora News Channel, 8:48–9:06.

59. African Diaspora News Channel, 8:47–9:46.

60. "Debunking the Media Lies Fueling War in Ethiopia, w/ Journalist Hermela Aregawi," BreakThrough News, November 4, 2021, https://www.youtube.com/watch?v=jeBsFcqAvhA.

61. "Hermela Aregawi: Why 'I Had a Responsibility to Speak Out' on Ethiopia," BreakThrough News, January 5, 2022, https://www.youtube.com/watch?v=LXQa_xo26eQ.

7

"Read, Write, Execute"

Edward Snowden and the New History of the Whistleblower

MATTHEW STEVEN BRUEN

Introduction: Edward Snowden's Emergent Democratic Authorial Identity

Most commentaries and analyses of Edward Snowden begin in 2013, the consequential year in which Snowden removed classified information from the National Security Agency (NSA), fled from the United States, and released the stolen documents to journalists Barton Gellman, Glen Greenwald, Laura Poitras, and Ewen MacAskill. Most of the Snowden revelations dealt with the American surveillance regime, particularly programs conducted by the NSA such as PRISM (a data collection program aimed at gaining access to information held by Internet and technology companies) and XKeyscore (sweeping tool for surveilling Internet communication). The primary concern for Snowden—as well as the aforementioned journalists—was that the US government was breaching foundational civil liberties by using the NSA to spy on American citizens and their allies. Other revelations showed that US intelligence agencies surveilled all Internet activity, no matter where it occurred. As important and fascinating as these subjects are, however, the focus of this essay begins in December 2014 when the (in)famous whistleblower did something quite pathbreaking: Edward Snowden joined Twitter.

Although there are other whistleblowers on social media, Snowden immediately differentiated himself by the manner in which he used Twitter to contribute to political discourse. His notoriety allowed him to garner millions of followers almost overnight. And he tweeted . . . a lot. He discussed familiar subjects such as government surveillance of civilians and US abuses of power in its wars in Iraq and Afghanistan. He also commented on topics like cryptocurrency, the future of the Internet, economics, parenting, and geopolitics. Within weeks of his online debut, Snowden received massive engagement (tens of thousands of likes on Twitter, countless mentions in articles, etc.) and began the process of transitioning from whistleblower to author.

Snowden did not stop with Twitter. Shortly after arriving in Moscow,[1] he began work on his autobiography: *Permanent Record*.[2] Many Snowden observers, myself included, expected that Snowden's book would deal predominantly with the events prompting his revelations. And while much of the text covers his decision-making in the years before his exile, my scholarly interest was piqued when I discovered the book also contained much commentary about the Internet's history, constitutional philosophy, and how the online world shaped his identity. This was no ordinary autobiography; it was the formal debut of Edward Snowden, professional writer.

Snowden leveraged his new position as a respected author into a successful Substack in the summer of 2021. Titled *Continuing Ed*, Snowden's Substack contains sixteen essays (as of December 20, 2023, on diverse material like a future American-issued Central Bank Digital Currency, the coronavirus pandemic, and conspiracy theories).[3] He engages more deeply with the subjects of his Substack essays than he does with the topics he discusses on Twitter, a process that provides a more penetrating look into his mindset and worldview. He is also more humorous and sarcastic in the Substack pieces than in his other publications. Being funny and snarky in his online writing appears to be a calculated move meant to endear him to readers, catch their attention, and have them poised to come back for more. As good writers eventually tend to do, Snowden has learned to cultivate and cater to his enormous reading audience.

After Snowden joined Substack, I realized that something entirely new in the history of whistleblowing was taking shape. Here was a whistleblower who had made great use of online platforms and managed to stay relevant even after the dust had settled from his initial revelations. Snowden, through his shrewd usage of Twitter, Substack, and his autobiography, had positioned himself as an important source on a wide array of important issues. If other, previous whistleblowers had blown the whistle and then put that whistle away for good, Snowden did the opposite; he blew the whistle once, and then, in a manner, he did it again, and again, and again.[4] In fact, not even the Russian invasion of Ukraine has completely silenced Snowden. After a dark period of over two months, he reappeared on Twitter on May 3, 2022, to comment on the leak of the US Supreme Court decision that ultimately overturned *Roe v. Wade*. Snowden's persisting authorship complicates traditional conceptions of whistleblowing. In other words, might we consider the status of whistleblower as enduring beyond the immediate revelations?

This essay's analysis of Snowden's emergent writerly identity thus establishes a new perspective on one of the most famous whistleblowers of recent times. Through my analysis of Snowden's autobiography, Twitter, and Substack, I will chart his development as an author and show how it has enabled him to continue his protest against authoritarian abuses perpetrated by so-called democratic governments. Snowden initially turned to whistleblowing to protest the robust surveillance regime of the US, but as he has matured as an author, Snowden has taken his protest to new heights. This observation about Snowden's pathbreaking, post-whistleblowing rhetoric helps demonstrate how "the convergence of whistleblower and civic protest rhetoric" augments "the progression of democratic ethics and human rights writ large."[5]

Over the course of this chapter, I will explore the meaning-making processes of Snowden's post-whistleblowing writings and provide what I call a "new history" of the American whistleblower, one centered on Snowden's evolving role as a successful author and political commentator. I will also demonstrate how his new identity dovetails his democratic ideals. Indeed, his shrewd usage of Internet writing platforms is consistent with his vision of the Internet as a liminal space under constant tension between state interests and individual liberties.

The mode of critical inquiry that I employ in this essay is book history (sometimes also called "print culture studies"). Book historians specialize in the analysis of reading and writing, often focusing on the historical and cultural conditions under which these literary practices occurred. Robert A. Gross writes that book history "help[s] to track the dissemination of ideas in learned and popular cultures, to recover lost *mentalités* of subordinate classes, and to assay the impact of print on the spread and uses of literacy, the production and communication of knowledge, the power of church and state, the growth of nationalism and the extension of empire, and the conduct of everyday life in the face-to-face communities in which the vast majority of humanity once lived."[6] I am particularly interested in the history of authorship—its practitioners, its contexts, its conditions, and its methods, among other things.[7] Some print culture historians, such as Elizabeth McHenry, seek to recover information about forgotten groups, thereby further filling in the historical record. McHenry's research subjects are African American literary societies of the nineteenth century, Black women writers of the early twentieth century, and contemporary reading groups like Oprah's well-known book club.[8] These subject areas have not received thorough critical inquiry, so by recovering, contextualizing, and analyzing the writerly and readerly physical materials associated with these groups, McHenry is able to produce new knowledge about the ways Black Americans have achieved, maintained, and spread literacy.

I have identified a similar gap in Snowden scholarship and commentary. Most, if not all, books on Snowden engage his dramatic escape to Hong Kong and Russia, his earthshattering revelations, and the ways he undermined the US surveillance regime. A historical analysis of Snowden's emergent writerly identity thus represents a new case study in the practice of post-whistleblowing public discourse. This essay, therefore, documents, contextualizes, and analyzes this new history of whistleblowing authorship Snowden invented and ushered into the world.

Part I. Twitter: @snowden

In late 2014, a Twitter account named @snowden appeared. At the time, many believed this to be yet another impostor seeking to capitalize on Snowden's newfound fame. However, the account actually belonged to Snowden and represented his early foray into professional writing, albeit in 140-character increments.[9] He offered his first tweet in September 2015, which contained his trademark humor: "Can you hear me now?"[10] At that time, there had been much speculation about Snowden's post-whistleblowing intentions, but he had kept his plans quiet. Several Twitter accounts were created with his name during this relatively dark period, but none had really been him. Once Twitter officially verified the identity of @snowden, however, the political and scholarly world took notice. A new Edward Snowden had arrived on the global stage, one who had shed his identities as a government employee, as a self-described spy, and even as a fugitive. He was now a promising new writer.

The first few months of Snowden's Twitter career followed a predictable pattern. He frequently commented on mass surveillance, hacking, encryption, and other familiar topics. This, of course, was his wheelhouse. He also committed one of the all-time great examples of trolling (a term used to describe something that is intentionally provocative and seeks to inspire some form of a reaction) when he decided to follow just one other Twitter account: @NSAGov, the official account of the National Security Agency.[11]

Things began to change in 2016. During this period, Snowden wrote about stopping the killing of people with albinism in Malawi.[12] He waded into the protests that rocked Washington, DC, during the women's marches at the beginning of the Trump presidency.[13] He commented on the role of torture in America's "forever wars."[14] He entered into the debates surrounding privacy and Google, Facebook, and other social media entities. And he supported many other whistleblowers who had come both before and after him. By 2018, Snowden had successfully established his new role as a writer with a specialty in digital surveillance regimes, but also one who would cover a broad multitude of subjects.

Snowden used his Twitter account to announce his autobiography in September of 2019. As he mentions in the following tweet, Snowden recognized that Twitter was only a start, but that he had matured while writing his book: "I had set out merely to write a book, but when the manuscript was completed, it had become more—a work of literature. It took the better part of my year, drafting from night to noon, for that picture to come into focus. But at the outset, I was hardly an author."[15] As a historian of reading and writing, I struggle to find another moment when an author brazenly declared a recently completed manuscript as "a work of literature." Much more commonly, writers have the opposite reaction. For example, as Herman Melville was finishing *Moby-Dick: Or, The Whale* he famously lamented, "All my books are botches."[16]

Between December 2014 and September 2019, Snowden considered himself "hardly an author."[17] At the risk of parsing his words too much, it seems clear that he saw himself as a nascent writer during that time frame, but that he did not consider his tweets to amount to a serious body of written work. Once he completed his autobiography, however, he felt comfortable labeling himself a complete and legitimate writer. From that point on, Snowden regularly tweeted about his current writing process. For example, on August 8, 2021, Snowden said on Twitter: "Currently writing: Under His 'i,' " a Substack essay on Apple and privacy.[18] Aside from cross-platform promotion, Snowden usually alerts his audience when he is putting pen to paper, so to speak. By being forthcoming about his writing process, Snowden primes his audience for the written work he will soon release. In many ways, he is a natural at the hype process, a key factor in driving readers to texts.

Twitter thus served an important role in Snowden's emergence as a writer and commentator by presenting a kind of training ground: He wrote hundreds of tweets in the years leading up to the publication of his memoir. Even though tweets are, of course, short pieces of writing, when taken in the aggregate, Snowden wrote thousands upon thousands of words. As I can attest as an instructor of collegiate-level composition, practice does, in fact, make you a better writer. Snowden's years of experience on Twitter taught him how to encapsulate ideas in a pithy and short package and how to interact through writing with a receptive audience. It helped him build an enormous reading audience through his engagement in political debates and his conversations with other, more established writers and thinkers. It enabled him to cross-promote his other work, including his autobiography and Substack. Finally, Twitter provided Snowden with practice. Snowden's thousands of tweets therefore laid the groundwork for him to become a successful author, one capable of producing "a work of literature."[19]

Part II. The Autobiography: *Permanent Record*

In September of 2019, Snowden's autobiography, *Permanent Record*, was finally published. It is a fascinating look into Snowden's personal history, replete with stories about his employment with the Central Intelligence Agency and his time as a contractor for the NSA. It also details first-hand experiences of his dramatic escape from Hong Kong to Moscow and provides his perspective on the failures of the American law enforcement, intelligence, diplomatic, and military systems to catch and stop him.

However, I focus predominantly on the preface to *Permanent Record*. In this opening piece of writing, we see Snowden officially position himself as a whistleblower who has become a champion of perpetual public protest in the name of democratic rights, someone who will write and comment on any and all pertinent issues that may come across his writer's desk.

The following analysis of Snowden's autobiography is based in part on my training in the print cultures of the American autobiography. In many ways, Snowden is participating in an American tradition that hearkens back to Benjamin Franklin[20] in the eighteenth century and Frederick Douglass[21] in the nineteenth century. Scholars of the autobiographical tradition, including the important researcher of the slave narrative William L. Andrews, argue that the American memoir is intimately tied with concepts of freedom and liberty. As Andrews contends about the nineteenth-century autobiographies of enslaved and formerly enslaved peoples, "During the evolution of this tradition, autobiographers demonstrate through a variety of rhetorical means that they regard the writing of autobiography as in some ways uniquely self-liberating, the final, climatic act in the drama of their lifelong quests for freedom."[22]

Furthermore, the eminent historian David Waldstreicher has argued that Franklin's autobiography shows us that American memoirs are almost always about the development of liberal identity.[23] As Waldstreicher notes in the first chapter of his book on Franklin, "In so many ways, American freedom often depended on running away."[24] Although Snowden is obviously not an ex-slave nor does he occupy the lofty historical position of a Benjamin Franklin, he nevertheless taps into the same literary practices. So much of Snowden's 339-page memoir is concerned with freedom: his own, that he found online, that of his fellow Americans, and that of proponents of democracy worldwide. Of course, the climactic moment of Snowden's story is his flight from Hawaii to Hong Kong and then hairbreadth escape to Moscow.[25]

Indeed, Snowden is deeply concerned with upholding democratic principles surrounding liberty and explicitly states that he perceives himself as a proponent of the democratic process. Consider the following paragraph-length sentence from the preface: "The freedom of a country can only be measured by its respect for the rights of its citizens, and it's my conviction that these rights are in fact limitations of state power that define exactly where and when a government may not infringe into that domain of personal or individual freedoms that during the American Revolution was called 'liberty' and during the Internet Revolution is called 'privacy.' "[26] There is little reason to doubt Snowden's sincerity; he appears genuine in his desire to help America actualize its founding ideals and augment democratic rights globally. That said, positioning himself as a champion of democratic rights is also very beneficial to Snowden's post-revelations authorial career. It allows him to write with authority on any and all issues related to freedom, democracy, the US Constitution, privacy law, and many more analogous subjects.[27]

Snowden begins his self-positioning in the very first paragraph of his autobiography. Here, he makes clear how he sees himself:

> My name is Edward Joseph Snowden. I used to work for the government, but now I work for the public. It took me nearly three decades to recognize that there was a distinction, and when I did, it got me into a bit of trouble at the office. As a result, I now spend my time trying to protect the public from the person I used to be—a spy for the Central Intelligence Agency (CIA) and National Security Agency (NSA), just another young technologist out to build what I was sure would be a better world.[28]

There is a lot to unpack in these lines. To begin, he wastes no time establishing himself as someone who is in it for the long haul. When he states "now I work for the public," Snowden is directly referring to the writing that he performs on a near-daily basis. This is his declaration of writerly independence: "I am not going anywhere," he says, "and you must listen to me."[29]

In keeping with Snowden's authorial voice, the euphemism of stealing government secrets that "got [him] in a bit of trouble at the office" represent his hallmark style of righteous indignation and biting humor. It is also a style that one often encounters on Internet platforms like Twitter, Reddit, and many others. As such, it typifies the language of "young technologist" millennials like Snowden. Of course, the Internet is Snowden's preferred means of executing his post-whistleblowing political project. In another passage a few pages into the preface, Snowden addresses the foundational role that the Internet played for him. He writes that, in its origination, "the Internet was a very different thing. It was a friend, and a parent. It was a community without border or limit, one voice and millions, a common frontier that had been settled but not exploited by diverse tribes living amicably enough side by side, each member of which was free to choose their own name and history and customs."[30] Understanding Snowden's personal history with computers and the Internet is essential to understanding the way he invented a new form of whistleblowing authorship for himself in his post-revelations life. For Snowden, the Internet was more than just a source of information or a place to play video games; it was a community of like-minded young people who celebrated an individual's right to self-determination, it was a stand-in for absent parental figures, and it was a place where the young Snowden found a degree of belonging that he never experienced in school or elsewhere. It was, to put it simply, home.

Snowden expresses severe dismay and disenchantment with what the Internet became in the first decade of the twenty-first century. With the advent of social media and the multitudinous ways that our online lives can be tracked and surveilled, Snowden's home caught fire: "Our attention, our activities, our locations, our desires—everything about us that we revealed, knowingly or not, was being surveilled and sold in secret."[31] This was not the Internet that Snowden fell in love with, nor was it the comforting parental figure he admired. It was rapidly becoming yet another arena for the US to exploit for its own gain. As Snowden writes, "The American government, in total disregard of its founding charter, fell victim to precisely this temptation, and once it had tasted the fruit of this poisonous tree it became gripped by an unrelenting fever."[32] Snowden's revelations—as outlined by the journalists listed in the first sentence of this essay—rather clearly illustrate the point he makes in the previous quotation. The US government, through its two powerful intelligence agencies, had indeed conducted surveillance on citizens in the name of national security.[33] The fact that it had used the Internet to do this deeply hurt Snowden and one can read his use of Internet platforms to spread his postrevelations message as a way of attempting to seize back control of that space and render it once again a bastion of free speech and democratic exchange.

As Snowden's preface reaches its conclusion, he includes one additional piece of information that is relevant to his new identity as an author: He believes that journalists and the press at large are under attack from the same governmental entities that violate one's right to privacy. Speaking about the rise of authoritarianism and global crackdowns on the freedom of the press, Snowden states the following: "Nowhere has this regression been more apparent than in the relationship of governments to the press. The attempts by elected officials to delegitimize journalism have been aided and abetted by a full-on assault on the principle of truth. What is real is being purposefully conflated with what is fake, through technologies that are capable of scaling that conflation into unprecedented global confusion."[34] Snowden had a good reason to be concerned about this development: Glen Greenwald—the most prominent of the journalists to whom Snowden provided classified documents—watched as his partner was detained in the United Kingdom under false pretenses, and with the US government's approval.[35] This move was widely regarded as retaliation for Greenwald's Snowden-related publications.

Snowden's decision to become an author and de facto journalist himself was motivated partly by these events. As he states near the end of the preface, "They were able to say so much, and so freely, in large part because I refused to defend myself. From the moment I came forward to the present, I was resolute about never revealing any details of my personal life that might cause further distress to my family and friends, who were already suffering enough for my principles."[36] Despite concerns about his social circle and kin, Snowden did, in fact, move forward with the publication of his memoir. In many ways, this outcome was a foregone conclusion. He had already tasted notoriety and attention from Twitter. Writing a book detailing his decisions and establishing his postrevelations writerly identity was a logical next step.

Snowden's autobiography ends with scenes of him in Russia.[37] Many of them include moving descriptions of the trials and tribulations of his wife, Lindsay, and their life together in exile. But near the end of the book, Snowden provides a perfect glimpse into his new life as a whistleblower-turned-author. Writing about his day-to-day experiences, Snowden states: "When people ask me what my life is like now, I tend to answer that it's a lot like theirs in that I spend a lot of time in front of the computer—reading, writing, interacting."[38] Consider that list of verbs at the end of his sentence. Motivated partially by a desire to claim his own voice in the face of governmental obfuscation, Snowden has completely transformed from a self-described computer geek into a respected and highly sought-after writer and shaper of public discourse.

Permanent Record merely formalized the path that Snowden had set for himself when he started his Twitter account. In so doing, he rewrote the playbook for a post-whistleblowing life in the public eye: using Internet platforms to bring his writing directly to the people, authoring an autobiography that justifies and explains past and future acts of protest, and, above all else, positioning himself at the forefront of debates regarding hot-button issues. The key to all of this, of course, is writing. Snowden's original whistleblowing actions were themselves a type of authorial process, despite his desire to have journalists do most of the publishing. He researched, created narratives, and delivered those narratives in many, many interviews. In so doing, he positioned himself as an intellectual engaged in protest against antidemocratic surveillance regimes. It thus made sense for him to assume the mantle himself after the dust cleared from his initial revelations. What began as an act of protest against governmental infringements of liberty has turned into a permanent role as one of America's most outspoken authorial voices.

Part III. Substack: *Continuing Ed*

In June of 2021, Snowden launched a Substack entitled *Continuing Ed.* Substack is an online writing platform started by the technologist Chris Best. An innovative way for authors to bypass traditional publishing gatekeepers, Substack allows for direct distribution of writing to audiences. Some authors choose to make their Substacks subscription-based, but the financial results and the general impact can be mixed.[39] That being said, Substack works for writers, like Snowden, who already have a massive audience that will follow them anywhere.[40]

In his first essay published to *Continuing Ed*, Snowden details his motivations for joining the site. They are directly related to his newly crafted identity as a writer and commentator. According to Snowden, "I'd like to do my part in encouraging a return to longer forms of thinking and writing, which provide more room for nuance and more opportunity for establishing consensus or, at the very least, respecting a diversity of perspective and, you know, science."[41] Although he does not directly state it, he is reacting to the shortness and pithiness of tweeting. He rightly identifies that Twitter fosters polemics and enables people to entrench within their de facto ideological camps. At the very least, Snowden gives the impression that he wishes to rise above the fray of partisan politics as an author and suggests Substack as his vehicle to do so.

As he mentions repeatedly in his autobiography, Snowden is inspired by the early days of the Internet. He is thus a nostalgic writer in some ways, wishing to return to a time when individuals had the freedom to share their views online without fear of government reprisal:

> I want to revive the original spirit of the older, pre-commercial
> internet, with its bulletin boards, newsgroups, and blogs—if
> not in form, then in function. . . . The utopianism of these
> blogs might seem as quaint today as the sites' graphics (and
> glamorous MIDI audio), but whatever those outlets lacked in
> sophisticated design, they more than made up for in curiosity
> and intelligence and in their fostering of originality and exper-
> imentation. They were, when it comes down to it, not curated
> and templated "platforms" so much as direct expressions of the
> creative primacy of the individual.[42]

This is the overarching point of Snowden's Substack: It is a place where
he can take his time, deeply explore important issues in his writing, be
curious and open, experiment with written form, and, above all, express
himself in as pure a way as possible. This unadulterated and direct form of
writing is itself reflective of the democratic concerns that Snowden places
at the center of his politics: individuals should be free from governmental
(in this case, editorial) interference.

Although he will never be anonymous like he was during the early
days of the Internet, his use of Substack offers himself plenty of advantages. For one thing, the way in which Substack connects authors to readers enables Snowden to mostly bypass editors and publishers.[43] Consider
the ending to his first Substack essay:

> For the past eight years, I've spoken out in defense of speech
> freedoms on various platforms, but none has been a home. I've
> been edited by editors, moderated by moderators, crammed
> into newspaper and magazine columns next to the ads for fancy
> wristwatches; I've had my thoughts contorted by character-
> limitations and tripped-up by threads, even before they were
> taken out of context and misinterpreted, accidentally and
> willfully. Platforms should ensure a writer has full control over,
> and full ownership of, their intellectual property, so I'm glad
> to help give this one a fighting chance.[44]

Snowden is right to worry about his words being taken out of context;
in fact, it seems to happen to him quite frequently. Some of this may
be his own fault. Indeed, Snowden is not immune to a poorly worded
tweet that ignites a firestorm. But, a lot of the controversy and vitriol that

surrounds Snowden comes from a source outside of himself. He is something of a blank canvas, if you will, on which people of different political persuasions project their own positions, ideas, and feelings.[45] For example, politicians as ideologically different as Alexandria Ocasio-Cortez and Rand Paul—who can barely agree on the sky being the color blue—both support Snowden and his desire for a presidential pardon. Likewise, it is also easy to find Democrats and Republicans who think Snowden should be severely punished for his actions.[46]

Continuing Ed thus allows Snowden to remove ambiguity. It also frees him to discuss issues beyond the realm of surveillance and governmental abuses of privacy rights. In many ways, Snowden's Substack is his true debut as an unfettered writer. Snowden's writerly identity can perhaps be most clearly witnessed in his essays on the future of an American Central Bank Digital Currency (CBDC) and climate change.

On October 8, 2021, Snowden published a piece called "Your Money AND Your Life: Central Banks Digital Currencies Will Ransom Our Future," a fascinating take on a form of electronic money that might be issued by the US government in the future. In this essay, Snowden begins to carve what I like to call an interest matrix—a collection of subjects that any given writer returns to again and again. Writing about CBDCs makes a lot of sense for a budding author of Snowden's profile as it is a topic that connects to the government, to potential violations of privacy, and, of course, to the Internet itself.

At the very beginning of the essay, Snowden dispels any notion that this new money is a "digital dollar"; instead, he sees it as a boldfaced attempt to tighten the American surveillance regime. The American dollar is *already digital*, Snowden argues. How else do you explain web banking and payments made online? This is an important distinction to make, because should the US move forward with such a change to its monetary makeup and policy, it will likely attempt to claim that the proposed change is no different than what Americans do with their money on a regular basis. Snowden argues a US CDBC would also not qualify as a cryptocurrency, but is "closer to being a perversion of cryptocurrency, or at least of the founding principles and protocols of cryptocurrency—a cryptofascist currency, an evil twin entered into the ledgers on Opposite Day, expressly designed to deny its users the basic ownership of their money and to install the State at the mediating center of every transaction."[47] Here we see a familiar rhetorical side to Snowden: the one deeply skeptical of government and its motivations. The difference is that he has taken his general philosophy regarding limits on state power and used it as a rhetorical lens to explore a range of different subject areas, including this take on a potential US-based digital currency. In addition to playing to his audience's preconceived notions of his politics, this approach again positions Snowden as a staunch defender of the US Constitution—as effective an audience-building technique as perhaps exists, at least in an American context.

In an essay on the danger of our climate future, Snowden covers a different set of topics, further establishing his writerly interest matrix. Here, we see him astutely concerned with the actual communication of negative subject matter than with the problem of climate change itself: "When we decide the situation is so bad that there's nothing to be done, we succumb to a kind of civic paralysis. An overwhelming concatenation of negativity, communicated as constantly unfolding catastrophe, leads even the most conspiracy-immune into apathy—and willful ignorance. And now here's the baddest news: it leads us into apathy and willful ignorance *whether or not we believe the science.*"[48] Notably, Snowden does not offer solutions to this problem. To use a medical metaphor, Snowden is acting more as a diagnostician in this essay than as a prescriber of medicine. In many ways, this mirrors his democratic approach to the distribution of US intelligence documents; he blows the whistle/highlights a problem and then allows members of the public to decide for themselves.

Conclusion: The Russia-Ukraine Tweets

Through his successful transition from whistleblower to professional writer, Edward Snowden forged a new path for future whistleblowers. His example will likely be replicated, in part because such a playbook keeps the whistleblower squarely in the public eye, enabling a form of protest that will last as long as the whistleblower is willing and able to write. However, accurate reporting is paramount to whistleblowing, which leads to a downside in the Snowden strategy. What if what you write is not just wrong, but egregiously so? This exact scenario took place two months before the writing of this chapter.

On February 24, 2022, Russia again invaded Ukraine.[49] In the leadup to the invasion, US President Joseph R. Biden Jr. revealed unprecedented intelligence to the general public about Russian intentions. For observers like myself, the writing was on the wall. If the US president, backed by the world's foremost intelligence agencies, says that one country is going to invade another, the odds are overwhelmingly in favor of that event coming to pass.

Snowden, sitting in exile in Moscow, felt differently. Consider the following tweet made about a week before the Russian invasion began: "Now that the promised invasion has failed to materialize, maybe we could take another look at the story that was breaking when the White House was suddenly overcome with a mysterious and inexplicable desire to change the news cycle."[50] Here, we see Snowden writing that the US government was hyping the threat of war in order to distract from unsavory news. He also heaped blame on journalists for reporting on Biden's ominous warnings: "If there's an invasion tomorrow, dunk on me because I have been spectacularly wrong. But remember, too [*sic*] that the source of my skepticism is that the US IC has (again) been making truly spectacular claims without presenting any evidence—because you did not require it of them."[51] The "you" in the second sentence refers to journalists, whom Snowden criticizes for not asking hard enough questions of US intelligence agencies. In perhaps the most controversial tweet of this era, Snowden seems to directly blame the press for the possibility of war. Garnering over one hundred thousand likes, the tweet reads: "There is nothing more grotesque than a media pushing for war."[52] To put it mildly, the tweet did not age well.

In this and the aforementioned tweets, Snowden let his biases (and his idealistic vision of global affairs) get the better of him. In the aftermath of Russian tanks rolling across the international border with Ukraine, Snowden thus had a choice. Would he admit he was wrong? Would he use his new platform as a respected author to argue against Russia's brutality?[53] On February 27, 2022, Snowden issued the following mea culpa: "I'm not suspended from the ceiling above a barrel of acid by a rope that burns a little faster every time I tweet, you concern-trolling ghouls. I've just lost any confidence I had that sharing my thinking on this particular topic continues to be useful, because I called it wrong."[54] Once again, Snowden packaged his acknowledgment of his tremendous mistake in his trademark biting humor. But at least he did what was right: He admitted he was wrong. This raises an interesting issue. The new post-whistleblowing revelation of wrongdoing inaugurated by Snowden is less bound by concrete evidence than conventional whistleblowing and contains ample room for error. One hopes that future practitioners of this new art will follow Snowden's lead and acknowledge their mistakes.

Moving forward, the ability to take responsibility for his words and actions will be of paramount importance. Taking accountability and demonstrating the capacity to change his mind will ensure that he maintains a high level of credibility in the eyes of most of his readers. This reader-writer dynamic is something that Snowden appears to be learning in real time. If readers do not trust the author, especially one who has placed democracy, freedom, and so on, at the center of his writerly identity, these readers will disappear. And without a public audience, a writer writing social and political commentaries is not really worth much. Snowden's decision to acknowledge his egregiously bad tweet about the Russian invasion shows that he understands the perils of closed-mindedness and what it might mean for his future as a writer.

This rather infamous tweet was followed by public silence. It seemed that the prolific writer had lost his pen. Many worried he had been imprisoned by Russian intelligence or that he was about to be used as a pawn in negotiations with the West. But, he appeared again on Twitter two months later and started covering the following topics, which are in line with his previous interests: government overreach, surveillance abuses, the benefits of digital currency, among others. Then, on May 3, 2022, to support the person who leaked the impending Supreme Court decision to overturn *Roe v. Wade*, Snowden wrote: "Someone may have put a lot on the line to warn you of this. It doesn't matter who they are or why they did it: their role is complete. What matters now is how you respond."[55] It is hard not to see Snowden's post-whistleblowing turn to writing as filled with meaning, creating linkages that somehow bind the otherwise solitary activity of blowing the whistle. From one whistleblower to another, with love.

Notes

1. When Snowden initially fled the United States, he went to Hong Kong first. He then boarded a flight to Moscow, Russia. In the midst of that flight, the US State Department canceled his passport. His residency in Moscow is thus not one he voluntarily chose, but one that was forced on him by the geopolitical actions of the American and Russian nation-states.

2. Edward Snowden, *Permanent Record* (London: Pan Books, 2020).

3. Substack is an online platform that bypasses standard journalistic practices, such as editorial review. It allows writers to directly engage their audiences, but in long-form writing as opposed to the short, pithy posts made on X (Twitter). I find it useful to think of it as long-form X.

4. Here, I am using *whistleblowing* to refer to an act that protests against some perceived injustice, specifically through the lens of a subject's personal experience and expertise.

5. Joshua Guitar and Alan Chu, "Racing to (Dis)Own Whistleblowers and Protests: Theorizing *Amongness* in the Shared Rhetorical Spaces of Democratic Agency," chapter 1 in the present volume, 1.

6. Robert A. Gross, "Texts for the Times: An Introduction to Book History," in *Perspectives on American Book History*, ed. Scott E. Casper, Joanne D. Chaison, and Jeffrey D. Groves (Amherst: University of Massachusetts Press, 2002), 2–16.

7. In print culture studies, "authors" are generally anyone who writes, even nonliterate individuals who dictate their stories to someone else and writers of text messages.

8. Elizabeth McHenry, *Forgotten Readers: Recovering the Lost History of African American Literary Societies* (Durham, NC: Duke University Press, 2002).

9. Twitter went to 280 characters in 2017.

10. Snowden, Twitter post, September 29, 2015, 12:00 a.m.

11. Snowden removed classified material from this agency and later released it to journalists.

12. Snowden, Twitter post, December 10, 2016, 10:53 a.m.

13. Snowden, Twitter post, January 21, 2017, 12:06 a.m.

14. Snowden, Twitter post, June 22, 2017, 11:09 a.m.

15. Snowden, Twitter post, September 30, 2019, 11:45 a.m.

16. Herman Melville to Nathaniel Hawthorne, June 1851, http://www.melville.org/letter3.htm.

17. Snowden, Twitter post, September 30, 2019, 11:45 a.m.

18. Snowden, Twitter post, August 8, 2021, 4:20 p.m.

19. Snowden, Twitter post, September 30, 2019, 11:45 a.m.

20. Benjamin Franklin, *The Autobiography of Benjamin Franklin*, 1791.

21. Frederick Douglass, *Narrative of the Life of Frederick Douglass*, 1845.

22. William L. Andrews, *To Tell a Free Story: The First Century of Afro-American Autobiography, 1760–1865* (Chicago: University of Chicago Press, 1986), xi.

23. Liberal as in a member of a free society.

24. David Waldstreicher, *Runaway America: Benjamin Franklin, Slavery, and the American Revolution* (New York: Hill and Wang, 2004), 6.

25. There is an irony here, especially because Snowden fled to a nonliberal state. It is worth noting that Russia was not meant to be his permanent destination.

26. Edward Snowden, *Permanent Record* (New York: Metropolitan Books, 2019), 6–7.

27. It also helps him deflect the criticism he regularly faces, such as: Jeffrey Toobin, "Edward Snowden's Real Impact," *New Yorker*, August 19, 2013, https://www.newyorker.com/news/daily-comment/edward-snowdens-real-impact; Zachary Keck, "Yes, Edward Snowden Is a Traitor," *Diplomat*, December 21, 2013, https://

thediplomat.com/2013/12/yes-edward-snowden-is-a-traitor/; Damon Linker, "The Case Against Snowden," *Week*, September 23, 2016, https://theweek.com/articles/650407/case-against-snowden.

28. Snowden, *Permanent Record*, 1. Citations to this source here and below are to the US (Metropolitan Books) edition.

29. There is an obvious tension here. Snowden (in Moscow, not the US) declares he works for the public, but he does not hold public office and was not selected by the public for this position.

30. Snowden, *Permanent Record*, 4.

31. Snowden, *Permanent Record*, 6.

32. Snowden, *Permanent Record*, 5.

33. Snowden's actions are worth debating, but the facts are not. US state surveillance happened.

34. Snowden, *Permanent Record*, 7.

35. Guardian Staff, "Glenn Greenwald's Partner Detained at Heathrow Airport for Nine Hours," *Guardian*, August 18, 2013, https://www.theguardian.com/world/2013/aug/18/glenn-greenwald-guardian-partner-detained-heathrow.

36. Snowden, *Permanent Record*, 7.

37. I have chosen not to spend much time in the middle of Snowden's autobiography because most of it contains known information. More relevant here are the ways he frames his actions and how he thinks of himself as an author—these parts are found at the beginning and the end.

38. Snowden, *Permanent Record*, 333.

39. Jen Doll, "Inside Substack, Where Authors Are Suddenly Making Serious Money in the Newsletter Game—but It's Publish or Perish," *Fortune*, October 7, 2021, https://fortune.com/2021/10/07/substack-writers-newsletters-how-much-money-do-they-make/; Tiffany Hsu, "Substack's Growth Spurt Brings Growing Pains," *New York Times*, April 13, 2022, https://www.nytimes.com/2022/04/13/business/media/substack-growth-newsletters.html.

40. It is unclear whether Snowden makes money from his Substack. He does not include a subscription fee, but an agreement with Substack itself is not unusual. It is possible that Snowden came to a financial agreement with the site. However, this remains unreported as of this writing.

41. Edward Snowden, "Lifting the Mask: On Liberty, on Privacy, and on Substack," *Continuing Ed*, June 15, 2021.

42. Snowden, "Lifting the Mask."

43. Substack includes a Terms and Conditions section and reserves the right to remove someone.

44. Snowden, "Lifting the Mask."

45. Joshua Guitar makes a similar argument in *Dissent, Discourse, and Democracy: Whistleblowers as Sites of Political Contestation* (Lanham, MD: Lexington Books, 2021).

46. Mike Rogers and Dutch Ruppersberger, "No, Edward Snowden Does Not Deserve a Pardon, President Trump," *Washington Post*, August 18, 2020, https://www.washingtonpost.com/opinions/2020/08/18/edward-snowden-deserves-trial-not-pardon/.

47. Edward Snowden, "Your Money AND Your Life: Central Banks Digital Currencies Will Ransom Our Future," *Continuing Ed*, October 8, 2021.

48. Edward Snowden, "Covid, Climate, and the New Denialism; Denying Facts: Bad. Denying Hope: Worse," *Continuing Ed*, September 1, 2021.

49. Russia invaded Crimea in 2014 and the Donbas region in 2015. It has held land internationally recognized as belonging to Ukraine since these events.

50. Snowden, Twitter post, February 16, 2022, deleted.

51. Snowden, Twitter post, February 15, 2022, 1:00 p.m.

52. Snowden, Twitter post, February 11, 2022, 2:46 p.m.

53. Snowden, Twitter post, September 30, 2019, 11:45 a.m.

54. Snowden, Twitter post, February 27, 2022, 4:37 p.m.

55. Snowden, Twitter post, May 3, 2022, 2:20 a.m.

8

From Solidarity to Suspicion

The Case of Javier Esqueda

Sarah Walker-Riftkin

On May 25, 2020, Minneapolis police officer Derek Chauvin knelt on George Floyd's neck for more than eight minutes while Floyd asphyxiated on the street. In the aftermath of Floyd's death, protests against police misconduct erupted worldwide, prompting responses from leadership across all levels of government. Utilizing a common but covertly racist depiction of Black men, Bob Kroll, then president of the Police Officers Federation of Minneapolis, characterized Floyd as a "violent criminal" in internal letters to union membership. Kroll's commentary on Floyd drew journalists' attention where his comments were scrutinized. Public outcry and calls for his resignation eventually prompted Kroll to retire in January 2021, four months earlier than his planned retirement date. Not all deaths of Black men are so carefully documented, and the opinions of police union presidents rarely receive such public criticism. While police are called to "protect and serve" every member of the communities they police, the protection and service seems to hang on an understanding that the police are above questioning.

A more obscure case that began months before George Floyd's murder demonstrates the fragility of police officer solidarity. On January 28,

2020, Eric D. Lurry Jr., a thirty-seven-year-old Black man, died of an apparent narcotics overdose while in the custody of Joliet, Illinois, police officers Jose Tellez and Andrew McCue. According to *USA Today*'s investigation into police activities, Joliet police arrested Lurry on January 28, 2020.[1] Police apprehended Lurry on drug charges, obstructing justice, and resisting a police officer.[2] Officers placed Lurry in the back of a police cruiser, which was being recorded by a body-cam-style video camera. Shortly after being placed in the vehicle, Lurry appeared to swallow several bags.[3] Lurry then began to suffer symptoms of a narcotic overdose. The video showed officers reaching into the back of the squad car to slap Lurry, instructing him to "wake up, bitch."[4] Officers then proceeded to hold his nose in an attempt to get Lurry to open his mouth. Lurry was "eventually taken to a local hospital, where he was pronounced dead."[5] NBC 5 Chicago's report on the matter did not get published until nearly twenty-one months after Lurry's arrest, noting that the cause of death was an accidental overdose: "The Will County Coroner's Office determined that Lurry had 'fatal doses' of heroin, fentanyl and cocaine in his system."[6]

The incident went largely unnoticed until May of 2020, when an internal investigation prompted Joliet Police Department (JPD) Sgt. Javier Esqueda to look at the video footage of the back of the squad car. After viewing the footage, Esqueda suspected the department was concealing the details of Lurry's death and decided to blow the whistle. By deciding this, Esqueda discovered how tenuous the bonds of the police force can be when he suddenly found himself excluded from them. In short, Sergeant Esqueda highlighted the consequences of critiquing an organization to which he belonged and demonstrated how solidarity cannot be rhetorically extended to both a formal organization and a community.

I contend there are two primary reasons to study the internal rhetorical effect of whistleblowing on police misconduct. First, close examination of events like Esqueda's expulsion permits scholars a look into the mechanics of a theory as they are applied to the real world. By examining the rhetorical situation encasing Esqueda, and untangling the rhetorical pressures revealed in the Joliet Fraternal Order of Police Supervisors Association's (JFOPSA) response, we can piece together and explain the communication strategies at play and evaluate the rhetorical implications of excommunicating police whistleblowers from an organizational culture that prioritizes solidarity. Esqueda personifies a kind of purposeful step into the complicated dance that is Rancière's in-between;[7] a step that is both demanded by his role as protector and public servant, and constrained against his loyalty to his own coworkers and subordinates. Second, though much has been said about the limits of observation and critique on hegemonic institutions, activism begins with understanding. By highlighting the rhetoric police unions use to protect, or expel, their members, we commit to a more critical perspective of the institution as a whole and establish measures and procedures for better due process for whistleblowers in other hierarchical structures such as politics, finance, or technology. Given that McKerrow expressly called for rhetoricians to challenge structures of power, lest they change us in our engagement with them,[8] I argue it is vital to investigate just how rhetorically protected—or indeed, unprotected—its members are when they choose to indict their organizations. Effectively then, this Esqueda case serves as a reminder that all institutions should be questioned, and that sometimes under questioning, these institutions falter.

I see the limits of solidarity, constitutive rhetoric, and identity as especially well articulated through the expulsion of Esqueda from JFOPSA, his local police supervisor's union, in November 2021. In what follows, I contextualize how solidarity conceptually connects unions and social movements and examine the ousting of Esqueda as a demonstration of solidarity to a specific, identity-branded in-group, rather than to a single member or the community to which they belong. I identify the strategic value of solidarity as a rhetorical tool, what events transpired to encourage Esqueda's whistleblowing, and how that act informed retaliation from the very union he expected to protect his actions. Specifically, I am interested in the sense of solidarity usually afforded to members of a union, the rhetorical limits of that solidarity, and how those limits demonstrate warning signs for members of social movements and social movements as a whole. The removal of Esqueda for blowing the whistle, rather than the perpetrators of Lurry's abuse, indicates how the margins between a community-oriented organization like the police and the community itself become sites for democratic and antidemocratic acts.

Brotherhood in Blue: Theoretical Considerations

Given the context of this chapter, it seems prudent to establish a definition of a social movement. Sociologists Ralph H. Turner and Lewis Killian loosely define a social movement first by what a group of individuals do, which they call collective behavior.[9] Collective behaviors may be inspired by social or societal problems.[10] Killian further clarifies a social movement as a "loosely organized but sustained campaign in support of a social goal, typically either the implementation or the prevention of a change in society's structure or values."[11] The broad applicability of a term like *social movement* is intentional, as social movements tend to develop in response to a context, rather than finding a problem to apply their collective behavior. A social movement then, is a tactical, persuasive response from a collected group of people to a larger society. Examples include such diverse actions as the Protestant Reformation, the civil rights movement, and Occupy Wall Street.

Labor movement action in the US fulfills Turner and Killian's estimation of a social movement. Labor unions are collections of individual people who engage in collective action in response to societal norms. Unions are traditionally born of an agreement between workers of a particular context, or with specific skills or specialties, that they will negotiate as a group rather than as individuals. The workers then collectively negotiate with their management or employer to improve their wages, hours, and working conditions. These negotiations serve to protect the individual workers from exploitation or undue discipline and ensure for the employer that negotiations will be governed by rules and regulations. In general, a labor union is understood by its members to be protecting individuals from harm through use of collective democratic behavior. By projecting a legal, procedural, and ethical "shield" around the collection of workers that constitutes the whole, a union directly engages in meaning-making and a shared understanding of collective goals. Unions are further sutured to the larger human activity of decrying authoritarian power structures and actualizing democratic agency, strengthening the rhetorical and material impression that union membership is as much about human rights as it is protection from managerial malfeasance. Child labor restrictions, Occupational Safety and Health Administration regulations such as requiring accessible fire extinguishers and first aid equipment, affirmative action, and weekends are all results of collective action taken by unions in response to problems and tragedies workers experienced in US workplaces.[12]

Scholars and policymakers have noted that labor unions have frequently participated in, lent resources to, and encouraged other prominent social movements.[13] Intersecting principles and community needs often push labor unions to develop values that counter racism, sexism, homophobia, and ableism—all issues of enormous and increasing importance in the late twentieth and early twenty-first centuries. Practically, unionist action creates or contributes to social movements by organizing like-minded but untrained individuals to act in concert to effect change. Because unions are active organizations, interested primarily in preventing or reducing harm to its members, a union's collective knowledge of law, bureaucracy, and power structures often provides a blueprint for social movement groups. The prominent 1960s civil rights organization known as the Student Nonviolent Coordinating Committee modeled its own structure from labor unions, as did "gay rights" organizations like the Mattachine Society. Clearly then, social movements and unionism are intertwined in conceptual and practical ways. Labor and social movements both engage theorist Chantal Mouffe's conceptualization of democracy as inherently combative.[14] The act of communicating similar goals and acting in concert against an institution—the management in a labor movement, and the government in a social movement—demonstrate how labor and social movements are antagonistic by design.

As it happens, solidarity is a vital component in both unionism and social movements as both need a unified understanding of an issue in order to enact change. Sociologists and labor scholars have examined solidarity in some detail, typically emphasizing the slippery nature of the term. Sociologist Émile Durkheim described solidarity as a feeling or influence that ties individual people to a society.[15] In his 1893 work *The Division of Labor in Society*, Durkheim analogizes solidarity as the cooperation between organs in a living body. When all the organs effectively specialize in their own action and also cooperate with their neighbor organs, the body is healthy and vital. Complicating Durkheim's views on solidarity, political theorist Lawrence Wilde argued, "On the one hand it has connotations of unity and universality, emphasising responsibility for others and the feeling of togetherness. On the other hand it exhibits itself most forcefully in antagonism to other groups, often in ways which eschew the possibility of compromise."[16] In other words, Wilde views solidarity as a normalizing tool, a way to make in-groups and out-groups. Wilde might be drawn into Durkheim's analogy by considering solidarity as the liver and kidneys of an organization—providing stability and unity, while identifying and providing a convenient route to remove unwanted material. Making in-groups and out-groups *is* a concept well known to rhetoric scholars.

Solidarity is a key rhetorical term, which is informed by rhetorician Maurice Charland's theory of constitutive rhetoric. Charland uses an example of conceptual collectivization to illustrate how individual people are encouraged to rhetorically associate themselves with interest or activism groups in essentially three interlocking pieces.[17] First, a rhetor must determine and align the professed beliefs of the group to the identity markers and beliefs of the people the rhetor is recruiting.[18] Second, the rhetor must narrativize the life of the group for the new members.[19] Put another way, members of the movement must be certain that if they follow the direction of the group, their needs and wants will be satisfied. Third, rhetors must produce a story that inspires others not just to identify with the group, but to take action that will benefit the group's end-goals.[20] In other words, the narrative of a social movement or organization must have a beginning, middle, and satisfactory end. When enough individuals are convinced that a group's narrative is achievable and desirable, the group can be considered constituted, created by the interests of the members. I argue that solidarity holds Charland's constituted groups together.

Police unions occupy an interesting rhetorical space in which they have co-opted the language and hierarchy of unionism but remain dedicated arms of the state placed in opposition to the communities they "protect and serve." Theorist Louis Althusser directly links police with the state in his conceptualization of repressive state apparatuses, or RSAs.[21] In his work, Althusser posits that state authority is reified by two categories of institutions designed to centralize power.[22] Ideological state apparatuses (ISAs) expand the state's authority to rule by instilling particular values and beliefs about the state in the citizenry. Schools, churches, and bureaucracy tend to fall into this category. Althusser directly contrasts ISAs with RSAs and uses the police as his demonstrative example of an RSA, arguing that RSAs funnel power to the government with violence and threats of violence, making resistance to the state impractical by giving citizens a literal, visible show of power to repress the populace.

Police unions function to build connections and trust among officers, but they do not function to build trust between communities and the police against the establishment in the way union organizers have joined public outcry with critiques of the state. Instead, police unions act as protection for officers against city councils, citizen watch groups, and federal investigators. Indeed, while co-opting the name and structures of democratic institutions, and thus accessing some of the same good will afforded to labor unions, police unions function to maintain distance between the public and the police, effectively building rather than tearing down hierarchy. To return to Derek Chauvin's murder of George Floyd as a recent example, the Minneapolis police union prioritized protecting Chauvin and the other officers at the scene from scrutiny instead of reassuring public trust in policing. Unlike other labor unions, the membership in police unions consists primarily of armed officers of all levels of police hierarchy. Police are trained to think of themselves as law enforcement, which in turn encourages a perspective of the public as potential criminals.[23] Just as Althusser positioned the police as central to RSA, law enforcement recruits are trained in situational awareness techniques that specifically encourage them to see people as potential threats in any situation.[24] This perspective differs significantly from the mindset of other labor organizations—who tend to view their workers as members of a community. The relationships between unions and communities are informed by the mutual trust that each has the best interests of the other in mind. Thus, many labor unions do not tend to view the public as an enemy, but as allies in the betterment of their collective conditions. In fact, though police unions are often included in labor discussions, state and federal labor councils have expressed concern about police union goals and whether their implicit position as agents of law enforcement places them at odds with other union goals that are often critical of state or business practices.[25]

There are a few moving pieces in Charland's theory[26] that are complicated by the specifics of the Esqueda case. It is my supposition that the act of identifying as a police officer implies an association with others as a police officer—replete with the expectations, prejudices, and threats that a law enforcement officer might meet. The institution of policing in the US has generally accepted the expectation that police are to "protect and serve." By ideologically reinforcing this expectation, police draw an explicit connection between who the public should expect a police officer to be, how they should act, and what they should uphold.[27] The identification as police is more mutable than identification as, say, a racial or ethnic marker. Though an internal identification as an officer is always present, external identification as an officer is reliant on that officer wearing a uniform or carrying a badge. As Judith Butler succinctly notes, our identities are performative and our values are constituted in part by the groups and societies to which we belong.[28] In other words, when a person carries an identification with their job, they imply a certain loyalty to the ideals of that job because that job has constituted them as a member of their ranks.

The rhetorical pressure of solidarity results in a coerced choice between solidarity to a community the police are "sworn to serve" or solidarity with the collection of individuals employed as law enforcement officers. This forced division implies that a person must disengage from solidarity with one of the opposed forces. Mentally disengaging holds rhetorical significance—an act of disidentification from the goals, interests, and values of a group gives a whistleblower freedom from cognitive dissonance but may also cut someone off from a community that once held important significance for them. Since Charland[29] argues that the narrative of a group's beliefs, goals, and tactics are what draw people to identify with them, the expulsion of whistleblowers implies that the narrative that constitutively folded someone in is not strong enough to maintain them. The division of solidarity into an agonistic mentality complicates our perspective of unionism, police, and whistleblowing. Such a complication demands exploration into the rhetorical pressure to conform to the pain of being isolated.

The Fraternal Order: Contextual Considerations

As the rhetorical situation in this case is complex, it is important to convey some facts that are significant to this case. First, as a sergeant, Esqueda's job was to supervise and train officers, including some who we will discuss. Second, Esqueda disobeyed orders from his superiors by leaking footage of Lurry's arrest. Third, Esqueda is visibly not white.

Esqueda told *USA Today* that he initially struggled with the decision to blow the whistle on his own officers.[30] He was a twenty-seven-year veteran with JPD when he saw the video of Lurry's arrest, treatment by the police, and fatal overdose on May 2020. He supervised the training of at least one of the officers involved in Lurry's death. Esqueda's promotion to sergeant, position as a trainer, and his nearly three-decade tenure with the department demonstrated his good standing among the ranks of JPD.[31] Esqueda noticed several procedural problems with Lurry's treatment as well as the documentation of Lurry's arrest.[32] Esqueda alerted his commanding officer of the video, especially after investigations into the death stalled, but was told to "shut up when he tried to explain his qualms about the arrest."[33] As the supervisor of the officers in question, Esqueda does not cleanly fit into the traditional conceptualizations of whistleblowing; however, considering the support his officers enjoyed from the JFOPSA and Esqueda's superiors, Esqueda clearly and quickly became the disempowered party in this situation. To apply Guitar and Chu's definition, Esqueda became a vulnerable member of an institution who was motivated by democratic ethics to "truthfully expose violations of human rights and abuses of power."[34]

Esqueda shared the footage of Lurry's arrest with a local news outlet in July 2020. *USA Today* reported that within days of that act, Esqueda was placed on administrative leave.[35] The leak brought public attention to the Joliet Police Department, and internal investigations were performed. All officers shown engaging with Lurry in the video received minor disciplinary action, including a six-day suspension for Tellez, who turned off the sound recording on the camera. Journalist Ascha Lee noted that Illinois Attorney General Kwame Raoul used the footage to open an investigation into the practices and policies of the Joliet Police Department.[36]

In the intervening eighteen months since Esqueda's leak, the former Joliet police sergeant has been made "a pariah" at his place of work.[37] Police chief Al Roechner arrested Esqueda on two official misconduct charges in October of 2020.[38] One of the charges pertained to illegally using his JPD-issued laptop to view the footage of Lurry's arrest and death.[39] Esqueda disputed this charge to *USA Today* by noting that typically only closed case material is available to be viewed by login on the JPD system, and that he had both heard of the footage and grew concerned because one of his trainees was involved.[40] Esqueda's lawyer Jeff Tomczak told journalist John Ferak, "What is most sad about this is that this is a clear message from Chief Roechner to the frontline officers that should they see actions they believe are misconduct by fellow officers, they must keep their mouths shut and stay quiet or they will be charged with a felony."[41] In addition to felony misconduct charges, in November 2021, Esqueda was removed from membership in JFOPSA in a 35 to 1 vote for his expulsion.[42]

JFOPSA has not released any information about the internal politicking of Esqueda's removal, but some important observations can be extrapolated from their vote. First, there is no indication that the primary responding officers Tellez or McCue were ever considered for expulsion from the union, though Esqueda and others have identified that the officers were not trained to handle overdoses in the way they demonstrate in the cruiser footage. Additionally, Tellez and McCue were not disciplined by Chief Roechner. According to the Joliet Patch, Tellez was placed on a six-day suspension only after Roechner retired and was replaced by Dawn

Malec in January 2021, who also upheld the department's discipline of Esqueda. Second, Esqueda's reporting and public disclosure of the details are likely the reason for his expulsion. The timing of the vote, the extensive discussion that appears to have occurred among officers between the leak and the expulsion, and the secrecy surrounding the reasons for the expulsion indicate the union acted in some kind of solidarity with one another, a commitment that they did not expect the public to understand.

"I Don't Regret It": Analysis of Esqueda and JFOPSA

As noted in the preceding context, Lurry's death incited subsequent actions by both Esqueda and the police department. Esqueda's long tenure with JPD prior to these events indicates an identification with the department's stated goals, or at least an uncritical acceptance of a shared meaning in terms like *protect* and *serve*. These terms, regardless of their connotations, are anchor points for identification with the values of the constituted group known as the police. Belief in the importance of protection and service to a community has been established as a value held in common among law enforcement officers. The narrative of that belief does not preclude members from acting in contradiction of that value, but it does create a point of shared identity that officers are expected to at least acknowledge when they choose to enter the profession. The police union in Joliet offers a fairly standard advantage: solidarity. In the case of a police union however, solidarity is used to ensure loyalty to the ideology of policing.

Esqueda makes it clear that he experienced a break with the department's claims when he told *USA Today* that he thought "this is a cover-up."[43] Esqueda did not state his intention to leave the police force, but his actions rhetorically signaled his ideological break with JPD. This rhetorical tension is important. In the wake of George Floyd's murder, citizens were demanding transparency from officers, and JPD's decision to keep quiet about the video and circumstances of Lurry's death created a mutually exclusive choice for Esqueda. His first option was to show solidarity with the department by performing the narrative given by his captain, which avoided the implication that JPD officers engaged in misconduct while omitting evidence to the contrary. Esqueda's other option was to break with the department and alert the media, a step that was directly contrary to department wishes. Though logic dictates this situation was not inherently limited to two exclusive choices, JPD's insistence that Tellez's and McCue's actions be ignored in favor of maintaining silence precluded other departmental or procedural responses. Esqueda could not rely on the chain of command; he could not use intra-departmental channels to resolve the situation. When Esqueda blew the whistle, he did so knowing the footage contradicted the narrative of the events the department had built. The department clearly intended to depict Lurry's death as an accidental overdose, thus rhetorically blaming Lurry for his own death and absolving the officers of wrongdoing while ignoring the more damning video evidence.

Yet, Esqueda saw police misconduct in the video. He told CBS News Chicago, "I can't think of anywhere where I was taught CPR or in the academy where you slap a man, call him a bad name, cut off his airway, go for his throat."[44] Esqueda told USA Today that he counted the number of seconds Lurry's airway was restricted.[45] He revealed to CBS News Chicago that pinching someone's nose and opening their mouth is itself police misconduct. He stated, "That's been written in the law for a few years . . . You can't do that anymore to try to get them to cough up any kind of drugs in their system."[46] Police Chief Roechner ordered that Esqueda write a memo corroborating department findings of an accidental overdose death. This order indicates that department leadership knew that the footage troubled their version of events and acted to protect their officers—a key indicator of where their solidarity lies.[47]

The mutually exclusive choice that Esqueda faced implies a larger troubling of police solidarity by linking the concept of trust and mutual action to an identification marker. The solidarity of the police unions rests on officers identifying with their role as public servants, and on protecting those officers from harm. This conception of solidarity is in line with other trade union and social movement notions. However, by punishing whistleblowers, the police union adds an additional feature of solidarity not often found in other unionist structures—silence. Labor unions have historically worked against the silencing of their members and the communities to which they belong. When someone agrees to be silent about wrongdoing, they remove the power of the collective to correct or mitigate that wrongdoing, effectively permitting it to continue. If it were true that loyalty to a group is mutually exclusive, as JFOPSA implies with their ousting of Esqueda, then leaders of groups constituted by an identification with a job or a political position are effectively placed above scrutiny. By labeling whistleblowers as enemies of a cause or group,

group members implicated for misconduct undercut accountability to a greater concerned public, ensuring that a person can be loyal to only one group at a time.

Tension caused by Esqueda's choice to keep or break department orders illustrates a break or divide in understanding of the term *solidarity*. For JPD, solidarity in this situation meant maintaining the department's incomplete account of their officers' wrongdoing. The union, and the department's connotation of the term, is clearly defined through Esqueda's supervisor's response to the evidence. Esqueda does not provide us with a direct definition of solidarity, but we can clearly see his priorities in his ultimate actions. The officers involved in arresting Lurry that night were under Esqueda's supervision. Esqueda told *USA Today*, "I was taught that when people are in our custody, they're in our care, we are the caretakers . . . You don't treat a man that way, you know. He was a human being."[48] Choosing to hold officers accountable rhetorically indicates to the citizenry that police institutions can be trusted to expose and expunge problem officers—a nod to a solidarity with the community over Esqueda's police affiliation.

Esqueda also demonstrated a continued rhetorical connection with JPD, noting that he wanted the office to be a safe place for the community. He told CBS News Chicago journalists, "I want people to know that they can trust the Joliet Police Department and the officers—not be afraid of them . . . If anything, I want the department to be reformed."[49] In contrast, while being questioned in a deposition about Joliet PD's practices, former union President Patrick Cardwell invoked union privilege several times in regard to Lurry's death, telling prosecutors, "I'm going to exercise union privilege . . . I'm going to exercise my stance, as far as when I was union president, and exercise union member, or union privilege on not discussing these matters."[50]

The consequence of choosing to blow the whistle on JPD is encapsulated in Cardwell's letter to Esqueda in October 2021. The letter is short, beginning, "In accordance with the by-laws of the Joliet Police Supervisor's Association, we are serving you notification of our intent to proceed with your expulsion from our Association."[51] Note that the minds of the executive board seem final in this sentence, not as if the matter is up to a vote of the membership. This is a clear narrativization of Esqueda as a part of the out-group. The language demonstrates finality, as if the story of this vote were already decided. The vote in November clearly demonstrates the length to which an organization will stretch to distance itself from a perceived traitor. The constituted group that is Joliet police officers forcibly acted to remove Esqueda from their ranks, and did so almost unanimously, indicating that in order to be in good standing with JFOPSA, a member should vote to remove whistleblowers. Esqueda told *USA Today* in a follow-up interview, "They all wanted me charged, they all want me gone, and by doing this, it's self-gratification for them."[52]

Removing Esqueda from the union makes little sense unless JFOP-SA's motivation is specifically to punish Esqueda for breaking with the department line. Esqueda contacted his supervisor, explained his concerns, and acted with an interest to public safety: ostensibly everything the public expects from a police officer. The irritant for JFOPSA must therefore be the betrayal of other officers to the public. Furthermore, JFOPSA leadership has refused to comment on the union's actions, reasons, or evidence for the vote—even in sworn depositions in other investigations—citing union privilege as a kind of Fifth Amendment protection.

JFOPSA presidents who handled Esqueda's case appeared not to be certain of the grounds on which they based their expulsion, though all agree it was not exclusively Esqueda's whistleblowing. Bear in mind that if the decision to expel Esqueda was based on unrelated misconduct, then the timing of his expulsion vote was only further suspect, as more than a year had passed since Esqueda was in a position to engage with the public in the capacity of a police officer. There are some important rhetorical signals in the uncertainty around Esqueda's expulsion: Whistleblowers and police do not share narratives and should not be constitutively linked together. Whistleblowing is antithetical to the solidarity required to maintain police unions. Because Esqueda's sense of ethics encouraged him to act in favor of transparency, he could not continue to identify with JFOPSA, who demonstrated that their ideological bent is toward protection at the direct expense of transparency with the community.

The Thin Blue Line: Conclusions from Joliet

Whether Esqueda was treated fairly by his workplace and his union depends on the affiliations of who you ask. Joliet police officers have reported that Esqueda was actually removed for a failure to supervise his charges in an unrelated incident. Esqueda's lawyer and Lurry's family seem to think that the department's discipline was retaliatory and an unfair labor practice. No matter who is right, I contend that trust in the Joliet

Police Department has been gravely injured from within and without. Esqueda's view on the matter remained unwavering: "After everything that's happened, do I really want to be associated with them?"[53]

Lurry's death and Esqueda's whistleblowing may not seem note-worthy to someone who knows the complicated position police hold in the US. However, there are two conclusions that merit mentioning as nuances to the rhetoric of state apparatuses, and to the mitigating rhetoric of whistleblowing on social movements and state actors. First, to return to Althusser's conceptualization of repressive state apparatuses, Esqueda's whistleblowing illuminates a peculiar complication: The police are also an ideological state apparatus. From the standpoint of JPD, whistleblowing destroys public trust in the institution of policing, a problem the department cannot fix with overt violence. JPD's standing in the community hinges upon an ideological belief that police are there to help—that police will treat everyone with dignity and will act to save someone, regardless of their guilt. In order to uphold that ideology, the police must maintain a unified image of justice, due process, and compassion. If even one person cracks that image, they must be removed from a position to avoid further harm. Just like a religious organization (Althusser's exemplar of an ISA) might cut out members who question their teachings, the police must remove officers who question the decisions of the state.

In a keen irony, it should be noted that the ideology of the police in Joliet would protect the officers who insulted a dying man before protecting the officer disturbed by that breach of dignity. For some officers in Joliet, their jobs, and the identities they carry with them to those jobs, now come with a new unspoken rule: Misconduct remains internal. Esqueda's treatment by the department and the union will surely make the next officer who spots potential misconduct pause before they report on their fellows.

Second, JFOPSA co-opts solidarity from unionism and other social movements to further protect its members from scrutiny or questioning. The drive for self-preservation further erodes police narratives of solidarity with the communities where they enforce laws. The same could be true for other organizations who choose to remove rather than protect whistleblowers. Unless the constituted group who identifies with the narratives of a social movement are provided the freedom to question the structure, beliefs, and narratives, then social movements become performative traps in which social expectation forces particular behavior. Further, the very act of stifling a whistleblower rhetorically empowers repressive state apparatuses to erode the voice of anyone who would stand in-between.[54] To deny members the ability to question the institution is to make constitutively and narratively defined ideology more important than the actual members of a defined body. Whistleblowers are necessary to the health and transparency of a movement, especially if the state is as entangled with that movement as Joliet is with its police. In short, as distrust of police institutions grows, and as police unions continue to protect some officers and expel others, dilemmas like Esqueda's may be normalized. Police recruits, officers, and leadership may be expected to know where their loyalty lies, and there is no certainty that their solidarity would be to their communities over their colleagues. And without action to ensure that misconduct is addressed and duly punished, the secrecy, and implied threat of retaliation, may keep some officers protecting and serving only their own interests.

Notes

1. Daphne Duret, "Whistleblower Featured in *USA Today* 'Behind the Blue Wall' Series Ousted from Police Union," *USA Today*, November 12, 2021.

2. Duret, "Whistleblower Featured."

3. NBC 5 Chicago, "Family of Man Who Died in Custody Applauds Illinois AG's Investigation into Joliet Police Practices," NBC 5 Chicago, September 2, 2021.

4. NBC 5 Chicago, "Family of Man."

5. NBC 5 Chicago, "Family of Man."

6. NBC 5 Chicago, "Family of Man."

7. Jacques Rancière, *Dis-agreement: Politics and Philosophy*, trans. Julie Rose (Minneapolis: Minnesota University Press, 1999).

8. Raymie E. McKerrow, "Critical Rhetoric: Theory and Praxis," *Communication Monographs* 56 (1989): 91–111.

9. Ralph H. Turner and Lewis Killian, *Collective Behavior* (Englewood Cliffs, NJ: Prentice-Hall, 1987).

10. Turner and Killian, *Collective Behavior*.

11. Lewis Killian, "Social Movement," Brittanica.com, updated September 1, 2022.

12. AFL-CIO, "Know Your Workplace Rights," aflcio.org.

13. "A Strong Labor Movement Is Critical for Civil Rights—Testimony of Wade Henderson," The Leadership Conference on Civil and Human Rights, March 10, 2009.

14. Chantal Mouffe, "Deliberative Democracy or Agonistic Pluralism?," *Social Research* 66, no. 3 (1999): 745–758.

15. Émile Durkheim, *The Division of Labor in Society* (New York: Free Press, 1933).

16. Lawrence Wilde, "The Concept of Solidarity: Emerging from the Theoretical Shadows?," *British Journal of Politics and International Relations* 9, no. 1 (2007): 176.

17. Maurice Charland, "Constitutive Rhetoric: The Case of the *Peuple Québécois*," *Quarterly Journal of Speech* 73, no. 2 (1987): 133–150.

18. Charland, "Constitutive Rhetoric."

19. Charland, "Constitutive Rhetoric."

20. Charland, "Constitutive Rhetoric."

21. Louis Althusser, "Ideology, and Ideological State Apparatuses (Notes Towards an Investigation)," in *Lenin and Philosophy and Other Essays* (New York: Verso, 1970).

22. Althusser, "Ideology."

23. Seth Stoughton, "Law Enforcement's 'Warrior' Problem,'" *Harvard Law Review* 128 (April 2015): 225–234.

24. Richard Fairburn, "Cooper's Colors: A Simple System for Situational Awareness," Police1.com, July 2017.

25. Ria Modak, "Police Unions Are Anti-Labor," *Harvard Political Review*, August 2020.

26. Charland, "Constitutive Rhetoric."

27. Rich Morin, Kim Parker, Renee Stepler, and Andrew Mercer, "Police Views, Public Views," Pew Research Center, January 2017.

28. Judith Butler, "Performative Acts and Gender Constitution: An Essay in Phenomenology and Feminist Theory," in *Performing Feminisms: Feminist Critical Theory and Theatre*, ed. Sue-Ellen Case (Baltimore: Johns Hopkins University Press, 1990).

29. Charland, "Constitutive Rhetoric."

30. Duret, "Whistleblower Featured."

31. Dave Savini, "Sgt. Javier Esqueda, Joliet Police Sergeant Who Blew Whistle on Eric Lurry's Death in Custody, Talks About Retaliation He Says He's Faced," CBS News Chicago, July 19, 2022.

32. Daphne Duret, Brett Murphy, and Gina Barton, "Officer Exposed Death, Now Faces Prison Time; He Breached Police Code of Silence, Is Now Paying Price," *USA Today*, September 8, 2021.

33. Duret, Murphy, and Barton, "Officer Exposed Death."

34. Joshua Guitar and Alan Chu, "Racing to (Dis)Own Whistleblowers and Protests: Theorizing *Amongness* in the Shared Rhetorical Spaces of Democratic Agency," chapter 1 in the present volume, 2.

35. Duret, Murphy, and Barton, "Officer Exposed Death."

36. Ascha Lee, "Protesters Demand Investigation into Death of Man Who Overdosed While in Joliet Police Custody," WBBM Newsradio Chicago, September 18, 2021.

37. John Ferak, "Joliet Police Supervisors: Sgt. Esqueda Faces Expulsion," *Patch*, October 20, 2021, https://patch.com/illinois/joliet/esqueda-faces-expulsion-joliet-police-supervisors-union.

38. CBS Chicago, "Joliet Police Sergeant Who Alleged Police Misconduct in Death of Eric Lurry Has Been Arrested," CBSNews.com, October 21, 2020.

39. Duret, "Whistleblower Featured."

40. Duret, "Whistleblower Featured."

41. John Ferak, "Joliet Police Whistleblower Charged with Misconduct in Lurry Case," *Patch*, October 20, 2021, https://patch.com/illinois/joliet/joliet-police-whistleblower-charged-misconduct-lurry-case.

42. Duret, "Whistleblower Featured."

43. Duret, "Whistleblower Featured."

44. CBS Chicago, "Joliet Police."

45. Duret, Murphy, and Barton, "Officer Exposed Death."

46. CBS Chicago, "Joliet Police."

47. Savini, "Sgt. Javier Esqueda."

48. "Illinois AG Launches Investigation into Joliet Police Department; Sergeant Who Exposed Circumstances of Eric Lurry's Death in Custody Has High Hopes," CBS Chicago, September 8, 2021.

49. "Illinois AG Launches Investigation."

50. John Ferak, "Sgt. Cardwell Must Pay $500, Redo Deposition in Dave Jackson's Suit," *Patch*, March 13, 2022, https://patch.com/illinois/joliet/sgt-cardwell-must-pay-500-redo-deposition-dave-jacksons-suit.

51. Ferak, "Joliet Police Supervisors."

52. Duret, "Whistleblower Featured."

53. Duret, "Whistleblower Featured."

54. Guitar and Chu, "Racing to (Dis)Own."

9

Should Political Appointees Have Whistleblower Protection?

The Case of Kevin Chmielewski

CHRYS EGAN AND JOHN PATRICK MURPHY

Kevin Chmielewski (pronounced "shim-uh-less-ski") was born and raised on the quiet, scenic Eastern Shore of Maryland and dreamed of a professional career in Washington, DC, politics. Despite establishing a promising trajectory in pursuit of this goal, an unanticipated act of whistleblowing cost him his career, reputation, identity, and financial stability.[1] He paid an extremely high price for following his conscience and directions from President Donald Trump. Although Chmielewski suffered a fate common to whistleblowers, his case is nonetheless unique. According to him, he was not aware of what a "whistleblower" was until he was labeled as one, and he never envisioned his actions as whistleblowing. Rather, he maintains that he simply completed the responsibilities given to him by the Trump administration.[2] His story illustrates the need for increased attention to whistleblower protections and free speech in the political sphere. More directly, his case raises the question of whether political appointees should receive whistleblower protections.

In 2017, Chmielewski was appointed by Trump to the Environmental Protection Agency (EPA) as the Director of Scheduling and Advance. He claims he was directed by Trump to share any useful information about controversial EPA Director Scott Pruitt, whom Trump also appointed.[3] By 2018, Chmielewski shared evidence about Pruitt's alleged abuse of office, including gross overspending on travel and other items, creating business opportunities for his family members, misusing security detail, unauthorized pay raises, and more.[4]

An unknown source publicly outed Chmielewski as a "whistleblower" to Congress and the media. As a result, Chmielewski was asked to testify on Capitol Hill, which ultimately led to fourteen federal investigations into Pruitt's ethical and financial practices.[5] Pruitt was offered the choice to either resign without investigation, or to face potential criminal charges and termination. Unsurprisingly, Pruitt resigned. Although there was some media coverage of Pruitt and his alleged wrongdoings, he left the EPA relatively unscathed, without any legal charges, continuing to hold his law license, and prospering as an environmental consultant for international coal sales. In fact, Pruitt believes his professional reputation was strong enough that he ran for US Senate in his home state of Oklahoma but lost in the 2022 Republican primary election by a wide margin.[6]

However, Chmielewski's experience at the EPA and subsequent years could not be more different than Pruitt's in terms of reputation and consequences. As an EPA staffer, Chmielewski was invested in the work and felt concern about both the information the EPA was receiving and Pruitt's apparent disregard for environmental data.[7] In addition, according to Chmielewski, multiple EPA staffers noted Pruitt's habitual overspending on travel and attempts to use his authority toward his and his family's gain. Chmielewski states he shared some concerns directly to Vice President Mike Pence, Pence's chief of staff and deputy chief of staff, and high-ranking Trump officials about Pruitt's activities, as he had been directed by the Trump administration. Shortly after, Chmielewski was outed as a source, yet he does not know who shared his name or why.[8] Even more dramatically, Chmielewski was removed from the EPA grounds by an armed guard, instantly denied access to his work files, blackballed by all his DC connections, and unable to continue working in DC politics. His entire life changed overnight. Chmielewski moved back to Maryland's Eastern Shore and reported, "I live paycheck to paycheck."[9] While subsequent government investigations confirmed most of Chmielewski's whistleblowing allegations, he has been unable to recover any financial remuneration from the government, or receive reinstatement as a federal employee because he was a political appointee.

Whistleblowing as Rhetoric

At its core, this book examines the complexities of whistleblowing, meaning-making, and democratic tensions.[10] Chmielewski recalls hearing himself referred to as a "whistleblower" and wondering what that meant. The National Whistleblower Center states: "On the simplest level, a whistleblower is someone who reports waste, fraud, abuse, corruption, or dangers to public health and safety to someone who is in the position to rectify the wrongdoing. A whistleblower typically works inside of the organization where the wrongdoing is taking place."[11] This general definition certainly applies to Chmielewski, who admits, "I had no idea really what a whistleblower was, what their rights were, when all this stuff was happening. It is still weird to say I am a whistleblower. It feels like it is a dirty word."[12]

However, legal considerations tend to be far more complex. One gray legal area concerns whistleblowers who are political appointees. Chmielewski states he was appointed by Trump to the EPA with the understanding that he was to inform the administration about another one of Trump's appointees—Pruitt. Chmielewski contends that Trump administration officials told him they had misgivings about Pruitt's conduct. While the Whistleblower Protection Act of 1989 and the Whistleblower Protection Enhancement Act of 2012 are designed to protect federal employees who report wrongdoing, Chmielewski discovered that as a "political appointee," these whistleblower protections did not cover him in the same way as other employees.

We argue that Chmielewski's story exposes the practice of politics in Washington, DC: People are supposed to do the right thing when they serve in important positions, but the system, especially for political appointees, is stacked against them, and the cost is high to challenge it. There has been limited media coverage about the retaliation against Chmielewski and, therefore, there has been little public outcry about the injustice. We use this chapter to inspire interest in Chmielewski's unique case as a whistleblower, and to further explore how a post-hoc or forensic examination of past actions can affect the rhetorical positioning of a personal narrative.

We explore this case study on whistleblowing costs and protections within the context of a universal human and civil right to freedom of speech. We use the evolution of whistleblowing laws in the US, where this case occurred; relevant media records on Chmielewski, Pruitt, and Trump; and an in-person interview conducted with Chmielewski on November 15, 2021. A challenge of conducting a rhetorical analysis of Chmielewski's public whistleblowing rhetoric is that he never intended his information to be public, therefore, there is limited documentation on what Chmielewski actually said about Pruitt and the EPA to the Trump administration. Yet, because someone unknown to Chmielewski shared his EPA concerns to the media and Congress, the case garnered some public attention and documentation.

While there are no publicly available transcripts of these congressional meetings, we have enough consequent public discourse to analyze. For instance, we have an April 12, 2018, letter to Trump and the letter to Pruitt authored by Rep. Elijah E. Cummings (D-MD), Rep. Gerald E. Connolly (D-VA), Rep. Donald S. Beyer Jr. (D-VA), Senator Tom Carper (D-DE), and Senator Sheldon Whitehouse (D-RI).[13] The letters share a few statements about what Chmielewski reportedly said in these meetings. The letter to Trump states, "While Mr. Chmielewski described himself as a lifelong Republican and a strong supporter of yours and the Vice President, he painted an extremely troubling picture of wasteful spending, unethical behavior, and improper retaliation against EPA staff on the part of EPA Administrator Scott Pruitt."[14] That letter also states: "Mr. Chmielewski said to us when explaining his decision to speak out against Administrator Pruitt that, regardless of political party, 'right is right, and wrong is wrong.' "[15] With attention to freedom of speech as a democratic right, we explore these public letters, media statements from Chmielewski, and our personal interview with Chmielewski through three rhetorical concepts: deontic logic, epideictic rhetoric, and forensic rhetoric.

We argue that Chmielewski's whistleblowing rhetoric demonstrates the deontic view, where whistleblowing is a *duty* related to the ordinary expectations of people in a legitimate organization.[16] According to this view, ethical people will feel like they should report the wrongdoing. Chmielewski explicitly shares this sentiment as quoted in the letter to Trump from the congressional meeting: "Right is right, and wrong is wrong." Chmielewski declares the moral situation as being plain and simple. In Chmielewski's case, his deontic view is that he did what any decent person should do in the same situation—share concerning information about a supervisor's mismanagement of the agency, funds, and public trust.

Where the rhetorical analysis gets more interesting is in the counterbalance of forensic and epideictic rhetoric. Whistleblowing generally is theorized as a form of forensic rhetoric or communication related to legal or civic issues. Considering whistleblowing as forensic is a logical designation because the revealed content likely has legal or civic impact, and certainly the act of whistleblowing itself is debated within a legal or civic context. In Chmielewski's case, the forensic argument is baked into the unusual circumstance: He was serving as a political appointee of the president, reporting information about another political appointee—within and about a federal agency—that ultimately was shared in congressional meetings and letters. The conceit could be entirely forensic.

However, Chmielewski's ultimate uniqueness may be as an epideictic whistleblower. Epideictic rhetoric is public oratory of praise or blame seen in a new light.[17] While epideictic rhetoric is often understood in terms of eulogies and other forms of ceremony, Chmielewski's case of compelled whistleblowing informs a series of important questions: Who was on display? (Chmielewski); By whom? (the Trump administration); For what purpose? (seemingly, Chmielewski was put on display as a whistleblower by the Trump administration as a cautionary tale to others in DC not to be publicly identified as whistleblowers). As a political appointee, Chmielewski occupies the precarious position as a politically appointed whistleblower, a compelled subject of epideictic oration, who then is publicly blamed by Trump for fulfilling his role as directed. Further, this rhetorical view illustrates that the problem lies not with the whistleblower, but with flaws in the organizational culture, in this case, with the EPA, the Trump administration, whistleblower protection, and the federal government writ large.

How Kevin Chmielewski Became an Unintentional Whistleblower

In our personal interview with Chmielewski on November 15, 2021, he shares colorful stories of how he grew up in the Ocean City, Maryland, resort area. He was raised by his single mother who made ends meet by working as a bartender in this beach town that swells to over three hundred thousand visitors during the summer from eight thousand permanent residents year-round. While his mother worked hard to keep the household financially stable, Chmielewski found life at the beach to be fun, including opportunities for youthful trouble. He spent his free time skateboarding and surfing in his teen years, plus developing friends and mentors who saw his bright potential. One mentor was a police officer, and former Marine and Secret Service employee who befriended Chmielewski to help him more than once with problems he found himself in. Chmielewski describes himself as an average or below average student who did not aspire to attend college. However, among Chmielewski's strengths is that he is instantly warm, generous with his time and talents, intelligent, and palpably enthusiastic.[18]

Chmielewski pursued his interests to help his community by entering public service. After graduating high school in 1998, he joined the Coast Guard and the Merchant Marines. He began working in politics for the Republican Party in 2003, doing unglamorous behind-the-scenes logistical campaign work for Rick Perry, George W. Bush, Dick Cheney, John McCain, and Mitt Romney, ensuring that such work unfolded smoothly.[19] He assisted with campaign planning, security, and general support of the candidates and their campaigns. Likely, the name Kevin Chmielewski would have remained unknown to most people, as a man who helped things happen in the background. That is, until Donald Trump drew attention to him.

The first media record and public event connecting Chmielewski to Trump was on April 20, 2016. During Trump's 2016 campaign for the presidency, Chmielewski arranged for Trump to visit the small town of Berlin, Maryland, to speak at Stephen Decatur High School, Chmielewski's alma mater. Among his accomplishments in arranging this visit, Chmielewski somehow convinced Trump, his security detail, and the FAA to allow Trump's personal Boeing 757 airplane to land at the diminutive Salisbury-Ocean City Regional Airport. This airport is so small that it only has two gates and a much shorter runway than is commonly used by such a large jet. In addition, Maryland's Eastern Shore is not a campaign stop that other presidential candidates had made before, but Chmielewski was able to convince Trump to land there and travel thirty minutes by car with police escort to speak to attendees at this area high school, which was packed with cheering supporters. This story illustrates Chmielewski's ability to impress Trump by managing difficult logistics and getting tasks accomplished.

In the *Delmarva Now* local media event photo of the Stephen Decatur High School rally, a younger, more naïve version of Chmielewski stands at the podium next to and looking at Trump, who is speaking to a large crowd. In the twenty-minute *Delmarva Now* video recording of the event, at the 12:25 mark, Trump publicly refers to Chmielewski in his remarks.

> You know one of my men—a great—went to this school. Kevin! Where's Kevin? Where is Kevin? He is the star. Get Kevin in here. Kevin. Watch this. Kevin, Kevin, Kevin . . . [Trump gets the crowd to chant Kevin's name over and over.] We gotta get him. Get up here. Get up here Kevin. [Chmielewski appears on stage at the 12:50 mark, with Trump putting his hand on Chmielewski's shoulder.] I don't know what they produce at this school, but this guy's a champ. He's tough as hell. Whenever there's a problem, he's not supposed to, he runs right in like full blast, runs in. He is a wild man. Is everybody like that at this place? Say hello Kevin.

Chmielewski instantly backs away from the microphone that Trump points at him, then hesitantly adds: "Thank you. Thank you, guys." Trump concludes his remarks about Chmielewski: "He is a great speaker too. He is a great speaker. He is great. He has been with me right from the beginning. He is tough as hell and he's great and he has energy, you know. He's not a low energy person. You understand that right? He's got a lot of energy. Great guy." This public, high praise from Trump in 2016 is important to remember in contrast to Trump's silence in 2018 as armed guards forcibly escorted Chmielewski from the EPA, which ended his career in DC.[20]

During Trump's 2016 presidential campaign, Chmielewski became a personal assistant and a "senior advance," managing logistics needed in any situation. Having demonstrated his value to Trump, upon election in 2016, Trump appointed Chmielewski to a staff position with Homeland Security, which was Chmielewski's first-choice assignment because of his interest in law enforcement. However, in May 2017, Trump changed Chmielewski's appointment to the Environmental Protection Agency, where he remained until forced to leave on March 18, 2018. Chmielewski was pleased to work at Homeland Security and would have stayed there, but he was loyal to Trump and willing to serve at the EPA since Trump said he needed him there to watch his fellow appointee, EPA Director Scott Pruitt. Pruitt served as EPA director from February 2017 until he resigned on July 5, 2018. Chmielewski first served as EPA Director of Scheduling and Advance, and then as Deputy Chief of Staff of Operations.[21]

Chmielewski claims he was asked to be Trump's watchdog on Pruitt, whose troubled reputation already created concern.[22] Pruitt was a "knucklehead," Chmielewski remembers Trump telling him. "He's doing a lot of stuff we don't agree with," a White House official told him. "We need one of our guys to rein him in."[23] Although whistleblowers tend to be framed within a lens of forensic rhetoric, these commands from Trump position Chmielewski as an epideictic rhetor as he is asked to voice what is already known of Pruitt's character. Since Chmielewski had no particular educational training or career background in environmental protection, he believes his appointment to this role relates to his demonstrated value to Trump during the campaign and his established loyalty to Trump. He worked hard, long hours in this job, filled with many meetings, reports, and travel.[24]

In a short time frame, Chmielewski shared internal information directly to senior officials in the Trump administration about Pruitt's questionable activities, such as his misuse of funds, unethical conflicts of interest and cronyism, and improper use of federal employees for personal business, to name a few issues. Soon thereafter and unbeknownst to Chmielewski, someone leaked his name as a whistleblower to both Congress and the media.[25] Chmielewski is unsure who leaked his activities, but he feels it was politically motivated to prevent potential damage to the administration's reputation.[26] Further, he believes that sharing his name was done in violation of whistleblower policies that should have protected his good faith efforts requested by the Trump administration, but that instead made him an instant target. As a result, Chmielewski met with elected officials on Capitol Hill, leading to multiple federal investigations into Pruitt's ethical and financial practices.[27] The investigation charges include:

> receiving a lucrative deal on a condominium rental from the wife of an energy lobbyist, ordering government employees to do private work for him, granting an unauthorized pay raise to one of his employees, ordering an expensive soundproof box, arranging for needlessly expensive travel for himself on the taxpayers' dime, meeting with energy executives regularly since the start of his tenure and punishing employees who attempted to blow the whistle on his controversial activities, allegedly attempted to help his wife open up a Chick-fil-A franchise.[28]

During his tenure at the EPA, Pruitt is best known for his tactics to dismantle sustainability efforts initiated by President Barack Obama's administration to combat "climate change," a phrase that EPA staffers were not allowed to say under Pruitt. Pruitt made no attempt to disguise his overwhelming support of industry interests to undo regulations considered too high a cost to their businesses.[29] He also is known for committing over a dozen possible ethical violations during his short EPA service. These issues and others led to Pruitt either having to face inquiry into these allegations or choose an early resignation. On July 5, 2018, Pruitt resigned.[30]

Yet, according to Chmielewski, what is publicly known about Pruitt and the EPA during this time is "just the tip of the iceberg."[31] During interviews, Chmielewski claims he is unable to discuss the details due to national security and ongoing legal battles. Yet, Chmielewski tells us that, as a father and someone who lives in a resort beach area that depends on the ecosystem for its economy, he was alarmed about Pruitt's lack of interest in the environment, health, and safety, and that his conduct created national security concerns.[32]

Pruitt's disregard for rules, odd behavior, overspending, and subversive management of the EPA was publicized in the media at the time, yet surprisingly there was no initial media coverage about retaliation against Chmielewski for blowing the whistle. First, Chmielewski was "dismissed" from the EPA, but he claims even that is questionable since he spent significant time in limbo. He did not resign, although another staff member wrote a resignation letter for Chmielewski and used intense pressure for him to sign and submit it. Chmielewski refused. During this time, he also was not yet terminated. He no longer received a salary, but temporarily maintained his benefits and had not received a termination notice. In this career limbo, he was unable to do any work because he was denied access to the EPA facility, technology, and information.[33] In rhetorical terms, Chmielewski began experiencing the customary outgrowth of parrhesia, where a speaker of uncomfortable truths faces punishment or danger.[34] In DC politics, Chmielewski faced blame, if not explicitly by Trump's administration, then implicitly by blackballing him from Republican circles, essentially silencing his voice.

When the official EPA dismissal claim came, the reason given was that Chmielewski did not file his required political appointee financial disclosure forms during his first thirty days in the Trump administration. The value of these forms is for appointees to show transparency and potential conflicts of interest. Although appointees can request an extension in filing these forms, there is no record of Chmielewski making a request or submitting the forms.

This official EPA dismissal reason is suspicious because Chmielewski did not start working at the EPA until over a year into his initial appointment by Trump, which was after working for Homeland Security, and far past the thirty-day filing deadline. If the thirty-day deadline was so vital, Homeland Security, where Chmielewski worked during his first month as an appointee, should have insisted on receiving the forms then. When Chmielewski was transferred to the EPA, the EPA should have requested a review within the first thirty days. While Chmielewski should have filed these forms in that time frame, it is unlikely this was the reason he was terminated a year later. Chmielewski was terminated on a technicality, while his superiors committed more egregious acts with little repercussion. We argue his termination clearly demonstrates retaliation for whistleblowing.

To his personal and professional detriment, Chmielewski did the right thing. He continues to fight for whistleblower and free speech rights. This is precisely what attracts us to Chmielewski's story: He was an ordinary person who became an unsuspecting victim in a multiyear, ongoing battle with the federal government for being honest about another person's wrongdoing. Chmielewski was simply tasked into compelled whistleblowing and became entangled in extraordinary circumstances.

Chmielewski's whistleblowing rhetoric started at the most basic level, without even knowing what a "whistleblower" was. That he was labeled as a "whistleblower" by an unknown source, thrusting him suddenly in the public eye and out of his career, is perhaps one of the more unique circumstances of his story, and one in which the post-hoc recontextualization of his identity exposes how some whistleblowers come to understand their own actions. He did his best to share, document, and defend his claims, but his ethical action came at an unacceptable cost to his finances, family, and well-being. This deontic view of Chmielewski's case may resonate with readers who hope they too would do the right thing in difficult circumstances. But without stronger whistleblower protections, we can understand the fear, intimidation, and hesitancy that potential whistleblowers feel. If whistleblowers are "vulnerable members of institutions who, motivated by democratic ethics, truthfully expose violations of human rights and abuses of power,"[35] stronger protections are necessary to protect people who speak truth to power.

We contend these protections should be grounded in the freedom of expression. As Foucault explains, parrhesia connotes freedom of speech, where speakers reveal the truth for the sake of revealing the truth.[36] In this case, Chmielewski revealed to the Trump administration all that he knew about potential misconduct by Pruitt at the EPA, perhaps less information to Congress when called to appear, and certainly less to the media and public. In this difficult position as an internal whistleblower appointed by the US president and knowing classified information, Chmielewski felt allegiance to reveal the whole truth to Trump first, being more strategically guarded with others. Yet, in turn, Trump never revealed the whole truth about Chmielewski's appointment by him as an internal whistleblower, instead leaving Chmielewski exposed and discarded. Deontic logic compounds this complexity, creating a unique intersection of ethos and logos regarding who owns what information and with whom it can be shared.

Between a Rock and a Hard Place: Political Appointee Whistleblowers

To offer a safer pathway for potential whistleblowers, Congress passed the 1989 Whistleblower Protection Act (WPA) to "strengthen and improve protection for the rights of federal employees, to prevent reprisals, and to help eliminate wrongdoing within the Government."[37] One advantage of this act was clarifying the whistleblowing process for employees to report workplace concerns without retaliation. The act also specified roles for the Office of Special Counsel and the Merit Systems Protection Board.[38] The aim of the act was to protect federal whistleblowers from retaliatory actions for bringing to light violations of law, regulations, management, funds, or public health and safety.[39]

In 2012, the Whistleblower Protection Enhancement Act (WPEA), signed by President Obama, amended the WPA by strengthening protections for federal employees who blew the whistle on waste, fraud, and abuse. It further attempted to clarify that nondisclosure agreements (NDAs) would not prevent an employee from sharing concerns in these areas. The "enhancements," as the name of the act indicates, were stronger protections against retaliation and clarifying the role of NDAs in the whistleblowing process.[40]

While the WPA and the WPEA, at least on the surface, improved the rights of federal employees as whistleblowers, the acts left certain people uncovered. Nonfederal employees, in public and private industries, need to rely on other avenues like the Occupational Safety and Health Administration (OSHA), where relevant. Labor union employees also receive fewer protections. Protections in individual states vary, as well. As is most relevant to Chmielewski's case, the whistleblower acts of 1989 and 2012 did not specify provisions to support political appointees. If Chmielewski had been hired by the EPA as a staff member, he would have, in theory, been protected by federal whistleblower statutes. Because Chmielewski was appointed by Trump, he did not receive whistleblower protection under existing policies.

Although the details of Chmielewski's story are distinct, his vulnerable situation is also common to many whistleblowers. Readers may be more familiar with high-profile cases like that of Chelsea Manning and Edward Snowden, who shared thousands of classified documents with public sources, believing they were exposing political and military corruption. By contrast, in Chmielewski's case, if he shared any classified documents, he did so only with superiors who had access to that information anyway. Chmielewski contends he did not share any sensitive information with the public, but only, as directed, with members of the Trump administration.

Chmielewski reasonably expected protection and support for doing the task requested of him by the Trump administration, but he learned that like many other whistleblowers, there are troubling gaps in protection. For instance, the Government Accountability Office said in a 2009 report that whistleblower employees do *not* receive enough protection from retaliation by their employers.[41] Further, OSHA documented in 2007 that only 21% of the 1800 whistleblower cases they reviewed had "a favorable outcome" for the whistleblower.[42] This lack of support leaves whistleblowers in a highly vulnerable situation, and likely has a chilling effect—discouraging free speech through fear or threats—on potential whistleblowers who are afraid to speak.

While it is understandable that political appointees may be different in certain aspects of their roles from traditionally hired federal employees, all employees deserve whistleblower and other basic legal protections in a democratic system where officials serve the public and must be accountable to them. However, political appointees are treated differently from civil service employees in several key ways, including typical length of service based on who is in the administration, ethics restrictions during and after employment, and a lack of certain legal protections under the Civil Rights Act of 1965 and Whistleblower Protection Enhancement Act. Unfortunately, existing whistleblower guidelines are unclear, at best, about exceptional circumstances, like political appointees, and how much they must shed their free speech and civil rights upon appointment.

Chmielewski's personal and legal argument is that, regardless of *how* he was offered the position at the EPA, he documented compelling evidence of serious infractions by his supervisor that he reported to other superiors. Ideally, those superiors should have immediately addressed Pruitt's conduct and protected Chmielewski from retaliation. A democratic system should be designed to uphold ethical action and freedom of speech. As the Supreme Court noted in *Tinker v. Des Moines*, citizens do not "shed their constitutional rights to freedom of speech or expression" when entering an institution.[43] While there are certain time, place, and manner restrictions, and privacy agreements, those must not infringe on a citizen's right to report potential illegal or dangerous action.

To give context to the need for stronger whistleblower protection acts, consider that President Ronald Reagan's term in 1981 made him the first president to take office after whistleblowing is formally mentioned in US legal code with the Civil Service Reform Act of 1978. Since then, contemporary presidential stances on government whistleblowers have ranged from insensitive to hostile. The tension against government whistleblowers grew in the George W. Bush administration after 9/11, where Homeland Security measures took on a new fervor of chilling effect on free speech and retaliation against dissent under the USA Patriot Act of 2001, which enhanced surveillance and expanded the list of crimes that could be classified as terrorist activities.[44] It is important to note that both Democrat and Republican presidents have persecuted whistleblowers over the past forty years.

This modern presidential attitude toward whistleblowers began with Reagan and continues through the modern presidency. "In essence, the Reagan administration significantly narrowed the scope of government whistleblowing to insulate the State, rather than expose it."[45] The strategy was to keep government whistleblowers internal rather than public by requiring nondisclosure agreements, reclassifying previously declassified information, and shaving away protections in the Civil Service Reform Act. During Reagan's two terms, of the thousands of whistleblowers' appeals, only four cases were decided in favor of the whistleblower.[46] This White House stance of confining whistleblower speech away from the public sphere continues.

Consider the whistleblower stances of Obama and Trump. It is noteworthy that since 1917, eight of the thirteen people charged with treason under the Espionage Act were whistleblowers during Obama's terms, including Manning and Snowden.[47] "President Obama, a constitutional-law scholar, weaponized the Espionage Act against whistleblowers like no administration before" so that "sharing secret information leaves a whistleblower vulnerable to being charged under the Espionage Act of 1917."[48] The Espionage Act was designed to protect the US from inappropriate sharing of information related to defense or the military, which might apply to Manning and Snowden but certainly not to Chmielewski, who uncovered financial fraud and abuse of office that he did not share publicly until called to do so by Congress.

Heightening this rhetoric of treason, Trump disavowed all whistleblowers if they did not conform to his agenda, going so far as demanding that he know the identity of the anonymous whistleblowers who triggered his first impeachment. "The president and his defenders consistently conflate the definitions of whistleblowing and spying, clouding the difference between shedding light on wrongdoing and betraying the country."[49] As with Obama, Trump's association of whistleblowing as treasonous should not apply to the types of offenses that Chmielewski privately documented against Pruitt. We view modern presidential stances on whistleblowing as a free speech–chilling effect by using fear of the Espionage Act as a broad brush to conflate legitimate whistleblowing with spying and treason. While sharing some forms of military and security information could be legally equivalent to spying or treason, more common examples of whistleblowing content relate to individual fraud, corruption, discrimination, and harassment, which would tend to be outside the scope of treason.

Another limitation in understanding and utilizing whistleblower information is the lack of context often provided by the government, industry, or media reporting the story. "In creating charges against whistleblower-leakers, Presidents Obama and Trump seem to be working to separate the whistleblowers from the context of their complaints."[50] This artificial separation of the person from the circumstances and messages runs counter to the entire value of whistleblowing: exposing the truth for the sake of informing a democratic public. In a democratic society, the validity of the message should protect the messenger.

Individual whistleblowers must be considered within their situational contexts. All are operating in a system that too often fails to protect whistleblowers, especially those with access to classified and sensitive information that could cause public embarrassment and criticism for the US from its citizens and the rest of the world. For example, in Manning's case, she ostensibly was not protected because she used WikiLeaks as her public outlet. For Snowden, he was not protected due to his status as an NSA subcontractor, as opposed to being an NSA employee. In Chmielewski's case, he was not protected because he was a political appointee. For each of these whistleblowers, the focus was on the individual and the technicalities to deny protection, rather than on the search for truth and correction of wrongdoing.

Whistleblowing keeps all of us safer, not just in the US, but globally. The Organisation for Economic Co-operation and Development (OECD), of which the US and thirty-seven other nations are members, states emphatically the essential value of whistleblowing worldwide:

> Encouraging employees to report wrongdoing and to protect them when they do, is essential for corruption prevention in both the public and private sectors. Employees are usually the first to recognise wrongdoing in the workplace. Empowering them to speak up without fear of reprisal can help authorities both detect and deter violations. In the public sector, protecting whistleblowers can make it easier to detect passive bribery, the misuse of public funds, waste, fraud and other forms of corruption. In the private sector, it helps authorities identify cases of active bribery and other corrupt acts committed by companies, and also helps businesses prevent and detect bribery in commercial transactions. Whistleblower protection is essential to safeguard the public interest and to promote a culture of public accountability and integrity.[51]

As a result, the OECD advocates for international standards on whistleblower protection, guidance on whistleblower rights, national data on whistleblower protection, and protected reporting systems free of retaliation. In an increasingly globalized and interconnected world, international best practices for whistleblower rights would shine the light of public scrutiny on national practices and offer the most protection for individuals willing to report wrongdoing.

Current Status of Chmielewski and Whistleblowing Acts

Chmielewski continues to fight against the dichotomy between political practice and public service as he pursues his rights to compensation and whistleblowing status in federal court, with the help of attorneys from the Government Accountability Project. Further, he works toward whistleblower protections that include political appointees, testifying to Congress about this matter and his experience.[52] His legal case against the federal government in federal court for whistleblower protection and back compensation is ongoing.

Chmielewski saw progress in June 2021 with the proposed Whistleblower Protection Improvement Act (WPIA) and the Periodic Listing Updates to Management (PLUM) Act. The WPIA stated it "would make long overdue reforms to ensure that whistleblowers are protected from retaliation and to provide equitable remedies when whistleblowers do face retaliation." The PLUM Act stated it "would make our government more transparent for the American people by providing timely information about senior government officials who are making decisions that impact the lives of millions."[53]

In July 2021, the US House Committee on Oversight and Reform voted to approve the WPIA and the PLUM Act. Committee chair, New York Rep. Carolyn Maloney (D), shared these strong statements on behalf of the committee:

> Federal whistleblowers provide critical information on government corruption and wrongdoing, including by providing information to Congress. Their disclosures safeguard taxpayer dollars, improve federal programs, and save lives. The Whistleblower Protection Improvement Act would make long overdue reforms to ensure that whistleblowers are protected from retaliation and to provide equitable remedies when whistleblowers do face retaliation. The PLUM Act would make our government more transparent for the American people by providing timely information about senior government officials who are making decisions that impact the lives of millions. This bill also includes legislation to require reports that summarize the demographics of political appointees, which would further enhance transparency and ensure that our senior leaders are diverse and representative of America.[54]

During the time spent writing this chapter, there have been important updates in Chmielewski's case that officially corroborate his allegations and support his whistleblowing efforts. The EPA's Criminal Enforcement Division released a long-awaited report, as identified in a recent letter to

President Biden from the US Office of Special Counsel. It summarized its findings from years of investigations raised by Chmielewski about Pruitt's conduct while he was head of the EPA. This letter substantiated many of Chmielewski and the other whistleblowers' allegations of wrongdoing. This report had not been released until 2022, despite separate reports by the General Accountability Office in 2018 concluding there were spending violations by Pruitt, and another report in 2019 by the EPA's inspector general that concluded Pruitt had spent excessively on travel arrangements.[55] This 2022 development supports and substantiates Chmielewski's case as a political appointee whistleblower who was blackballed, discredited, and silenced for four years, who continued to fight to bring the truth to light and is starting to see that happen. In this report, there were several EPA whistleblower claims substantiated, including excessively spending $123,942 on travel in violation of the Federal Travel Regulation and the EPA's own policies, spending excessively and improperly on security in violation of the Antideficiency Act, a $52,407 soundproof privacy booth, an improper increase of EPA personnel salaries, and endangering public health and safety by directing his protective service detail (PSD) to use emergency lights and sirens while driving at excessive speeds in nonemergency situations, and wrongfully removing a PSD member from his position after he refused to violate the rules.[56]

Samantha Feinstein, International Director at the Government Accountability Project, concluded of Chmielewski and his EPA whistleblower colleagues:

> We cannot forget that the EPA whistleblowers were retaliated against for telling the truth. This vindication comes four years after their initial disclosures in 2018. . . . In fact, they continue to make Kevin Chmielewski's life hell. That is their choice, but it is an ironic one coming from the same agency whose report contains findings of significant wrongdoing, brought to light thanks to the four courageous whistleblowers. . . . Kevin sacrificed his career to restore good government, but the EPA shows no signs of stopping their mission to destroy Kevin for reporting the unequivocal truth.[57]

In May 2022, the Government Accountability Project was able to publicly share that seven of Chmielewski's claims against Truitt and the EPA were substantiated. Some of the original allegations had a lack of conclusion due to accused wrongdoers retiring or resigning.[58] Unfortunately for Chmielewski, these 2022 advancements are too little, too late. According to him, he has yet to receive compensatory renumeration for his efforts. Chmielewski, with the help of the Government Accountability Project and the Justice Department, seeks restitution because the EPA and the Biden administration are unwilling to give Chmielewski his EPA position back due to his status as a political appointee in the previous administration.[59]

Despite this experience, Chmielewski expressed feeling relieved and vindicated that some of these details finally are being made public. Simultaneously, he also feels disappointed that his former supervisor, Pruitt, has paid a small price for his malfeasance while Chmielewski suffered significantly for telling the truth.[60] Chmielewski has been unable to get a federal job since 2018. He had to settle for a position that is outside of his chosen career field. He describes this situation "like a kick in the face," for doing the right thing.[61] He feels he acted as any American citizen should in reporting wrongdoing in a position with the US federal government.

When drawing conclusions on the importance of Kevin Chmielewski as a whistleblower, several rhetorical lenses bring the concepts into sharper focus. First, the deontic view places whistleblowing as a duty of ordinary people in difficult situations, which certainly applies to Chmielewski and ideally to all of us. Second, epideictic rhetoric of public praise or blame connects to Chmielewski in a unique, unfortunate manner as a rare politically appointed whistleblower. He privately shared negative information with his supervisors at their behest, then was publicly outed as a whistleblower, which has a chilling effect on free speech. Third, whistleblowing is often conceptualized as forensic rhetoric around legal and civic issues, while Chmieleski's case is more epideictic as he believed he was doing the right thing in private by providing information to the president to which he was loyal.

The fact that Chmielewski is the first known presidentially appointed whistleblower makes him a singularly unique case in the documented history of whistleblowers. This case illustrates another example of when someone tries to speak the truth from a disempowered position, while repeated attempts are made to obstruct democracy. In the context of this book, Chmielewski's feelings of certainty of his actions and ambiguity—or perhaps uncertainty, of his identity as a whistleblower—illustrate how the meaning-making processes of one's self is consistently in a state of movement. This is worth further inquiry, especially as it is applied to the study of individual whistleblowers and collective protest.

Notes

1. Kevin Chmielewski, personal interview, November 15, 2021.

2. Kevin Chmielewski, personal interview, November 15, 2021.

3. Coral Davenport and Eric Lipton, "Trump Picks Scott Pruitt, Climate Change Denialist, to Lead E.P.A.," *New York Times*, December 7, 2016, https://www.nytimes.com/2016/12/07/us/politics/scott-pruitt-epa-trump.html.

4. Kevin Chmielewski, personal interview, November 15, 2021.

5. Laura Strickler and Adiel Kaplan, "Ex-EPA Chief Scott Pruitt Spent Nearly $124,000 on 'Excessive Airfare,' Agency Says," NBC News, May 16, 2019, https://www.nbcnews.com/politics/politics-news/ex-epa-chief-scott-pruitt-spent-nearly-124-000-excessive-n1006491.

6. Timothy Cama, "Pruitt Loses Okla. Senate Primary; Casten Beats Newman," *E&E Daily*, June 29, 2022.

7. Kevin Chmielewski, personal interview, November 15, 2021.

8. Kevin Chmielewski, personal interview, November 15, 2021.

9. Andy Kroll, "He Helped Bring Down a Top Trump Crony. Now He's Driving for Uber," *Rolling Stone*, October 14, 2021, https://www.rollingstone.com/politics/politics-features/trump-whistleblower-scott-pruitt-epa-justice-1239197/.

10. Joshua Guitar and Alan Chu, "Racing to (Dis)Own Whistleblowers and Protests: Theorizing *Amongness* in the Shared Rhetorical Spaces of Democratic Agency," chapter 1 in the present volume, 1.

11. "What Is a Whistleblower?," National Whistleblower Center, n.d., https://www.whistleblowers.org/what-is-a-whistleblower/.

12. Kroll, "He Helped Bring Down a Top Trump Crony."

13. Committee on Oversight and Accountability, Top Dems Release Detailed New Info from Senior EPA Whistleblower, ["Press Release"] https://oversightdemocrats.house.gov/news/press-releases/top-dems-release-detailed-new-info-from-senior-epa-whistleblower.

14. Committee on Oversight and Accountability, "Press Release."

15. Committee on Oversight and Accountability, "Press Release."

16. Emanuela Ceva and Michele Bocchiola, *Is Whistleblowing a Duty?* (Cambridge: Polity Press, 2018).

17. Aristotle, *The Rhetoric of Aristotle: A Translation* (Cambridge: Cambridge University Press, 1909).

18. Kevin Chmielewski, personal interview, November 15, 2021.

19. Dereck Kravitz and Alex Mierjeski, "Trump Body Man Turned EPA Whistleblower Is Violating Ethics Rules, the Agency Says," *ProPublica*, April 12, 2018, https://www.propublica.org/article/kevin-chmielewski-trump-body-man-turned-epa-whistleblower-is-violating-ethics-rules-the-agency-says.

20. Mitchell Northam, "Decatur Grad Had a Hand in Bringing Trump to Berlin," *Delmarva Now*, April 12, 2016, https://www.delmarvanow.com/story/

news/local/maryland/2016/04/21/decatur-grad-had-hand-bringing-trump-berlin/83331996/.

21. Kravitz and Mierjeski, "Trump Body Man."

22. Kevin Chmielewski, personal interview, November 15, 2021.

23. Kroll, "He Helped Bring Down a Top Trump Crony."

24. Kevin Chmielewski, personal interview, November 15, 2021.

25. Strickler and Kaplan, "Ex-EPA Chief Scott Pruitt."

26. Kevin Chmielewski, personal interview, November 15, 2021.

27. Juliet Eilperin and Brady Dennis, "EPA Watchdog Suggests Agency Recover $124 Pruitt's Trips at the Time," *Washington Post*, May 16, 2019, https://www.washingtonpost.com/climate-environment/2019/05/16/epa-watchdog-suggests-agency-recover-pruitts-excessive-travel-expenses/.

28. Matthew Rosza, "Scott Pruitt Aide Resigns from EPA Amid Chick-fil-A, Trump Mattress Scandals," *Salon*, June 6, 2018, https://www.salon.com/2018/06/06/scott-pruitt-aide-resigns-from-epa-amid-chick-fil-a-trump-mattress-scandal-report/.

29. Brady Dennis and Juliet Eilperin, "How Scott Pruitt Turned the EPA into One of Trump's Most Powerful Tools," *Washington Post*, December 31, 2017, retrieved January 2, 2018, https://www.washingtonpost.com/national/health-science/under-scott-pruitt-a-year-of-tumult-and-transformation-at-epa/2017/12/26/f93d1262-e017-11e7-8679-a9728984779c_story.html.

30. Justin Anderson, "Focus on Scott Pruitt's Scandals Ignores the Biggest of All: Destruction of Environmental Safeguards," *Salon*, May 25, 2018, https://www.salon.com/2018/05/25/focus-on-scott-pruitts-scandals-ignores-the-biggest-of-all-destruction-of-environmental-safeguards/.

31. Kevin Chmielewski, personal interview, November 15, 2021.

32. Kevin Chmielewski, personal interview, November 15, 2021.

33. Kevin Chmielewski, personal interview, November 15, 2021.

34. Michel Foucault, *Discourse and Truth: The Problematization of Parrhesia, University of California at Berkeley, October-November 1983.*

35. Guitar and Chu, "Racing to (Dis)Own Whistleblowers and Protests," 00.

36. Foucault, *Discourse and Truth.*

37. United States Congress, Whistleblower Protection Act of 1989, S 20, https://www.congress.gov/bill/101st-congress/senate-bill/20.

38. United States Congress, Whistleblower Protection Act of 1989.

39. Anderson, "Focus on Scott Pruitt's Scandals."

40. United States Congress, Whistleblower Protection Act of 1989.

41. United States Congress, "GAO: Nation's Whistleblower Laws Inadequately Enforced, Needs Additional Resources," http://democrats-edworkforce.house.gov/media/press-releases/gao-nations-whistleblower-laws-inadequately-enforced-needs-additional-resources. Committee on Education and the Workforce, February 26, 2009, https://edlabor.house.gov/media/press-releases/gao-nations-whistleblower-laws-inadequately-enforced-needs-additional-resources.

42. United States Congress, "GAO: Nation's Whistleblower Laws."

43. *Tinker v. Des Moines Independent Community School Dist.*, 393 U.S. 503, 1969.

44. United States Congress, Uniting and Strengthening America by Providing Appropriate Tools Required to Intercept and Obstruct Terrorism (USA Patriot Act) Act of 2001, Public Law 107-56, October 26, 2021.

45. Joshua Guitar, *Dissent, Discourse, and Democracy: Whistleblowers as Sites of Political Contestation* (Lanham, MD: Lexington Books, 2021).

46. Thomas M. Devine, "The Whistleblower Protection Act of 1989: Foundation for the Modern Law of Employment Dissent," *Administrative Law Review* 51, no. 2 (1999): 531–579.

47. Brittany Gibson, "All the President's Whistleblowers," Prospect, October 18, 2019, https://prospect.org/justice/all-the-presidents-whistleblowers/.

48. Gibson, "All the President's Whistleblowers."

49. Gibson, "All the President's Whistleblowers."

50. Gibson, "All the President's Whistleblowers."

51. Organisation for Economic Co-operation and Development (OECD), "Whistleblower Protection," https://www.oecd.org/gov/ethics/whistleblower-protection.

52. Kevin Chmielewski, personal interview, November 15, 2021.

53. Carolyn B. Maloney, "Oversight Committee Approves Legislation Strengthening Whistleblower Protections and Transparency of Political Appointees," House Oversight Committee, June 29, 2021, https://oversight.house.gov/news/press-releases/oversight-committee-approves-legislation-strengthening-whistleblower-protections.

54. Maloney, "Oversight Committee."

55. Eric Lipton, "Trump E.P.A. Director 'Endangered Public Safety' by Ordering His Drivers to Speed," *New York Times*, March 26, 2022, https://www.nytimes.com/2022/05/26/us/politics/scott-pruitt-epa-report.html.

56. Government Accountability Project, "U.S. Special Counsel Findings Vindicate Government Accountability Project Client Kevin Chmielewski, Whose Whistleblowing Exposed Scott Pruitt's Corruption," ["Press Release"] May 27, 2022, https://whistleblower.org/press/press-release-u-s-special-counsel-findings-vindicate-government-accountability-project-client-kevin-chmielewski-whose-whistleblowing-exposed-scott-pruitts-corruption/.

57. Government Accountability Project, "U.S. Special Counsel Findings."

58. Government Accountability Project, "U.S. Special Counsel Findings."

59. Lipton, "Trump E.P.A. Director."

60. Kevin Chmielewski. Personal Interview, November 15, 2021.

61. Lipton, "Trump E.P.A. Director."

10

Breaking the Blue

Whistleblowing on Those Tasked to Protect and Serve

COLIN H. CAMPBELL

Even as police departments around the US consider reforms after the killing of George Floyd in May 2020, police accountability advocates have expressed concerns that undesirable behaviors will continue unless officers or other influential people within police departments feel confident to report misconduct among their own ranks. Police who conceal or distract from those who engage in unethical and/or illegal behavior of their colleagues is not a novel concept, and neither is the ostracization that whistleblowers, be it from officers or whistleblowers surrounding police, experience after exposing such wrongdoing in the efforts of protecting human rights.

Traditionally, whistleblowers have navigated myriad agencies to hold law enforcement agencies accountable. Human resources departments, the federal government, the National Labor Relations Board (NLRB), the Equal Employment Opportunity Commission (EEOC), state labor boards, and other official entities have been used to mitigate the backlash that whistleblowers could receive in retribution for exposing misconduct.[1] Organizations like police departments make whistleblowing challenging, making accountability less likely. Police officers face a high amount of pressure to resist exposing other officers. For some law enforcement whistleblowers, the cost to force police officers to operate within the law is too high. Whistleblowers are often perceived as threats to the police order and as violators of implicitly understood codes. Whistleblowers who report on fellow police could be displaced from their departments if their colleagues retaliate as a response to feeling betrayed by reporting against their colleagues. Like most whistleblowers, truth-telling officers face various forms of retribution, such as job termination and even death threats. Private citizens who report the police to other authorities could also face repercussions such as harassment or even worse.[2]

Whistleblowing against police malpractice ascended to saliency in the early 1970s when Paramount Pictures released *Serpico*, a biographical crime drama.[3] The film, based on a true story, followed protagonist Frank Serpico's struggle to report police corruption. While Serpico's intentions may have been noble, he soon discovered that he was a target because of what he attempted to expose about other police officers on the force. In cases where art imitates life, whistleblowers regularly find themselves in these real-life circumstances.

This chapter will discuss the rhetorical dynamics of whistleblowers who hold police accountable and experience associated backlash. It will extrapolate the experiences of one private citizen and two former officers: Darnella Frazier, Javier Esqueda, and Austreberto Gonzalez, all of whom exposed police wrongdoing and faced negative consequences for doing so. Their actions, which expose a recurring and overlapping rhetorical tension[4] specific to whistleblowing surrounding police, articulate how the act of bearing witness, regardless of organizational membership, is itself a responsibility to a larger social collective.

Historical Perspectives

Whistleblowing in America has been considered a part of civic responsibility to promote and benefit the public good through augmenting human rights.[5] Benjamin Franklin is recorded as one of the first American whistleblowers in 1773 when he revealed clandestine communication between England and the colonies striving for independence. The royally appointed governor of Massachusetts was caught in a scandal for misleading Parliament to boost the number of troops against a burgeoning militia in American colonies.[6]

During the Civil War era, unchecked war profiteering and venality disrupted Union and Confederate armies. Armies were sold broken equipment, disabled beasts of burden, and spoiled food that resulted in sick and malnourished troops. Congress passed the False Claims Act on March 2, 1863, to counter these unlawful and corrupt activities.[7] Federal courts within competent jurisdictions ruled that complainants called "relators" could sue an accused corrupt contractor for the benefit of the US government.[8] Private citizens could file suits on behalf of the government (called "qui tam" suits) against those who have defrauded the government.[9] It was also decided that private citizens who successfully brought qui tam actions may receive a portion of the government's recovery. Successful plaintiffs were entitled to receive half of the money retrieved by the government. The objective was to uncover the largest plots to defraud the government. Early cases demonstrated an effectiveness at protecting the country's interests financially and otherwise while holding perpetrators accountable. It proved to be a cost-effective way to hold those who stole from the US Department of the Treasury liable for their crimes.[10]

At the same time Congress was codifying what could be described as early whistleblowing policies with government contractors, a new but tenuous relationship was being created between white-dominated authorities and Black communities. Social scientists suggest that this often disparate power dynamic between "law enforcement" entities and vulnerable Black communities leads to social issues related to the policing of Black communities and the whistleblowers who act in ways to protect the marginalized and vulnerable within these communities.[11] The history of this relationship established the tone for continued hegemonic sustention represented by the controlling class upon subaltern groups, in this case descendants of enslaved Africans. This antagonism was fueled by a long history of slave patrols that asserted dominance on Black individuals with little opportunity for abusers to be held accountable.

To understand currently entrenched cultural norms that are antipathetic to whistleblowers whose revelations served members of minority communities, a basic understanding of slave patrols is necessary. Slave patrols started in South Carolina around 1704.[12] Authoritative policing in Southern slave-holding states were grounded in slave patrols.[13] Empowered white volunteers were entrusted to enforce laws related to the lifestyles of the enslaved. They often were charged with tracking down escaped slaves and returning them to their respective slave masters or plantations.[14] The reward for finding these enslaved Black people was higher when the enslaved were accused of retaliation against their masters or engaged in slave uprisings.[15] These patrolmen were also tasked with punishing enslaved people, suppressing potential uprisings, and punishing recalcitrance under the enforcement of plantation rules. Slave patrollers swore an oath: "I [patroller's name], do swear, that I will as searcher for guns, swords, and other weapons among the slaves in my district, faithfully, and as privately as I can, discharge the trust reposed in me as the law directs to the best of my power. So, help me, God."[16]

According to historian Gary Potter, slave patrols served three main functions: "(1) to chase down, apprehend, and return to their owners, runaway slaves; (2) to provide a form of organized terror to deter slave revolts; and (3) to maintain a form of discipline for slave-workers who were subject to summary justice outside the law."[17] Potter suggests that the objectives of these slave patrols that often carried out slave surveillance with impunity were fairly simple: to control the movements and behaviors of enslaved populations.[18] This form of organized policing allowed members of these groups to impose control on Black populations, often without the need to answer to a higher power in cases of misconduct or excessive violence.[19]

Slave patrols were given the authority to impose physical violence and terrorize families to act as shocking deterrents from rebellion or revolt. Patrollers often received financial compensation to control enslaved people's actions, which included forced sexual dominance. This concept of sexual agency over Black men and women to dissuade was pervasive. White men used sexual assault against enslaved men's women partners as a way to embarrass Black men and maintain power against the potential of retaliation.[20] Early slave patrols were oppugnant to Black resistance, establishing an authoritative cultural dynamic for generations.[21] Slave patrols would exist for more than 150 years, extending their presence even after the Civil War and into the Reconstruction era. Sally Hadden contends that there are comparisons between deputized slave patrollers before the Civil War and the extrajudicial stochastic terrorist acts used by vigilantes and groups such as the Ku Klux Klan.[22]

Modern police departments are derived from this reinforced framework initiated by North American slave patrols and their treatment of Black Americans and other groups. Southern police departments started the modernization of this by practicing the same objectives as early patrols.[23] Scholars have traced the legacy of structural racism that started with slave patrols while examining how structures support conventional systems that marginalize members of nonwhite communities.[24] These established systems of power were used as future models of policing. Policing in Southern states that held slaves preserved some of those organizational cultural conventions in nuanced ways that differed from their Northern policing compatriots. Indeed, Southern slave patrols progressed more directly into Southern police departments.[25] Part of the early police's post–Civil War responsibilities was monitoring newly freed slaves. These slaves often returned to plantations or land owned by whites if they were unable to procure land.[26]

Yet, publicly funded police departments were also formed in Northern cities in the 1830s to perform law enforcement with a focus on Black populations.[27] Without delving too deeply into the incremental shifts in policing, the systemic desire to uphold a racial power imbalance was constantly sustained and reinforced over time, at times violating basic human rights to exacerbate subculture group detriment.[28] The first Black Codes were passed in 1865 following the Civil War. These were codes that addressed how Black Americans could work, where they could work, how often they could work, and how much these forced Americans through enslavement should be compensated. These "codes" also dictated where Black people should live and how they could vote in elections. Grievances coming from these communities were rarely addressed, while reporting abuses of power to embolden accountability could be responded to with punishment. It was an extension of slavery without the name.[29]

At the end of the nineteenth century and into the twentieth century, a newer form of slave codes started to take effect as Jim Crow laws, which emphasized segregation that was often separate and unequal. These revised laws taken from the codes restricted Black people from sharing public spaces including libraries, schools, restaurants, or bathrooms. Anyone found breaking these rules could be answered with severe force that was condoned by the power of the authorities.[30] Jim Crow laws stood for decades until the landmark verdict in 1954 *Brown v. Board of Education of Topeka, Kansas.* This ruling clarified that, even if segregated schools are otherwise equal in quality, segregation was declared unconstitutional and a fundamental violation of human rights.[31] In addition, the civil rights movement that galvanized to abolish institutional racial segregation and discrimination followed soon after and into the 1960s.

Yet, systemic racism persisted at the hands of executive power. Richard Nixon, the thirty-seventh US president, focused heavily on the antiwar masses and Black people. In the 1980s, the war on drugs pushed more aggressive police officers and agents into the homes of Black Americans.[32] Then in 1994, President Bill Clinton signed the Violent Crime and Law Enforcement Act. This legislation put an extra one hundred thousand police officers in communities and placed a "three strikes" mandatory life sentence for repeat offenders. This only further augmented police aggression. This surge in policing became concomitant with overpolicing without supporting accountability to follow the increase of patrols in communities. During this era, private prisons and mass incarceration grew exponentially—changing the Black population into a new type of industry that economically benefited a white power structure.[33]

As a result of these race-based policies encouraging a socioeconomic divide between Black and white Americans, inequality spread in more complex ways.[34] Taking these disparities into account, a comparison of traditional policing methods and the push for community policing, or the basic dynamic of the relationship between people and policing, has created an oppositional approach. This dynamic has created mistrust and hostility between racialized groups and the status quo demographic tasked with the challenges of civil oversight. Groups such as Black Lives Matter and the National Coalition on Black Civic Participation have pointed to aggressive policing policies as part of the reason for their ongoing activism.[35] This is an indication that the policing of Black communities has often been strained because of maintained perceptions and deleterious policing policies that risk the safety of marginalized communities. As such, whistleblowing surrounding the police is framed in the context of centuries of patterned behavior intended to protect executive, white institutions of power, regardless of cost.

The following three cases of whistleblowing against illegal police corruption and activities that occurred during the year 2020 explore misdirected authoritative power as inequity that sustains cultural hegemony. The year of Floyd's death sparked "calls for reform" and a "renewed focus to community policing."[36] These three cases also hold in common where whistleblowers exposed allegations or actions of misconduct while facing different levels of condemnation. These cases highlight instances where whistleblowers sought to hold police accountable and were later subject to reprisal or retribution as intrinsic or extrinsic members of analyzed law enforcement members. This research contributes to the literature by studying the challenges and the potential penalties of whistleblowers who expose wrongdoing in police organizations and helps to clarify the lived experiences of whistleblowers who expose the corrupt behavior that exists among police department ranks.

Research Methods

Gramsci's theory of cultural hegemony offers a theoretical approach to analyze the ideological and antipathetic relationship within authoritarian systems, such as police officials' ranks, when whistleblowers report officer duplicity after their interactions when dealing with the public.[37] Gramsci adjusts the position of classical Marxist positivistic history and discusses how disempowered persons can use their agency to initiate social change to protect marginalized populations. Predominantly, Gramsci interrogates the concept of hegemony.[38]

Gramsci describes hegemony as the preeminence of one social class over another.[39] His conceptualization includes political, economic, and social controls exerted by a dominant class through its prevailing objectives of experiencing advantageous societal relationships that can, at times, encourage corrupt behavior.[40] Consequently, Gramsci views rebellion, or behaviors that counter the status quo, as part of a natural progression within a sociopolitical order. He defined the concept as a system of class order in which a "hegemonic class" asserted political leadership over "subaltern classes" by "winning them over."[41] In this, the proletariat had to free itself of its class corporatism to embrace other classes, notably the peasants, in a system of alliances within which it could then genuinely become the leading element in the society.

Gramsci elaborates on hegemonic conceptualization by referencing two areas. First, his conjecture starts with classist structure that observes the interests of groups that occupy a space of dominance over subaltern groups. The dominant class is forced to make concessions that are in line with its corporate interests. Gramsci also discusses hegemony as a "fundamental class."[42] The understanding of this principal class underlies the relations of power situated within the owners or non-owners of production. In a hegemonic system, the subaltern, but fundamental class pushing for systemic change, must force its objective against the dominant class while trying to assimilate to the conditions of other subaltern classes.

Gramsci posits that a hegemonic system possesses a "subaltern" class that is aspiring for state power by challenging the dominant class while conforming itself to the proclivities of the other subaltern classes.[43] This constitutes a predominance set by consent and, consequently, a status of influential legitimacy by other subaltern classes. Within this dynamic, there is a constant struggle for power that Gramsci describes as a process of consent given by a majority of the population controlling the social life of the subaltern group. The subaltern class must push to attain equality by constantly conforming to the interests and endeavors of the upper classes.

While the concept of hegemony can be studied through a multitude of means, I employ critical narrative analysis and combine it with Gramsci's fundamental concepts of puissant dynamics within culture to understand the plight of those maligned by their workplace spaces. To better understand the theoretical grounding connected to whistleblowers' actions, critical narrative analysis (CNA) helps to examine participants' roles in hegemonic frames.[44] It is a vehicle to better understand the narratives of prevailing power disparities at the macro-levels of social, historical, and political contextualization.[45] CNA helps us analyze power relations within, particularly as they expose power discrepancies while adding to our critical awareness.[46] As Souto-Manning elucidates, CNA is especially well suited for examining media narratives.[47]

CNA dismantles, questions, and investigates the ideological groundings that have assumed conventionality over a span of time.[48] This methodology performs an intense evaluation by exploring social theory and rhetorical expression to inspect the interaction of ideologies and power in various discourses. Marshall and Rossman suggest using CNA when describing the meaning of experiences for those who are often marginalized or oppressed while re-creating new personal narratives.[49] In theorizing CNA, Souto-Manning's methodological development builds an important bridge between narrative analysis as a rhetorical method, and also critical discourse analysis (CDA), a prominent postpositivist method.[50] Although rhetoric and postpositivism maintain some ontological conflicts, Souto-Manning recommends that narrative analysis, when used in conjunction with CDA, can illuminate important, critical insights.[51]

Although officially outside of rhetorical studies, CDA boasts a robust history of helping scholars better understand power dynamics. CDA brings social analysis into language studies by targeting "discourse and relationship between discourse and other social elements that include (power relations, ideologies, institutions, social identities, and so forth)."[52] CDA shows how discourses can reinforce systemic organizational hegemony.[53] Analyzing the use of CDA is helpful to contextualize the relationship between whistleblowers and established systems of power because of its ability to reveal how the relationship dynamic further suppresses or decreases voices of those who are in vulnerable positions against authority. It has also been studied that those who are oppressed by the role of systemically controlled rhetoric might not fully process their oppression because the discourse has been ingrained into the organization's culture. This is especially pertinent since whistleblowers often endure consequent antagonistic responses from the prevailing agents and institutions of power. These interrogative processes are uniquely illuminative when paired with rhetorical inquiry.

The use of CNA in this study, as a combination of narrative analysis and CDA, combines discursive details that assemble the accounts of whistleblowing participants' experiences and the influence that their revelations had on their lives. The method situates and interprets lived experiences against cultural and political environments within their respective organizational structures. CNA operates as a guide to help us understand the motivations of whistleblowers discussed in this chapter, the responses they received, and where improvements may be better recognized to support those who speak truth to power to strengthen human and civil rights.

This chapter focuses on three cases relating to whistleblowers in policing. The cases demonstrate whistleblower vulnerabilities and the perils they face despite their intentions of justice. In following the lead of scholars such as Kim[54] and Riessman,[55] once I collected the necessary data from each case, I examined each situation for emergent themes using a combination of narrative analysis and CDA. Like other critical narrative researchers, I analyze texts for thematic structure, plotlines, and sociocultural referencing.[56] There are numerous parts to the stories and each section may possess its own set of implicit narratives categorized by the specific circumstance. Through analysis, it is possible to examine whole experiences represented through the stories. Most descriptions must be reconstructed from the accounts that were reported from each incident. These parts can inform understanding of the whole.

Darnella Frazier: The Unintended Whistleblower

On May 25, 2020, Minneapolis police officers arrested a forty-six-year-old Black man named George Floyd. Floyd was arrested after being suspected of trying to use a counterfeit $20 bill. The main arresting officer, Derek

Chauvin, knelt on Floyd's neck during the arrest for nearly ten minutes, ultimately killing Floyd. Several other officers who were present at the time of the arrest prevented bystanders from intervening. Bystanders and security cameras that recorded video from the fatal arrest needed to be viewed and contextualized to understand with more detail the series of events that led to Floyd's death. Law enforcement officials and legal advocates later determined that the videos demonstrated that officers on that day involved in the commission of Floyd's arrest engaged in a series of actions that violated policies of the Minneapolis Police Department, which turned an otherwise routine detention into a fatal event. Floyd's death was ruled as a homicide due to his suffocating to death under Chauvin's knee.[57] The video that was released through social media sparked outrage around the world.

Darnella Frazier, who was seventeen years old at the time of Floyd's death, has been widely considered a hero for recording the video that led to Chauvin's murder conviction and manslaughter charges. The video ended up being used in court. Frazier, who rarely does interviews, said she recorded the scene en route to get victuals with her younger cousin. Although traditional conceptualizations could preclude Frazier from assuming status as a whistleblower, the reframing of conventional perceptions of whistleblowing can help us better interrogate the necessity of including Frazier's case despite the differences from the other examples in this chapter. Despite not having formal membership in a police organization, Frazier cleanly fits other characteristics of whistleblowing that traditionally include the reporting of an individual from within the offending organization. Yet, if we recognize Frazier's citizenship within a community policed by members of that community, Frazier's membership within a democratic body can still establish the access and influence of a type of insider. As such, Frazier exemplifies Guitar and Chu's[58] conceptions of whistleblowing action, which in turn connects various bodies of literature that interrogate impediments to democratic systems.

Frazier functioned as a whistleblower by reporting the illegal actions of an established system deputized by officials serving as the dominant power structure. Understanding this power dynamic through a Gramscian lens, Frazier became the de facto disruptor of the preeminent fundamental class ideology, which is often associated with the protection of the police while also receiving the benefit of the doubt. Qualified immunity, which protects police from lawsuits when injurious actions or deaths occur during the execution of their jobs, is predicated upon the notion of giving members of law enforcement deference even at the exploitation of the common citizenry. Failed civil suits that challenge the concept of qualified immunity substantiate the notion that police operate in a way that is above what the average citizen can engage.[59]

The family of George Floyd filed a lawsuit against the Minneapolis Police Department and the officers involved in his death. The suit specifically named former Police Officer Derek Chauvin as well as the three other officers who were involved in Floyd's fatal arrest. None of this would have been possible without the deliberate videography of the event from Frazier, which functioned as a representation of a counterhegemonic contingent of the police culture itself—an ethos so corruptive in nature that it prevented other officers from interfering in the arrest even as Floyd's life slowly slipped away. Frazier has since been awarded for her courage as a whistleblower who captured and reported Floyd's last minutes alive. Angela Harrelson, Floyd's aunt, in an interview with CNN, expressed the importance of Frazier's video: "It really doesn't surprise me that much, with police cover-ups, because they've always had done that, especially towards Black and Brown people . . . The sad thing is if it hadn't been for that 17-year-old girl Darnella, it would have been another Black man, who was killed by the police, his own fault, and they would have said, 'Oh, it was drugs, oh it was this.' And we would never have had the story we would have and wouldn't be here today."[60]

Frazier's through-the-lens eyewitnessing and whistleblowing against the Minneapolis police officers did not come without a price, however. She said she had trouble processing her trauma. "I couldn't sleep properly for weeks. I used to shake so bad at night my mom had to rock me to sleep," she said.[61] Frazier faced many questions about why she recorded the video. Some criticized her over why she didn't do more to stop Chauvin from killing Floyd. Comments for and against Frazier played out throughout the media. Frazier discussed the immense pressure she felt, especially because of her age and the awareness of the case in the era of social media. "I don't expect anyone who wasn't placed in my position to understand why and how I feel the way that I do," Frazier wrote on Facebook.[62]

After Floyd's death, Frazier struggled to maintain a normal life. Frazier said reporters would show up at her residence early in the morning. She said she was unable to get a restful night's sleep for weeks. She was ravaged by panic and anxiety attacks whenever she saw a police car. She said she would only get rest after her mother rocked her to sleep. Frazier's divulgences and subsequent anxieties indicate there needs to be protections and encouragement for those who are at risk when reporting police incidents that may be illegal or threatening to vulnerable people.

Frazier was forced to face criticism and questions over her motives as a result of her recording of George Floyd's murder. In the aftermath of mass outrage, protests, and demonstrations over George Floyd's death, Frazier received threatening messages online. Even though Frazier took the video as proof of the realities surrounding police brutality and the concerns felt by thousands across the country, she became the subject of harassment. She still deals with the trauma of what she witnessed and the comments she received afterward.[63]

My analysis indicates that Frazier's disclosures confronted entrenched police policy that tends to protect the activities of those in power. This is further evidenced by the condemnation Frazier faced after her video's release and the threatening environment that she hid from. Using Gramscian principles as a guide, Frazier utilized her agency in alignment with a vulnerable group responding to a misappropriation of power. Because of her antiestablishment stance, which led her to take action, she faced reprisal. This would be easily predicted through Gramsci's analysis of a member of a "subaltern" class challenging the dominant class against accepted authority. Despite Frazier's young age at the time, she exhibited a level of temerity by using her mobile phone to call out injustice and consequently force change.

Javier Esqueda: Blue Wall Whistleblower

In a different scenario from young Frazier, Sgt. Javier Esqueda experienced a more severe form of repudiation from those who objected to his whistleblowing from within an Illinois police department. Sergeant Esqueda was a twenty-seven-year veteran of the Joliet Police Department who was placed on desk duty after being arrested on felony charges related to official misconduct in the summer of 2020. Esqueda blew the whistle on fellow officers who, he alleged, were connected to Eric Lurry's death.[64] He believed the police department was engaged in a cover-up.

Esqueda told reporters that he had been ostracized by his coworkers since July 2020 when he shared footage of his fellow police officers mistreating Lurry, a thirty-seven-year-old, who was handcuffed in the back of a car when officers reportedly shoved a baton in his mouth allegedly to retrieve small bags of drugs. Esqueda was accused of leaking squad car camera footage to the media that showed members of the Joliet Police Department choking and physically abusing Eric Lurry while he was being held in custody. Lurry suffered fatal injuries as a result, but police union leaders said it was Esqueda's conduct that was "reprehensible."[65]

The "disgraced" officer started to feel the pain of his whistleblowing actions. Esqueda faced twenty years in prison after department officials opened a criminal investigation and he was charged with four counts of official misconduct.[66] According to Joliet Police Chief Dawn Malec, Esqueda's violations included improper release of evidence and making public statements about the department without prior permission from the police chief.[67] Ironically, the officers involved in Lurry's death were never charged and three were allowed to continue working on the force. While the power structure remained, the whistleblowing disruption was maligned.

Esqueda has continued to speak out against the actions of the officers despite being continuously humiliated as a result of holding people in power accountable. It was not until after Esqueda spoke to the media that any of the police officers involved in the incident received any type of minor disciplinary action. Video from various camera angles may have recorded what happened that day, but any such footage was allegedly destroyed. One officer turned off the recording of the audio function after Lurry was accosted. Despite all of these missteps, accidental or not, it was Esqueda, the challenger to official authority, who had his badge and gun taken away. The disgraced former sergeant was also placed on desk duty and then he was arrested for making the video public. Esqueda asserted that the Joliet Police Department wanted him charged so fervently that it went outside of the usual jurisdictional boundaries to seek felony misconduct charges against him. Esqueda found support when the online community created an electronic petition to restore him to regular duty.[68]

The hegemonic dynamic between Esqueda and his former employer is represented in a complicit political culture concomitant with forced collective ideology. In many ways, it is akin to a dominant prevailing ruling class where others operate as a subordinate state within the dominant culture. As Gramsci suggests, hegemony is often augmented by forces that can take on cultural forms such as law enforcement operating as a repressive group. Gramsci defined two methods of gaining hegemony, the first being when a social group emphasizes its own interests in the effort of neutralizing other appendant social groups. The second being when a social group promotes its interests to embolden the full development of all the preferred sectors of society.[69] Gramsci, in his study of Italian political practice, realized the bourgeoisie had used the first method, by managing to create a group of allies to accord with the pursuit of its own interests. This notion is reflected in US society where the high arrest rates of Black Americans and other members within the BIPOC (Black, Indigenous, and people of color) community are used to justify augmented policing efforts and aggressive incarceration methods.

Austreberto Gonzalez: Whistleblowing from the Inside

Austreberto Gonzalez says when he reported that a secret cabal of police officers was operating above the law in the fall of 2020, he was dismissed by his departmental superiors and harassed by those in his police department. The retired Marine and former sheriff's deputy said that a gang of other sheriff's deputies attacked him, which included an assault by a coworker, for exposing their illegal activities.[70] Gonzalez, like others in his position who challenged improper organizational practices, set himself up for departmental retribution.

Gonzalez claimed in a court filing that the officers who targeted him tattooed themselves with Nazi imagery, engaged in a corrupt mindset that committed civil rights abuses against the public, celebrated the shootings of other officers, and initiated work slowdowns when not given preferred work assignments.[71] After Gonzalez filed his report he received a text message with a photo of graffiti at the station, he said. The graffiti reportedly said, "ART IS A RAT."

Former Deputy Gonzalez was considered a whistleblower after filing a claim that roughly a fifth of the one hundred deputies at the Compton Station, Los Angeles County Sheriff's Department (CPT) were a part of an exclusive group called "The Executioners." Gonzalez referred to this group as a gang. Gonzalez said that after he made an anonymous complaint, he was threatened, forced to resign from his field training officer position, and left exposed after being denied a policing partner—leaving him to book threats from hostile coworkers alone.

Researchers have suggested that the response Gonzalez received is emblematical of an oppressive power structure that is exposed by its malfeasance.[72] Social theorists interpret this reaction as the construction of an alternative ideological position based on critically enhanced knowledge based on experiential influences. Consequently, this comprehension skill set results in progressive understanding in the conventional practice from a previous hegemonic standard.[73] This theoretical interpretation supports Gonzalez's claim that some of his colleagues adopted a white nationalist ideology and, thus, his whistleblowing actions against them made him a target of aggression from members of the station. In a reverse set of circumstances, Gonzalez then claimed he became a target, prompting him to legal action. In a lawsuit reinstated by his attorney, Gonzalez claimed that he continued to be a target of retaliation even further beyond initial threats and intimidation.[74] Gonzalez was also "passed up for better assignments and not given a better work schedule so he could care for his daughter, who has medical needs."[75] Gonzalez said he kept records showing that he had a schedule that was constantly being rearranged by bullying supervisors. The retaliation that Gonzalez faced was not unusual. In Gramscian tradition, whistleblowers' challenges suggest that the disputes between supported established systems were incited by a culture supported by an adamantine power dynamic.

The concept of ideological power structures (rather than tangible ones) is grounded in the belief that cultural values reinforce class relations and suppress philosophical contradiction especially if that refutation is not generated from a dominant group. It is widely recognized that some classes within a hierarchy engage in a superior social status while other disaffected groups from the dominant structure are diminished in their acknowledgment and influence. In many cases, the superior class holds strong political power, and subordinate groups support this puissance. Gramsci would most likely contend that the push for dominance in a controlled civil system can only be challenged with consciously deliberate purpose. The challenging party will always face backlash from the dominant power structure as a consequence because it disrupts conventionally held beliefs and actions. However, without this disruption, hierarchical intractability remains despite its potentially pernicious societal effects. This observable phenomenon suggests that protections should be considered for the vulnerable. Gonzalez left on disability due to work-related stress. A judge later tossed his case and barred him from providing further evidence regarding "Executioner's" activities.

A Call to Action

From the cases provided in this chapter, I further demonstrate that whistleblowers face serious risks of retribution despite integrous objectives. The reluctance to empower whistleblowers within and around some police departments indicates that current systems are structurally deficient because they leave other members of the citizenry vulnerable. Organizations that do not emphasize a protected environment for whistleblowers allow for dominant culture advantages to augment at the exploitation of others. Agents of whiteness have historically established these entrenched systems that now have become normalized while contemporaneously oppressing other racialized groups. This racial structuralism has endured generations from the enslavement of Africans who were terrorized by slave patrols until today when discussing issues such as disproportionate recipients of police aggression.[76]

In the Gramscian tradition, the dynamics leading to this tiered hegemony are similar to the conditions of structural racism or white hegemony. The analysis of meaning-making processes observed by this hierarchical structure interrogates the racial dynamics necessary to understand the overall impact between the original offender and inevitably the aggrieved whistleblower. White hegemony encourages structural racism to benefit the majority culture at the exploitation or disadvantage of other groups without racial privileges. This racist form of structuralism is exemplified in myriad forms as this chapter indicated. Consideration of minority oppression within policing institutions makes it apparent that systemic hegemonic sustenance is often controlled by the dominant group comprised of agents of whiteness. This categorization is often performed by grouping people largely based upon skin color. As the white hegemonic structure has been sustained for generations in US culture, there is little surprise that organizations that operate within this system without the full regard of other groups emulate the established and supported ethos. Only when organizational culture is modified to accept and encourage vigilance among the ranks of police can we make steps to minimize or eradicate hegemonic dynamics.

While some companies promote professional development and workplace fairness, those investments with intentions of organizational success can be wasted without the proper channels for proper whistleblowing procedures and necessary protections. A strong ethical organizational environment has the potential to increase whistleblowing revelations and increase accountability and improved safety for the public at large.[77] The charge to protect the public in an organizational climate that dismisses ethical judgment makes the quest for justice more challenging amid whistleblowing apprehensions.[78]

Groups such as the Montana Innocence Project point to an endemic problem where "some police officers openly engage in unethical, immoral, and even illegal behavior, but they are often protected by what is known as the blue wall of silence."[79] These intrinsic unofficial police policies shared between departments and members of law enforcement often encourage fellow officers to look the other way and not contest misconduct to the detriment of a victim of police malfeasance. The lack of holding fellow officers accountable also enables police corruption through exercising biases and miscarriages of justice. Whistleblowers push the boundaries of the police code of silence culture by releasing information that is believed to be vital or important to a case despite caustic demands not to expose fellow officers' criminality. But because of anxieties or retaliatory fears, whistleblowers' admissions may not be easily facilitated because of ingrained cultural defensiveness regarding police tradition.[80]

There are current movements to change prevailing culture. Police reforms drafted to address unlawful action more than they had been in the past were once again pushed into the spotlight after 2020 under new US Department of Justice leadership. Legal experts are revisiting whether the issue of whistleblowing should be promoted within the public. There is a great amount of pressure for police officers to expose malfeasance from other officers coming from civil rights advocates. However, the threat whistleblowers like Frazier, Esqueda, and Gonzalez face from the public and their colleagues, such as isolation, retaliation, threats, harassment, and/or judgment, are deterrents that are challenging to overcome.[81] Being a whistleblower can often put citizens and officers in difficult positions because they may be the only eyewitnesses to an officer's criminality while on the job.

The stories of Frazier, Gonzalez, and Esqueda indicate some of the issues whistleblowers face who endeavor to hold specific members within systems of power, such as police departments, accountable. While these narratives indicate how individual and collective attempts to actualize democratic agencies inform police whistleblowing, it is perhaps in the narratives of Frazier, Esqueda, and Gonzalez that opposition to such agency is made most apparent. Just as consequentially, the victims of professional impropriety also encounter delayed or denied justice.

If police culture by and large, continues to dissuade from full transparency, questionable actions that endanger members of the public will become even more difficult to confront. We already know that official records are often doubted and testimonies have made court cases obfuscatory,[82] and that anonymous reporting is scrutinized and stifled by regulations outlined by police union and collective bargaining agreements.[83] Current policies only go so far as whistleblowing protections ostensibly highlight the need for witnesses to have an outlet to make a report, but they often fall short of breaking the wall of reticence often associated with police departments. In the name of human rights, it is crucial that democratic societies find ways to augment protections for members of communities who blow the whistle against police as it may be one of the only ways to curtail the enduring ideology of police violence against subaltern societies and communities.

Notes

1. Ashley Savage, "Whistleblowing in the Police Service: Developments and Challenges," *European Journal of Current Legal Issues* 22, no. 1 (2016), https://api.semanticscholar.org/CorpusID:156953941.

2. Melissa Jones and Andy Rowell, "Safety Whistleblowers Intimidated," *Safety and Health Practitioner* 17, no. 8 (1999): 3.

3. Amaka Okechukwu, "Watching and Seeing: Recovering Abolitionist Possibilities in Black Community Practices of Safety and Security," *Du Bois Review* 18, no. 1 (2021): 153–180.

4. Joshua Guitar and Alan Chu, "Racing to (Dis)Own Whistleblowers and Protests: Theorizing *Amongness* in the Shared Rhetorical Spaces of Democratic Agency," chapter 1 in the present volume, 6.

5. Lars Lindblom, "Dissolving the Moral Dilemma of Whistleblowing," *Journal of Business Ethics* 76 (2007): 413–426.

6. John L. Smith Jr., "Benjamin Franklin: America's First Whistleblower," *Journal of the American Revolution* (2013).

7. "The False Claims Act," US Department of Justice, 2022, https://www.justice.gov/civil/false-claims-act.

8. "The False Claims Act," National Whistleblowers Center, 2022, https://www.whistleblowers.org/protect-the-false-claims-act/.

9. Evan Caminker, "The Constitutionality of Qui Tam Actions," *Yale Law Journal* 99 (1989): 341.

10. "False Claims Act," US Department of Justice.

11. Philip L. Reichel, "Southern Slave Patrols as a Transitional Police Type," *American Journal of Police* 7, no. 2 (1988): 51.

12. Sally E. Hadden, *Slave Patrols: Law and Violence in Virginia and the Carolinas* (Cambridge, MA: Harvard University Press, 2003).

13. K. B. Turner, David Giacopassi, and Margaret Vandiver, "Ignoring the Past: Coverage of Slavery and Slave Patrols in Criminal Justice Texts," *Journal of Criminal Justice Education* 17, no. 1 (2006): 181–195.

14. Mark A. Yanochik, Bradley T. Ewing, and Mark Thornton, "A New Perspective on Antebellum Slavery: Public Policy and Slave Prices," *Atlantic Economic Journal* 29 (2001): 330–340.

15. Yanochik, Ewing, and Thornton, "New Perspective."

16. "Slave Patrols: An Early Form of American Policing," National Law Enforcement Officers Memorial Fund, https://nleomf.org/slave-patrols-an-early-form-of-american-policing/.

17. Gary Potter, "The History of Policing in the United States," *EKU School of Justice Studies* 1 (2013), https://onenation502.org/wp-content/uploads/2020/08/eku-the-history-of-policing-in-use.pdf.

17. Potter, "History of Policing."

18. Potter, "History of Policing."

19. Marlese Durr, "What Is the Difference Between Slave Patrols and Modern-Day Policing? Institutional Violence in a Community of Color," *Critical Sociology* 41, no. 6 (2015), http://dx.doi.org/10.1177/0896920515594766.

20. Larry H. Spruill, "Slave Patrols, 'Packs of Negro Dogs' and and [*sic*] Policing Black Communities," *Phylon* 53, no. 1 (2016): 42–66.

21. Harvey Wish, "American Slave Insurrections Before 1861," *Journal of Negro History* 22, no. 3 (1937): 299–320.

22. Hadden, *Slave Patrols.*

23. Potter, "History of Policing."

24. Tonia Poteat, "Navigating the Storm: How to Apply Intersectionality to Public Health in Times of Crisis," *American Journal of Public Health* 111, no. 1 (2021): 91–92.

25. Durr, "What Is the Difference."

26. Connie Hassett-Walker, "How You Start Is How You Finish? The Slave Patrol and Jim Crow Origins of U.S. Policing," *Human Rights* 46, no. 6 (2021): 6–8.

27. David M. Anderson and David Killingray, "Consent, Coercion and Colonial Control: Policing the Empire, 1830–1940," in *Policing the Empire: Government, Authority and Control, 1830–1940*, ed. David M. Anderson and David Killingray (Manchester: Manchester University Press, 1991).

28. Durr, "What Is the Difference."

29. Thomas N. Ingersoll, "Slave Codes and Judicial Practice in New Orleans, 1718–1807," *Law and History Review* 13, no. 1 (1995): 23–62.

30. Hadden, *Slave Patrols.*

31. Richard Kluger, *Simple Justice: The History of Brown v. Board of Education and Black America's Struggle for Equality* (New York: Vintage Books, 2004).

32. Deborah Small, "The War on Drugs Is a War on Racial Justice," *Social Research* 68, no. 3 (2001): 896–903.

33. Bryan J. McCann, *The Mark of Criminality: Rhetoric, Race, and Gangsta Rap in the War-on-Crime Era* (Tuscaloosa: University of Alabama Press, 2017).

34. R. Khari Brown, Angela Kaiser, and James S. Jackson, "Worship Discourse and White Race-Based Policy Attitudes," *Review of Religious Research* 56, no. 2 (2014): 291–312.

35. Kim Barker, Mike Baker, and Ali Watkins, "In City After City, Police Mishandled Black Lives Matter Protests," *New York Times*, June 28, 2021, https://www.nytimes.com/2021/03/20/us/protests-policing-george-floyd.html.

36. Candice Norwood, "Calls for Reform Bring Renewed Focus to Community Policing, but Does It Work?," PBS, September 18, 2020, https://www.pbs.org/newshour/politics/calls-for-reform-bring-renewed-focus-to-community-policing-but-does-it-work.

37. Benjamin Levin, "What's Wrong with Police Unions?," *Columbia Law Review* 120 (2020): 1333–1401.

38. Antonio Gramsci, *Further Selections from the Prison Notebooks*, trans. Derek Boothman (Minneapolis: University of Minnesota Press, 1995).

39. Antonio Gramsci, *Prison Notebooks*, trans. Joseph A. Buttigieg with Antonio Callari (New York: Columbia University Press, 1992).

40. Maria Pentaraki and Janet Speake, "Grassroots Solidarity Structures in Greece as Counterhegemonic Practices Contesting the Dominant Neoliberal Hegemony," *Journal of Studies and Research in Human Geography* 16, no. 1 (2022): 5–21.

41. Antonio Gramsci, *The Southern Question*, trans. Pasquale Verdicchio (Chicago: Guernica Editions, 2005).

42. Gramsci, *Further Selections from the Prison Notebooks*.

43. Gramsci, *Prison Notebooks*.

44. Mariana Souto-Manning, "Critical Narrative Analysis: The Interplay of Critical Discourse and Narrative Analyses," *International Journal of Qualitative Studies in Education* 27, no. 2 (2014): 163.

45. Mary Elizabeth Curran, "Narratives of Relevance Seizing (or Not) Critical Moments," in *The Research Process in Classroom Discourse Analysis: Current Perspectives*, ed. Kim Marie Cole and Jane Zuengler (New York: Routledge, 2008).

46. Souto-Manning, "Critical Narrative Analysis," 163.

47. Souto-Manning, "Critical Narrative Analysis,"

48. Peter Teo, "Racism in the News: A Critical Discourse Analysis of News Reporting in Two Australian Newspapers," *Discourse and Society* 11, no. 1 (2000): 7–49.

49. Catherine Marshall and Gretchen B. Rossman, *Designing Qualitative Research*, 6th ed. (New York: Sage, 2014).

50. Souto-Manning, "Critical Narrative Analysis."

51. Souto-Manning, "Critical Narrative Analysis."

52. Norman Fairclough, "Critical Discourse Analysis," in *The Routledge Handbook of Discourse Analysis*, ed. James Paul Gee and Michael Handford (New York: Routledge, 2013), 9.

53. Ruth Wodak and Michael Meyer, "Critical Discourse Analysis: History, Agenda, Theory, and Methodology," in *Methods for Critical Discourse Analysis*, ed. Ruth Wodak and Michael Meyer (New York: Sage, 2009).

54. Jeong-Hee Kim, *Understanding Narrative Inquiry: The Crafting and Analysis of Stories as Research* (New York: Sage, 2015).

55. Catherine Kohler Riessman, *Narrative Methods for the Human Sciences* (New York: Sage, 2008).

56. Kim, *Understanding Narrative Inquiry.*

57. Derek A. Applewhite, "A Year Since George Floyd," *Molecular Biology of the Cell* 32, no. 19 (2021): 1797–1799.

58. Guitar and Chu, "Racing to (Dis)Own Whistleblowers and Protests."

59. "Constitutional Law—Qualified Immunity—Third Circuit Holds Bystanders Have First Amendment Right to Record Police but Grants Qualified Immunity to Officers Involved 'Fields v. City of Philadelphia,' 862 F.3d 353 (3d Cir. 2017)," *Harvard Law Review* 131, no. 7 (2018): 2049.

60. Joe Hernandez, "Read This Powerful Statement from Darnella Frazier, Who Filmed George Floyd's Murder," NPR, May 26, 2021, https://www.npr.org/2021/05/26/1000475344/read-this-powerful-statement-from-darnella-frazier-who-filmed-george-floyds-murd.

61. Hernandez, "Read This Powerful Statement."

62. Tiffanie Drayton, "Teen Who Recorded George Floyd Video Says She's Getting Attacked Online," *Daily Dot*, May 28, 2020, https://www.dailydot.com/irl/darnella-frazier-george-floyd-video-online-attacks/.

63. Elly Belle, "The Traumatized 17-Year-Old Who Filmed George Floyd's Killing Is Already Being Harassed," *Refinery29*, May 29, 2020, https://www.refinery29.com/en-us/2020/05/9846485/darnella-frazier-filmed-george-floyd-death-harassment.

64. Sun-Times Wire, "Joliet Police Sergeant Who Leaked Video of Man's Death in Custody Placed on Desk Duty," *Chicago Sun-Times*, July 7, 2020, https://chicago.suntimes.com/2020/7/7/21316874/eric-lurry-joliet-police-death-sgt-javier-esqueda-desk-duty.

65. Daphne Duret, "Whistleblower Featured in *USA Today* 'Behind the Blue Wall' Series Ousted from Police Union," *USA Today*, November 12, 2021.

66. Duret, "Whistleblower Featured."

67. Anisah Muhammad, "Blue Wall of Backlash—Cops Punished for Trying to Do the Right Thing," *Final Call*, September 14, 2021, https://new.finalcall.com/2021/09/14/blue-wall-of-backlash-cops-punished-for-trying-to-do-the-right-thing/.

68. Dave Savini, "Sgt. Javier Esqueda, Joliet Police Sergeant Who Blew Whistle on Eric Lurry's Death in Custody, Talks About Retaliation He Says He's Faced, CBS Chicago, July 19, 2022, https://www.cbsnews.com/chicago/news/sgt-javier-esqueda-joliet-police-sergeant-whistleblower-retaliation/.

69. Ernesto Laclau and Chantal Mouffe, *Hegemony and Socialist Strategy: Towards A Radical Democratic Politics* (London: Verso, 2014).

70. John Rogers, "LA Sheriff Probes Deputy-Gang Claim, Seeks to Punish Dozens," *Washington Post*, August 13, 2020, https://www.washingtonpost.com/national/la-sheriff-probes-deputy-gang-claim-seeks-to-punish-dozens/2020/08/13/6225f87a-dda9-11ea-b4f1-25b762cdbbf4_story.html.

71. Paula Froelich, "'Executioner' Gang Controls Compton Sheriff's Department: LA County Deputy," *New York Post*, August 3, 2020, https://nypost.com/2020/08/01/gang-controls-compton-sheriffs-department-la-county-deputy/.

72. Maria Pentaraki, "COVID-19 Response—Lessons Learned: Challenging the Neoliberal TINA Discourse Through Social Work Education," *Social Work Education* 42, no. 7 (2023): 1002–1018.

73. Pentaraki and Speake, "Grassroots Solidarity."

74. Savini, "Sgt. Javier Esqueda."

75. Louis Casiano, "LASD Has Been 'Permeated' by a Violent Deputy Gang with Matching Tattoos Called the 'Executioners,'" Fox News, August 3, 2020, https://www.foxnews.com/us/lasd-has-been-permeated-by-a-violent-deputy-gang-with-matching-tattoos-called-the-executioners.

76. Brendan McQuade, "World Histories of Big Data Policing: The Imperial Epistemology of the Police-Wars of U.S. Hegemony," *Journal of World-Systems Research* 27, no. 1 (2021): 109–135.

77. Derek Dalton and Robin R. Radtke, "The Joint Effects of Machiavellianism and Ethical Environment on Whistle-Blowing, *Journal of Business Ethics* 117, no. 1 (2013): 153–172.

78. Julia Zhang, Randy Chiu, and Liqun Wei, "Decision-Making Process of Internal Whistleblowing Behavior in China: Empirical Evidence and Implications," *Journal of Business Ethics* 88, no. 1 (2008): 24–41.

79. Montana Innocence Project, "The Blue Wall of Silence Perpetuates Racist Policing, Wrongful Convictions," https://mtinnocenceproject.org/the-blue-wall-of-silence-perpetuates-racist-policing-wrongful-convictions/.

80. John Hagan, Bill McCarthy, and Daniel Herda, "Racist Torture and the Code of Silence: A Situational Analysis of Sidebar Secrecy and Legal Cynicism in the Trial of Jon Burge," *Du Bois Review* 19, no. 1 (2022): 31–60.

81. Ana Popovich, "New Research Examines Retaliation Against Police Whistleblowers," *Whistleblower Network News*, November 16, 2021, https://whistleblowersblog.org/government-whistleblowers/new-research-examines-retaliation-against-police-whistleblowers/.

82. Laura Rose Matteis, "Stay Away from the Neck: Why Police Chokeholds and Other Neck Restraints Violate International Human Rights," *Thomas Jefferson Law Review* 38 no. 1 (2015): 101–141.

83. David Lewis and Wim Vandekerckhove, "Trade Unions and the Whistleblowing Process in the UK: An Opportunity for Strategic Expansion?," *Journal of Business Ethics* 148, no. 4 (2018): 835–845.

11

Tragic Responses to Whistleblowing a Tragedy

A Burkean Analysis of the Flint Water Crisis

CRAIG M. HENNIGAN

Whistleblowing is one way that the contradictions of neoliberalism can be revealed. Flint pediatrician Mona Hanna-Attisha's whistleblowing in Flint, Michigan, led to broader protests and investigations into water systems worldwide. As more infrastructure fails when governance is guided by financial calculations rather than service to people, the cracks in the system are made evident through the act of exposing wrongdoing and sustained through public protest.

Neoliberalism, while a slippery term, has undeniably influenced many aspects of public life. One such aspect includes how whistleblowing can expose the inherent contradictions of neoliberal governance at a state and municipal level in addition to its more common association in unveiling institutional misconduct. Austerity politics affects critical infrastructures required to maintain public services expected by citizens. This chapter analyzes the rhetoric of a whistleblower and her opponents in one of the most devastating results of austerity in recent US history, demonstrating how citizens occupy the space between conventional boundaries in a manner often attributed to whistleblowers and protests.

The following pages review some of the ways that we, in this volume, define whistleblowers and add to the literature by examining how whistleblowers "truthfully expose violations of human rights and abuses of power."[1] The analysis begins by addressing how neoliberal municipal governance has been causing infrastructural decay through austerity, resulting in disastrous outcomes. A discussion follows about what constitutes an insider when defining a whistleblower. After that, I review Kenneth Burke's guilt redemption cycle[2] as a way to explain the response by the State of Michigan to the Flint water crisis. Then, using the autobiography of whistleblower Mona Hanna-Attisha,[3] mainstream newspaper articles, and congressional hearings, I explicate how various stakeholders often respond to public whistleblowing by attempting to relieve guilt rhetorically through denial and scapegoating.

Neoliberalism and the Flint Water Crisis

Approaching the Flint, Michigan, water crisis requires an interrogation into the neoliberal calculations that helped cause it. Neil Smith's work on urban gentrification attributes neoliberal policies to the relocation of marginalized communities.[4] Drawing upon David Harvey, neoliberalism is "a theory of political economic practices that proposes that human well-being can best be advanced by liberating individual entrepreneurial freedom and skills within an institutional framework characterized by strong private property rights, free markets, and free trade."[5] The role of the state under a neoliberal governmentality is to facilitate the movement of capital and foster accumulation. A neoliberal logic reduces governance decisions to financial calculations as a foremost priority. In other words, the neoliberal ideology facilitates privatization and financial accumulation in all sectors.[6] Municipalities, then, are guided by competitiveness, as local officials have to try and attract capital to maintain job growth and economic profitability. Mobilization of capital enhances earnings for companies as they relocate to places with cheaper labor or less environmental restrictions, even with the foreknowledge that their departure can devastate local economies.[7] Struggling cities often resort to austerity measures to remain financially solvent and avoid receivership.[8] There is no shortage of academic work on Flint's water crisis and its connection with neoliberal municipal governance.[9] The Flint water crisis is one of the most extreme examples of what capital departure and prioritization on financial accumulation can do to public utilities. While much of the work explores the austerity politics and its effects, none focuses on the role of the whistleblower and the state's response.

Unquestionably, the auto industry's disinvestment from Flint levied the harshest consequences. General Motors closed multiple automobile plants in Flint throughout the 1980s and 1990s. Plant closings included the home of the famous "sit-down strikes" at Fisher Body Plant Number One, and various part manufacturers like AC Delco.[10] Over seventy thousand workers for GM lost their jobs through plant closings while ancillary companies that manufactured auto parts also left Flint to relocate in places like Mexico, where there are more relaxed labor and environmental restrictions.[11] The city of Flint lost a large amount of its tax base. Poverty accelerated, but officials still had to maintain an infrastructure for a city larger than its population warranted. In response, urban decision-makers in Flint typified neoliberal governance as they made savings a priority and shifted their rhetorical strategies to emphasize the need for cutting costs. When neoliberalism is employed as such, officials reshape public services to earn profit rather than simply serve the public. Harvey explicates how neoliberal economics is not simply about reducing regulation alone but making a conscious decision to privilege financial institutions over the well-being of the urban population:

> The municipal government was no longer about benefiting the population, the municipal government had to address creating a good business climate. That was the goal, create a good business climate. And if there is a conflict between creating a good business climate and the well being of this or that segment of the population, then to hell with this or that segment of the population. New York City became a divided city in the 1980s; an incredible crime wave took over. If you are going to privatize everything, why not privatize redistribution through criminal activity.[12]

In terms of Flint's water services, it is not simply a change in how services are rendered that is neoliberal in nature. Indeed, opting to save money is good governance when it is beneficial to the community. This chapter instead examines problematic aspects of austerity regarding how the change occurred, the execution of the change, and the state's response when things went awry.

The Detroit, Michigan, public water system, now under a regional authority, is one of the largest metropolitan water systems in the US, serving millions of customers with thousands of miles of lines.[13] Prior to regionalization, communities receiving water and sewerage services from that system would pay Detroit. As the next section shows, the causes and nature of the Flint water crisis provide necessary context to Hanna-Attisha's actions as a whistleblower.

The City of Flint was one of the customers of the Detroit water system. During the water crisis, Darnell Earley, an emergency manager (EM), was running Flint. The EM law in Michigan was controversial because it stripped the authority of the elected body in a city and replaced them with an appointee of the governor. As an appointee, there is no accountability to any local governmental body, only the governor. EMs are installed because of fiscal difficulties within a municipality or school district. EMs have complete local control over the entirety of city operations. They are sent in to cut costs, bring a city back to solvency, and avoid receivership.

A major cost to the City of Flint was payment to the City of Detroit for water and sewerage services. Because of this, Earley decided to switch water services from Detroit to a new system called Karegnondi. That system would pull water from Lake Huron to supply Flint, but the infrastructure to Lake Huron would not be completed for two years. The EM decided a temporary switch to the Flint River would accommodate the city while the infrastructure was built to Lake Huron. However, the Flint River has very corrosive water and requires extra corrosion control agents. Unfortunately, the City of Flint did not add corrosion control to the water and that decision caused leaching of lead from Flint's pipes. Leaded water flowed across schools and residences all over Flint, creating a public health emergency.[14]

On September 29, 2015, Governor Rick Snyder acknowledged that the state needed to act on the water issue, and on October 1, 2015, he announced measures to provide filters and water for affected Flint residents.[15] At first, Snyder avoided the appearance of scapegoating, but later he decided to blame the people representing the Environmental Protection Agency (EPA) and the Michigan Department of Environmental Quality (MDEQ)—a department also likely responsible for the Flint disaster. Numerous public protests occurred throughout the crisis as citizens, particularly those in Flint, demanded clean water as a fundamental human right.

Meeting a Definition of Whistleblower

As insiders, whistleblowers report corruption and problems in the state and other institutions. While members of an institution, whistleblowers lack the organizational power to correct the wrongdoing of those above their position. As a result, they often publicly blow the whistle outside their institution to demand change. Whistleblowers often cite that their motivations to expose wrongdoing are rooted in democratic ethics.[16] Whistleblower information is typically classified or reserved for internal use, so going public puts the whistleblower at risk since they are breaking policies, or possibly the law, in dispensing secret information publicly.

This description is not the only model of whistleblower, however. Greene, Horvath, and Browning[17] acknowledge multiple definitions of the whistleblower based on how the layperson or professional interprets the actor. Either way, whistleblowing is a communicative act.[18] What it communicates may warn of a risk of harm to others, a potential violation of human rights, or corruption and malfeasance.[19] Bok and Elliston both focus on the conflict in loyalties toward an organization and personal ethics when a whistleblower decides to act.[20] The motivation of a whistleblower, according to Jubb, may be altruistic and pertain to the ethics of the greater good, or entirely motivated through self-interest. However, for Jubb, motivation does not qualify a whistleblower.[21] The motivation of the whistleblower, however, is a part of the way they view themselves as an actor. This is often overlooked in much of the scholarship because of how rare it is to have such access to the actor. In this case, Hanna-Attisha embodies democratic agency in her motivation to preserve human rights to clean water and health.

Guitar relies on a characteristic of being an insider as a requirement of whistleblowing.[22] This would rule out media entities performing investigative reporting as whistleblowers. It is useful to further interrogate the definition of an insider, however. Many whistleblowers report wrongdoing of the state, for example, but how far removed from state departments can a whistleblower be? Most people would not consider the state officially investigating its own departments to be whistleblowing. However, what if a state employee notices problems with the actions of another part of the state and assumes professional or personal risk when revealing the problem publicly? Most would consider that person a whistleblower.

For the purpose of this chapter and to advance the definition of this volume,[23] a broader view positions whistleblowers as a relational condition. Hanna-Attisha's relationship to the agency that she blew the whistle on is perhaps more tangential than others, but she still remained at great personal and professional risk. In this case, we also have the opportunity to look at the interpretation of the whistleblower themselves. How they feel about their status as whistleblower should not be overlooked. It is uncommon to have access to the internal thoughts of the whistleblower, and while memories are always flawed and there are biases when considering the individual, Hanna-Attisha's example gives a unique opportunity to embrace those biases in order to understand her internal decision to blow the whistle.

In her autobiography, Hanna-Attisha first noticed lead poisoning increases and considered alerting government officials, although at the time she did not perceive herself as a whistleblower. Her older brother Mark Hanna placed the title upon her when discussing the situation at a family gathering on September 21, 2015. Mark is a public interest lawyer who often represented whistleblowers in his practice. Hanna-Attisha realized that she was a whistleblower when she discussed the issue with Mark. He explained the risks of working as an employee in a public hospital and how the state could retaliate against her:

> "Just so you know what's ahead," Mark went on, "it could get rough. Many whistle-blowers, even if they're successful in exposing fraud, have their lives destroyed. They become obsessed, sometimes paranoid, sometimes with good reason. And it's often a years-long fight. Many are retaliated against. I have clients who have lost their homes and friends, their marriages destroyed. One even killed himself. That's why I always counsel new clients—even though they're doing the right thing—that they need to seriously consider the costs. You have to be prepared for the worst.[24]

Mark's label of whistleblower and Hanna-Attisha's internal struggle offer additional reasons to qualify Hanna-Attisha as a whistleblower. They create their own definition of what whistleblowing means in contesting power but also the conditions that grant them such a title. The potential threats to her career and well-being are similar to more typical insider whistleblowers. The information she was revealing to the public also had high stakes attached.

In this respect, the relational condition that defines a whistleblower is perhaps best seen between actors like news reporters, the whistleblower themselves, their contacts, and their opposition. Defining relies on agreement in meaning; it is discursive. The language creates meaning and symbolic action. This chapter continues to aim at expanding academic interpretations of whistleblowing beyond conventional understandings to embody a co-constructive process of becoming, or to be.

Symbolic Action and Guilt Redemption

Kenneth Burke informs us about how rhetoric is a form of symbolic action.[25] Burke's approach is especially apt for critiquing the rhetoric surrounding whistleblowers as symbolic action means that rhetoric does more than simply deliver information through messages; it frames situations to create a reality by using symbols to explain events. In short, rhetoric is active worldmaking. A whistleblower does more than simply reveal information. They have the capacity to create a world through how they expose their secrets. People exposed will contest that vision of the world and respond with their own active mobilization of symbols. Revealing corruption and potential harm to the populace creates a form of guilt that rhetors are called to resolve. Redemption is the final resolution of guilt, which Burke calls a guilt redemption cycle.

In Burke's terminology, guilt is a reference to the Original Sin but is extended beyond the religious to explain the cause of rhetoric.[26] Guilt begins a tragic frame, where opponents are seen as malevolent enemies and a purgation of guilt is needed to get back into a comic frame. The comic frame allows us to self-examine and accept transgressions by others as mistakes and lessons rather than offenses intentionally taken against us.[27] Guilt is an exigency, and rhetoric can purge guilt in a few different ways. The whistleblower is one who reveals guilt. They bring it to the public and create a rhetorical situation that warrants a response. There are a number of strategies a rhetor can employ to mitigate the guilt revealed by a whistleblower.

The common way to deal with guilt is associated with victimage. The guilt can be transferred to another cause or person through scapegoating. The origin of the scapegoat is one of sacrifice. A sin or transgression by a party in Biblical times was transferred upon a goat, and to cleanse the souls of guilt, that goat is killed.[28] Rhetorically, Burke suggests a person may use public speaking to transfer guilt onto another party, making them a scapegoat and purging themselves of guilt in order to move forward. When a whistleblower exposes a great sin, those accused may attempt to scapegoat the whistleblower themselves. If a whistleblower accesses privileged information in a manner that is illegal, then the state may scapegoat the whistleblower and punish them for revealing information that was secret. Alternatively, an institution accused by the whistleblower may try to find other parties to lay the guilt upon in order to deflect blame.

As a whistleblower like Hanna-Attisha alerts people to the guilt of a social problem, Burke informs us that scapegoating is a powerful mechanism to purge guilt. Finding a scapegoat to transfer guilt justifies actions in a variety of social problems. For instance, Robert Ivie writes that scapegoating is an effective strategy to mobilize nations to continue war actions.[29] As another example, when we feel guilty because of social problems associated with the war on drugs, we may look to find a scapegoat like drug cartels or illicit drug dealers at home.[30] Scapegoating is not found simply in rhetoric of wars and battles, but in countless contexts, like French and Brown's examination of the rhetoric surrounding weight loss and sexual assault, or Blain's work in how politics of victimage can lead to real-world violence against target groups like the LGBTQ+ community.[31] Burke informs us that scapegoating is a preferred method of purging guilt because it allows people to fight an enemy outside of the self, rather than perform a self-examination of our own potential responsibility for guilt.[32]

The more difficult journey to purge guilt is by mortification. This also involves sacrifice, but it is sacrifice of the self. Burke explains that mortification comes from within.[33] It is to purify the soul by denial of a problematic part of the self, a temptation or desire that is closed off. Mortification avoids passing guilt to a scapegoat and purges it by creating victimage internally. This is also accomplished rhetorically, however. There can be no purging of guilt without sacrifice, so through rhetoric a person admits guilt and the rhetor engaged in mortification sacrifices themselves. That sacrifice is not necessarily a mortal sacrifice of life, but a public reckoning with guilt and opening oneself up to punishment. The sacrifice of mortification is redemptive to the rhetor, through actual physical retribution or representational penance.

Finally, is a strategy where the rhetor transcends guilt. The guilt is redefined as a positive trait, rather than a negative one. Brummett addresses this strategy in his comparison of presidential speeches by Carter and Reagan about overproduction and consumption. Carter viewed those traits as guilt to be purged through mortification, while Reagan's speech placed these practices as laudable and worthwhile.[34] For a whistleblower, an institution may react by indicating that the transgression or guilt was necessary for a higher purpose, or that something viewed as corruption was somehow a protection to the public.

Before any of these strategies to purge guilt can be attempted, a rhetor may engage in guilt denial. Rather than find a scapegoat or perform self-sacrifice to admit and purge guilt, a rhetor may simply deny that the guilt exists. If there is no guilt, then there is no need for mortification or victimage. Most often, rhetors will try to transfer guilt onto a scapegoat rather than pursue the process of mortification. In what follows, I show how the State of Michigan denied guilt as long as possible until the facts are established on the side of the whistleblower. Then, the dance of finding a scapegoat began.

Mona Hanna-Attisha—Creation and Denial of Guilt

Hanna-Attisha is a pediatrician who works at Hurley Medical Center in Flint, Michigan. Residents of Flint had complained about the water switching from Detroit to the Flint River for months prior to Hanna-Attisha's entry into the story. Residents felt the MDEQ did not listen to their concerns.[35] Hanna-Attisha, through her work, had noticed an uptick in blood lead levels affecting children in the Flint area. She found the initial increase in lead levels through anecdotal evidence with the patients coming through her office.

When she realized that she had access to lead screenings for Medicaid patients in Flint, she pursued further research to try and find the extent of lead poisoning in the city.[36] By controlling for outside variables, she could link lead level increases in children's blood to Flint's change in water source. At this point, Hanna-Attisha had to choose whether to reveal her work, at personal risk, or to go through a slower process of peer review and verification through bureaucratic channels to report her findings. She decided that, due to the danger of the situation and her ethical obligations as a pediatrician, she had to present her findings quickly. Through publicizing her work, she sparked feelings of negativity and anger in both Flint residents and governmental officials. These feelings are what Burke refers to as guilt. Hanna-Attisha initially revealed her findings in a meeting with public officials in Flint, including Mayor Dayne Walling. Walling, who was powerless governmentally due to the authority of the EM, still had social capital in Flint. Hanna-Attisha explains in her autobiography that she felt Walling did not take the lead issue seriously.[37] When she wanted to have a press conference immediately so the public could be alerted of the issue, Walling did not attend and instead took an opportunity to visit the Vatican and meet Pope Francis. Later, Walling expressed regret over that decision, while still justifying his actions: "I thought that the doctors would be the most kind of credible and effective advocates based on the work she had done, and the city's job was to do what it could with the water system." Walling says now, "Politically, I look back on that, and I think, I should have been at the press conference, but in my mind, I was supportive of her work."[38] Hanna-Attisha acted without Walling and revealed her findings in a press conference on September 24, 2015.[39] Hanna-Attisha's alert to the media spread the negative feelings of guilt to the public, but she also informed people they must stop drinking the water. The response by local and state governmental officials attempted to deny guilt and prevent its distribution.

Walling at first denied guilt in his belief that presenting the findings for lead in the Flint water was not his responsibility. It is worth noting that Walling was the person who changed the water source in Flint from Detroit to the Flint River by flipping a ceremonial switch in a press event. It is possible he felt that acknowledging the failure of the water system would point back to him politically. In the aforementioned retrospective interview in 2018, he seemed to experience what Burke would call the process of mortification when he expressed regret over visiting the pope. Walling "will tell you he thinks 'every day' about how he wished he had conducted himself differently—by joining the City Council in calling for a return to Detroit's water system, or refusing to drink that water on TV and acknowledging residents' 'legitimate concerns.' "[40] Yet, he continues scapegoating and shirking the responsibility of the guilt onto the MDEQ. Even as late as 2022, he testified in court that the fault of the lead poisoning lies with the engineering companies that were acting as consultants during the transition to a new water source.[41] This is not to say that Walling is solely responsible for the Flint disaster, just that his mortification is inauthentic since he is moving blame away from himself. Instead, he continues to engage in scapegoating others in order to avoid any responsibility.

After Hanna-Attisha presented her findings in 2015, representatives of the state initially denied the existence of a problem with the water system. The state responses came from three main spokespeople: Brad Wurfel, spokesperson for MDEQ, Angela Minicucci, for the Michigan Department of Health and Human Services (MDHHS), and Sara Wurfel, spokesperson for the office of Michigan Governor Rick Snyder. Brad Wurfel's response claimed both that the lead content in the water was within acceptable levels and that Hanna-Attisha's findings were "irresponsible" and "unfortunate."[42] Minicucci said Hanna-Attisha's work was not congruent with the data of the state, and that seasonal changes could affect lead levels.[43] Sara Wurfel claimed that the research had been "spliced and diced."[44] The initial collective response by multiple representatives of the Michigan government denied Hanna-Attisha's findings.

It is at this stage that the state was both denying that a lead problem existed in the water and attempting to scapegoat Hanna-Attisha and the Hurley Medical Center for creating panic in the citizenry. The state has an interest in Hanna-Attisha's findings being incorrect. A massive failure is an indictment on the austerity politics the state is relying upon. Burke tells us that there are two main ways we can rhetorically respond to guilt: through mortification and victimage.[45] Scapegoating is the domain of victimage, creating a scapegoat to take on the sin of guilt. The phrasing of "spliced and diced" calls into question the science and numbers presented by the whistleblower. Not only was the whistleblower framed as unethical for presenting information irresponsibly to stir public fear, but Sara Wurfel undermined Hanna-Attisha's competence as a scientist. The framing of the response is in Burke's tragic frame, in that the state suggested that Hanna-Attisha had intentionally caused discord in an already scared populace. A comic frame views our opponents as mistaken, but a tragic frame sees our opposition as malevolent.

Brad Wurfel, just after the whistleblower press conference, said the water crisis had reached "near hysteria."[46] As a spokesperson for MDEQ, he presented data from the department indicating that seasonal changes could affect lead levels as children stay inside during winter months and are more exposed to lead paint. The following day, however, the data released by the state intending to show that seasonal changes can affect lead levels actually supported the conclusions by Hanna-Attisha when the *Detroit Free Press* reviewed the numbers.[47] Over a number of years, the data released by the MDEQ showed a downward trend in the number of children with elevated lead levels in Flint. This trend reversed after the change in water supply. Because of the credibility and irrefutable evidence brought forward by Hanna-Attisha and MDEQ itself, state officials had to capitulate and admit that guilt, in this case elevated levels of lead poisoning caused by the water change, does exist. Where to assign that guilt, however, is a worthwhile exploration into scapegoating and mortification.

Scapegoating

Kenneth Burke's comic and tragic frames are a part of his larger theory of Dramatism, which implies that our rhetoric responds to a world that resembles a stage.[48] Snyder is a relevant actor in the Flint drama as he is the person who appointed the EMs to various cities and school districts in the state. The EM has near autocratic power over a city's functions, and Snyder is the only person who can remove or give orders to an EM. There is little doubt that Snyder is partially responsible for the lead poisoning of Flint's children.

An indicator of scapegoating is the usage of the word *blame* and the phrase *blame game*, which appear in multiple newspaper articles covering the crisis.[49] With community leaders blaming the EM, the Snyder administration shifting blame to the EPA, and some members of the media blaming Snyder, there was a rush to condemn various other scapegoats. Unfortunately, while the blame was being shifted, there was no critical self-examination of broader systems that Burke requires for true mortification to take place.[50]

When Brad Wurfel began by questioning the numbers and calculations of the whistleblower, it rhetorically shifted blame and transferred the whistleblower into a scapegoat. But, when the *Detroit Free Press* investigated and confirmed the data from Hanna-Attisha, the state began to look for other agencies at the local and federal level to either shift or share responsibility. Brad Wurfel could no longer make claims to the epidemiological data that Hanna-Attisha revealed. Hanna-Attisha had access to blood records that showed the lead levels for all children on Medicaid in the area.[51] This access and her status as a public employee within the Flint community made her an insider, and her expertise in assembling research allowed her to reveal findings as a whistleblower that put her in conflict with the state. After her research was confirmed, Hanna-Attisha was cast as a credible whistleblower by local media. This development made it impossible for the state to deny the existence of the guilt. So, representatives instead began to transfer guilt in an attempt to gain redemption. When guilt can be successfully placed onto a scapegoat, no introspection of systemic change is needed and the state can be redeemed. For agents of the state, the blame becomes something to assign on people for political gain. Hanna-Attisha would not allow appointees of Governor Rick Snyder to mitigate or shift guilt elsewhere, however.

In January of 2016, Governor Snyder and appointees gave a press conference about the status of the Flint disaster.[52] Among the people standing behind Snyder and his entourage was Hanna-Attisha. As Nick Lyon, then head of the Michigan Department of Health and Human Services, spoke, Hanna-Attisha was seen on camera shaking her head multiple times. She was in disagreement with how Lyon was supposedly underreporting numbers of children who had been suffering from lead exposure. The focus of the press conference shifted to the reaction by the whistleblower as the state aimed to downplay its guilt. Hanna-Attisha not only was directly addressing the statement of Lyon with her nonverbal actions, but she was also sharing the stage with Snyder, making one of the most direct responses to his administration. Snyder placed Hanna-Attisha with him during the press conference but did not anticipate resistance from her. After the presser, she sent emails directly to Snyder's office explaining how the presser was misinforming the public about the scope of the crisis.[53] Shaking her head in a silent, simple, but very public protest, she continued to produce agonism needed to hold the state responsible for its actions while also continuing to engage with the administration she blew the whistle on. The attempts to purge guilt continued to cause more frustration at a federal congressional hearing in March of 2016.

On March 17, 2016, Snyder sat before the US House Committee on Oversight and Government Reform to explain the failures that caused the Flint water crisis. Members of the committee immediately drew partisan lines in their questioning of each witness.[54] Maryland Democratic Representative Elijah Cummings alluded to the shortcomings of neoliberal governance in his opening statement by critiquing the idea of Snyder "running the State of Michigan like a business."[55] As he critiqued the capitalist nature of Snyder's style of governance, EPA representative Gina McCarthy also noted a possible racial component when she said, "As a country, we have a systemic problem of underinvesting in environmental justice communities, and make no mistake about it, this is an environmental justice community."[56] As environmental racism often occurs in impoverished minority communities like Flint, McCarthy's suggestion of racist policies was given weight. Additionally, cities with the largest Black populations were often the ones selected for EM oversight in Michigan, including Benton Harbor, Pontiac, and Detroit.[57] Even while making note of the greater systemic flaws that led to the crisis, the hearing almost instantly redirected to assigning blame to various characters from the state of Michigan and the EPA.

Snyder engaged again in a false mortification, claiming in his opening statement: "I'm not going to point fingers or shift blame. There's plenty of that to share, and neither will help the people of Flint."[58] Just a few paragraphs after that, he indicated that the problem in his MDEQ was "bureaucrats created a culture that valued technical competence over common sense."[59] Often, Snyder blamed unidentified "career bureaucrats," which he mentioned five times in the hearing. Snyder's false mortification shifted guilt away by claiming that while he was taking responsibility, he should also be absolved from fault. This rhetorical move aligns with established neoliberal ideology that positions governance at fault. Neoliberalism is sometimes characterized as an aversion to regulatory government and laissez-faire approach to the economy, or the creation of a regulatory system that enhances the ability of private entities to accumulate capital.[60] Ironically, Snyder somehow attempted to separate himself from that government bureaucracy even though he served as governor and ostensible leader of the state.

Snyder testified that MDEQ bureaucrats "created a culture of technical compliance over common sense,"[61] which led to the catastrophe. His attacks extended to the "inefficient, ineffective, and unaccountable bureaucrats at the EPA,"[62] but he stopped short of attacking the EM, an unaccountable bureaucrat in his employ. For all of the blame being laid upon career bureaucrats, Snyder positioned Hanna-Attisha outside of that status. Snyder instead blamed public employees and the state's experts at MDEQ and MDHHS. Snyder characterized Hanna-Attisha, however, as a "third-party expert"[63] even though she is also a public employee and possessed inside information that led to her whistleblowing. It is especially curious that Snyder still tries to frame Hanna-Attisha as an ally after her appearance shaking her head in the aforementioned press conference.

Snyder's characterization is unusual because he refused to act against the whistleblower and instead praised her work. While a whistleblower places themselves in danger from authorities like Snyder, Hanna-Attisha now appeared shielded against retaliation. The guilt redemptive cycle can explain in part why this is the case. Hanna-Attisha has a close connection with the victims of the Flint water crisis through her work as a pediatrician. Her connection to the victims makes it harder to transfer guilt upon her to scapegoat. Her position places her among the first to assist those affected most by the water crisis. Proximity to those affected by guilt gives a shield from attack. Her story, as was told in local newspapers, made her a protagonist and advocate for victims.[64] The state was unable to continue trying to undermine Hanna-Attisha through rhetoric once the *Detroit Free Press* confirmed her findings.

Witnesses and politicians both use the anti-scapegoating rhetoric of wanting to avoid a "blame game." However, without going through a process of true mortification, where they throw themselves at the mercy of those they have wronged and willingly accept the penance for their transgressions, they will remain in a tragic frame of victimage. Mortification allows a critical examination of root causes that can bring discourse back into a comic frame. That would require accountability not only to themselves, but to greater systems that create conditions that allow things like the Flint water crisis to occur. Neoliberalism conditions people to look toward other causes that are nonfinancial to scapegoat for its underlying contradictions.

Officials for the State of Michigan attempted to admit some kind of fault in what had happened in Flint. While doing so, however, they aimed to share or deflect much of the blame onto others. When they acknowledged the missteps they made, they only pointed toward the actions of a few individuals as if these missteps were an isolated event. Neoliberalism and studies in environmental justice show that the risk to racial and income marginalized communities has always been heightened due to neglect by the state.[65] While a couple of representatives of Michigan made a nod toward larger systems, they tried to mitigate the harm without upending these governmentalities entirely.

Hanna-Attisha, however, clarified that the need for blame is not simply about finding a responsible party for the crisis; it is also about understanding the underlying systems that create conditions that caused the Flint water crisis to happen. Her autobiography on the incident recognizes the systemic problems in the introduction of her work:

> Because the real villains live underneath the behavior, and drive it. The real villains are the ongoing effects of racism, inequality, greed, anti-intellectualism, and even laissez-faire

neoliberal capitalism. These are powerful forces most of us don't notice, and don't want to. These villains poisoned Flint with policy—with decisions that were driven by lack of hope in government. If we stop believing that government can protect our public welfare and keep all children safe, not just the privileged ones, what do we have left? Who are we as a people, a society, a country, and a civilization?[66]

Hanna-Attisha, went beyond simply revealing information; she identified root causes that are much deeper than simple policy errors. Naming neoliberal capitalism explicitly makes her perspective unique even among other types of whistleblowers.

Hanna-Attisha alerted citizens of the lead water crisis. She also, arguably, blew a post-hoc whistle regarding guilt created by state malfeasance. This action is ongoing as Hanna-Attisha continues to address government officials of the risk that comes with decaying infrastructure due to the failures of municipal governance. In 2016, Hanna-Attisha testified in front of the US House Democratic Steering and Policy Committee about the Flint crisis.[67] She attested that nobody has been redeemed of the guilt, as the response to the crisis was "two years too late."[68] However, she made some policy suggestions that were framed as moral responsibility to provide services that may reduce cognitive problems in children who have been exposed to lead. She called for more nurses in schools, noting that Flint had not been adequately doing so. She included a critique of underfunding rooted in a governmental style that cuts cost over benefiting citizens in her statement: "Tragically, Flint schools have one general nurse for every 6500 students (1:6500). Unfortunately this is a state-wide problem—Michigan ranks last in the nation in nurse to student ratio. Finally, early interventions (Early On), which provide early developmental services for children with delays, is hamstrung by chronic underfunding. This has created limited capacity and long waitlists for an important program to tackle these problems head on."[69]

Implications

The Flint water crisis redefined what it means to be a citizen in Flint. Even today, the phrase "Flint still does not have clean water" is repeated as the final pipes were supposed to be completed in August of 2023 but doubts remain as to whether or not the job is done.[70] To be a citizen of Flint means to be a victim of state malfeasance, which only began to be acknowledged due to the stand taken by a singular pediatrician who dared to blow a whistle.

After her data initially went public, she was subjected to having her research and competence questioned. Once vindicated, new efforts were made to transfer guilt to another acceptable scapegoat. Many of the people involved in this story resigned due to the crisis. A civil suit against the State of Michigan resulted in more than $600 million in damages.[71] More consultants who had worked on the water switch are in an ongoing civil suit, with some settling out of court.[72] Former Governor Snyder, as well as former EMs, faced criminal charges but those charges have since been dropped.[73] Mortification, and the self-critical evaluation of actions and systems, is unlikely to come soon.

By deliberately occupying the contested space between her duties as pediatrician and as a member of a loosely defined group of city residents, Hanna-Attisha challenges the conventional understanding of a whistleblower. She is a person who has information about actions of the state that have harmed citizens. She is an employee of a public hospital, effectively making her a member of the state health system and member of the Flint community. She revealed her information at great risk to her professional career, but in the name of human rights. Her positioning as a whistleblower began discursively with a conversation she had with her brother and later on through her relational positioning by media outlets. Multiple newspaper articles call her a whistleblower, so even if some of the academic literature may exclude her from technical definitions, it is time to expand those definitions. In this, we gain more understanding of not only these terms and actions more broadly, but we can also study the rhetorical processes of democracy as they unfold. Whereas Hanna-Attisha spoke truth to power from a vulnerable position and in the name of democratic ethics, she contested the antidemocratic power structures of the status quo.

When considering the rhetoric of both Hanna-Attisha and representatives of the state through a Burkean lens, this case reveals that whistleblowers are uniquely positioned to sound the alarm of guilt. Through rhetoric, we aim to purge that guilt through either scapegoating or mortification. For the Flint crisis, scapegoating is the preferred route of guilt redemption, first to the whistleblower, then to various state officials, to the EPA, and to the governor. Even though a resignation was tendered at

MDEQ, that is not enough to redeem the state from its guilt in causing a city to be exposed to lead poisoning. The impact of the crisis is too high. Hanna-Attisha continues advocacy on water infrastructure today and is sounding an alarm about how cities are starved of water infrastructure funds. Her greater warning is to the system of neoliberal economics and epistemology that make it possible to ignore the needs of citizen health in favor of financial solvency.

Burke and the guilt redemption cycle, then, is useful for analyzing the rhetoric of the whistleblower as they bring awareness of guilt to the wider public. Scholars may consider how parties that have the whistle blown against them react to guilt. Will organizations be able to engage in mortification and take on guilt in order to redeem themselves? Or will they continue to scapegoat and find ways to avoid responsibility for their actions? Through Burke, we can recognize how whistleblowers create exigencies through guilt. They are a catalyst of spreading the knowledge of guilt, to which organizations then must respond. Through scapegoating a whistleblower, other members of an organization, or outside parties, attempt to purge guilt. It is unlikely that many institutions would choose to begin work on mortification and self-sacrifice without being prompted first by an authority of unequal influence.

Notes

1. Joshua Guitar and Alan Chu, "Racing to (Dis)Own Whistleblowers and Protests: Theorizing *Amongness* in the Shared Rhetorical Spaces of Democratic Agency," chapter 1 in the present volume, 2.

2. Kenneth Burke, *Permanence and Change: An Anatomy of Purpose*, 3rd ed., with a new afterword (Berkeley: University of California Press, 1984).

3. Mona Hanna-Attisha, *What the Eyes Don't See: A Story of Crisis, Resistance, and Hope in an American City* (New York: One World, 2018).

4. Neil Smith, *The New Urban Frontier: Gentrification and the Revanchist City* (London: Routledge, 1996).

5. David Harvey, *A Brief History of Neoliberalism* (Oxford: Oxford University Press, 2007), 2.

6. Harvey, *Brief History of Neoliberalism*.

7. Jefferson Cowie, *Capital Moves: RCA's Seventy-Year Quest for Cheap Labor* (Ithaca, NY: Cornell University Press, 1999).

8. David Fasenfest, "A Neoliberal Response to an Urban Crisis: Emergency Management in Flint, MI," *Critical Sociology* 45, no. 1 (January 2019): 33–47.

9. Brian McKenna, "The Agony of Flint: Poisoned Water, Racism and the Specter of Neoliberal Fascism," *Anthropology Now* 10, no. 3 (September 2, 2018): 45–58; Fasenfest, "Neoliberal Response to an Urban Crisis"; Terressa A. Benz, "Toxic Cities: Neoliberalism and Environmental Racism in Flint and Detroit Michigan," *Critical Sociology* 45, no. 1 (January 2019): 49–62; Laura Pulido, "Flint, Environmental Racism, and Racial Capitalism," *Capitalism Nature Socialism* 27, no. 3 (July 2, 2016): 1–16.

10. Jan A. Zverina, "GM to Close Flint Parts Plant," UPI, January 22, 1990, https://www.upi.com/Archives/1990/01/22/GM-to-close-Flint-parts-plant/3509632984400/; Shaun Byron, "Fisher 1 Retirees Mark Closed Plant's 25th Anniversary," mlive, December 14, 2012, https://www.mlive.com/news/flint/2012/12/fisher_1_closing_in_flint_his.html.

11. Jeremy Allen, "A Look Back on the History of Delphi Flint East," mlive, November 2, 2013, https://www.mlive.com/business/mid-michigan/2013/11/a_look_back_on_the_history_of.html; Peter Bourque, "Remembering When GM Employed Half of Flint, Michigan," *Arizona Daily Star*, August 2, 2009, https://tucson.com/lifestyles/remembering-when-gm-employed-half-of-flint-michigan/article_e4176079-2b6b-591e-bd13-3ca041c9dcf2.html.

12. David Harvey, "Neoliberalism and the City," *Studies in Social Justice* 1, no. 1 (March 5, 2007): 8–9.

13. "Great Lakes Water Authority—Michigan's Source for Water," GLWA, accessed June 7, 2022, https://www.glwater.org/.

14. Mark Brush et al., "Timeline: Here's How the Flint Water Crisis Unfolded," Michigan Radio, December 21, 2015, http://michiganradio.org/post/timeline-heres-how-flint-water-crisis-unfolded#stream/0.

15. "Key Moments in Flint, Michigan's Lead-Tainted Water Crisis," AP News, May 14, 2021, https://apnews.com/article/us-news-health-michigan-rick-snyder-flint-7295d05da09d7d5b1184b0e349545897.

16. Davia Sills, "What Motivates a Whistleblower?," *Psychology Today*, October 20, 2021, https://www.psychologytoday.com/us/blog/learning-at-work/202110/what-motivates-a-whistleblower; Ronald Walter Greene, Daniel Horvath, and Larry Browning, "Truth-Telling and Organizational Democracy: The Rhetoric of Whistleblowing as an Act of Parrhesia," in *Whistleblowing, Communication and Consequences: Lessons from the Norwegian National Lottery*, ed. Peer Jacob Svenkerud, Jan-Oddvar Sørnes, and Larry Browning (New York: Routledge, 2021), 31–45.

17. Greene, Horvath, and Browning, "Truth-Telling and Organizational Democracy."

18. Frederick A. Elliston, "Anonymity and Whistleblowing," *Journal of Business Ethics* 1, no. 3 (August 1982): 167–177.

19. Sissela Bok, "Whistleblowing and Professional Responsibilities," in *Ethics Teaching in Higher Education*, ed. Daniel Callahan and Sissela Bok (Boston, MA: Springer US, 1980), 277–295; Elliston, "Anonymity and Whistleblowing";

Norman E. Bowie, *Business Ethics*, Occupational Ethics Series (Englewood Cliffs, NJ: Prentice-Hall, 1982).

20. Bok, "Whistleblowing"; Elliston, "Anonymity and Whistleblowing."

21. Peter B. Jubb, "Whistleblowing: A Restrictive Definition and Interpretation," *Journal of Business Ethics* 21, no. 1 (August 1999): 77–94.

22. Joshua Guitar, *Dissent, Discourse, and Democracy: Whistleblowers as Sites of Political Contestation* (Lanham, MD: Lexington Books, 2021).

23. Guitar and Chu, "Racing to (Dis)Own Whistleblowers and Protests," 2.

24. Hanna-Attisha, *What the Eyes Don't See*, 205.

25. Kenneth Burke, *A Rhetoric of Motives* (Berkeley: University of California Press, 1969); Kenneth Burke, *Language as Symbolic Action: Essays on Life, Literature and Method* (Berkeley: University of California Press, 1966).

26. Burke, *Permanence and Change*.

27. Kenneth Burke, *Attitudes Toward History* (Berkeley: University of California Press, 1984).

28. Calum Carmichael, "The Origin of the Scapegoat Ritual," *Vetus Testamentum* 50, no. 2 (2000): 167–182.

29. Robert L. Ivie, "Images of Savagery in American Justifications for War," *Communication Monographs* 47, no. 4 (November 1980): 279–294.

30. Susan Mackey-Kallis and Dan Hahn, "Who's to Blame for America's Drug Problem? The Search for Scapegoats in the 'War on Drugs,'" *Communication Quarterly* 42, no. 1 (January 1994): 1–20.

31. Michael Blain, "The Politics of Victimage: Power and Subjection in a US Anti-Gay Campaign," *Critical Discourse Studies* 2, no. 1 (April 2005): 31–50; Sandra L. French and Sonya C. Brown, "It's All Your Fault: Kenneth Burke, Symbolic Action, and the Assigning of Guilt and Blame to Women," *Southern Communication Journal* 76, no. 1 (February 8, 2011): 1–16.

32. Burke, *Rhetoric of Motives*.

33. Kenneth Burke, *The Rhetoric of Religion: Studies in Logology* (Berkeley: University of California Press, 1970).

34. Barry Brummett, "Burkean Scapegoating, Mortification, and Transcendence in Presidential Campaign Rhetoric," *Central States Speech Journal* 32, no. 4 (December 1981): 254–264.

35. Melissa Denchak, "Flint Water Crisis: Everything You Need to Know," NRDC, November 8, 2018, https://www.nrdc.org/stories/flint-water-crisis-everything-you-need-know; Ryan Felton, "What General Motors Did to Flint," Jalopnik, April 28, 2017, https://jalopnik.com/what-general-motors-did-to-flint-1794493131.

36. Hanna-Attisha, *What the Eyes Don't See*.

37. Hanna-Attisha, *What the Eyes Don't See*.

38. Edward McClelland, "Dayne Walling Flipped the Switch That Set Off the Flint Water Crisis. Now, He's Trying to Make a Comeback," *Politico*, August 5, 2018, https://politi.co/2AIJ4K0.

39. Ron Fonger, "Elevated Lead Found in More Flint Kids After Water Switch, Study Finds," mlive, September 24, 2015, https://www.mlive.com/news/flint/2015/09/study_shows_twice_as_many_flin.html.

40. McClelland, "Dayne Walling Flipped," para. 30.

41. Joey Oliver, " 'Gigantic Omission': Former Flint Mayor Walling Says of Engineering Firm Report That Didn't Mention Lead," mlive, March 30, 2022, https://www.mlive.com/news/flint/2022/03/gigantic-omission-former-flint-mayor-walling-says-of-engineering-firm-report-that-didnt-mention-lead.html.

42. Hanna-Attisha, *What the Eyes Don't See*, 259.

43. Robin Erb, "Flint Doctor Makes State See Light About Lead in Water," *Detroit Free Press*, October 10, 2015, https://www.freep.com/story/news/local/michigan/2015/10/10/hanna-attisha-profile/73600120/.

44. Hanna-Attisha, *What the Eyes Don't See*, 261.

45. Burke, *Permanence and Change*; Burke, *Rhetoric of Religion*.

46. "Doctors Urge Flint to Stop Using Water from Flint River," *Crain's Detroit Business*, September 28, 2015, https://www.crainsdetroit.com/article/20150928/NEWS01/150929872/doctors-urge-flint-to-stop-using-water-from-flint-river.

47. Nancy Kaffer and Kristi Tanner, "State Data Confirms Higher Blood-Lead Levels in Flint Kids," *Detroit Free Press*, September 26, 2015, https://www.freep.com/story/opinion/columnists/nancy-kaffer/2015/09/26/state-data-flint-lead/72820798/.

48. Kenneth Burke, *A Grammar of Motives* (New York: Prentice Hall, 1945).

49. Erb, "Flint Doctor"; Curt Guyette and Keith Owens, "Flint's Water Crisis Is Snyder's No-Blame Game," *Michigan Chronicle*, October 17, 2015, https://michiganchronicle.com/2015/10/17/snyders-no-blame-game/; Todd Spangler, "State Questions EPA's Flint Order but Will Comply," *Detroit Free Press*, January 22, 2016, https://www.freep.com/story/news/local/michigan/flint-water-crisis/2016/01/22/inspector-looking-epas-handling-flint-water/79170150/.

50. Burke, *Rhetoric of Religion*.

51. Hanna-Attisha, *What the Eyes Don't See*.

52. Hanna-Attisha, *What the Eyes Don't See*, 299–300.

53. Hanna-Attisha, *What the Eyes Don't See*.

54. Amber Phillips, "The 9 Most Heated Moments from Rick Snyder's Congressional Hearing on the Flint Water Crisis," *Washington Post*, March 17, 2016, https://www.washingtonpost.com/news/the-fix/wp/2016/03/17/the-9-most-heated-moments-from-rick-snyders-congressional-hearing-on-the-flint-water-crisis/.

55. "Examining Federal Administration of the Safe Drinking Water Act in Flint, Michigan, Part III, 114th Congress" (Washington DC: O'Brien & Bails Court Reporting & Video, March 17, 2016), 3.

56. "Examining Federal Administration," 12.

57. "Emergency Manager Law," ACLU of Michigan, October 2, 2017, https://www.aclumich.org/en/cases/emergency-manager-law.

58. "Examining Federal Administration," 5.

59. "Examining Federal Administration," 6.

60. Jamie Gough, "Neoliberalism and Localism: Comments on Peck and Tickell," *Area* 28, no. 3 (September 1996): 392–398; Jamie Peck and Adam Tickell, "Jungle Law Breaks Out: Neoliberalism and Global-Local Disorder," *Area* 26, no. 4 (December 1994): 317–326.

61. "Examining Federal Administration," 6.

62. "Examining Federal Administration," 6.

63. "Examining Federal Administration," 76.

64. Erb, "Flint Doctor."

65. Alfredo Huante, "Planning the Barrio: Racial Order and Restructuring in Neoliberal Los Angeles," *Urban Affairs Review* 58, no. 4 (July 2022): 996–1027; Patrick Bigger and Nate Millington, "Getting Soaked? Climate Crisis, Adaptation Finance, and Racialized Austerity," *Environment and Planning E: Nature and Space* 3, no. 3 (September 2020): 601–623.

66. Hanna-Attisha, *What the Eyes Don't See*, 14.

67. "The Flint Water Crisis: Lessons for Protecting America's Children," Washington, DC, Speaker.gov, February 10, 2016.

68. "Flint Water Crisis: Lessons for Protecting America's Children," 1.

69. "Flint Water Crisis: Lessons for Protecting America's Children," 2.

70. While the city has made a claim that service line pipes had all been replaced, residents have doubts to the veracity of those claims. The city also still has web portals open for requests to replace residents' service lines. See James Felton and Hannah Mose, "Flint Residents Want Answers After Pipe Replacement Deadline," WNEM.com, August 2, 2023, https://www.wnem.com/2023/08/02/flint-residents-want-answers-after-pipe-replacement-deadline/; Ron Fonger, "Concerned Pastors Say There's New Evidence Flint Failed to Complete Service Line Work," mlive, November 13, 2023, https://www.mlive.com/news/flint/2023/11/concerned-pastors-say-theres-new-evidence-flint-failed-to-complete-service-line-work.html; "Get the Lead Out," City of Flint, November 20, 2023, https://www.cityofflint.com/get-the-lead-out/.

71. Paul Egan, "Federal Judge Approves $626.25M Settlement in Flint Water Crisis," November 10, 2021, https://www.freep.com/story/news/local/michigan/flint-water-crisis/2021/11/10/federal-judge-approves-settlement-flint-lead-poisoning-case/5556131001/.

72. Ron Fonger, "Judge Gives Initial Approval to Engineering Company's $8M Flint Water Crisis Settlement," mlive, November 17, 2023, https://www.mlive.com/news/flint/2023/11/judge-gives-initial-approval-to-engineering-companys-8m-flint-water-crisis-settlement.html.

73. Zahra Ahmad, "Ex-Gov. Rick Snyder, 4 Others Charged in Flint Water Crisis Must Testify," Bridge Michigan, March 21, 2022, https://www.bridgemi.com/michigan-government/ex-gov-rick-snyder-4-others-charged-flint-water-crisis-must-

testify; Ed White, "Flint Water Crisis Charges Dismissed Against Ex-Gov. Snyder," AP News, December 9, 2022, https://apnews.com/article/health-crime-michigan-indictments-rick-snyder-ccdb4cea9e892c0a5a6f1d6bac80247e.

12

See Someone, Say Someone

Doxing Vision as Usurping the Rhetoric of Whistleblowing

KELLIE MARIN

> Our country is in a state of mourning. Some of us must say, "Let's step back for a moment, let's just pause, just for a minute, and think through the implications of our actions today, so that this does not spiral out of control."
>
> —Barbara Lee[1]

On September 14, 2001, Representative Barbara Lee cast the sole opposing vote to House Joint Resolution 64 that would grant the US Armed Forces almost unlimited military power in foreign intervention to capture any supporters or actors involved in the attacks three days earlier. She was met with death threats, accusations of treason, and *The Washington Times* called her "a long-practicing supporter of America's enemies."[2] Time would evidence Lee's caution given the ongoing, unbridled nature of military intervention, occupation, and surveillance within the US and abroad. Nearly twenty years later, insurrectionists violently stormed the Capitol on January 6, 2021. Certainly, we should lament such an assault on democracy, but Lee's cautionary tale braces a rhetorical confliction where the methods of achieving appropriate justice deserve as much critique as the insurrectionists themselves.

The January 6 attack sparked a blitz of online investigations. For example, the US Federal Bureau of Investigation (FBI) called for the "public's assistance in identifying individuals" on their "Most Wanted" web page.[3] Embedded on their website are videos and images of the rioters for people to peruse and report if they recognize someone. The FBI is only one entity retrieving, curating, and archiving millions of hours of videos from that day. Austrian netizen (habitual internet user) @donk_enby hacked into the Parler database before it was shut down by Amazon, saving over eighty terabytes of raw data, which were then used by research centers and the US government.[4] The nonprofit news source *ProPublica* published over five hundred videos so that people can view footage of specific areas of the Capitol Building and surrounding grounds and submit a tip.[5] The Instagram account @homegrownterrorists has posted screenshots of images and videos from that day, leading to arrests by the FBI.[6] These collective efforts are neither exhaustive nor quantifiable as the data archives continue to grow across the web.

In this chapter, I argue that these public efforts to identify Capitol rioters and publish their personal information, an act of doxing in online spaces, is perpetuated through a rhetoric of whistleblowing. Evoked by the state and media platforms, such rhetoric usurps tenants of whistleblowing reserved for the demos to garner participation in the surveillance and identification of rioters. Whistleblowers are, as defined in this volume, "vulnerable members of institutions who, motivated by democratic ethics, truthfully expose violations of human rights and abuses of power."[7] Doxing refers to the publishing of personal information of individuals online, leading to outcomes from the innocuous (ordering unpaid pizzas to a person's home) to the deeply disturbing and violent (sexual harassment, stalking, and threatening individuals by organized online communities of trolls).[8] Due to its close association with anonymous and pseudonymous hackers, doxing has often been labeled as a form of violent vigilantism.[9] While distinct, whistleblowing and doxing are mechanisms of exposure. The former is linked to exposing wrongdoings of individuals and organizations, while the latter is often linked to exposing individuals who others *perceive* as wrongdoers. Thus, the rhetorical linkages between whistleblowing and doxing become a slippery and dangerous slope, with consequences to the concept of democracy and practical governance alike.

Throughout this chapter, I argue that through a rhetoric of whistleblowing, civilians are encouraged to dox others in service of the state. Such rhetorical framing does not overtly refer to the actions and tools to report others as whistleblowing or doxing. Instead, the call to identify, police, and report insurrectionists is framed as democratic and, like whistleblowing, as necessary to holding people accountable.

This activity normalizes doxing and is problematic to democracy for two reasons. First, the state and its aligned media usurp whistleblowing principles foundational to a democratic citizenry through the rhetoric of holding those in power accountable. Second, not everyone at the Capitol committed a crime. The calls for doxing do not depend on what citizens deem as suspicious—authorities and the public have already defined Capitol rioters as wrongdoers—but on the simple act of identification. In fact, most did not commit a crime. Yet, the rhetoric of doxing as whistleblowing depicts anyone at the Capitol as *guilty until proven innocent.* So, while we should question the motives of those who attended the January 6 event, democracies must afford citizens the rights of speech and assembly. In a volume of scholarship exploring the rhetorical linkages that unite whistleblowers and protests in the name of democratic rights, this chapter explores how rhetoric frames antidemocratic actions under the guise of democracy.

To advance these arguments, I demonstrate how the public's and the state's rhetoric about the Capitol rioters evokes tenets of whistleblowing by framing doxing as democratic. Next, I analyze public and government databases and social media accounts to reveal how doxing is fundamentally undemocratic by promoting citizen surveillance in service of the state. To do so, the rhetoric of the sites depend on what I call "doxing vision," where civilians are encouraged to view, share, and speak out against rioters. I conclude that the normalization of doxing following the insurrection has intensified the contemporary culture of surveillance in a way that diminishes democratic potential rather than promoting it.

Rhetorically Usurping Whistleblowing to Promote Doxing

In democracies, whistleblowing is said to be essential to protecting disempowered people who have the courage to speak out against corrupt institutions.[10] Whistleblowing is not only a practice but a rhetorical event in which, Sarah Riddick argues, "a rhetor discloses information to one or more audiences about concerning institutional activities."[11] If Trump supporters represent authoritarian sympathizers, the call to disclose information about them online and to authorities in an effort to uphold democratic principles represents a rhetoric of whistleblowing.

After the insurrection, the state and citizens hailed one another to become an army of doxers dedicated to revealing the personal details of rioters. These processes did not function as whistleblowing but rather were advanced through a rhetoric of whistleblowing. While many participants were "inspired believers," the prominent organizing of the insurrection originated from antigovernment organizations like the Oath Keepers and Three Percenters who supported Trump's authoritarianist claims that the election was "stolen."[12] Within this context, calls to dox insurrectionists are steeped in framing rioters as antidemocratic.[13] By usurping a rhetoric of whistleblowing, doxing acts gain moral righteousness,[14] and in the process, rhetorically shift the historically violent associations of doxing to an activity good for democracy. Authorities and organizations aiding the FBI do not explicitly say "doxing" is morally right or even use the term to describe their politicization of the public. Through a rhetoric of whistleblowing, doxing authoritarian sympathizers (rioters) is positioned as preserving democracy.

The state has routinely asked citizens to report suspicious activities and people. Inspired by the "If You See Something, Say Something" campaign by the New York Metropolitan Transportation Authority, the Department of Homeland Security (DHS) propagated a nationwide campaign, now ubiquitous in almost any public space, that shares similarities with doxing. As well, in the aftermath of the Boston Marathon bombing, Reddit users started a page where many users misidentified innocent people as suspects, revealing their information online. Such invalid suspicions can have detrimental effects for the accused individual and democracy writ large.

After the insurrection, it was not vigilantes enacting state practices of seeing and saying something based on reporting suspicious activities—like a person leaving a suitcase unattended at an airport—but of reporting and revealing individuals' information online. As the events at the Capitol unfolded, the FBI released a call "seeking information that will assist in identifying individuals who are actively instigating violence in Washington, D.C. The FBI is accepting tips and digital media depicting rioting and violence in the US Capitol building and surrounding area in

Washington, D.C." While neither the FBI, nor any similar calls, use the term *doxing*, they are asking netizens to engage in the same activity by identifying someone from the footage circulating after January 6. What changes in the case of the insurrection, however, is not just that authorities utilize the calls of post-9/11 "See Something, Say Something" rhetoric to garner the help of civilians, but that those calls support the act of doxing, whether intentionally or not.

The call to dox neither reflects an act of whistleblowing nor is it democratic. On the same day the FBI released their call, then President-elect Joe Biden responded to the insurrection by framing it as an attack on democracy, stating, "The certification of the Electoral College vote is supposed to be a sacred ritual. We affirm—the purpose is to affirm the majesty of American democracy. But today's reminder, a painful one, is democracy is fragile."[15] The next day, on January 7, 2021, FBI Director Christopher Wray released a statement confirming these efforts in the name of democracy: "Such behavior betrays the values of our democracy. Make no mistake: With our partners, we will hold accountable those who participated in yesterday's siege on the Capitol."[16] The immediate framing of rioters as antidemocratic positions the collective efforts to dox them as democratic through a rhetoric of whistleblowing.

Scholars of whistleblowing portray it as a civic duty and a key tenet of a democratic community. Joshua Guitar and Alan Chu, for example, argue whistleblowers are "vulnerable members of institutions who, motivated by democratic ethics, truthfully expose violations of human rights and abuses of power."[17] By using a rhetoric of whistleblowing to promote doxing as a civic duty to democracy, state agents position doxing as a legitimized, and democratically ethical, practice. It is not abuses of power that are being exposed to the public—the news, and rioters themselves, have already broadcasted the insurrection—it is the identification and naming of those insurrectionists to the public and officials that makes it an act of doxing, albeit under the framing of whistleblowing. Even if the information is not accurate or the doxed individual is not guilty of a crime, doxing becomes rhetoricized as a necessary whistleblowing act to shed, as Frederick Elliston claims, "the spotlight [on] abuses that threaten the public interest."[18] In this case, Trump's abuse on democracy by claiming the election as illegitimate informs the call for citizens and netizens to identify the January 6 participants as a service to public interest.

To aid the FBI in what is potentially its biggest investigation in its history, nonprofit organizations and civilians circulated rhetoric framing doxing as a patriotic act. Sedition Hunters, both a website and Twitter (now known as X) account, positioned themselves as a "global community of open-source intelligence investigators (OSINT) working together to assist the US FBI and Washington D.C. Capitol Police in finding people who allegedly committed crimes in the January 6 Capitol Riots."[19] On their Twitter page, they are more dependent on collective participation because of the ability to share. One tweet reads: "Not everyone has the time to spend researching with #SeditionHunters but you can help in a HUGE way just by retweeting out #Doyouknow images. The more people who see them the more opportunity to identify. Thanks to everyone who helps!!!! #DCRiots #CapitolRiots #wewillnotgiveup."[20]

Others created social media accounts asking for help in identifying rioters to preserve democracy. The Instagram account @Homegrownterrorists was born on the day of the insurrection and advertises itself as "Gossip Girl, but for democracy." Even the handle "Homegrownterrorists" infers that the rioters were acting from antidemocratic ideologies. To combat terrorism and preserve democracy, framing doxing through a rhetoric of whistleblowing encourages civilians to out those who would act in service of authoritarianism.

Even well after the attack on the Capitol, the surrounding rhetoric persisted under the guise of whistleblowing. On the eve of the first anniversary of the Capitol riot, US Attorney General Merrick Garland stressed, "The Justice Department remains committed to holding all January 6th perpetrators, at any level, accountable under law—whether they were present that day or were otherwise criminally responsible for the assault on our democracy."[21] Biden is even more explicit, calling out Trump's authoritarian power and the necessary response to preserve democracy. Biden stated, "[Trump] values power over principle, because he sees his own interests as more important than his country's interests and America's interests, and because his bruised ego matters more to him than our democracy or our Constitution."[22] Further, he stressed that the rights given by the US Constitution come with responsibilities "to see that America is an idea—an idea that requires vigilant stewardship."[23] Today, that vigilantism runs strong in the effort to dox insurrectionists. @Homegrownterrorists has almost four hundred thousand followers and has successfully identified some rioters. The FBI's website and *ProPublica* continue to elicit tips by circulating footage and images and providing updates on who has been identified and their respective charges. As Vice President Kamala Harris claimed on the anniversary of the riot,

"The fragility of democracy is this: That if we are not vigilant, if we do not defend it, democracy simply will not stand; it will falter and fail."[24] Yet, doxing and the defense of democracy are not congruent. Doxing threatens fundamental democratic rights, like freedom of expression as it enables monitored speech, and equality as it positions people as guilty until proven innocent.

The evolution from reporting suspicious activities to reporting suspicious identities is particularly instrumental in upending the democratic notion that one remains innocent until proven guilty. As an extension of the "If You See Something, Say Something" campaign, doxers are not called to reveal suspicious activities of the insurrectionists—those who have already put themselves on display across various social media channels—they are called to verify the identities of the individuals. According to the rhetoric that calls on citizens to reveal rioters' identities—even those who lawfully protested—rioters are presumed guilty in a court of public opinion. Thus, one need not scrutinize what they were doing in the videos and images to determine if their suspicion is warranted; they just need to identify someone they know.

The implications of framing doxing as morally righteous and democratically necessary through a rhetoric of whistleblowing have been met with criticism by some. Paraphrasing research director of Harvard's Shorenstein Center on Media, Politics and Public Policy Joan Donovan, reporter Issie Lapowsky states, "Twitter detectives aren't just running the risk of misidentifying innocent people; they may also unknowingly be putting themselves at risk by publicly pursuing potentially dangerous people."[25] This argument and my following criticism stress the dangers that the post-insurrection intensification of security practices represents both to one's self and to the civic debate about the state and citizen surveillance.

Significantly, criticisms like this also position doxers as vulnerable subjects. Whereas whistleblowers exist as inherently vulnerable members of institutions, agents of the state rhetoricize democratic citizens who out insurrectionists as similarly vulnerable. Doxers are empowered to reveal insurrectionists' identities through a rhetoric of whistleblowing that frames them as disempowered and vulnerable, and that rhetoric is emphasized not just by Donovan but online resources for security. On the Sedition Hunters website, they provide links to "research tools" that include links to how to stay more secure online. One research tool, labeled "Anti Doxxing Guide for Activists Facing Attacks," states that their guide is to support activists "getting slammed by right wing forces around

266 | Kellie Marin

the world for resisting white supremacy, Islamophobia, casteism, and all strains authoritarianism."[26] While the guide is to help prevent activists from being doxed, the activists are ironically doing the doxing.

The rhetorical call for civilians' help extends beyond the discourse I have previously discussed by transforming the ways we are invited to see, share, and speak out about someone we know. In the following section, I analyze the rhetoric of state agencies and vigilante netizens who promoted doxing rioters as democratic. I argue that doxing of identities online becomes legitimized through a rhetoric of whistleblowing that depends on sharing and using the tools of the state to preserve "democracy." By giving citizens the tools of the state, they are granted access to otherwise foreclosed spaces of surveillance. Ultimately, these mechanisms shift our public culture from one of reporting suspicion to one of conviction.

Doxing Vision: See Someone, Share Someone, Say Someone

My following analysis examines the state, public, and civilian efforts to promote doxing through a rhetoric of whistleblowing. Rhetoric, in this sense, is not limited to discourse but also considers how users are enlisted to become subjects of state surveillance efforts. In post-9/11 culture, this approach to rhetoric aimed at identifying insurrectionists examines how users are encouraged to become the state's "eyes and ears" and speak out.[27] It is through rhetorics that encourage viewing, sharing, and identifying the perpetrators—practices legitimized within an authoritarian surveillance state—that doxing is legitimized as a democratic act against authoritarian sympathizers. In other words, US officials have framed their authoritarian actions as democratic to warrant their search for other authoritarians.

SEE SOMEONE

The troves of videos and images of rioters across various platforms facilitate a "need" for more eyes on more videos. While a plethora of footage may promise to capture perpetrators, it also demands more labor to sort through the data. The FBI was not shy in asking for the public's assistance, but the efforts of authorities neither encapsulate the larger efforts of online netizens against rioters nor, alone, qualify their calls as doxing. It is instead a collective rhetorical effort. Law enforcement, nonprofit organizations, and social media accounts created archives of images and videos promoting viewers to be "inside agents" with atypical access to social media data. By granting access to the data, civilians are equipped with the information needed to report who participated in the sedition efforts. This rhetorical move aligns viewers with the functionality of surveillance technologies. This way of viewing rioters is what I call "doxing vision": a way of looking that aligns viewers with the technologies that promote the identification of individuals.

One of the most prominent ways the rhetoric of these platforms encourages users to "see" and dox others is through mimicking surveillance tools such as geolocation. *ProPublica* videos are not only posted online but are cataloged according to time and location around the Capitol. The first video starts at 12:01 p.m. and shows a sea of red hats, puffy coats, and numerous flags ranging from "TRUMP 2020," the American flag, the Gadsden flag, and various others. *ProPublica* curated these videos in chronological order, visualizing where the bulk of the videos were produced and at what time of day. In addition to when the videos were published, *ProPublica* also enables viewers to analyze where the videos were recorded in proximity to the Capitol, with helpful titles such as "Around D.C.," "Near Capitol," and "Inside Capitol."

These curations create online mapping that enlists users to be active analysts, thereby aiding the authorities in the doxing of individuals. Databases, like *ProPublica*'s, exert rhetoric to perpetuate certain ways of engaging with and inventing responses to the databases.[28] *ProPublica* encourages participants to analyze where rioters were located, with color groupings to indicate areas of congestion: neutral (gray), warning (yellow), and danger zones (red). Curated in such a fashion, this mapping aligns the viewers' gaze with that of the state's technological capacities to surveil one's whereabouts based on geolocation in devices civilians carry. In doing so, the website's database "weaponizes" viewing by linking it with surveilling, identifying, and reporting insurrectionists to authorities. By linking viewing to reporting to the state, such mechanisms diminish, as Roger Stahl claims, "the civic impulse to deliberate matters of state violence."[29] Instead of discussing the implications of sharing someone's identity online or determining if what they did at the Capitol warrants arrest, user reports instead insinuate guilt.

In the right-hand corner of each video, that weaponization is evident as viewers are directed to "send us a tip" or "share" the images with others to participate in the activity of surveillance, with the goal of punishment. By being encouraged to identify and turn someone in, users become a kind of state agent. Weaponization, as Stahl argues, "shuttles the citizen to the end of the chain of command" instead of being a deliberative participant in the means of the site in the first place.[30] Such a rhetorical move is antidemocratic even as the discourse about countering the Capitol riots evokes a rhetoric of whistleblowing that appears democratic. The verdict of whether those present at the insurrection are guilty is already decided in the rhetoric of the database: all that one views is illegal, and the sharing of perpetrator identities aids authorities and safeguards democracy. Indeed, some of the Capitol rioters are standing trial for alleged crimes; however, the site rhetorically constructs users as the judge and jury to determine and turn in any attendee as guilty prior to their day in court. This acquiescent rhetoric is central to war rhetoric in post-9/11 culture. Whereas Jeremy Engels and William Saas argue that authorities tell us "*Don't worry, we've got this,*"[31] the ways netizens can use and interact with the database means that authorities handle what comes after the civic duty of identification.

While a rhetoric of whistleblowing frames the websites and actions as a means to uphold democracy in the face of authoritarianism, rhetoric within these databases provides only one antidemocratic way to do so. While this form of crowdsourcing is not new to post-9/11 culture,[32] its aim is to transform the surveilling subject from feeling suspicious about a person's activities to a speaking subject willing to disclose the identity and relinquish responsibility for the proceeding actions taken by the state.[33] Even if the Capitol rioters are all antidemocratic seditionists, such processes problematically evoke an assumption of guilt without a trial. As an important aside, I am not implying a defense of the actions of Capitol rioters; rather, I contend that the normalization of assuming guilt severely threatens the future of authentic democratic protest.

The modes of perceiving one another that these sites and calls evoke evolve out of "See Something, Say Something,"[34] absolving suspicion and replacing it with the conviction that warrants doxing. Alone, "seeing someone" is not enough to perpetuate doxing culture. These rhetorics depend not only on seeing as guilty, but they depend on *sharing* images, videos, and databases and *saying* who insurrectionists are to the public and state authorities.

Share Someone

Shared information has played an integral role in the investigative process. Of those charged, 83 percent of the charges referenced evidence found on social media.[35] Adam Scott Wandt states, "While it's not unheard of for criminals to brag about their crimes on social media, what is unique about this particular incident is the treasure trove of information that was released by the subjects themselves in the form of both video, pictures and conversations on different social media platforms."[36]

Data sharing, while "unique" to this incident, has long been part of a surveillance culture. Surveillance culture depends on a subject's consent to have their data surveilled so that they may share their data on online networks. Clare Birchall argues that the surveillant networks of data sharing, like social media, represent "shareveillance": a term that captures "the conditions in which subjects are asked to consume shared data and produce data to be shared [and] are required to be surveillant and surveilled as elements of control."[37] To identify rioters, citizens must opt in to the systems of surveillance and share the data with the hope that another user will identify the insurrectionists. Sharing is, as Birchall claims, "not something we do after possessing data; rather, it is the basis on which having any relation with that data can be possible at all."[38] As shareveillant subjects, we engage with government surveillance through open data sharing and obtaining access to the information of others to turn them in to authorities. "The democratic character of such participation," according to Mark Andrejevic, "is supplemented by the promotion of a shared sense of civic responsibility."[39] As democratic as participation may seem, both Birchall and Andrejevic note that to share means to subject yourself to citizen and state surveillance, which naturally begets the question: How democratic can sharing be?

To further rhetoricize these shareveillance actions as democratic, authorities claim they cannot conduct surveillance of rioters without the help of individuals and data sharing sites. In a press release on the FBI website, Steven M. D'Antuono, assistant director in charge of the Washington Field Office, stated, "As we have seen with dozens of cases so far, the tips matter. Tipsters should rest assured that the FBI is working diligently behind the scenes to follow all investigative leads to verify tips from the public and bring these criminals to justice."[40] As a common refrain for authorities, such rhetoric implies the rioters were indeed criminals. I do not claim that the FBI is not following all leads, but with the amount of footage and images circulating, the more surveillance data to sift does not always lead to effective justice for criminals.[41] While *ProPublica*'s archive of videos are embedded in their site, not disclosing the origins of the footage, the FBI hosts their videos on YouTube. The connection among state surveillance and private communication networks is not new, as

Edward Snowden's 2013 revelations indicated, but the way they both track data and produce sharing subjects, seeped in a logic of "see something, say something," culminates to a culture of doxing after the insurrection.

Netizen social media accounts plead with the public to share so there are more eyes on rioters. Of the almost eight hundred rioters who were charged, it is unclear how many were identified by authorities versus that of netizens, and the public cannot track how many images are being shared or how many tips have been reported. Nevertheless, it is exactly this inaccessibility to knowing that necessitates sharing. The opening quote of account @Homegrownterrorists states, "Without you, I'm nothing—please reshare." This quippy line is indicative of the value sharing has not only for state efforts to identify, but for the networks to function effectively. It is not just one image like those shown in the previous section, but the vast images and videos shared across various disconnected users that necessitate *more* sharing to achieve the goal of identification.

The power of these rhetorics to promote sharing lies not in their call or even who is in the picture, but in the circulation and repetition of that call. As Catherine Chaput argues, rhetoric's "persuasive power can be seen as deriving from the repetition of values added and exchanged through disparate communicative acts."[42] Each post, whether on the FBI's website, YouTube, Instagram, or Twitter, shared by users across these same sites are disparate in that one would be taxed to find who shared what and where it circulated after the original post.[43] The rhetorical success of the call to share is not measured with quantifiable data then,[44] but by what Brian Massumi calls "the coming-together or belonging-together of processually unique and divergent forms of life."[45] By sharing to one's followers, regardless of what others do, one can guarantee they have done their part so that more eyes can potentially identify and dox individuals. This value placed on collectively sharing upholds the surveillance state's efforts to track individuals and enlists users to track each other. This is, as Lee Johnston argues, the responsible way for citizens to enact their citizenship online—one that is "both sanctioned and sponsored by the state."[46] Doxing, as the end goal of sharing someone, becomes legitimized by the state to uphold "democracy" in the face of antidemocratic seditionists. State-sanctioned doxing, while rhetorically framed as democratic, increases authoritarian oversight of online speech.

Not only does the act serve the efforts of state surveillance, but this activity of sharing is validated by various online accounts. After scrolling through @Homegrownterrorists's account, it becomes clear that the posts that once asked for assistance in spotting individuals had been updated with information that rioters had been identified and/or arrested. One caption says: "Identified: Jenna Ryan a real estate broker (Jenna Ryan Realty) and domestic terrorist from Frisco, TX . . . Being a REALTOR is all based on ethics. @realtors @txrealtors what do you have to say about this licensee who broke the law and committed acts of sedition?"[47] This explicit reference to "ethics" perpetuates the idea that doxing is morally right. One of the images even labels Ryan as a "terrorist," and thus, judgment is already rendered as to her guilt.

While social media operate on an assumption that there are more opportunities to speak out against antidemocratic practices,[48] the act of sharing posts and doxing personal information reifies state surveillance of and by netizens. Such sharing engulfs users in a relationship with state surveillance practices. The activity of "shareveillance," as Birchall notes, "delimits the political experience and agency of subjects called on to share their data in order to be watched, and to watch and act on data shared by the state."[49] While users are seemingly given vigilante agency to "blow the whistle" on insurrectionists through collective doxing, the nature of surveillance becomes a covertly political practice in which one subjects themselves to, and enacts surveillance for, the state. This diminishes critical attention as to how these practices have been violently enacted toward subjects who may very well be innocent.

SAY SOMEONE

The call to collectively dox rioters at the insurrection through a rhetoric of whistleblowing, frames all individuals present that day as guilty. What is uncertain is what crimes they committed. Of the various efforts by authorities and netizens alike, the FBI offers the most direction in what and who is deemed worthy of being subjected to doxing. On their website, the FBI defines the criminals they seek to prosecute: person(s) responsible for placing pipe bombs in Washington, DC, on January 5, 2021, and individuals associated with assault on federal officer (AFO) or assault on media (AOM) personnel. Within the directions on their website is a hyperlink that takes visitors to a page on reporting tips "warning" people that tips with "no investigative value will" not be considered and that "providing false information could subject [one] to fine, imprisonment, or both (Title 18, US Code, Section 1001)."[50] Under each video or image is a reference number and either "AFO" or "AOM" identifying the unlawful act occurring. As netizens and journalist entities took up the call to share and identify individuals, the same diligence to define the parameters of what and who participated in illegal activity diminished.

Much of the rhetoric on social media sites reverts to uncritical practices of doxing individuals. One image posted on @Homegrownterrorists, for example, is indicative of doxing without parameters or considerations that justify identifying people. Like other posts from this account, @Homegrownterrorists asks, "Do you recognize this 'Patriot'?" One of the responses from follower @resistbutvote reads, "To all the idiots posting false names. It's ok. We can take all postings and the FBI can check. Easier to start there than from scratch with nothing. So who cares! The site is phenomenal!"[51] While I would not go so far as to say this statement is representative of the sentiments of all the doxers, it is an accurate description of how these platforms promote saying *someone*, whether guilty or not. To be sure, this is problematic in a democratic culture where one cannot trust that they will be presumed innocent until legally proven guilty.[52] Whereas whistleblowing focuses on exposing wrongdoings supported by evidence, in the case of @Homegrownterrorists and others like it, it is the information of individuals that is exposed. Even if we are rightfully appalled by the actions of the insurrections, succumbing to doxing does not uphold democracy, especially as it fosters false accusations.

Misidentification, done unintentionally or purposefully, has long been a staple of crowdsourcing citizen watchers to aid authorities. Reeves, in *Citizen Spies*, notes this as a "primary danger with crowdsourcing technologies: [That] they can easily lead vigilant citizens to mobilize against false or even imagined enemies."[53] On *ProPublica*'s webpage, unlike the FBI's website, there is no direction on what is considered a crime and thus who should be identified. The videos are chronologized and geolocated, but there is no guidance regarding what actions should be reported or which individuals to identify. The rhetorical mechanisms of websites like *ProPublica* amplify the danger of misidentification by not linking the call to dox individuals in videos to specific crimes—perpetuating the sense that doxing anyone visible is justified. Whereas @Homegrownterrorists mentions some of the alleged crimes, it is not supported with evidence. In one example, a video published of an insurrectionist at the riot yelling about how everyone in the Capitol Building "is a treasonous traitor" is claimed to be a crime: "Do you recognize this 'Patriot'? He beat a cop down with an American Flag, saying, 'Death is the only remedy for what's in that building. #homegrownterrorists."[54] The video does not show any crime being committed and is not verified by the FBI, which, if it was, would be classified as an AFO.

The websites, social media accounts, and calls by authorities and netizens perpetuate that collectively participating in doxing all individuals involved in the insurrection is the appropriate measure, regardless of actual criminal behavior. Founder of the Social Media the Internet and Law Enforcement conference, Lauri Stevens states, "Social media is like community policing on steroids. It's a force multiplier."[55] The various dedicated entities on a mission to identify accumulate with every like, share, and tip. Collectively, these responses to January 6, 2021, promote doxing *any* individuals without encouraging critical attention to what they did and what the effects of sharing their identity might have.

The Evolution of "If You See Something, Say Something"

Democracy is heralded as a beacon of good and an immutable marker of national identity,[56] yet, the core foundations of this myth are wrought with enduring ethical tensions. Watching swarms of people storm the Capitol Building, beaming with pride while they smashed a symbol of democracy—no matter how incoherent its ideals are with its practices[57]—mobilized a collective response to identify the individuals as antidemocratic seditionists. The US Constitution protects the right to protest under the First Amendment, but when those "protests" contradict democracy and, in fact, support authoritarianism as the insurrectionists did, the collective response poses an ethical dilemma. As part of this volume dedicated to the "important relationships that emerge *among* individual and collective attempts at actualizing democratic agency,"[58] my chapter demonstrates how well-meaning attempts to counter authoritarianism can promote problematic tenets of surveillance culture. In this chapter, I have labeled January 6 participants not as "protesters" but as "insurrectionists" and in so doing have argued that their "democratic assembly" sought authoritarian ends. Even so, I have argued that a rhetoric of whistleblowing that promotes doxing is a cautionary tale for the future of democracy.

Insurrectionists who committed crimes at the Capitol are rightfully being prosecuted, but the promotion of doxing an assembly violates core tenets of democracy. Doxing is a means of control by those in power to silence others. In online spaces, this operates by silencing marginalized groups, but, in the aftermath of the Insurrection, doxing functions by

274 | Kellie Marin

upholding state power. I have argued that the state and media platforms evoke a rhetoric of whistleblowing that usurps the act of speaking out to injustice by perpetuating doxing. These rhetorics do so by equipping citizens and netizens alike with the tools to surveil. These processes necessitate the sharing of identity information that frames all individuals involved with the January 6 events as antidemocratic criminals. Curbing free speech on- and offline typifies a central tension within democracy, blurring, for instance, the line between rights and hate speech.[59] Those who targeted and participated in efforts to dox individual identities show authoritarianism cannot survive when collective agency attempts to uphold democracy. But, as my chapter illustrates, those attempts themselves can be antidemocratic and uphold state power by legitimizing surveillance culture.

Long has surveillance rhetoric functioned by operating on fear, evoking citizen participation, and diminishing political discussion about surveillance or the effects they have on culture. "If you see something, say something" was a penultimate campaign with a logic dependent upon the fear of another terrorist attack. This rationale pervades and regulates how we see and participate in and with state surveillance practices.[60] Since 9/11 this logic has habituated ways of looking as being always-on-the-lookout for potential threats. Bradford Vivian discusses the way in which habituated practices in security heighten "anxieties at security checkpoints preced[ing] . . . contemplation or reflection."[61] Similarly, habituated practices of looking in post-9/11 led to reporting without more critical contemplation of the potential effects. In the aftermath of January 6, 2021, that logic is evolving to incorporate the vigilante practice of doxing.

Turning in, and framing, individuals as criminals is not new—from calls on "Wanted" posters to reporting individuals behaving in "suspicious" ways. What is novel about this collective doxing is that it frames individuals as *already* a criminal, regardless of that validity, and this framing warrants identifying and turning them in. "Wanted" posters describe perpetrators for what crime they did and, if known, the identity of the perpetrator. In this case of the insurrection, it is specifically about identifying, and in many cases publishing, individuals' personal information, a process that precedes knowing whether the behavior is suspicious, criminal, or even if individuals are wanted for a crime at all. By recognizing and sharing their information online and/or to authorities to combat antidemocratic actions, doxing becomes a tool for state surveillance *and*, in the court of public opinion, frames others as guilty until proven innocent. As Wendy Hesford has argued well before the Insurrection, recognizing and disclosing rioters' identities eliminates the democratic practice of due process.[62] While many might view insurrectionists as deserving of this action, it has serious ramifications to the future of authentic democratic protests. For instance, state surveillance targeted protesters of the Black Lives Matter (BLM) movement across the country by mapping protesters' whereabouts and using facial recognition technologies (FRT) to arrest protesters for crimes they may already be wanted for.[63]

Prior to January 6, 2021, doxing, while sometimes viewed positively when enacted against groups (like the KKK) who further marginalize others, was relegated to hackers, online networks, and anonymous spaces not well regulated by the state. By promoting doxing in service of democracy, the state normalizes the practice while simultaneously diminishing the discourses that are critical of state surveillance. In previous cases, such as Redditors using technologies to dox citizens as potential Boston Marathon suspects, Michael Bouzis observes, "Redditors were not criticizing the way in which the FBI and police exerted power over citizens, but only claiming that they could use technology to exert that power more quickly and efficiently."[64] Like Redditors, citizens are quick to utilize surveillance tools and demonstrate their ability to identify rioters deemed criminal and deserving of judgment without much discussion about the methods in which this data was curated and circulated. As one user commented on a @homegrownterrorists's post: "We will have facial recognition after January 6th. Honestly I wish we did."[65] A rhetoric of whistleblowing promotes civilians to partake in surveillance culture through doxing without discussion of the violence state surveillance does. The state will continue to develop more tools to curate, surveil, and harm. The actions of the insurrectionists remain indefensible as an overt attack on democracy. Yet, state-authorized doxing similarly threatens democracy, but in a far more clandestine manner. In this, such surveillance tactics present a harrowing future for the civil liberties of democratic citizens.

Notes

1. Statement in opposition to HJ Res. 64, American Rhetoric: Online Speech Bank, September 14, 2001, https://www.americanrhetoric.com/speeches/barbaraleeagainstinvasion.htm.

2. "Who Is Barbara Lee?," *Washington Times*, September 18, 2001, https://www.washingtontimes.com/news/2001/sep/18/20010918-025434-6670r/.

3. "Most Wanted: Capitol Violence," Federal Bureau of Investigation, accessed on March 15, 2022, from https://www.fbi.gov/wanted/capitol-violence.

4. Saumya Dixit, "Who is Parler Hacker @donk_enby? Deleted Posts Provide 'Very Incriminating' Evidence against US Capitol Riots," Meaww, January 11, 2021, https://meaww.com/who-is-parler-hacker-donkenby-deleted-posts-very-incriminating-data-dump-us-capitol-riots-trump.

5. Lena V. Groeger et al., "What Parler Saw During the Attack on the Capitol," *ProPublica | The Insurrection*, January 17, 2021, https://projects.propublica.org/parler-capitol-videos/.

6. City News Service, "Ex-Coronado Man Who Breached U.S. Capitol Gets 3-Month Prison Sentence," NBC San Diego, March 15, 2022, https://www.msn.com/en-us/news/us/ex-coronado-man-who-breached-u-s-capitol-gets-3-month-prison-sentence/ar-AAV68YC?ocid=uxbndlbing.

7. Joshua Guitar and Alan Chu, "Racing to (Dis)Own Whistleblowers and Protests: Theorizing *Amongness* in the Shared Rhetorical Spaces of Democratic Agency," chapter 1 in the present volume, 2.

8. Danielle Keats Citron, *Hate Crimes in Cyberspace* (Cambridge, MA: Harvard University Press, 2014), 53.

9. amanda b., "Doxxing," Know Your Meme, updated by Don, 2021, 2013, https://knowyourmeme.com/memes/doxxing.

10. *Transparency International: The Global Coalition Against Corruption*, transparency.org, accessed on December 18, 2022, https://www.transparency.org/en/our-priorities/whistleblowing.

11. Sarah Riddick, "Students' Social Media Disclosures: Reconsidering the Rhetorics of Whistleblowing," *Rhetoric Review* 41, no. 4 (2022): 282.

12. Lorenzo Vidino, Seamus Hughes, Alexander Meleagrou-Hitchens, Devorah Margolin, Bennett Clifford, Jon Lewis, Andrew Mines, and Haroro Ingram, " 'This Is Our House!' A Preliminary Assessment of the Capitol Hill Siege Participants," George Washington University's program on extremism, March 2021.

13. Joshua Guitar, "<Snowden> Is (Not) a Whistleblower: Ideographs, Whistleblower Protections, and Restrictions of <Free> Speech," *First Amendment Studies* 54, no. 1 (2020): 4.

14. David J. Ciuk and Joshua Rottman, "Moral Conviction, Emotion, and the Influence of Episodic versus Thematic Frames," *Political Communication* 38, no. 5 (2021): 520.

15. Joe Biden, " 'It's Not Protest, It's Insurrection': Biden Delivers Remarks on 'Siege' Upon U.S. Capitol," WBUR.org, January 6, 2021.

16. Christopher Wray, "Statement on Violent Activity at the U.S. Capitol Building," FBI National Press Office, January 7, 2021, https://www.fbi.gov/news/press-releases/press-releases/director-wrays-statement-on-violent-activity-at-the-us-capitol-building-010721.

17. Guitar and Chu, "Racing to (Dis)Own," 00.

18. Frederick A. Elliston, "Anonymity and Whistleblowing," *Journal of Business Ethics* 1, no. 3 (1982): 169.

19. "Welcome," Sedition Hunters, accessed on December 13, 2013, https://seditionhunters.org/.

20. Tweet posted to the @SeditionHunters account, Twitter, January 22, 2021, https://twitter.com/seditionhunters/status/1352662734874292226.

21. Tierney Sneed, "Merrick Garland on Capitol Attack: 'The Actions We Have Taken Thus Far Will Not Be Our Last," CNN Politics, January 5, 2022, https://www.cnn.com/2022/01/05/politics/merrick-garland-january-6-anniversary-speech/index.html.

22. Joe Biden, "Remarks by President Biden to Mark One Year Since the January 6th Deadly Assault on the U.S. Capitol," Whitehouse.gov, January 6, 2022, https://www.whitehouse.gov/briefing-room/speeches-remarks/202 2/01/06/remarks-by-president-biden-to-mark-one-year-since-the-january-6th-deadly-assault-on-the-u-s-capitol/.

23. Biden, "Remarks by President Biden to Mark One Year Since the January 6th."

24. Kamala Harris, "Remarks by Vice President Harris Marking One Year Since the January 6th Deadly Assault on the U.S. Capitol," White House, January 6, 2022, https://www.whitehouse.gov/briefing-room/speeches-remarks/2022/01/06/remarks-by-vice-president-harris-marking-one-year-since-the-january-6th-deadly-assault-on-the-u-s-capitol/.

25. Issie Lapowsky "Doxxing Insurrectionists: Capitol Riot Divides Online Extremism Researchers," protocol, January 16, 2021, https://www.protocol.com/doxxing-capitol-rioters.

26. Equity Labs, "Anti-Doxing Guide for Activists Facing Attacks," *Medium*, September 2, 2017, https://equalitylabs.medium.com/anti-doxing-guide-for-activists-facing-attacks-from-the-alt-right-ec6c290f543c.

27. See Joshua Reeves's "speaking subject," in *Citizen Spies: The Long Rise of America's Surveillance Society* (New York: New York University Press, 2017), 78.

28. Jeff Rice, "Urban Mappings: A Rhetoric of the Network," *Rhetoric Society Quarterly* 38, no. 2 (2008): 198–218.

29. Roger Stahl, *Through the Crosshairs: War, Visual Culture & the Weaponized Gaze* (New Brunswick, NJ: Rutgers University Press, 2018).

30. Stahl, *Through the Crosshairs*, 17.

31. Jeremy Engels and William O. Saas, "On Acquiescence and Ends-Less War: An Inquiry into the New War Rhetoric," *Quarterly Journal of Speech* 99, no. 2 (2013): 231.

32. Jeff Howe, "The Rise of Crowdsourcing," *Wired*, June 1, 2006, https://www.wired.com/2006/06/crowds/.

33. Reeves, *Citizen Spies*, 78.

34. I draw upon Kevin Michael Deluca and Jennifer Peeples's "public screen" idea in which new technologies shape perceptions: "From Public Sphere to Public Screen: Democracy, Activism, and the 'Violence' of Seattle," *Critical Studies in Media Communication* 19, no. 2 (2002): 131.

35. Vidino et al., " 'This Is Our House!,' "14.

36. Quoted in Rachel Axon and Katie Wedell, " 'Pics or It Didn't Happen': Experts Explain Why Capitol Rioters Posted Incriminating Videos and Selfies," *USA Today*, January 21, 2021, https://www.usatoday.com/story/news/investigations/2021/01/21/fbi-uses-selfies-social-posts-arrest-u-s-capitol-rioters/4203158001/.

37. Clare Birchall, *Radical Secrecy: The Ends of Transparency in Datafied America* (Minneapolis: University of Minnesota Press, 2021), 102.

38. Birchall, *Radical Secrecy*, 105.

39. Mark Andrejevic, *iSpy: Surveillance and Power in the Interactive Era* (Lawrence: University Press of Kansas, 2007), 179.

40. "FBI Washington Field Office Releases New Videos of Suspects in Violent Assaults on Federal Officers at U.S. Capitol, Seeks Public's Help in Identifying Them," FBI Washington, July 6, 2021, https://www.fbi.gov/contact-us/field-offices/washingtondc/news/press-releases/fbi-washington-field-office-releases-new-videos-of-suspects-in-violent-assaults-on-federal-officers-at-us-capitol-seeks-publics-help-in-identifying-them-070621.

41. Matthew Guariglia, "Too Much Surveillance Makes Us Less Free. It Also Makes Us Less Safe," *Washington Post*, July 18, 2017, https://www.washingtonpost.com/news/made-by-history/wp/2017/07/18/too-much-surveillance-makes-us-less-free-it-also-makes-us-less-safe/.

42. Catherine Chaput, "Rhetorical Circulation in Late Capitalism: Neoliberalism and the Overdetermination of Affective Energy," *Philosophy and Rhetoric* 43, no. 1 (2010): 14.

43. Birchall refers to this as "closed government data" that is "withheld from public view, whether in the interests of privacy diplomacy, or national security," in *Radical Secrecy*, 104.

44. Chaput, "Rhetorical Circulation in Late Capitalism," 19; Brian Massumi, *Parables for the Virtual: Movement, Affect, Sensation* (Durham, NC: Duke University Press, 2002), 255.

45. Massumi, *Parables for the Virtual*, 255.

46. Lee Johnston, "What Is Vigilantism?," *British Journal of Criminology* 36, no. 2 (1996): 226.

47. Homegrown Terrorists (@Homegrownterrrorists), "Identified: Jenna Ryan a real estate broker (Jenna Ryan Realty) and domestic terrorist from Frisco, TX," *Instagram*, January 7, 2021, https://www.instagram.com/p/CJwoxpgHO1U/.

48. A wrongful assumption Jodi Dean argues in "Communicative Capitalism: Circulation and the Foreclosure of Politics," *Cultural Politics* 1, no. 1 (2005): 58.

49. Birchall, *Radical Secrecy*, 12.

50. "FBI-Tips," FBI.gov, accessed on April 15, 2022, https://tips.fbi.gov/.

51. Homegrown Terrorists, "Do you recognize this "Patriot"? #homegrownterrorists," Instagram, January 6, 2021, https://www.instagram.com/p/CJuGtcPnY4P/.

52. Trust is central to communicating with others in a democratic culture. Whether one agrees, or is appalled, there should still exist a presumption of legal norm to uphold a democratic culture. Drawing on Danielle Allen, *Talking to Strangers: Anxieties of Citizenship Since* Brown v. Board of Education (Chicago: University of Chicago Press, 2004), 132.

53. Reeves, *Citizen Spies*, 42.

54. Homegrown Terrorists, "Do you recognize this Patriot? He beat a cop down with an American Flag, saying, 'Death is the only remedy for what's in that building.' #homegrownterrorists," Instagram, January 11, 2021, https://www.instagram.com/p/CJ7qk5AHWh8/.

55. Quoted in Alejandro Martínez-Cabrera, "Social Media a Police Weapon That Can Backfire," SFGate.com, September 25, 2010.

56. Robert Ivie, *Hunt the Devil: A Demonology of US War Culture* (Tuscaloosa: University of Alabama Press, 2015), 2.

57. Chantal Mouffe, *The Democratic Paradox* (London: Verso Books, 2000).

58. Guitar and Chu, "Racing to (Dis)Own," 5.

59. Mark Slagle, "An Ethical Exploration of Free Expression and the Problem of Hate Speech," *Journal of Mass Media Ethics* 24, no. 4 (2009): 240.

60. Michel Foucault posits "regulatory" power as not just disciplining of man as individuals, but as a "global mass," in "Society Must Be Defended," *Lectures at the Collège de France 1975–76* (New York: Picador, 1997), 242.

61. Bradford Vivian, *Commonplace Witnessing: Rhetorical Invention, Historical Remembrance, and Public Culture* (New York: Oxford University Press, 2017), 159.

62. Wendy Hesford, "Surviving Recognition and Racial In/Justice," *Philosophy and Rhetoric* 48, no. 4 (2015): 539.

63. "FW: "National Moment of Silence" and a list of Google Map locations posted by u/jandrewweb, "Interactive/Live Map of Ferguson Protests," August 10, 2014, https://www.reddit.com/r/StLouis/comments/2e196o/interactivelive_map_of_ferguson_protests/; George Joseph, "Exclusive: Feds Regularly Monitored Black Lives Matter Since Ferguson," *Intercept*, July 14, 2015, https://theintercept.com/2015/07/24/documents-show-department-homeland-security-monitoring-black-lives-matter-since-ferguson/.

64. Michael Bouzis, "Doxing or Deliberative Democracy? Evidence and Digital Affordances in the *Serial* subReddit," *Convergence: The International Journal of Research into New Media Technologies* 25, no. 3 (2019): 361.

65. Comment @Homegrownterrorists, "Do You Recognize this Terrorist? #FBI156AFO #UnderarmorDarkShades," March 17, 2021, https://www.instagram.com/p/CMiur_knaIB/.

13

Ninja Girl, Blow the Whistle and Poison Arrows!

An Epideictic Function of Entertainment Film and Its Applications for Whistleblowing

Noriaki Tajima and Satoru Aonuma

Once conceived as mere display oratory without practical consequences, scholars of epideictic have now turned their attention to its robust socio-political dimensions, recognizing its edifying, ideological, and constitutive functions.[1] In the foundational text *The New Rhetoric: A Treatise on Argumentation*, francophone rhetoricians Chaïm Perelman and Lucie Olbrechts-Tyteca noted the politicocultural utility of epideictic as it "strengthens the disposition toward action by increasing adherence to the values it lauds."[2] In North America, Gerald Hauser, a renowned US rhetorician, pointed to epideictic's "constitutive activity propaedeutic to action: reflecting on public norms for proper political conduct."[3] In Japan, Hideki Kakita also discussed the significance of epideictic rhetoric in the context of Isocrates's critique of a democratic polity.[4] A proud Athenian citizen and the logographer-turned-father of liberal arts, Isocrates considered epideictic as a discourse worthy of its cause, calling it the "highest" kind of oration, "which deals with the greatest affairs and, while best displaying the ability of those who speak, brings most profit to those who hear."[5] Epideictic was central to his rhetorical paideia, a model of education that accentuates the "ideal models" that "all individuals are bound to imitate, . . . to make each individual in the image of community."[6]

Like many other rhetorical acts, whistleblowing shares the same objective with epideictic in that it constitutes communal norms and strengthens popular democratic governance via symbolism. Prima facie, their respective routes to achieving that goal are different. Whereas epideictic attempts to do so by publicly displaying the virtue and vice of a certain individual or collective actions to the audience, whistleblowing is an act that causes an "organizational dissidence," and justice is done when the present or past organization members disclose and report "illegal, immoral or illegitimate practices" by leaders of that organization.[7]

Our interest lies in exploring such whistleblowing-like functions of epideictic. That is, we explore epideictic's critical-radical potentials not only by critiquing the status quo, but also by providing moral and pedagogical guidance for our democratic governance at the same time. As rhetorical scholars across the globe have found the significance of epideictic as a practical discourse, we focus on an example in Japanese fictional cinematography released in August 2021. Titled *Shu Shu Shu no Ko* (English title: *Ninja Girl*),[8] it is an entertainment fiction, depicting a girl who engages in the act of whistleblowing. First, by way of praise and blame, epideictic's typical topos, the film represents whistleblowing as an honorable and justified act. It powerfully demonstrates the effectiveness and legitimacy of whistleblowing and educates the viewing public that they themselves could also blow the whistle. It is worth noting that the story's protagonist possesses special skills as a member of a traditional ninja family. With her ninja skills, the girl enacts justice and punishes antagonists, positioning herself as a role-model whistleblower who brings justice to society. Furthermore, the film's comic frame realizes a unique and arguably rare instance of a fictional storyline of whistleblowing. This reflects and further contributes to the positive cultural image of whistleblowing in Japanese society.

Second, *Shu Shu Shu no Ko* is a film that in itself is a powerful act of epideictic rhetoric by the film's director Yu Irie. It is important to note that *Shu Shu Shu no Ko* is not merely a piece of fictional comedy; it is, in fact, a politically loaded cinematographic text that exposes real-life injustice in the guise of fictional entertainment. That is, by way of film production and projections, Irie critiques various wrongdoings by the political leaders, notably Shinzo Abe—the longest-serving prime minister in Japanese history—his wife, and his friends.[9] Through the discussion in this chapter, we claim that Irie's rhetorical act achieves the role of whistleblowing, for he engages in real-life injustices while also educating his audience to collectivize the civic agency against the political authority in the real world.

In this development, we intend to contribute to this volume by demonstrating that Irie's *Shu Shu Shu no Ko* develops a unique pathway for how whistleblowing can occur. It is a film in which political injustice was publicly exposed for entertainment, which avoided the dissidence that ordinary whistleblowing may cause. That is, whereas the movie is a fictional story of whistleblowing, Irie himself was also engaged in the activist-like rhetoric, or the act of (quasi-)whistleblowing of the sociopolitical injustice by film production. To better elucidate the activist nuances embedded in the work, we will discuss not only the film itself but also Irie's comments about the production during a personal interview with the filmmaker.[10]

Following this introduction, the chapter proceeds with the section introducing *Shu Shu Shu no Ko* to our readers, where information regarding the film itself, the director, as well as its production background will be provided. We then turn to the rhetorical analysis of blowing the whistle using epideictic rhetoric as our analytico-theoretical framework, first in terms of digital whistleblowing featured in the film, and second in terms of rhetoric-political critique enacted by the film. In doing so, we contribute to the study of epideictic as a powerful critical-public discourse and explore the similarity between "edutainment" rhetorics of motion pictures and symbolic effects of whistleblowing as *Shu Shu Shu no Ko* exemplifies. Such discourse illustrates how the rhetorical connections shared by whistleblowers and protests might emerge in texts that are unconventional, or perhaps less studied.

Shu Shu Shu no Ko: A Premiere

The project of *Shu Shu Shu no Ko* started in 2020, and the film was released in 2021. The film's protagonist, Miu, is a quiet, ordinary girl working at a local municipal office. One day, Mano, Miu's close friend since childhood and fellow city official, is ordered by a group of corrupt superiors to falsify the city's official documents on one controversial city ordinance. Later, Mano kills himself in regret and despair. Devastated, Miu is despondent and purposeless. Afterward, Miu's grandfather Goro tells her that she was born to a traditional ninja family, a family secret she did not know. He suggests that Miu train herself in this family tradition and take vengeance in justice's name. After hard training, Miu becomes proficient in sophisticated ninja skills. Taking advantage of the skills she acquired, she engages in a whistleblowing mission: stealing video footage that provides evidence of the superiors' crime and revealing it to the public. Following the format of a typical ninja film, *Shu Shu Shu no Ko* sets its climax as an act of revenge when she emerges from a shadow and punishes her antagonists with a poison blowpipe.

In part, Irie's production of *Shu Shu Shu no Ko* is a critical response to the Japanese government's ignorance of the financial crisis in movie theaters and low-budget filmmakers due to the COVID-19 pandemic crisis.[11] Instead of some other governments that launched lockdowns, the state restriction policy for people to stay where they are to avoid the spread of the COVID-19 virus, the Japanese government sporadically announced a "state of emergency" three times to various parts of the country that "strongly advised" its population to refrain from "unnecessary and non-urgent" interactions. In the name of self-quarantine, the Japanese people were "strongly suggested" to stay home and refrain from engaging in various out-of-home activities, including visiting movie theaters. Accordingly, some businesses were hard hit as they were "advised" to close temporarily. Unlike France, Germany, and other countries where various cultural and artistic activities were supported by public money during the lockdown periods, the Japanese government had been reluctant to offer subsidies or other forms of financial assistance to the film industry (including production, distribution, and theaters). Whereas so-called cinema complexes, multiple-screen theaters mainly for blockbuster movies, were financially supported by the national fund after a while, small theaters, typically holding only a few screens and managed independently from large media complexes, were forced to run without monetary support. As a result, small domestic theaters lost 30 to 40 percent of their net income since the pandemic, putting many on the edge of bankruptcy.[12] Even though Irie had already shifted his attention to domestic blockbuster films and national television network drama series by then, his affection for small theaters and low-budget movie culture made him decide that *Shu Shu Shu no Ko* would premier exclusively at these theaters all over the country, and that part of the ticket sales be donated to a private fund for saving small theaters.[13]

While his project was enthusiastically welcomed by small theater owners, doing so also allowed him to explicitly take a critical stance against the national government, which itself is rare in the domestic cinematic scene. At the time, it was increasingly difficult to criticize or question the political situation in Japan directly, and Irie targeted his critique for this exact politicocultural climate. As McCormack notes, "Despite public opposition often at levels of 70 percent or more, [Abe's] governments have enacted—often by forcing through the Diet—major legislation, especially bills with serious implications for security and human rights and freedom of expression."[14] This, in turn, has created a sociopolitical climate where publicly raising critical voices against the government and other public authorities becomes much more precarious. That is, the majority of Japanese citizens have been conditioned by authorities to overlook any abuse of power. McCormack continues: "The Abe government has been practicing the politics of post-truth, in which those who hold power determine what is to be known as truth. The same Japan where Treasury officials would order the doctoring of official documents to help the government out of a predicament of its own making . . . and where the Prime Ministerial will was a key political consideration . . . also saw other revelations of official, high-level deception and obfuscation or data fixing."[15] Transparency in the political process and democratic governance thus deteriorated, while the power base for Abe and his friends in the government continued to remain firm and intact. In short, the recent Japanese national government established a political context in which acts of whistleblowing would be increasingly difficult. However, as we will explicate, Irie's fictional story serves as a corollary to more conventional whistleblowing acts in this specific cultural and political context created by Abe's administration and political party.

We now turn to specific rhetorical features of the film. At first glance, the film appears to be a clear, fictional work of entertainment. However, those aware of Irie's past works recognize the visual signatures as reference points to his sociocultural interest. Stressed in the film's flier and trailer was a series of landscapes such as a riverbank, vegetable fields, and soaring metallic towers with high-voltage lines between them. Whereas these are what we can typically see throughout Japan (especially in medium- to small-size local cities outside large metropolitan areas such as Tokyo and Osaka), these landscapes are part of Irie's visual signatures found in many of his previous works, most notably in the critically acclaimed *SR Saitama no Rappā* (English title: *8000 Miles*) trilogy (2009–2012) about Japanese-language rappers, which brought him to the major blockbuster scene. The works Irie filmed in the past almost always feature the complexity of tensions and interrelations between the local versus the national, the private contra the public, and the conflict between civil rights and authoritarian power. Through this landscape, cinephiles watching *Shu Shu Shu no Ko* would almost instantly recognize these signs as cues for struggles between the haves and have-nots.[16]

Epideictic No. 1: A Ninja's Poetic Justice

NINJA ON OUR SIDE

In the simplest term, *Shu Shu Shu no Ko* is a story of the political idealization of whistleblowers. In the film, the protagonists Miu, Goro, as well as Mano are on the side of justice. The antagonists are the city mayor behaving dictatorially for his own benefit, his loyal followers and collaborators, and corrupt city hall officials supporting them. Like this, the virtue and vice are clearly assigned and fixed throughout the film. Given these roles or subject positions assigned to the main characters, most, if not all, critics and analysts trained in the rhetorical tradition would expect praise and blame, epideictic's typical topos, to be found in the film. That is, the film proposes a moral guidance and educates the audience according to the specific roles and actions assigned to characters in the movie.[17]

To fully understand the epideictic that *Shu Shu Shu no Ko* embodies, however, it is essential to know ninja film as a genre in cinematography. While we now see a torrent of popular images of ninja in contemporary transnational popular culture (such as in *American Ninja, Teenage Mutant Ninja Turtles, Naruto,* and *Lego Ninjago*), it should be noted that they have their origin in entertainment films produced and released in 1960s Japan. During this period, Japan experienced a so-called domestic "ninja-film boom," where the ninja emerged as an imaginary movie hero and became (re)contextualized against the particular historico-cultural backdrop for the first time.[18] S. A. Thornton, a film critic, outlines the several distinct characteristics of ninja around that time, two of which we will discuss later.[19] First, ninja appeared as resistance soldiers against the powers that be. In many first-wave ninja films, their archetypical enemy was an atrocious autocracy, specifically the warlord samurai with the ambitious aim of conquest and domination. Fighting against the enemy and protecting the peasants alongside a smaller number of the lesser but good samurai, ninja engaged in various covert missions in their efforts. Akin to certain clandestine actions of contemporary whistleblowers, ninja would, for example, sneak into the warlord's castle, obtain the evidence of their crime, and disclose those secrets to the public. As guerrilla fighters, they were also engaged in quasi-military missions against outside enemies, often disturbing their plans, destroying their facilities, obstructing their fighting capabilities, and even assassinating them. By way of these representations, the ninja as a guardian of justice has become part of a heroic narrative in various popular cultural artifacts, and in entertainment films in particular. On this point, Teru Shimamura offers an interesting observation: The ninja boom in Japanese popular culture is attributed to the popularity of one short ninja novel originally appearing in *Akahata*, a newspaper published by the Japanese Communist Party.[20] Shimamura explains that the socioeconomic settings of the story coincided with the modern-day working-class experience. He also states that readers of the novel cheered for the ninja heroically engaging and completing the mission, as if the ninja in the story had made their never-realized dream a reality. We also contend that Shimamura's observation applies to the other popular cultural representations of ninja that came after the novel, including *Shu Shu Shu no Ko*.

Other distinct characteristics of ninja, according to Thornton, include their superhuman abilities, extralegal status, and "shadow-like" figure. Due to then-innovative special effects technology, ninja were represented as possessing magical abilities and miraculous skills, such as walking up walls, running on water, leaping across tall buildings, and suddenly disappearing from view. Regarding what they can do, "there is no end of the possibilities."[21] Against cold-blooded aristocracy or greedy warlord samurai, they are on the side of justice by engaging in dangerous missions, including criminal and extrajudicial duties. During missions, ninja conceal their clan or boss so that the enemy's potential revenge should not be spurred beyond the ninja themselves, even when they are arrested.[22] Despite their powers, ninja take enormous personal risks, which correlate to the vulnerability that whistleblowers endure. Using their magical and supernatural skills, they can often quickly begin their mission and successfully complete it without anyone noticing. Whereas such characters appear incongruous with whistleblowers, we posit that the dexterous, amorphous characteristics of the ninja suggest a compelling analogy to the ideal image of whistleblowers.

From the traditional ninja film genre, *Shu Shu Shu no Ko* extracts an ideal image of whistleblowers, a perfect mission conductor compelled by a clear sense of personal duty. As an epideictic act, the film's ninja-hero selflessly serving the community's virtue while punishing vice illustrates how the film parallels certain whistleblowing actions, such as obtaining privileged information, eluding capture, and making the public aware of wrongdoing.[23]

DIGITAL WHISTLEBLOWING IN A COMIC FRAME

By positioning the epideictic rhetoric characterizing *Shu Shu Shu no Ko*, we demonstrate a deeper connection between ninja and whistleblowers. Central to the film's plot is the act of whistleblowing by the film's two central characters: Miu and her grandfather Goro. When Mano was forced by his corrupt superiors to falsify the official documents, he digitally recorded what he did and the conversation he had with his superiors. After forging the documents, Mano visited Goro on his way home and confessed what he did; he also told Goro that he recorded the crime scene and stored it on a flash drive. The following day, Mano leaps off the roof of City Hall.

In this development, Goro plays a key role. Without his advice and help, Miu would not be able to become a ninja and accomplish the mission of whistleblowing. In the first place, it was Goro who suggested that Miu train herself in her family's traditional ninja art. At this point, neither of these two knew where exactly Mano had left the USB flash drive containing the video footage of the crime.

As it turns out, Goro is not only a ninja master but also a computer expert. At first, he appeared as an infirm older man lying in bed and requiring care, as he could hardly stand or sit up by himself. After Miu obtained the flash drive and a password to open the video file, however, Goro responds, "I will upload the video on the Internet cloud with limited viewership settings, . . . I have been high-tech-oriented. Since the MS-DOS era." Then, he quickly gets up from bed and briskly types letters on his laptop. Here, the audience finds it humorous that he suddenly uses highly technical terms such as Internet cloud, limited viewership setting, and MS-DOS. Also comical is bedridden, sick Goro suddenly being awakened and working on the laptop to complete the digital work. Irie inserts such comical scenes occasionally so that the audience associates heroes with humor. While vengeance in the first-wave ninja film was typically conducted in a serious and dark tone, in *Shu Shu Shu no Ko*, the two modern-day ninja do their mission with a sense of joy and lightness.

We claim that the effect of Irie's comic frame is twofold. First, as Kenneth Burke notes, the comic frame enables socialization. By "transcending" different ideological values, the comic frame forms "both private and public relationships" between the speaker and the audience.[24] For instance, this scene is made familiar to those watching the film, as this framing made Miu and Goro relatable to the audience. Second, the comedy's satiric aspect takes on a rhetorical character as the audience interprets certain specific names, attitudes, events, or institutions as being held up to ridicule.[25] While we recognize that Burke's comic frame does not strictly denote contemporarily popular conceptions of comedy, Irie's use of the comedic helps solidify the epideictic roles of virtue and vice within the film. Namely, *Shu Shu Shu no Ko* is a comical play of whistleblowing. Whereas the heroes holding intimacies with the audience successfully completes the whistleblowing mission, the film's antagonists are not only antiheroes but also are subjected to satirical representations in the story. Taken together, *Shu Shu Shu no Ko* is a film that projects a positive image of whistleblowing.

Consequently, the comic frame and the narrative archetype of ninja movie ameliorate the cruel nature of the violent scene at the climax. Toward the end of the story, the corrupt city mayor and his followers are "punished." As Miu and Goro's whistleblowing mission is successfully executed, city corruption is widely reported by major media, which they learn during an informal party gathering. Then, all the lights suddenly turn off, and Miu in a ninja outfit emerges from the shadow, sticking them all with poison arrows. However, the negativity involved in Miu's action is made palatable because the likable and relatable hero is simply "punishing"—not killing—those responsible.[26] Thus, the scene reads as a typical ninja drama, with the violence rationalized as an honorable and justified act by which to bring peace.

Epideictic No. 2: Yu Irie as an Orator-Filmmaker

Having discussed the poetic justice praising the act of whistleblowing in *Shu Shu Shu no Ko*, we now turn to the epideictic rhetoric of Irie. One of the most critically acclaimed filmmakers in Japan, Irie largely situates his productions in the dialogical tensions between different and conflicting ideologies. As we have already discussed briefly, his artistic production is a means not only of self-expression but also of sociopolitical interrogation and intervention, incorporating tensions and ideological conflicts into comic entertainment.

In this section, we critically explore the sociopolitical interplay Irie loaded into *Shu Shu Shu no Ko*. His particular activist-like positioning implicated in this film is clear and obvious. In a published interview, he also verbally expressed his intention to make this film to represent "the voice of the modern people using a motif [ninja] quite commonly found in old domestic films."[27] By making and releasing this film, we see Irie engaging not only in meaning-making but also in meaning-problematizing, meaning-critiquing, and meaning-provoking. He further invites those watching the film to become accomplices in his ambitious rhetorical project.[28] In *Shu Shu Shu no Ko*, Irie offers a set of epistemic challenges of envisioning a political status quo in certain ways, as well as radical political agendas to change that reality.[29] In what follows, we discuss such rhetorical dimensions of Irie's making of this film, first as a powerful reminder to the public of the real-life injustices committed by those in power, and second, as a projection of the ideal against status quo injustices.

POWER CORRUPTS

As we have already described, *Shu Shu Shu no Ko* features the story of a public servant falsifying official documents and later killing himself. This, in fact, mirrors a real-life event. In 2018, a "cronyism" scandal involving then prime minister Abe and his wife Akie made national news: A piece of state-owned land in Osaka had been sold to Yasunori Kagoike, an operator of a kindergarten, at a price far below the ordinary market value. Later, the media revealed that the school operator had very close personal ties with the Abes. Given the kindergarten's hard-headed nationalist educational practices (such as training the children to give a prewar-style, military-like salute to the emperor), it was suspected that the Abes' favoritism enabled the extraordinarily huge discount the school operator enjoyed. However, "versions of the original and doctored documents [regarding this questionable land deal] made public by opposition lawmakers appeared to show passing references to Abe were scrubbed, along with several references to his wife Akie and finance minister Taro

Aso."[30] Abe stated that he and his wife had nothing to do with this land deal. He also claimed that he never ordered these changes in the official documents, shifting the blame to the Kinki Local Finance Bureau, a branch of the national government directly involved in this land sale. Nobuhisa Sagawa, then chief of the Financial Bureau, was reported to the parliamentary investigation session on this matter, publicly testifying the "alleged innocence" of both Shinzo and Akie. Bracketing these events, however, was the suicide of local Finance Bureau officer Toshio Akagi. It was reported that, before killing himself, Akagi had been suffering from depression as he was forcefully made by his superiors to falsify the financial record and meeting minutes regarding that land sale.[31]

This political scandal is clearly reflected in the film's plotline. Going analogically and by making the story in the film very similar to the Abes' cronyism scandal, Irie aimed to turn the "fictional" story into a powerful political critique. In the film, one of the mayor's secretaries who directly ordered Mano to falsify the document is named Nobuhi*to* Sagawa. This is a mirror image of one of the figures central to the real-life cronyism scandal, Nobuhi*sa* Sagawa. While Irie inserted several jokes to ridicule him and others in *Shu Shu Shu no Ko*, the film culminates in a particularly satirical critique when the fictional Sagawa proudly boasts to his fellow, corrupt city official that the anti-immigration bill passed the city congress because he "rewrote the official records" and that it is okay to do so because "revisions are quite normal in the central government." Given the country's judicial inability or hesitance to prosecute, or even interrogate, the real-life Sagawa or the Abes for the crime they allegedly committed and then attempted to cover up, this scene makes a powerful rhetorical appeal to the Japanese audience's sense of fear that falsifications at the highest level of the government may already be normalized and spread across the country without any recourse.

Irie's meaning-critiquing and meaning-provoking rhetoric becomes evident when he highlights the bureaucrats' corruption. That is, by mimicking real-life corruption in his fictional work, Irie emphasizes the potential scale of corruption that may not have been exposed to the public. As O'Gorman extrapolates, amplification is one major function of epideictic discourse: "Epideictic . . . provides for the polis through lexis as phantasia images of honor and shame or virtue and vice, that can be 'sized up' and interpreted according to a logic of scale."[32] Rice also suggests that rhetoric of magnitude leads the audience to make aesthetic responses, the response beyond just fulfilling the logical responsibility of evidentiary evaluations, because "the evidence has been transfigured, it has shifted, into something awe-full."[33] Given these insights, it is reasonable to understand that Irie's epideictic amplification serves in a fiction adjacent to whistleblowing by compelling the audience to recognize the pervasiveness of the problem and to be more critically engaged in national and local politics.

In this development, Irie's satirical rhetoric targets Abe more directly, pointing to another real-world scandal concerning the cherry-blossom viewing party, or *sakura o miru kai*. Immediately after the fictional Saga-wa's boast, the mayor joins them at a local bar to celebrate the passing of the anti-immigration bill. The mayor gives an informal speech to his supporters, which starts:

> MAYOR: This town will finally become a zero-immigrant city with the "Japanese-first" principle. We, the Japanese, should take over our city's tradition, culture, and discipline from the past and teach them to our Japanese children for our bright future. Well, this is a bit too formal on this occasion. Hey, everyone, celebrating this, why not have a big *sakura o miru kai* at Sengen Shrine next year? [Audience responds positively, applauding.]
>
> ONE OF THE AUDIENCE: Now? Is he serious? [Joyously and jokingly.]
>
> MAYOR: Are there any gangsters here? If so, you can't join us. You, you are not a gangster, are you? [The audience laughs.]

Viewing cherry blossoms (*sakura o miru*) and having a party (*enkai* or simply *kai*) under cherry trees in full bloom is popular in the Japanese spring. Yet, hearing someone use the phrase *sakura o miru kai* functions as a double entendre in Japan as it was the name for one controversial event officially sponsored by the prime minister. This annual event started in the spring of 1952 with the intent to hold a gathering under the cherry trees to honor Japanese nationals who accomplished significant achievements in the world or made significant contributions to the country in the previous year. Gradually, however, this event began to be abused for the personal benefit of the prime minister. During his term, for instance, Abe is said to have invited over 850 individuals from his own electoral district, most of whom had no particularly notable accomplishments or contributions that should merit the government honor.[34] It was also reported that those invited by the Abe administration included yakuza gangsters and those involved in illicit businesses.[35] When these facts were disclosed and made public in 2020, the government quickly abolished this event. Given these real-life happenings, we suspect that almost all Japanese who watch *Shu Shu Shu no Ko* could identify the mayor in the film as Abe's metonymical reference.

After providing these comparisons between the fictional and (alleged) real-life villains, Irie sets up a scene of revenge. Whereas the revenge at the climax is almost a convention in classic ninja films, the scene is rhetorically "amplified" to the contemporary audience: atrocious and agonizing, yet still satirical, surrealistic, and funny. By the rhetoric of amplification, the virtue-vice roles are represented more clearly as the film draws upon "affective ground" or "phantasmata, that, . . . underlie, inform and direct political deliberation," reminding one of how injustice is to be punished.[36] For instance, Miu's poison arrows hit the critical spots of two of the most prominent villains, namely Sagawa's forehead and the mayor's throat. Devising the strategy of amplification both on what the vice is doing and how they eventually perish, Irie's rhetoric insists that injustice costs the most severe "punishment" and that it is the evil that should be blown away at the end. At the same time, however, a series of overreactions by city officials helps the scene be more fictional and thus less cruel, fitting itself into the comic frame of the movie.

Overcoming Racism

It is important to note that the protagonist Miu is not only on the side of her friend Mano but also on the side of those marginalized or oppressed. More specifically, it was the anti-immigration act Mano was forced to falsify that signals Miu's allegiance. Therefore, the grand narrative to justify Miu's revenge was not just the counterblow against her grandfather and a friend but also the means to bring civic justice. For Irie, drawing this plotline is an epideictic work to function as a counterdiscourse to the cultural norms upheld in the status quo.[37] That is, as Agnew noted, epideictic rhetoric has the potential to provide alternative values to further enhance civic virtues.[38] Here, we can find Irie's adamant stance against racial and ethnic discrimination, given that it is rampant in populist and xenophobic politics. Thus, overcoming this discriminative climate is necessary for his mind.

Despite its apparent egalitarianism, Japan is a country deeply and insidiously stratified. In this, "immigrants," including foreign laborers without Japanese citizenship, are in the lowest strata, as the government does not officially acknowledge them possessing legitimate political rights and dignities. Also, they are frequently the targets of hate speeches, many of which are unregulated.[39] The Committee on the Elimination of Racial Discrimination in the United Nations International Convention on the Elimination of All Forms of Racial Discrimination reported the following regarding the current state of human rights abuses in Japan:

> The Committee is concerned about reports of the spread of hate speech including incitement to imminent violence in the State party by right-wing movements or groups which organize racist demonstrations and rallies against foreigners and minorities, in particular Koreans. . . . The Committee is further concerned by propagation of hate speech and incitement to racist violence and hatred during rallies and in the media, including the Internet. Furthermore, the Committee is concerned that such acts are not always properly investigated and prosecuted by the State party.[40]

With the belief that overcoming this racism is the foundation for the future of Japan, Irie crafted a plotline in which a modern ninja stands against the various discriminations against immigrants. To Irie, immigrants deserve fundamental human rights and humane treatment.[41] Thus, Miu finds the password to open the video from Mano's close friend, who happens to be an immigrant worker oppressed by city politics. Just as the old ninja defended the life and rights of underprivileged people in the classic ninja movies, Irie sets oppression against immigrants as additional reasons for Miu's actions.

This posture is most evident when Irie made what Sullivan called "allusions to historical events or works and thereby identified themselves with the tradition," a typical example being when a ninja defends the civil rights of local citizens.[42] Right before the climactic scene when Miu and Goro sit on the veranda of their house in the late evening, Miu asks Goro why he was once so intensely against the anti-immigrant act when he was a news reporter. This is when Irie articulates real-life historical facts within the fiction:

> GORO: You know, there was a huge-scale massacre of Korean immigrants after the Great Kanto Earthquake [in 1923]?

MIU: Yes.

GORO: Then, do you know how far the massacre in Tokyo spread around? This town is on the northern rim. The rumor reached this town, and the evacuees from Tokyo were slaughtered. We shouldn't repeat that. [Goro stands up] If no one responds to your call, then go your own way alone."[43] This is my favorite Indian poem.

This is Goro's final line. The next morning, his house is vandalized by the followers of corrupt workers, and soon after, Goro passes away. Thus follows Miu's retaliation scene in the climax, which operates as the revenge of Goro and Mano, as well as the immigrants in the city.

Using Goro, Irie manifests the virtue of antiracism using two examples. The first one is the mass murder of Korean immigrants evacuated from the earthquake in Tokyo, or the so-called Kanto Massacre, that happened in the region this work was filmed. The second is a line from *Ekla Chôlo Re*, a famous song by Nobel laureate and composer of India's and Bangladesh's national anthems Rabindranath Tagore. We see these two examples from history rhetorically and powerfully contrastive. While the former is the vice that should be blamed and not be repeated, the latter represents the virtue of antiracism, with a sense of urgency to defend human rights even if others do not agree with the actor. As Sullivan noted, epideictic discourse displays the example, or *paradeigma*, of virtue from history.[44] Thus, Irie advances his position against populist nationalism and xenophobia while showing ethical pathways that the audience is also invited to follow.[45]

For filmmakers, making films such as this one involves significant risks, one financial and the other political. On the financial risk, during the interview, Irie said he would need at least two to three years just to convince all those involved to start such projects and would likely face postponement or cancellation by corporate sponsors and other stakeholders.[46] He explained that the Japanese entertainment film industry is allergic to fictional films making political claims. However, *Shu Shu Shu no Ko* was completely of Irie's own. He not only wrote, produced, and directed the film, he also successfully secured finance for this film by using private and crowd funding.[47] Namely, for this production, he did not have to be bothered by corporate sponsors and others with financial stakes in the film because there were none.

The second risk a filmmaker would face in premiering this type of film would be political. Foreign workers and immigrants are regularly the target of racist demonstrations and rallies organized by right-wing movements and other hate groups. Although relatively small, artistic exhibitions, productions, and other events have been blackmailed, disrupted, and obstructed by demonstrations and rallies by hate groups.[48] To avoid the risk of such public censures and consecutive turmoil, Irie used the trick of entertainment suspense by hiding key plotlines during its premiere. On the film's official website and film booklet, Irie appealed to the audience not to disclose the critical plotline, including the fact that Miu is a ninja, that the city is corrupted, and that the city's politics is an analogy of real-world national politics. The official booklet sold at the ticket booth at local movie theaters spends about twenty pages, two-thirds of the whole volume, on the "spoiler" chapter, exclusively for the audience who already saw the movie. Says Irie at the very end of the chapter, "Caution!! . . . Once you see the movie, you are also a member of this covert clan: Don't disclose the information here to the future audience!"[49] Irie uses the spirit of the fandom that attempts to avoid spoilers to satisfy a desire to join with ninja. In other words, the ninja as a whistleblower analog fulfills an idealized function to counter real-world political corruption.

Irie's unique and creative ways of producing and premiering *Shu Shu Shu no Ko* suggest that he, as a whistleblower-producer of the social and political injustice, has taken his available means to decrease the risks he would have faced otherwise. By that, he counterproposed his own ideal to Japanese society. Yet, Irie's actions as a member of the film community and Japan citizenry place him in a precarious position as an insider who blew the whistle on abuses of power through the construction of a "fictional" whistleblower.

End Credits: Ninja Girl, Please Bring the Justice to Us!, or, Let's Bring the Justice Together!

In this chapter, we have explored the potential of fictional entertainment in terms of its whistleblowing functions. Using epideictic rhetoric as our analytico-theoretical framework, we explicated what *Shu Shu Shu no Ko* showed in response to the sociopolitical status quo in Japan. We demonstrated that this ninja film is a political exposé powerfully critiquing the status quo. Thanks to Miu, the protagonist, justice prevails, and authoritarianism perishes. Our analysis also suggests that, albeit fictional, the film embodies whistleblowing and ethical guidance for democratic governance. *Shu Shu Shu no Ko* is a product of Irie's artistic creativity and superb filmmaking skills that enabled the politically powerful mixing of sociopolitical tensions and ideological conflicts with the popular cultural discourse of entertainment. By framing the whistleblowing story within a comedic framework and turning it to a ninja film, he succeeds in making his own political claim more accessible to a larger audience.

Two important notes are in order before closing. First, the film reflects Irie's ambivalent subject position between a popular filmmaker and a citizen-activist. Whereas Irie intended this film to be a piece of entertainment comedy, as a concerned Japanese citizen he also wanted to say something about the current state of Japanese politics. Irie's rhetorical tactic was to employ a mouthpiece for the film and let Miu, the ninja hero, speak and blow the whistle on his behalf. Both funny and politically encouraging at the same time, *Shu Shu Shu no Ko* was the film many people had waited for. The film had been shown exclusively at small-scale movie theaters throughout Japan and attracted those thirsty for unrivaled entertainment and political exposé.

Our second and closing comment is on whistleblowing. This chapter points to the possibility that the image of whistleblowing as a solitary battle against a huge organizational force can be effectively translated into a hero narrative. We argue that such entertainment may enhance social mobility that seeks democratic justice both individually and collectively. That is, whistleblowing comedies like *Shu Shu Shu no Ko* can push forward a whistleblowing culture in politically silent cultures like Japan's. Also, we understand that finding the politically enabling potential of fictional works such as *Shu Shu Shu no Ko* is important in that they can change the signification of future whistleblowing acts and our political engagement in the real world. That is, whistleblowing stories, along with the whistleblowing acts, can increase the possibility of safeguarding whistleblowers and nurture a whistleblowing culture within society. As a medium of enhancing the acts of whistleblowing, whistleblowing stories, therefore, possess a possibility of decreasing social injustice. We hope our discussion of the film can also make a modest contribution to this cause, not only for better "understanding" but also for strengthening "the rhetorical linkage among solitary whistleblowing acts and public protests"[50] in the name of (radical) democracy and (poetic) justice.

Notes

1. See Bernard K. Duffy, "The Platonic Functions of Epideictic Rhetoric," *Philosophy and Rhetoric* 16, no. 2 (1983): 79–93; Christine Ovarec, " 'Observation' in Aristotle's Theory of Epideictic," *Philosophy and Rhetoric* 9, no. 3 (1976): 162–174; Takis Poulakos, "Isocrates's Use of Narrative in the *Evagoras*: Epideictic Rhetoric and Moral Action," *Quarterly Journal of Speech* 73, no. 3 (1987): 317–328.

2. Chaïm Perelman and Lucie Olbrechts-Tyteca, *The New Rhetoric: A Treatise on Argumentation* (Notre Dame: University of Notre Dame Press, 1969), 50.

3. Gerard A. Hauser, "Aristotle on Epideictic: The Formation of Public Morality," *Rhetoric Society Quarterly* 29, no. 2 (1999): 17.

4. Hideki Kakita, *Rinri no Performance: Isocrates no Philosophy to Minshushugi Hihan* (Ethics of performance: Isocrates's philosophy and critique of democracy) (Tokyo: Sairyusha, 2012).

5. Isocrates, "Panegyricus," in *Isocrates: The Loeb Classical Library*, vol. 1, trans. George Norlin (London: William Heinemann, 1928), 123.

6. Werner Jaeger, "Paideia: The Ideals of Greek Culture," in *Nobility, Tragedy, and Naturalism: Education in Ancient Greece*, ed. Joseph James Chambliss (Minneapolis: Burgess, 1971), 10.

7. Marcia P. Miceli and Janet P. Near, *Blowing the Whistle: The Organizational and Legal Implications for Companies and Employees* (New York: Lexington Books, 1992), 18.

8. In Japanese, *ko* is a girl, the protagonist Miu. *Shu* ("fwip" or "swish") is a Japanese onomatopoeia, the sound of something suddenly or swiftly appearing or passing. While the audience is unsure about what exactly makes this sound at the onset, they find out during the film that the term, given three times in succession, is a sound of poison arrows blown by Miu.

9. It should be noted that the murder of Mr. Abe on July 8, 2022, was *not* politically motivated and hence had nothing to do with his and his government's political wrongdoings discussed in this film or this chapter. It has been reported widely by various domestic and international media that the suspected gunman targeted and killed Abe "because his life and family had been ruined as a result of his mother's large donations to [the Unification Church] to which Abe had apparent close ties. The Unification Church confirmed that [his] mother is a longtime member and that it had received donations from her." Michelle Ye Hee Lee and Julia Mio Inuma, "As World Gathers to Honor Abe, Japan Grapples with Church's Influence," *Washington Post*, online ed., September 26, 2022,

accessed September 29, 2022, https://www.washingtonpost.com/world/2022/09/26/japan-unification-church-shinzo-abe-assassination/.

10. Also, Irie generously provided the film for our research purposes, enabling us to doublecheck all scenes and plotlines. The film is not yet released commercially on DVD or Blu-Ray, or listed on any movie subscription services. All translations of the film and interview are ours.

11. Yu Irie, *Shu Shu Shu no Ko* (Tokyo: Brocco Films, 2021), 6, 10, 18–19; and Yu Irie, "Interview" by Noriaki Tajima and Masaya Yoshida, online, February 16, 2022.

12. "Kyoryoku-kin naki Jitan, Kukyo, Eigakan ya Sports Shisetsu Shunyu-gen 'Isso Kyugyo Yosei o'" (Orders of shortening opening hours to movie theaters and sport facilities without subsidies: Owners, "Tell us to close and give us money"), *Nippon Keizai Shimbun*, February 18, 2021, evening ed., 9.

13. Irie, *Shu Shu Shu no Ko*, 18–19.

14. Gavan McCormack, "Abe Shinzo and Japan's One-Strong (Ikkyo) State," *Asia-Pacific Journal* 18, no. 7.4 (2020), https://apjjf.org/2020/7/McCormack.html.

15. McCormack, "Abe Shinzo."

16. See his works *The Sun* (2016), *Vigilante* (2017), and *Gangoose* (2018).

17. Kathryn Summers, "Epideictic Rhetoric in the *Englishwoman's Review*," *Victorian Periodicals Review* 34, no. 3 (2001): 263.

18. Irie mentions he has loved classic ninja films since his childhood and tried to find opportunities to make his own. See Yu Irie, "Zenkoku no Eigakan to Issho ni Okoru Mirai o Kangaeru: Interview" (Imagine the future in which we all get angry with movie theater owners all over the country: An interview) in *Kinema Shumpo* 1874, September 2021, 125; Irie, "Interview." Also, although the ninja image before the popular films in the 1950s is sparsely witnessed in manga and novels for children and young adult readers, the ninja in these media are characterized as superheroes with supernatural powers yet no reasons or contexts as to why they became a ninja or how they have such skills. See Wang Zhi Song, "Han Nihon Bunkaron to shiteno Ninja Mono" (Ninja genre as an anti-Japanese culture theory), in *Ninja no Tanjo* (Birth of Ninja), ed. Katsuya Yoshimaru and Yuji Yamada (Tokyo: Bensei Shuppan, 2017), 250.

19. S. A. Thornton, *The Japanese Period Film: A Critical Analysis* (Jefferson, NC: McFarland, 2008), 92–93.

20. Teru Shimamura, "Ninja toiu Stance: *Shinobi no Mono* ni okeru Minzoku to Taishu" (Ninja is/as a stance: Ethnicity and the people in *Shinobi no Mono*), *Riyu Xuexi Yu Yanjiu* (Journal of Japanese language study and research) 140 (2009): 12–14.

21. Thornton, *Japanese Period Film*, 126–128.

22. Wang, "Han Nihon Bunkaron," 248; and Shimamura, "Ninja toiu Stance," 13–14.

23. Denise M. Bostdorff, "Epideictic Rhetoric in the Service of War: George W. Bush on Iraq and the 60th Anniversary of the Victory over Japan," *Communication Monographs* 78, no. 3 (2011): 296–323; and Nathan Crick, *Rhetoric and Power: The Drama of Classical Greece* (Columbia: University of South Carolina Press, 2015), 11–24.

24. Kenneth Burke, *Attitudes Toward History* (Berkeley: University of California Press, 1984), 170.

25. This function of comedy is discussed by Crick, *Rhetoric and Power*, 132.

26. Irie, "Interview."

27. Irie, "Zenkoku," 125.

28. See David Bordwell, *Making Meaning: Inference and Rhetoric in the Interpretation of Cinema* (Cambridge, MA: Harvard University Press, 1989), regarding the nature of meaning-making, -remaking, -problematizing, and -critiquing for cinematographic texts.

29. James Berlin, "Rhetoric and Ideology in the Writing Class," *College English* 50, no. 5 (1988): 488, https://doi.org/https://doi.org/10.2307/377477; and James A. Berlin, "Post-Structuralism, Semiotics and Social-Epistemic Rhetoric: Converging Agendas," in *Defining the New Rhetorics*, ed. Theresa Enos (Newbury Park: Sage, 1993), 137–53.

30. "Japan: Embattled Shinzo Abe Blames Staff over Land Sale Scandal," *Guardian*, March 19, 2018, accessed June 20, 2022, https://www.theguardian.com/world/2018/mar/19/japan-shinzo-abe-land-sale-scandal.

31. "Japan Gov't to Pay Damages over Bureaucrat Suicide Linked to ex-PM Scandal," *Kyodo News*, December 15, 2021, accessed December 12, 2022, https://english.kyodonews.net/news/2021/12/d9b96ce1eb43-japan-govt-to-pay-damages-over-bureaucrat-suicide-linked-to-scandal.html.

32. Ned O'Gorman, "Aristotle's 'Phantasia' in the 'Rhetoric': Lexis, Appearance, and the Epideictic Function of Discourse," *Philosophy and Rhetoric* 38, no. 1 (2005): 28, 33.

33. Jenny Rice, *Awful Archives: Conspiracy Theory, Rhetoric, and Acts of Evidence* (Columbus: Ohio State University Press, 2020), 95–96.

34. McCormack, "Abe Shinzo."

35. Jake Adelstein, "The Importance of Defining Organized Crime in Japan," *Japan Times*, January 4, 2020, accessed June 20, 2022, https://www.japantimes.co.jp/news/2020/01/04/national/media-national/importance-defining-organized-crime-japan/.

36. O'Gorman, "Aristotle's 'Phantasia,'" 31.

37. Cynthia Miecznikowski Sheard, "The Public Value of Epideictic Rhetoric," *College English* 58, no. 7 (1996): 765–794.

38. Lois Agnew, "The Day Belongs to the Students: Expanding Epideictic's Civic Function," *Rhetoric Review* 27, no. 2 (2008): 158–159.

39. McCormack, "Abe Shinzo."

40. Committee on the Elimination of Racial Discrimination, "Concluding Observations on the Combined Seventh to Ninth Periodic Reports of Japan," September 26, 2014, 4, http://tbinternet.ohchr.org/_layouts/treatybodyexternal/Download.aspx?symbolno=CERD%2fC%2fJPN%2fCO%2f7-9&Lang=en.

41. Irie, "Interview."

42. Dale L. Sullivan, "The Ethos of Epideictic Encounter," *Philosophy and Rhetoric* 26, no. 2 (1993): 123.

43. Bengali polymath Rabindranath Tagore's line in a song commonly called *Ekla Chôlo Re.*

44. Sullivan, "Ethos," 118.

45. Berlin, "Post-Structuralism," 152.

46. Irie, "Interview"; Irie, "Zenkoku," 125–126.

47. Irie, "Interview."

48. Tatsushi Fujihara et al., *Jiyu no Kiki: Ikigurushisa no Shotai* (Freedom endangered: Why do we feel suffocated) (Tokyo: Shueisha, 2021).

49. Irie, *Shu Shu Shu no Ko*, 15.

50. Joshua Guitar and Alan Chu, "Racing to (Dis)Own Whistleblowers and Protests: Theorizing *Amongness* in the Shared Rhetorical Spaces of Democratic Agency," chapter 1 in the present volume, 3.

Contributors

Satoru Aonuma, MA, University of Iowa; PhD, Wayne State University, is a professor of communication studies at International Christian University, Tokyo. He specializes in argumentation, critical communication studies, and rhetoric of dissent in modern Japan. His recent publications include: "Shinzo Abe's Not So Beautiful Lies, or How He Stopped Worrying About Embarrassing Himself in Public," in *Local Theories of Argument*, ed. Dale Hample, 2021; "Contentious Performance and/as Public Address: Notes on Social Movement Rhetorics in Post-Fukushima Japan," *International Journal of Communication* 13 (2019).

Matthew Steven Bruen is an associate professor of English and chair of the Department of Literatures and Languages at Young Harris College. He teaches classes in Early American Literature, Composition, the First Year Experience, African American Literature, and Environmental Cinema. Dr. Bruen maintains a wide array of research interests, including place theory, cultural representations of nature, American pantheism and atheism, nineteenth-century Black experiences of nature, whistleblowing in the digital age, and many others. His first book, *Keeper of Lost Places*, was published in 2024. His shorter writing has been published by the University of Chicago Press, Aeon.co, and Narrative.ly. He has begun work on a book that contains case studies of historical American women who have challenged or fled from oppressive situations, tentatively titled *Breaking Free from Repression*.

Ann E. Burnette earned her PhD in communication studies from Northwestern University. She is a Minnie Stevens Piper Professor and Regents' Teacher in the Department of Communication Studies at Texas State University. She has received the Southern States Communication Association

John Sisco Excellence in Teaching Award and the Texas State University Presidential Award for Excellence in Teaching. Her scholarship on freedom of expression issues, presidential rhetoric, campaign persuasion, women in public address, and historical social movements has been published in the *Journal of Argumentation in Context*, *First Amendment Studies*, *Communication Law Review*, *Journal of Contemporary Rhetoric*, and edited books. Her work has been awarded the James Madison Prize for First Amendment Studies. Dr. Burnette is a past president of the Southern States Communication Association.

Colin H. Campbell, PhD, is a professor, journalist, author, and technologist in the Washington, DC, metro area. He is currently a Frederick Douglass Institute Teaching Fellow at Shippensburg University in Pennsylvania. Dr. Campbell's research examines mass media effects, especially the phenomena involving journalism and artificial intelligence (AI), while encouraging the need for increased ethical AI vigilance. Dr. Campbell's latest book, *Automated Journalism at the Intersection of Politics and Black Culture: The Battle Against Digital Hegemony*, takes a critical look at the use of artificial intelligence in media. Dr. Campbell's research qualified him to be inducted into the Edward Alexander Bouchet Graduate Honor Society in May 2020. Dr. Campbell is a former president of the Maryland Communication Association (MCA) and the current president of the Capital Press Club (CPC). He is also the creator of PanAfricanReport.com, an online digital news aggregator highlighting Black diaspora news and its connections to US polisocioeconomic culture.

Alan Chu's research primarily focuses on whistleblower rhetoric. He has published articles on the subject in the *Quarterly Journal of Speech* and *Advances in the History of Rhetoric*. When not writing, Alan enjoys climbing, skateboarding badly, and petting his neighbors' dogs. Alan thinks often about moving abroad.

David R. Dewberry, PhD, Denver University, is a professor of communication at Rider University and was a visiting fellow of law at Harris-Manchester College, Oxford University. His work has been recognized with the Franklyn S. Haiman Award for Distinguished Scholarship in Freedom of Expression by the National Communication Association and the James Madison Prize for Outstanding Free Speech Scholarship by the Southern States Communication Association, and the Richard S. Arnold

Prize for First Amendment Scholarship from the University of Arkansas. He has also served as the editor of the *Communication Law Review* and *First Amendment Studies*. In his spare time, he enjoys visiting offbeat tourist attractions.

Chrys Egan, PhD, is the associate dean of the Fulton School of Liberal Arts and a Professor of Communication at Salisbury University. She is chair of the International Leadership Association's (ILA) Public Leadership Community, past chair of the ILA's Women and Leadership Community, past president of the Popular Culture Association in the South, and past president of the Maryland Communication Association. She has over forty academic publications and fifty popular press articles on communication, leadership, and culture. She is coeditor of the book *Pathways into the Political Arena: The Perspectives of Global Women Leaders*. She coedited a *Merits* international journal special issue on "Changing Realities for Women and Work." She is coediting an ILA book series, *Transformative Women Leaders*. She earned awards for President's Diversity, Outstanding Faculty, Alumni Faculty Appreciation, Outstanding Research Mentor, Distinguished Faculty, BEACON Scholar-in-Residence, University System of Maryland Excellence in Mentoring, Maryland Top 100 Women (twice), Leadership Maryland, and Women and Leadership Outstanding Practice with Local Impact.

Rebekah L. Fox, Texas State University, earned a PhD in communication from Purdue University in 2008. Her research focuses on organizational rhetoric and resilience among firefighters and nurses, as well as the rhetoric of environmental and political issues, specifically related to the First Amendment. Dr. Fox is the recipient of the James Madison Prize for First Amendment Studies, the Janice Hocker Rushing Early Career Research Award, and the Richard S. Arnold Prize in First Amendment Studies. She is a three-time recipient of the Presidential Award of Distinction for Scholarly/Creative Work at Texas State University and has been awarded the Texas State University Presidential Award for Excellence in Service. Her publications have appeared in *First Amendment Studies, Communication Law Review, Health Communication*, the *American Journal of Nursing*, and the *Journal of Contemporary Rhetoric*.

Joshua Guitar earned his BA in communication from Adrian College, and his MA and PhD in communication from Wayne State University. Joshua currently serves as an assistant professor of communication at Kean University where he teaches classes in rhetoric, critical media studies, and political communication. Joshua's research has been featured in communication journals like *Critical Studies in Media Communication, Communication and Democracy*, and *Western Journal of Communication*. Joshua recently authored a book entitled *Dissent, Discourse, and Democracy: Whistleblowers as Sites of Political Contestation*, published by Lexington Books in 2021. Joshua has also won a number of awards for his research, including the 2019 Top Paper Award in the Political Communication division of the National Communication Association, the 2022 James Madison Prize for Outstanding Research in First Amendment Studies, and the 2023 Robert M. O'Neill Top Paper Award in the Freedom of Expression division of the National Communication Association.

Craig M. Hennigan received a PhD in communication from Wayne State University and is the director of debate at the University of Nevada, Las Vegas. His research aims to unpack how people express citizenship as it relates to cities.

Azeb Nishan Madebo is an assistant professor in the Department of Communication and Media at the University of Portland. She is a critical media, technology, race, and cultural studies scholar who specializes in Ethiopia and the Black diaspora. Her work focuses on the appropriation and adaptation of communication technologies for sociopolitical ends like nation-building and the politics of identity (both racial and ethnic) in the African/Black diaspora. She received her PhD from the University of Southern California's Annenberg School for Communication and Journalism in 2022 and her BA in communication from the University of Washington, Seattle.

Marnie Lawler McDonough is an assistant professor of communication at Concordia University Wisconsin. She earned her PhD in rhetoric and public communication from the University of Wisconsin–Milwaukee and holds an MA in corporate and organizational communication from Fairleigh Dickinson University in Madison, New Jersey. Her research focuses on rhetorical leadership, specifically the rhetoric of and about organizational leaders, the public airing of corporate "dirty laundry," and calls for / responses to organizational change. Dr. Lawler McDonough's interest in organizational rhetoric is inspired and informed by her more than fifteen years of professional experience across various communication roles in television, media, and higher education.

Kellie Marin earned her PhD in communication and rhetoric from The Pennsylvania State University. She is an assistant professor of communication at Texas State University. Marin's research centers on the role of civic participation within the surveillance state. Her scholarship has examined the role of virtual reality's depiction of state violence, counterterrorism education initiatives, the use of facial recognition technology during social protests, and the evolution of citizen surveillance practices. You can find her work in *Communication and Critical/Cultural Studies*, *Surveillance and Society*, *Screen Bodies*, and *Rhetoric Society Quarterly*.

John Patrick Murphy is a lecturer of economics at the University of Maryland Eastern Shore and has worked as an adjunct professor in information systems and operations management at Salisbury University, teaching economics, finance, information systems, statistics, and digital media. Murphy is a graduate of Washington College and the University of Georgia with degrees in political science and agricultural economics. He has worked in the security systems industry for eighteen years. Murphy owns and operates InterAmerican Business Associates, an information technology and specialized security systems company. While serving as a volunteer in the Peace Corps in Central America, Murphy had his own whistleblowing experience that helped him relate to the important topic addressed in this book.

Noriaki Tajima, MA, University of Alabama; PhD, Wayne State University, is a professor at Kansai University, Osaka, Japan. He has published journal articles and book chapters on rhetoric, social activism, and argumentation and debate in Japanese and English, including "How Japan Neglects Workers of Foreign Nationalities: An Analysis of Immigration Control Controversies in the National Diet," in *Local Theories of Argument*, edited by Dale Hample, 2021. Sharing his hometown and high school with Yu Irie, the director of the film analyzed in this volume, he has also been a cinephile for a long time. His dream is that his parents would someday confess to him the family secret that only *they* know where one of the six infinity stones is.

Svilen Trifonov, PhD, University of Minnesota, is a lecturer in the Department of Communication Studies at the University of Georgia. As a public address scholar, his work centers on the concept and practice of citizenship, studying cultural texts and discourses related to immigration, race, social movements, and borders.

Sarah Walker-Riftkin got her doctorate from Detroit's Wayne State University in 2022. Her dissertation tracked the changes in rhetorical strategy of the Christian right in clashes with the LGBTQ+ community over four decades. As a career, she is the director of forensics and an assistant professor at Northern Arizona University in Flagstaff, Arizona. As a scholar she specializes in gender, religious rhetoric, and argumentation theory. When she isn't driving a van full of debaters or explaining the rhetoric of Christian fundamentalist literature to someone, she is probably reading something. Hopefully she will have a cup of coffee, and a cat on her lap.

Index